The Changing Constitution

In *The Changing Constitution*, Richard H. Fallon Jr. explores the constitutional law of the United States as reflected in decisions of the Supreme Court, including recent blockbusters. The author analyzes controversial rulings addressing topics such as freedom of speech and religion, the Second Amendment right to bear arms, abortion, affirmative action, gay rights, and the powers and prerogatives of the president. Examining modern controversies from a historical perspective, he argues that it is impossible to understand US constitutional law without recognizing the political and institutional forces that always have brought, and will continue to bring, innovations and occasional reversals in constitutional doctrine. Fallon also highlights distinctive aspects of the current era, including the judicial philosophies of the sitting justices. This intellectually sophisticated overview of constitutional law and Supreme Court practice additionally discusses anxieties about whether and how the justices, who can overrule their own precedents, are meaningfully constrained by law.

Richard H. Fallon Jr. is the Story Professor of Law at Harvard Law School and an affiliate professor in the Harvard Government Department. A former Rhodes Scholar and Supreme Court law clerk, he is a prize-winning teacher and the author of numerous books and articles about constitutional law.

The Changing Constitution
Constitutional Law in the Trump-Era Supreme Court

Richard H. Fallon Jr.
Harvard Law School, Massachusetts

Shaftesbury Road, Cambridge CB2 8EA, United Kingdom

One Liberty Plaza, 20th Floor, New York, NY 10006, USA

477 Williamstown Road, Port Melbourne, VIC 3207, Australia

314–321, 3rd Floor, Plot 3, Splendor Forum, Jasola District Centre, New Delhi – 110025, India

103 Penang Road, #05–06/07, Visioncrest Commercial, Singapore 238467

Cambridge University Press is part of Cambridge University Press & Assessment, a department of the University of Cambridge.

We share the University's mission to contribute to society through the pursuit of education, learning and research at the highest international levels of excellence.

www.cambridge.org
Information on this title: www.cambridge.org/9781009533980

DOI: 10.1017/9781009534024

© Richard H. Fallon Jr. 2025

This publication is in copyright. Subject to statutory exception and to the provisions of relevant collective licensing agreements, no reproduction of any part may take place without the written permission of Cambridge University Press & Assessment.

When citing this work, please include a reference to the DOI 10.1017/9781009534024

First published 2025

Cover image: Constitution of the United States (Fine Art / Contributor / Getty Images)

A catalogue record for this publication is available from the British Library

Library of Congress Cataloging-in-Publication Data
NAMES: Fallon, Richard H., Jr., 1952– author
TITLE: The changing constitution : constitutional law in the Trump-era Supreme Court / Richard H. Fallon, Jr., Harvard Law School, Massachusetts.
DESCRIPTION: Cambridge, United Kingdom ; New York, NY : Cambridge University Press, 2025. | Includes bibliographical references and index.
IDENTIFIERS: LCCN 2025014920 (print) | LCCN 2025014921 (ebook) | ISBN 9781009533980 hardback | ISBN 9781009534024 ebook
SUBJECTS: LCSH: Constitutional law – United States | United States. Supreme Court | Political questions and judicial power – United States | Judicial review – United States | Judicial power – United States | Executive power – United States | Trump, Donald, 1946–
CLASSIFICATION: LCC KF4550 .F33 2025 (print) | LCC KF4550 (ebook) | DDC 342.73–dc23/eng/20250421
LC record available at https://lccn.loc.gov/2025014920
LC ebook record available at https://lccn.loc.gov/2025014921

ISBN 978-1-009-53398-0 Hardback

Cambridge University Press & Assessment has no responsibility for the persistence or accuracy of URLs for external or third-party internet websites referred to in this publication and does not guarantee that any content on such websites is, or will remain, accurate or appropriate.

For EU product safety concerns, contact us at Calle de José Abascal, 56, 1°, 28003 Madrid, Spain, or email eugpsr@cambridge.org

For Jeanie, Jamie, Kenny, Dolly, Paddy, Vicky, and Danny

CONTENTS

Introduction *page* 1

1 The Written Constitution and the Emergence of Judicial Supremacy 18
   The Text and Framing of the Constitution 20
   Judicial Review under the Constitution and the Outsized Legacy of *Marbury v. Madison* 26
   The Political Foundations of Judicial Review 32

2 Historical Overview of Constitutional Adjudication by the Supreme Court 35
   The Marshall Era: 1801–1835 37
   The Taney Era: 1836–1864 42
   From Reconstruction through the New Deal (or "the *Lochner* Era"): 1865–1937 45
   The Supreme Court of the New Deal Settlement and the Civil Rights Revolution: 1937–1969 50
   The Post-Warren Court: 1969–2016 53

3 The Supreme Court Today 57
   Polarized Legal Culture 58
   Constitutional Originalism and the Conventional Norms of Constitutional Argument 61
   The Current Justices 66
      The Pre-Trump Conservative Justices 66
      The Trump-Appointed Conservatives 70
      The Liberal Justices 73
   The Difference That Six Makes 75

4 Freedom of Religion: The Crumbling "Wall of Separation" between Church and State 77
   Introduction to the Establishment Clause: Material Support for Religion 81

Government Sponsorship of Religious Symbols and
    Exercises   85
Religion in the Public Schools   88
The Free Exercise Clause   90
Voluntary Governmental Efforts to Accommodate Religious
    Practices   98
Conclusion   100

5   The Freedom of Speech: The Ascent of "The Persuasion
    Principle"   102
    Content-Based Regulation of Speech   104
        Remote Origins of Modern Doctrine: Historical
            Debates   104
        More Proximate Origins of Modern Doctrine   106
        The Rise of the Demand for Content Neutrality   111
        Shocking and Offensive Speech   115
        A Note on "Hate Speech"   116
        Commercial Speech   117
        Political Campaign Advertising   120
        The Right Not to Be Compelled to Speak   124
        Conflicts between Rights Not to Speak and
            Antidiscrimination Laws   125
        Platforms and the Question of Who Is a Speaker with First
            Amendment Rights   126
    Unprotected Categories of Speech   127
    Freedom of Association   131
    Managerial Domains in Which the Demand for Content
        Neutrality Does Not Apply   133
        Government Speech   134
        Regulation of Government Employees' Speech   135
        Speech in the Public Schools   136
        Selective Subsidization of Private Speech and the Public
            Forum Doctrine   136
        Regulation of the Broadcast Media   138
    Conclusion   139

6   The Expanding and Contested "Right to Keep and Bear
    Arms"   141
    Historical Background to Current Issues   143

The Origins of Modern Doctrine: *District of Columbia v. Heller*   145
The "Incorporation" of the Second Amendment against the States   149
Defining Rights by History and Tradition   151
A Partial Modification of the History-and-Tradition Approach   155
Concluding Observations and Pending Issues   159

7   The Equal Protection of the Laws: What It Once Meant and Now Means   161
Equal Protection and the Constitution   163
Issues Involving Race   167
   Invidious Discrimination   167
   From Invidious Discrimination to Affirmative Action   175
Rational Basis Review   180
Racially Disparate Impact   183
Sex Discrimination   185
Discrimination against Gays and Lesbians   190
Judicial Review of Governmental Classifications under the Equal Protection Clause: Concluding Observations   193
Fundamental Rights under the Equal Protection Clause: A Further Basis for Searching Judicial Review   194
   Voting Rights under the Equal Protection Clause: A Historical and Conceptual Introduction   196
   The One-Person, One-Vote Cases   198
   Vote Dilution: Race Discrimination and Majority-Minority Districts   200
   Vote Dilution: Political Gerrymanders   202
   Burdens on the Right to Vote: Voter Identification Laws   206
   Equality in the Counting of Votes: *Bush v. Gore*   207
   Equal Protection Voting Rights, the Supreme Court, and the Judicial Role   208

8   Substantive Due Process and Unenumerated Fundamental Rights after the Overruling of *Roe v. Wade*   210
Historical Background to *Roe*   213

    Substantive Due Process and the Fourteenth
        Amendment 213
    Substantive Due Process in the *Lochner* Era 215
    The Road to *Roe v. Wade* 220
  Roe v. Wade and Abortion Rights 222
    Roe and Its Immediate Aftermath 223
    Dobbs 226
    Abortion: Concluding Observations 229
    Rights of Sexual Autonomy 230
  Marriage 234
  Conclusion 237

9 The Shrinking yet Still Formidable Powers of Congress 239
  Historical Background to Modern Issues 243
    Proximate Origins of *NFIB* 243
    Critical Perspectives 246
  Political and Constitutional Realignment 250
  Congress's Regulatory Power under the Commerce Clause
      Today 251
  The Necessary and Proper Clause 254
  The Taxing and Spending Power 256
    Historical Evolution 256
    The Spending Power as a Lever to Influence or Compel
        Behavior 257
  Congressional Power to Enforce the Civil War
        Amendments 260
  Concluding Observations 267

10 The Powers of the President and the Executive Branch in a
    Period of Ferment 268
  The President and Executive Power in Historical
      Perspective 276
  Delegated Powers: Vague Agency Mandates and the
      Nondelegation Doctrine 281
  Appointment and Removal Powers 284
  Unilateral Claims of Executive Power 288
  Executive Privilege and Immunity 291
  Conclusion 293

11 Law and Change in the Supreme Court 295
  Law and Politics in the Supreme Court 299
  Appraising Constitutional Law and Constitutional
    Change 304

Index 307

INTRODUCTION

On February 13, 2016, Justice Antonin Scalia died in his sleep at the age of seventy-nine. At the time of his death, he was staying at Cibolo Creek Ranch, a remote resort in the Chinati Mountains of West Texas, for a weekend of hunting and sightseeing. An avid hunter, Scalia had joined other guests on a quail hunt the previous afternoon and turned in early after dining with the owner of the ranch. He was discovered the following morning, dead of natural causes.

Justice Scalia's death was a pivotal event in the history of the Supreme Court, not least because he was an epochal figure. On the bench, he exhibited a dominating personality, often playing for laughs. In his opinions, he was a brilliantly lively writer. Scalia also exerted an intellectually paradigm-shifting influence on Supreme Court decision-making. Both in his opinions and in extrajudicial writing, Scalia championed two interpretive methodologies that had previously seemed outrageous to mainstream thinkers both on the bench and in leading law schools. One was "originalism" – the idea, roughly, that the Constitution should nearly always be interpreted in the twentieth and twenty-first centuries in ways consistent with its original eighteenth- or nineteenth-century meaning. The other was "textualism" – the idea, roughly, that the meaning of legal texts, including both the Constitution and federal statutes, not only depends on but is also exhausted by what their words actually say. According to Scalia, legislative history purporting to record what the drafters of texts meant to say or achieve is a legal irrelevancy. Because only the written texts were enacted into law, judges should confine their intention to the meaning of those texts in the context of their promulgation.

It is a reflection of Scalia's influence that today even "liberal" justices – including Elena Kagan and Ketanji Brown Jackson – sometimes claim to embrace originalist methodologies.[1] In a similar acknowledgment, Justice Kagan said in November 2015 that "we are all textualists now."[2]

During Scalia's nearly thirty years on the Supreme Court, the substantive content of constitutional law changed a lot, too. Developments included rulings that the First Amendment encompasses a right of corporations to spend money on political advertising, that the Second Amendment protects individuals' rights to possess guns for purposes of self-defense (not just service in a "well regulated Militia"[3]), that the Establishment Clause does not preclude cities and towns from beginning public meetings with prayers, and that Congress's regulatory powers are subject to a variety of previously undefined constitutional limitations.

Nonetheless, during Scalia's years on the Supreme Court, constitutional law did not change as much or always in the ways that he would have liked. He argued repeatedly but futilely for the overruling of *Roe v. Wade* (1973)[4] – a development that came only later, after his death. He failed to persuade a majority of his colleagues to hold that race-based affirmative action policies were per se unconstitutional.

---

[1] Justice Jackson said in her confirmation hearings that "the Constitution is fixed in its meaning," and it is appropriate to look at its "original public meaning" to interpret it. Robert Barnes and Ann E. Marimow, "Ketanji Brown Jackson Declares Herself a Modest Jurist, Defends Record against Republican Criticism," *The Washington Post* (Mar. 22, 2022), www.washingtonpost.com/politics/2022/03/22/ketanji-brown-jackson-hearing-day-2/. Justice Kagan similarly asserted in her confirmation hearings that "we are all originalists." Confirmation Hearing on the Nomination of Elena Kagan to Be an Associate Justice of the Supreme Court of the United States: Hearing before the S. Comm. on the Judiciary, 111th Cong. 62 (2010) (statement of Elena Kagan). Justice Kagan has more recently qualified that statement, insisting that she is not "an originalist in the conventional sense of the word" and that the "original meaning" of the Constitution is that it is supposed to "evolve[]" with time. Josh Gerstein, "Kagan Hopes Supreme Court's Ideological Divide on Precedent Isn't Permanent," *Politico* (Sept. 22, 2023, 6:02 p.m.), www.politico.com/news/2023/09/22/elena-kagan-supreme-court-precedent-speech-00117760.
[2] Harvard Law School, "The 2015 Scalia Lecture Series: A Dialogue with Justice Elena Kagan on the Reading of Statutes," *YouTube*, at 08:29 (Nov. 25, 2015), https://youtu.be/dpEtszFToTg.
[3] U.S. Const., Amend. II.
[4] 410 U.S. 113 (1973).

He dissented when the Court refused to reconsider *Miranda v. Arizona* (1966),[5] a pathbreaking decision that effectively requires police to notify criminal suspects of their rights to remain silent and to have the assistance of a lawyer prior to the commencement of custodial interrogations.

The reasons for Scalia's failures along these and a number of other dimensions are complex. Through Scalia's years on the Supreme Court, "conservative" justices always outnumbered those typically counted as "liberals." As of 1992, when Scalia had served on the Court for six years and the Court reaffirmed *Roe*'s "central holding" over his vehement dissent in *Planned Parenthood v. Casey*,[6] Republican presidents had appointed eight of the Court's nine justices. At the time of Scalia's death in 2016, Republican presidents had appointed five of nine. Yet in 2016, as in 1992, the conservative majority included moderate or swing justices who sometimes voted with the Court's liberals in politically salient cases.

When Justice Scalia died, the Supreme Court's future hung in the balance. With nearly a full year left in Democratic President Barack Obama's term of office, it appeared that Obama would be able to nominate, and secure Senate confirmation of, a replacement justice who would tip the Court's longstanding conservative majority to a 5–4 liberal margin. If events had unfolded in that way, abortion rights and affirmative action would have remained safe. Liberals would have hoped for the overruling of a number of decisions of the Rehnquist and Roberts Courts – so called in reference to Chief Justices William Rehnquist (1986–2005) and John Roberts (2005–) – including *Citizens United v. Federal Election Commission* (2010),[7] which found that corporations have free speech rights to spend money on political campaign ads.

Instead, politics intervened. Even before President Obama had had time to nominate a successor to Justice Scalia, the Republican Senate majority leader Mitch McConnell announced that the Senate would refuse to consider any nomination that Obama might submit so close to the 2016 presidential election, which was approximately nine months away. After McConnell and his Senate Republican colleagues

---

[5] 384 U.S. 436 (1966).
[6] 505 U.S. 833 (1992).
[7] 558 U.S. 310 (2010).

stalled confirmation hearings until after the November election and the inauguration of President Donald Trump, Trump nominated and the Senate confirmed the conservative originalist Neil Gorsuch as Scalia's successor. As a result, no substantial realignment in the Court's 5–4 conservative balance of power took place.

A subtle but highly significant shift in the Court's ideological center then occurred when the "moderate" conservative Justice Anthony Kennedy retired in July of 2018. Kennedy was an ardent supporter of gay rights and had cast "swing" votes to save *Roe v. Wade* from being overruled and to preserve affirmative action. As Kennedy's successor, Trump chose Brett Kavanaugh, a judicial conservative who, like Gorsuch, had been recommended by the Federalist Society, an influential organization of conservative law students, lawyers, and judges. During Kavanaugh's confirmation process, women who had known him during his high school and college years lodged allegations of past sexual misconduct. At that point, the confirmation proceedings turned rancorous. Despite lingering questions in many minds, McConnell, still leading a Republican Senate majority, brought his party into line to support the nomination, and Kavanaugh – who was expected to be more reliably conservative than Kennedy – was confirmed on nearly a party-line vote.

A little more than a year later, the iconic liberal Justice Ruth Bader Ginsburg died on September 18, 2020. When Justice Scalia died substantially further in time before a presidential election, majority leader McConnell took the position that the opportunity to nominate a justice should go to the winning candidate, not the incumbent president. McConnell adopted a different stance when, following Ginsburg's death, Trump swiftly nominated Judge Amy Coney Barrett – another favorite of the conservative Federalist Society – to take Ginsburg's former seat. Within thirty-nine days of Ginsburg's death, and only weeks before a presidential election that Trump would lose, Barrett was confirmed.

With Barrett's appointment, the nation entered a new era of Supreme Court and thus of constitutional history. Acting in conjunction, Mitch McConnell and Donald Trump had arranged the creation of a 6–3 conservative supermajority. The era of that conservative supermajority is not new merely because it has begun to bring change. As this book will emphasize, change is more nearly a constant than an anomaly in Supreme Court interpretation of the Constitution.

The distinction is that we have already begun to witness conservative changes of unprecedented scope and consequence. These include the overruling of a right to abortion, a holding that the Equal Protection Clause prohibits public colleges and universities from practicing race-based affirmative action, a dramatic expansion of already broad gun rights under the Second Amendment, a further loosening of restrictions on governmental support for religious institutions, and an unprecedented holding that a website designer's free speech rights entitle her to an exception from a state law barring people engaged in commercial activities from discriminating on the basis of sexual orientation. More dramatic developments are surely in the offing.

The successful efforts of President Trump and Senator McConnell to shape the Supreme Court, when viewed in conjunction with the changes in constitutional law that the new conservative supermajority has already begun to implement, both provide the occasion for this book and illustrate a number of its central themes. The first of those themes, which I have prefigured already, is that change is a historical constant in US constitutional law. It is impossible to understand constitutional law without understanding the dynamics that render it vulnerable to change. We have a very old Constitution that is difficult to amend. Much of its language is cryptic and vague and invites interpretation. And interpretations not only can vary but have varied over time.

The possibility of reasonable disagreement about how to interpret the Constitution is what makes the Supreme Court as important an institution as it is today. Through its power to authoritatively interpret both constitutional language and judicial precedents that are themselves subject to reasonable interpretive disagreement, the Supreme Court functions as an ongoing agent of constitutional evolution. Indeed, to function as a change agent is perhaps the Court's central modern role. Unlike other federal courts, the Supreme Court gets to choose its cases. It typically agrees to decide about 70 cases a year out of roughly 5,000 requests. And the Court determines which cases to decide with an eye toward possibly changing the law. Sometimes, perhaps most often, the changes involve efforts to make the law clear on a point where it previously was not clear. When lower courts have reached disparate decisions about how either the Constitution or a federal statute should be interpreted, the Supreme Court may agree to review one or more of the conflicting rulings for the purpose of clarifying what the law (in its view) requires. But sometimes the Court takes cases in order to overturn its own prior decisions and, for all practical purposes, to reshape the constitutional law of the United States. It did so, for example, when it agreed to review the lower court decision in the *Dobbs v. Jackson Women's Health Organization* (2022),[8] which overruled *Roe v. Wade*, and in the cases that effectively overruled prior precedents upholding affirmative action programs involving university admissions.

A second theme is that although the Supreme Court is in many ways a lawmaking institution, which often chooses its cases for the purpose of contemplating or effecting changes in our constitutional law, it is not a lawmaker in the same sense as Congress, the state legislatures, or the conventions that drafted and ratified the Constitution. Depictions of the justices as so many "politicians in robes,"[9] merely executing party political programs, are therefore misleading in most if not all cases. Even when the Court considers whether to overrule decisions that bind all lower courts until the justices vote to reverse them, the nature of the judicial process requires the Court to justify its rulings as interpretations either of the Constitution's language or of prior cases interpreting it. In this sense, the Court's decisions, unlike those of legislatures, are necessarily and inherently backward-looking, grounded in texts that were written in the past. In addition, norms of legal argumentation subject the justices to disciplines, including requirements of publicly reasoned decision-making, that can be tested for principled consistency.

But if constitutional interpretation is always backward-looking, it is also, simultaneously, forward-looking. The justices both are and ought to be concerned about whether the interpretations that they reach, and the formulations that they articulate to implement those interpretations, will produce fair, reasonable, and workable patterns of decisions in the future. Insofar as the justices' eyes are on the future, concerned with the practical consequences of possible decisions that they might make, the justices are and have to be lawmakers. And nothing could be clearer than that their values inform the way that they decide many of their most important cases.

It is important to make neither too little nor too much of the banal truth that the justices' values influence and sometimes determine

---

[8] 597 U.S. 215 (2022).
[9] Richard A. Posner, *How Judges Think* (Cambridge, MA/London, UK: Harvard University Press, 2008), 8.

their decisions – which, it should be recalled, sometimes elicits vehement denials rather than nods of assent, especially at the justices' confirmation hearings. (Chief Justice John Roberts famously compared the job of a Supreme Court justice with that of an umpire in a baseball game.[10] And Justice Kagan maintained that judicial rulings are determined by law "all the way down" to the point of decision,[11] apparently even in the most controversial cases.) Recognizing that the justices of the Supreme Court are, willy-nilly, lawmakers – though not, I repeat, in the same sense as legislators – people who dislike Supreme Court rulings sometimes rail that we have "government by judiciary." But we clearly do not.

Although there are some domains in which the Supreme Court has stunning power, there are many more areas in which it has almost none – over the size of the federal budget, for example, or the interest rates set by the Federal Reserve Board, or what US policy toward China or Russia should be. In response to the question of why this should be so, political scientists sometimes say that judicial power, including the power of the Supreme Court, exists within "politically constructed bounds."[12] As I shall explain more fully in this chapter, history teaches that there are some claims of judicial power that the public and the nation's political leaders would not accept. Over time, the justices have internalized a series of unwritten and frequently unspoken understandings of what judges and justices can and cannot do. These boundaries have changed from one historical era to another. They may be changing right now. But at any particular time, the justices are very much constrained in their lawmaking capacities. (Try to imagine the justices ordering Congress to increase or decrease the size of the defense budget.)

A third theme, highlighted by Justice Scalia's championing of originalism and textualism, involves the relationship between the

---

[10] Confirmation Hearing on the Nomination of John G. Roberts Jr. to Be Chief Justice of the Supreme Court of the United States: Hearing before the S. Comm. on the Judiciary, 109th Cong. 55 (2005) (statement of John G. Roberts Jr.).

[11] Confirmation Hearing on the Nomination of Elena Kagan to Be an Associate Justice of the Supreme Court of the United States: Hearing before the S. Comm. on the Judiciary, 111th Cong. 103 (2010) (statement of Elena Kagan).

[12] Keith Whittington, *Political Foundations of Judicial Supremacy: The Presidency, the Supreme Court, and Constitutional Leadership in U.S. History* (Princeton, NJ: Princeton University Press, 2007), 4; Matthew C. Stephenson, "'When the Devil Turns ...': The Political Foundations of Independent Judicial Review," 32 *Journal of Legal Studies* 59, 60–61 (2003); Mark A. Graber, "Constructing Judicial Review," 8 *Annual Review of Political Science* 425, 425 (2005).

methodologies that the justices apply in interpreting the Constitution and their normative beliefs and commitments. No one can understand the current Supreme Court without understanding the individual justices' varied degrees of commitment to originalism and textualism, especially originalism. But the Court is not now and never has been consistently originalist. The Court's own precedents remain an important basis for the Court's decisions, including by justices who hold themselves out to be originalists. For example, in the recent case in which the Court held that race-based affirmative action in college admissions violates equal protection norms,[13] the majority opinion – which all six of the conservative justices joined – was almost entirely devoid of reference to the original meaning of the Fourteenth Amendment. As the outcome in that case would tend to indicate, the justices' normative values also influence their decisions – which, almost self-evidently, explains why we can so readily describe the justices as "conservative" and "liberal." Still, it would be equally mistaken to think that methodological premises never help to shape outcomes. Among other influences, some of the conservatives' commitments to originalism may fortify their sense of righteous resolve in overruling past nonoriginalist decisions even in the face of predictable outrage from liberals and moderates.

A fourth theme has a more dominant influence on this book's architecture than any other. It is that the changes that the justices of the Supreme Court effectuate in our constitutional law occur against and are gauged in relation to a framework of prior decisions that, up until their overturning, had enjoyed the status of constitutional law binding lower courts and other public officials throughout the nation. At any particular time, there is a lot of constitutional law, the details of which would not be obvious to anyone who just read the written Constitution. Much of that law ought to interest engaged citizens. My aim in this book is to array the Court's decisions – including ones that are lesser known or sometimes forgotten – into patterns that collectively constitute the current constitutional law of the United States. For the most part, I do so on a topic-by-topic basis.

Sometimes the patterns of decisions are coherent and, at least for now, stable. Aspects of free speech doctrine furnish a good

---

[13] *Students for Fair Admissions, Inc., v. President and Fellows of Harvard College*, 600 U.S. 181 (2023).

illustration. Over the past fifty years or so, the Supreme Court has established that statutes that single out speech for prohibition based on its content are virtually per se unconstitutional under the Free Speech Clause of the First Amendment unless the speech falls into a constitutionally unprotected category (such as obscenity, "fighting words," or true threats). There is a plausible, stable rationale for this rule, which David Strauss has dubbed the "persuasion principle": It would be a constitutionally intolerable affront to citizens' autonomy for the government to deny them access to speech based on the premise that citizens cannot be trusted to assess the truth or value of speech for themselves.[14] Though big chunks of free speech law seem settled for the time being, in other areas, the current pattern of Supreme Court decisions reveals tensions or inconsistencies. Such inconsistencies often signal that changes are underway. Sometimes such changes are easy to predict, but sometimes they are not.

A fifth theme is among the most challenging to develop and confront. It is that although constitutional change is a constant in the unfolding history of the United States, and although we can look to history for lessons about how change is likely to continue going forward, we are now in a new and unprecedented era. In the past, historians and political scientists broadly agree, the Supreme Court's stance toward the leading political and constitutional controversies of the day has frequently, perhaps typically, tended to track mainstream public opinion.[15] Among other factors, the explicitly political process by which justices are first nominated and then confirmed by politically accountable presidents and senators has tended to produce this result. Also, the Court has often adjusted its course of decisions in order to render them acceptable to aroused political majorities.

In our currently divided climate, however, it is unclear that there is a coherent mainstream of public opinion that the Supreme Court could please, even if it set out to do so. It is also far from clear that a majority of the current justices – whose methodological commitments

---

[14] David A. Strauss, "Persuasion, Autonomy, and Freedom of Expression," 91 *Columbia Law Review* 334, 334 (1991).

[15] For a pioneering development of this thesis, see Robert A. Dahl, *A Preface to Democratic Theory* (Chicago, IL: University of Chicago Press, 1956), 109–12. For a more recent reformulation, see Barry Friedman, *The Will of the People: How Public Opinion Has Influenced the Supreme Court and Shaped the Meaning of the Constitution* (New York, NY: Farrar, Straus, and Giroux, 2009).

to originalism and textualism may fortify their senses that there are "right" constitutional answers to controversial questions that they are duty-bound to reach – would want to conform their decisions to public opinion anyway. As a result, it is easy to imagine a future in which the Supreme Court careens to the right in a way unprecedented in our history.

At the same time, there are countervailing forces whose influence on the justices remains to be seen. Among them, the Court's public approval ratings hover close to an all-time low.[16] Some of the justices appear worried by this development. It thus seems imaginable that they will slow the pace of change – though likely not its direction – in response. From our current temporal vantage point, the most I can say with confidence is that we inhabit a new era in which we have to expect quite rapid changes in the substantive content of constitutional law, nearly all in a conservative direction, but that the details of change are often harder to predict.

A sixth theme, partly overlapping with several of those that I have advanced already, is that the justices of the Supreme Court view themselves as custodians of "the rule of law," and the public, by and large, looks to them to play that role. The Court's law-changing power raises questions, which will sometimes loom in the background of this book and sometimes demand explicit attention, about the nature of law in the nation's highest tribunal. In what sense is the Constitution law? Do the justices take seriously their obligation of constitutional fidelity? What mechanisms are there, if any, through which the justices' obligations of fidelity to law can be enforced? Anyone who wants to understand what we want to call constitutional law must confront these questions, even if they defy pat answers.

Having introduced six themes, I should now explain how they relate to each other and inform the plan of the book. This is a book about current constitutional law and about the dynamics of change that have shaped it in the past and will almost certainly reshape it in the future, including the very near-term future in which the Supreme Court must be expected to continue under the dominance of a supermajority of very conservative justices. The book is about constitutional law as it

---

[16] Jeffrey M. Jones, "Supreme Court Approval Holds at Record Low," *Gallup* (Aug. 2, 2023), https://news.gallup.com/poll/509234/supreme-court-approval-holds-record-low.aspx.

exists today. But it is written based on the humbling premise that the present is a fleeting moment shaped by dynamics that make change – sometimes for the better and sometimes for the worse – inevitable.

The book's narrative unfolds as follows. Chapter 1 outlines the content of the written Constitution and describes the emergence of "judicial supremacy," or the dominant role of the Supreme Court, in interpreting it. The Constitution of the United States was the first written national constitution in the history of the world. At the time of its ratification, many people believed that each of the branches of the national government would interpret the Constitution for itself. Moreover, the Supreme Court was not initially regarded as a particularly important institution. The first chief justice resigned his position, and later declined to accept reappointment, on the ground that the office lacked dignity and importance. Besides describing the events through which it came to be broadly accepted that the Court is the Constitution's definitive interpreter, Chapter 1 begins to flesh out the idea that the Court's power exists within and is constrained by politically constructed boundaries. To a first approximation, those boundaries are constituted by the willingness of other institutions and ultimately the American people to accept the Court's rulings as authoritative.

Chapter 2 provides a capsule history of the role that the Supreme Court has played over the course of American history. It divides that history into five eras, beginning with the Court's uncertain early years and ending with the moderately conservative period that immediately preceded the installation of the current conservative supermajority. Throughout, Chapter 2 emphasizes the ways in which political and cultural currents have influenced the Court.

Chapter 3 provides a preliminary sketch of the Supreme Court as it exists today. This chapter describes the distinctive political environment in which the sitting justices were appointed and in which they function. It highlights the role that a conservative legal organization, the Federalist Society, has played in vetting potential nominees and in ensuring that the sitting justices who were appointed by Republican presidents are reliably conservative in their commitments. Chapter 3 also discusses the rise of originalism as a theory of constitutional interpretation and frames issues about the relationship between originalist methodology and substantively conservative values that will be a focus of attention through the remainder of the book. Finally, it gives introductory, capsule biographies of each of the current justices. As subsequent chapters will emphasize, "the Supreme Court is a 'they,' not an 'it,'"[17] and it is impossible to understand the Court's dynamics without a grasp of how the individual justices, taken one by one, approach their jobs.

Chapter 4 traces the arcs of change that are visible in the interpretation of the First Amendment's Establishment and Free Exercise Clauses. To a rough approximation, the Supreme Courts over which Earl Warren and Warren Burger presided as chief justice (from 1954 to 1969 and 1969 to 1986, respectively) sought to enforce a "wall of separation" between church and state. That wall has crumbled in the decades since. As Chapter 4 details, the current Court has embraced the originalist position that historical understanding and practice define the exclusive limitations on the government's acknowledgment of and support for religion. Among the outstanding questions under the Establishment Clause is whether the Warren Court's iconic decisions banning prayer in the public schools will survive the ongoing doctrinal reconstruction.

The pattern of decisions under the Free Exercise Clause is complex, but current trends reflect a fascinating reversal of positions by judicial conservatives and judicial liberals alike. Justice Scalia epitomized the conservatives of his generation in holding that while the Free Exercise Clause shields religious institutions and practices from affirmatively hostile treatment, it does not require the government to exempt either religious organizations or individual believers from generally applicable laws that impede religiously motivated practices. When Scalia authored the majority opinion embracing that view in *Employment Division v. Smith* (1990),[18] the most prominent claimants to exceptions were members of relatively small minority religions. More recently, as the parties seeking exceptions have increasingly included conservative Christians, the current conservative supermajority has substantially revised the prevailing doctrinal structure to mandate more religious exemptions from otherwise valid laws. Chapter 4 summarizes and seeks to explain developments to date.

Chapter 5 considers First Amendment history and doctrine concerning the freedom of speech. It briefly discusses what can be

---

[17] See Adrian Vermeule, "The Judiciary Is a They, Not an It: Interpretive Theory and the Fallacy of Division," 14 *Journal of Contemporary Legal Issues* 549 (2005).
[18] 494 U.S. 872 (1990).

gleaned about original understandings of the Free Speech Clause and reviews formative debates about how that clause should be interpreted, largely in cases growing out of an Espionage Act that Congress enacted during World War I. Chapter 5 then moves briskly forward to provide an overview of more recent developments, mostly occurring since the 1960s and 1970s. Since then the United States has progressively recognized broader speech rights than any other country in the world. Prior to the 1960s, defense of free speech rights was widely recognized as a "liberal" position. The defining issues included stances toward the regulation of obscenity and protections for speech by Communists and anarchists. Over subsequent decades, support for expansive speech protections has migrated to the political right, with conservative justices embracing the position that, outside of a few historically defined and exceptional categories, all content-based regulation of speech is constitutionally suspect. As Chapter 5 explains, the resulting doctrine provides robust protection not only for a good deal of "hate speech" and some outright lies but also for commercial advertising and corporate expenditures to promote the election of political candidates. Revealingly, the current conservative supermajority has seldom sought to justify its doctrinal innovations – which recently included recognition of an absolute right of a commercial website designer to refuse to design a website celebrating a same-sex wedding[19] – as reflecting the original understanding of the Free Speech Clause. Rather, the principles that the Court has invoked to explain the central elements of modern doctrine are rooted in the libertarian skepticism of governmental regulation of speech "markets" that the "persuasion principle" embodies.

Chapter 6 considers the Supreme Court's approach to the Second Amendment right "to keep and bear Arms." The Second Amendment prefaces that guarantee with a clause referring to militia service: "A well regulated Militia, being necessary to the security of a free State ...." In light of that preamble, prior to 2008 the Court had never held that the Second Amendment protects a personal right to bear arms for self-defense or for other purposes unrelated to militia service. Chapter 6 describes the Court's controversial readings of the language and history of the Second Amendment as supporting personal rights to keep and bear arms in a string of cases beginning in

---

[19] *303 Creative LLC v. Elenis*, 600 U.S. 570 (2023).

2008. Among the diverse subfields of constitutional law, in none is the current Court's approach more devoutly originalist. In appraising the permissibility of regulating the exercise of many constitutional rights, including under the First Amendment, the Court frequently asks whether restrictions are "narrowly tailored" to important or "compelling" governmental interests. In interpreting the Second Amendment, the Court now insists that the permissibility of modern restrictions on gun ownership and carriage should depend exclusively on analogies to historically tolerated forms of firearms regulation. Chapter 6 explores the difficulties that the conservative supermajority has encountered in applying that approach, which may or may not furnish a paradigm for future application in other doctrinal areas.

Chapter 7 canvases the Supreme Court's historically evolving interpretation of the Fourteenth Amendment guarantee that no state may "deny to any person within its jurisdiction the equal protection of the laws." The Court's implementation of the Equal Protection Clause has seldom purported to be originalist, including in its most recent decisions. Chapter 7 examines the strands of doctrinal history that once tolerated governmentally enforced race discrimination under the notorious "separate but equal" formula; that initiated a reversal of course in *Brown v. Board of Education* (1954);[20] and that have produced a body of modern precedents with few roots in the original history of the Fourteenth Amendment. In a recurring pattern, the justices have historically condemned forms of discrimination – first on the basis of race, then sex, and then sexual orientation – only when public opinion began to view them as unjustifiably bigoted. Chapter 7 also surveys a branch of equal protection doctrine that strictly scrutinizes deprivations of rights that the Court deems "fundamental" under the Equal Protection Clause, centrally including voting rights. It explains continuities, but also revealing disparities, between the approaches to voting rights of the liberal Warren Court, on the one hand, and the conservative Roberts Court, on the other.

Chapter 8 analyzes the Supreme Court's practice, over approximately a century and a half, in identifying some rights that the Constitution does not specifically list as being protected against substantive abridgment by the Due Process Clause of the Fourteenth Amendment. The Due Process Clause stipulates that no state shall

[20] 347 U.S. 483 (1954).

"deprive any person of life, liberty, or property, without due process of law." On the surface, it looks like a guarantee of procedural, rather than substantive, rights. But the Court has repeatedly held otherwise. For roughly fifty years, a conservative Court protected contract rights in cases emblematized by *Lochner v. New York* (1905).[21] After an embarrassed climbdown from that approach in the 1930s, the Court reembraced the Due Process Clause as a source of "unenumerated" substantive rights in *Roe v. Wade*. When the current Court overturned *Roe* in *Dobbs v. Jackson Women's Health Organization*, many observers read *Dobbs* as condemning *Roe* on originalist grounds. As Chapter 8 explains, however, a close reading demonstrates that the *Dobbs* Court avoided a strictly originalist approach. It continues to affirm that the Due Process Clause protects a set of fundamental substantive rights that are grounded in tradition. Chapter 8 explores the conservative justices' reasons for adopting that position and its implications for issues likely to arise in the future.

Chapter 9 discusses the Supreme Court's decisions defining and circumscribing the powers of Congress, which can permissibly legislate only in domains in which the Constitution authorizes it to do so. The Court's rulings on the scope of Congress's authority present a case study in constitutional change. For a long span of constitutional time extending into the Great Depression and the New Deal, the Court struggled, often uncertainly, to cabin Congress's regulatory and taxing and spending powers under Article I. But the Court, seemingly in response to political pressures, substantially abandoned that effort beginning in 1937. Over ensuing decades, the justices upheld assertions of congressional power to prescribe minimum wages and maximum hours, protect the environment, regulate all activities with substantial effects on the national economy, pass national civil rights laws, and create largesse-dispensing programs that the Founding generation could never have imagined. At least since the 1980s, however, a substantial strain of conservative thinking has maintained that the modern, swollen, national government could find no legitimate justification in the original Constitution, which contemplated a Congress of limited powers only, and that a constitutional counterrevolution is called for. Chapter 9 addresses the Supreme Court's so-far halting efforts to implement such a counterrevolution and identifies the considerations

---

[21] 198 U.S. 45 (1905).

that have given pause even to conservative justices. It also describes the Court's more aggressive efforts to limit congressional power under the Thirteenth, Fourteenth, and Fifteenth Amendments, all of which include express authorizations of Congress to "enforce" their substantive guarantees with "appropriate legislation."

Chapter 10 addresses the Supreme Court's recent, partly paradoxical, lines of cases involving issues of presidential power. On the one hand, the Court has held that Article II of the Constitution and the Constitution's overall structure endow the president with sweeping authorities and prerogatives. These include powers to control the conduct of a "unitary" executive branch by removing officials who refuse to do the president's bidding and, separately, a prerogative-like "immunity" from prosecution for many unlawful official acts, including ones that would constitute serious crimes if committed by anyone else. On the other hand, the Court has sought to limit the powers of agencies within the executive branch, which the president heads, on the theory that post–New Deal agency officials were allowed to assume functions that the Constitution reserves either to Congress or to the courts. Nowhere, Chapter 10 explains, has the Court's conservative supermajority pursued, or does it seem more likely to continue to pursue, a doctrinally revisionist agenda with more sweeping practical consequences.

Chapter 11 takes a step back to consider the nature of constitutional "law" in the Supreme Court. If constitutional law is as amenable to Court-driven change, revolution, and counterrevolution as previous chapters suggest, in what sense is it law at all? Chapter 11 advances an answer to that question that many find unsettling. The Constitution is our nation's supreme law not because it says it is, nor just because the Founding generation adopted it, but because various relevant constituencies in the United States today accept it as the supreme law. The Constitution would cease to be law here, just as the dictates of the British Parliament did in the past, if enough people began to reject its claims to authority. To express one of the central claims of Chapter 11 in a single affirmative sentence, the foundations of law, and especially constitutional law, lie in acceptance. Moreover, because the Constitution does not include all necessary rules for its own interpretation, many of the most important norms that mark the limits of legally permissible constitutional interpretation by the Supreme Court must depend for their lawful status, just as the Constitution itself does, on patterns of acceptance by justices and judges and the acquiescence of a broader public. In other words, some of the most important legal norms that define and limit the scope of legally permissible constitutional interpretation by the Supreme Court, including the doctrine of stare decisis, are rooted in contemporary understandings of what are acceptable modes of constitutional interpretation. Those understandings are enforceable through various formal and informal mechanisms that could include defiance of Court decisions that were sufficiently widely perceived as beyond the justices' lawful authority to render. As even this abbreviated summary should suffice to convey, the legal norms that apply to constitutional interpretation by the Supreme Court bear few similarities to the kinds of binding law – ranging from stop signs to the tax code – that most of us encounter in our daily lives. In thinking about "law" in the Supreme Court, we need to recognize the distinctive nature of constitutional law and the capaciousness of the interpretive authority that the Court lawfully possesses.

Chapter 11 also ventures tentative normative assessments of the two principal stories of constitutional change – one focused on the long-term, the other on the current era – that earlier chapters tell. It offers a generally positive appraisal of the long-term narrative, which highlights adaptive judicial interpretations of an old Constitution to changing conditions across historical time. By contrast, Chapter 11 presents a more troubled assessment of the current period in the history of the Court and the country.

1 THE WRITTEN CONSTITUTION AND THE EMERGENCE OF JUDICIAL SUPREMACY

Few Americans had a larger impact on early constitutional history than John Jay. Along with James Madison and Alexander Hamilton, Jay coauthored *The Federalist Papers*,[1] which developed the most famous arguments advocating the Constitution's ratification and have achieved renown as a classic of American political theory. Jay served as the first chief justice of the United States. While still holding that office, he negotiated Jay's Treaty, which helped calm threats of renewed hostilities with Britain in the vulnerable early years of constitutional government. After leaving the chief justiceship, Jay continued in public service as the governor of New York.

Despite Jay's long list of accomplishments, his career in relation to the Constitution also contains revealing gaps and omissions. He did not attend the Philadelphia Convention at which the Constitution was drafted. The governor of New York, who appointed the state's delegation, snubbed Jay because of his known support for a strong national government. After the Constitution's ratification, Jay accepted an appointment as the first chief justice, but he resigned in 1795 after only five years on the bench. At the time, the Supreme Court held little of the power and prestige that it possesses today. Its role was

---

[1] James Madison, "No. 10: The Union as a Safeguard against Domestic Faction and Insurrection," in *The Federalist Papers*, ed. Clinton Rossiter (New York, NY: Mentor, 1999).

widely debated. Some doubted that the Court had the authority to engage in judicial review of the validity of acts of Congress. In 1795, Jay preferred to serve as governor of New York. Nor did Jay return to national service following his gubernatorial term. When President John Adams nominated Jay to become chief justice once again in 1800, Jay declined the post. The Court, he told Adams, lacked "energy, weight, and dignity."[2]

Today, John Jay is little remembered. Nonetheless, he is part of the origin story in light of which modern constitutional law and the functions of the Supreme Court need to be understood. So viewed, Jay teaches an important lesson about the relationship of our current constitutional order to events in the historical past. Many of the understandings and institutional roles that can appear natural and inevitable to contemporary Americans, as if they were hardwired into the Constitution at the time of its initial design, were unforeseen by Americans of the past, sometimes including figures who played leading historical parts. At many points, events might have taken a different course, and understandings and traditions that we now take for granted might never have emerged.

This chapter lays out selected aspects of constitutional history as a prelude to the examination of contemporary constitutional law. It briefly describes the written Constitution that emerged from the Constitutional Convention in 1787 and discusses the Supreme Court's initially uncertain place in the new scheme of government. Against the backdrop of historical uncertainties, the Court's emergence as the Constitution's ultimate expositor is a phenomenon that calls for explanation. In recounting the Court's rise, this chapter pauses to debunk a myth that has grown up around the celebrated case of *Marbury v. Madison* (1803),[3] which was decided shortly after John Jay declined the opportunity to become chief justice for a second time. Among the insights to be drawn from *Marbury*, realistically considered, is that American lawyers, judges, and Supreme Court justices sometimes, perhaps frequently, shape constitutional narratives with the aim of justifying current allocations of power and supporting constitutional conclusions that they think desirable. Another set of lessons involves

---

[2] Letter from John Jay to President Adams (Jan. 2, 1801), in 4 *Correspondence and Public Papers of John Jay*, ed. Henry P. Johnston (New York: G.P. Putnam's Sons, 1890–93), 284, 285.

[3] 5 U.S. (1 Cranch) 137 (1803).

the political foundations and the implied promises on which the Supreme Court's current authority has been constructed. If those foundations were to crumble or the implied promises were to be breached, there is no guarantee, even today, that the Court's status and power would endure.

The Text and Framing of the Constitution

At the center of American constitutionalism lies a text – the written Constitution – with known (though multiple) authors and a known history. Today, originalists claim that the decisions of nearly all modern cases should reflect the Constitution's original meaning. As we shall see, that claim turns out to be substantially more complex and qualified than appearances might suggest. But discussion of originalism can wait. Even nonoriginalists agree that text and history matter to constitutional interpretation.

The Constitution includes three main components: a set of seven original "Articles" written at the 1787 Philadelphia Convention; ten initial amendments, known collectively as the "Bill of Rights"; and seventeen subsequent amendments, including three that were adopted during Reconstruction. The seven original Articles are devoted primarily to establishing a national government and defining its powers. They contain only a few explicit guarantees of individual rights. During the ratification debates, critics contended that more guarantees were needed. The first Congress that convened under the new Constitution in 1789 therefore proposed, and by 1791 the states had ratified, the package of ten amendments that we now refer to as the Bill of Rights. The First Amendment forbids Congress from abridging the freedoms of religion and speech. The Second provides that "A well regulated Militia, being necessary to the security of a free State, the right of the people to keep and bear Arms, shall not be infringed." Subsequent provisions of the Bill of Rights forbid unreasonable searches and seizures, stipulate that the federal government may not deprive anyone of life, liberty, or property without "due process of law," grant various rights to criminal defendants, and forbid cruel and unusual punishments. Since 1791, seventeen further amendments have been added, with the most important coming during Reconstruction. The Thirteenth Amendment abolishes slavery. The Fourteenth provides that no state may deprive any person of life, liberty, or property without due process of law nor deny to anyone within its jurisdiction the equal protection of the laws. The Fifteenth Amendment stipulates that "the right of citizens of the United States to vote shall not be denied or abridged ... on account of race, color, or previous condition of servitude."

As originally written and ratified, the Bill of Rights created rights only against the federal government, not the states, nearly all of which already had bills of rights of their own. The First Amendment, for example, thus begins with the words "Congress shall make no law ...." Beginning in the twentieth century, however, the Supreme Court has held that the Fourteenth Amendment "incorporated" most of the provisions of the federal Bill of Rights and thereby made them applicable against the states.

Even today, the Bill of Rights does not create rights of private individuals against other private individuals. Nor does the Fourteenth Amendment's Equal Protection Clause. The rights of private citizens against other private citizens, businesses, and employers – where they exist – must come from sources other than the Constitution, such as state law and federal statutes enacted by Congress. To put the point slightly differently, with the partial exception of the Thirteenth Amendment's prohibition of slavery and involuntarily servitude, only governments and their officials can violate the Constitution. Lawyers and judges often refer to this limitation on the Constitution's protective reach as "the state action requirement."

As the relative paucity of amendments reflects, the written Constitution is very hard to alter. Amendments require the approval of two-thirds of both Houses of Congress and three-quarters of the states. The stringency of the latter barrier explains why it proved impossible in the early part of the twentieth century to add an amendment that would have authorized Congress to "limit, regulate, and prohibit the labor of persons under eighteen years of age" and why a proposed amendment guaranteeing equal rights to women failed to earn ratification within a congressionally specified seven-year window. The Reconstruction Amendments might appear to demonstrate that constitutional amendment is not too dauntingly difficult in times when the public mind is focused on a vital issue or issues. But in fact, they illustrate how difficult gaining approval for constitutional amendments can be. Representatives of the southern states, who otherwise would have opposed the Thirteenth Amendment, had not yet been readmitted into the Congress that proposed it, and the only southern states to vote to ratify the Thirteenth Amendment had federally imposed Reconstruction governments. After a number of southern states voted to reject the Fourteenth Amendment, Congress made ratification a condition of their readmission to the Union. To describe the situation bluntly, many of the states whose votes were necessary to ratify the Fourteenth Amendment approved it only because they were coerced into doing so.

Also contributing to resistance to constitutional amendments is the reverence in which many Americans hold the original Constitution and those who wrote it. Both in judicial opinions interpreting the Constitution and in popular works of history, the delegates to the Philadelphia Convention are almost invariably acclaimed as visionary statesmen, referred to either as "the Framers" or "the Founding Fathers." In many respects, their celebration is well deserved. It also bears mention, however, that constitutional interpretation characteristically aspires to depict the Constitution and its authors in the best possible light in order to support interpretations that yield just and practical outcomes and make the Constitution appear worthy of adherence in the present day. Aspects of mythologizing – both of the Constitution and of the Framers – sometimes attend this aspect of the interpretive process. But the mythologizing should not obscure four points that explain much about how our practice of constitutional interpretation has evolved over the course of history.

First, nearly all of the Constitution was written a long time ago by inhabitants of a very different world who had very different preoccupations from ours. The Founders were practical people who wanted to create a workable Constitution. The Articles of Confederation that preceded the Constitution had proved inadequate because they failed to create a national government with sufficient powers to meet challenges requiring collective action by all of the states. Even so, although the delegates to the Constitutional Convention explicitly voted at one point in their deliberations to create a national government with powers to legislate "in all cases to which the separate States are incompetent,"[4] the Framers could not have imagined the world of today or the issues that it presents. The Framers did not foresee the internet, air travel, or a tightly interconnected national economy. The average life expectancy

---

[4] 1 *Records of the Federal Convention of 1787*, ed. Max Farrand (New Haven, CT: Yale University Press, 1911), 21.

at the time of the Constitution's ratification was somewhere between one's late thirties and early forties; the Founding Fathers could not have imagined anything like the Social Security system. Medicine was crude; the Framers did not anticipate Medicare or Medicaid.

Perhaps more surprising from a modern perspective, the Framers did not anticipate the emergence of political parties. When parties took root, their arrival necessitated a number of adjustments. To take just one example, as originally written the Constitution called for the electors in the electoral college each to vote for two candidates for president and provided that the person with the most votes would become the president and the one with the second-most votes the vice president. After parties had first formed, and the respective candidates of the Federalist and Democratic-Republican parties contested the presidential election of 1800, all of the Democratic-Republican electors voted for both Thomas Jefferson, the party's preferred presidential candidate, and Aaron Burr, its proposed vice president. The resulting tie threw the race into the House of Representatives that had been elected two years earlier, where the outcome remained in doubt through thirty-five ballots and considerable surrounding political intrigue. Following that political and constitutional crisis, which culminated in Jefferson's selection, the Twelfth Amendment to the Constitution, which specifies that members of the electoral college should cast separate votes for president and vice president, was written with parties specifically in mind. Other adaptations to accommodate the Constitution to a party system have mostly occurred without formal changes to the written text.

Second, the delegates who gathered in Philadelphia to write the Constitution represented a relatively narrow slice of the population. No Blacks and no women attended. In no state were women allowed to vote. The Framers, who were overwhelmingly members of the propertied elite, also sought to rein in political democracy in various ways. They anticipated that members of the Senate would be elected by the state legislatures and provided for election of the president by an "electoral college" rather than a direct vote of the people in hopes that these indirect modes of election would yield senators and electors who possessed more mature judgment and were less prone to fleeting passions than the mass electorate.

Emphasizing the Constitution's democracy-restraining and property-protecting provisions, Michael Klarman describes the drafting and ratification of the Constitution as twin aspects of "the Framers' coup,"[5] through which they thwarted what James Madison termed "the rage for paper money [and] for an abolition of debts" that had emerged in some states.[6] This characterization may be too strong, but in the context of post-Revolutionary America, the Constitution as originally written is easy to portray – and has been portrayed by many – as a conservative document that erects multiple barriers to the enactment of federal legislation that would change the status quo. For a measure to become law requires separate approvals by the two Houses of Congress. The president has a veto power. And looming always in the background is the possibility of judicial review of an enactment's constitutional validity.

Americans like to think that they have the best constitution in the world. But the US Constitution has not tended to be a good model for other nations. When other countries have tried to copy the US Constitution, they have frequently found that American-style divisions of powers too often frustrate the enactment of legislation that political majorities support and occasionally demand, including through extralegal means.[7] In other modern democracies, parliamentary systems have proved much more popular.[8]

Third, although some of the Framers' aims in designing the Constitution were lofty and relatively timeless, a number of the agreements reflected in the Constitution resulted from hard, sometimes self-interested, bargaining. The delegates to the Constitutional Convention largely took it for granted that slavery must be allowed to continue, at least in the short term. Otherwise the slave states would never have signed on to the new Constitution. Following the Civil War, the Thirteenth Amendment repudiated slavery. But race-based oppression continued long after and has given rise to issues with which national politicians and the federal judiciary continue to struggle in the long shadow of the Framers' original bargain.

In the Congress that existed under the Articles of Confederation, each state had one vote, regardless of size. At the Constitutional

---

[5] Michael Klarman, *The Framers' Coup: The Making of the United States Constitution* (New York, NY: Oxford University Press, 2016).
[6] Madison, "No. 10," in *The Federalist Papers, supra*, 84.
[7] Bruce Ackerman, "New Separation of Powers," 113 *Harvard Law Review* 633, 644–64 (2000).
[8] David S. Law and Mila Versteeg, "The Declining Influence of the United States Constitution," 87 *New York University Law Review* 762, 791–92 (2012).

Convention, the small states' initial demand for a similar accommodation met predictable resistance. The resulting compromise provides for population-based apportionment of seats in the House of Representatives but guarantees each state equal representation in the Senate. This arrangement blatantly contradicts the "one-person, one-vote" formula that the Supreme Court has otherwise celebrated as a core requirement of democratic self-government.

Overall, the state-based elements of our electoral system – including state-based representation in the electoral college – contribute to what critics view as a serious democracy deficit in the US political system. Among possible manifestations, the presidential candidate who won the most votes lost the tally in the electoral college in both the 2000 and the 2016 presidential elections. In addition, more than half the members of the Senate come from states comprising only 18 percent of the national population.

Fourth, the Constitution that came out of the Philadelphia Convention in 1787 was vague and thus debatable in many respects. Partly this is because the Constitution is very cryptic in many of its most important parts. Another contributor to constitutional debate is that constitutional interpretation, like all interpretation of texts and verbal utterances, necessarily occurs in context. (If I read a reference to "the president," the context will normally alert me whether the text is talking about the president of the United States, the president of a university, or the president of a social organization.) And because most communication occurs between a speaker or writer and an audience who know a good deal about one another's likely background knowledge and assumptions, many aspects of an utterance's intended and understood meaning can literally go without saying. (If I tell my wife that I will be home by 6 p.m., it will ordinarily go without saying that I mean by 6 p.m. today, but in another context it might equally go without saying that I mean by 6 p.m. on some other day.)

In the case of the Constitution, it is often hard to know what members of the Founding generation took to be relevant aspects of the historical, social, and linguistic context on which the "meaning" of the Constitution – to the extent that it even had a clear meaning – would have depended. For example, many scholars have appealed to the overall linguistic context of the Constitution's specific grants of power to Congress in Article I and to the president in Article II to argue that those powers were originally understood and intended to be exclusive.

By contrast, at least one leading scholar has recently argued that the relevant context for identifying congressional and presidential powers included the eighteenth-century law of nations. According to him, members of the Founding generation predominantly understood the Constitution, by establishing a national government, to have vested in the national government all of the then recognized powers and prerogatives of sovereigns in the international community of nations.[9] Again based on evidence of what he takes to have been widely shared eighteenth-century background assumptions, Jonathan Gienapp has advanced the even more radical view that the Founding generation regarded the original written Constitution more as a sketch to be elaborated and possibly adjusted in the course of subsequent practice than as a set of canonical formulations to be adhered to in all events.[10] In a subsequent book, Gienapp elaborates by asserting that the Framing generation understood constitutions and constitutional law as comprising a range of unwritten background principles and understandings in addition to written text.[11] Other scholars disagree about these and many other matters.

In noting disagreements among scholars, we should not assume that questions about the Constitution's originally understood meaning necessarily have clear, determinate answers. The Framers had not thought everything through and knew that they had not. James Madison specifically observed in *Federalist No. 37* that the Constitution's meaning was vague in many respects and would need to be "liquidated" or settled through experience, practice, or precedent.[12]

Judicial Review under the Constitution and the Outsized Legacy of *Marbury v. Madison*

If the Constitution's meaning was vague or debatable in some respects and therefore needed to be settled or liquidated, two important

---

[9] John Mikhail, "The Original Federalist Theory of Implied Powers," 46 *Harvard Journal of Law & Public Policy* 57, 58–60 (2023).
[10] Jonathan Gienapp, *The Second Creation: Fixing the American Constitution in the Founding Era* (Cambridge, MA: Harvard University Press, 2018), 81 (arguing that the Constitution was viewed as a "'first draught' ... a work in progress, in need of activation and subsequent work – in essence an imperfect and unfinished object").
[11] Jonathan Gienapp, *Against Constitutional Originalism: A Historical Critique* (New Haven, CT: Yale University Press, 2024).
[12] James Madison, "The Federalist No. 37," in *The Federalist Papers*, supra, at 229.

questions were: Which institution or institutions of government would do the liquidating, and how? Today we mostly accept that the Supreme Court is the ultimate expositor of constitutional meaning. To many if not most people, however, this was far from obvious at the time of the Constitution's drafting and ratification.

At the Constitutional Convention, most of the delegates appear to have assumed that the courts would have the power to hold statutes unconstitutional and therefore unenforceable whenever issues of constitutional validity arose in cases otherwise within their jurisdiction. But not everyone, and perhaps not even anyone, anticipated the Supreme Court's modern role. Based partly on practice in the states, many friends of the Constitution seem to have anticipated that in appraising the constitutional validity of legislation, the courts would follow "the rule of clear mistake": That is, they would hold a statute invalid only if it so clearly violated the Constitution that the members of the Congress that enacted it could not reasonably have thought otherwise.[13]

A substantial number of contemporary observers also seem to have believed that the responsibility for interpreting the Constitution would be shared equally among the three branches or "departments" of the federal government. The central premise of "departmentalism," as this theory was called, was that the Constitution creates three coequal branches, each of which is equally responsible for interpreting the Constitution as necessary to discharge its proper functions.[14] To be slightly more specific, Congress must determine the scope of its powers in enacting legislation; the executive must make similar determinations in deciding when to veto legislation and, in some cases, to issue pardons; and the judiciary would need to interpret the Constitution to determine whether a law that it was asked to enforce was constitutionally valid. Under a departmentalist theory, however, judicial rulings

---

[13] See James Bradley Thayer, "The Origin and Scope of the American Doctrine of Constitutional Law," 7 *Harvard Law Review* 129, 144 (1893); see also Sylvia Snowiss, *Judicial Review and the Law of the Constitution* (New Haven, CT: Yale University Press, 1990), 60; Dean Alfange Jr., "*Marbury v. Madison* and Original Understandings of Judicial Review: In Defense of Traditional Wisdom," 1993 *Supreme Court Review* 329, 342–49 (1993); Gordon S. Wood, "The Origins of Judicial Review Revisited, or How the Marshall Court Made More out of Less," 56 *Washington & Lee Law Review* 787, 796 n.41 (1999).

[14] Larry D. Kramer, *The People Themselves: Popular Constitutionalism and Judicial Review* (Oxford, UK: Oxford University Press, 2004), 98–114.

would not necessarily establish precedents binding on Congress or the executive branch. For example, the president could refuse to enforce even those laws that the Court had ruled to be valid if the president adjudged them invalid. And perhaps a president could even ignore or defy judicial decrees if the president thought they violated constitutional norms.

Today, by contrast, it is widely understood that the Supreme Court's role in resolving constitutional issues is paramount and that, as it is sometimes put, our system is one of "judicial supremacy" in which officials of other branches must accede to the Court's interpretations of the Constitution. If one asks how we got to the modern regime of judicial supremacy, the answer is that it emerged less from original historical understandings of the Court's intended role than from felt needs and historically contingent events.

Interestingly, however, among lawyers and judges, a Founding myth of sorts has long prevailed. According to that myth, the case of *Marbury v. Madison* (1803) established the modern, judicial supremacist, understanding of the nature of judicial power and set a precedent that has been followed ever since. Among the things to note about *Marbury* is the date of its decision. As of 1803, fourteen years after the Constitution went into effect, the Supreme Court had still not ever clearly held that it had the authority to declare a law enacted by Congress invalid under the Constitution. Indeed, as of 1803, as John Jay pointed out in declining reappointment as chief justice, the job of a Supreme Court justice possessed little of the allure, authority, and prestige that it holds today. Among other drawbacks of the position, the justices sat together and issued rulings in the name of the Supreme Court of the United States only for a few months each year. During the remaining months, they headed off individually to "ride circuit" – that is, to travel to different parts of the country where they acted for all practical purposes as lower court judges.

In claiming the power of judicial review in *Marbury*, Chief Justice John Marshall largely echoed arguments that Alexander Hamilton had made in defending the Constitution in *The Federalist Papers*.[15] Among his arguments, Marshall maintained that the Constitution should be read as conferring the power of judicial review

---

[15] *The Federalist Papers, supra*, at 463–71 (spanning Alexander Hamilton's *The Federalist* Nos. 78 and 79).

on the courts, even though it nowhere describes that power explicitly, because the idea of a written constitution would be a fraud without judicial review. There would be no point in establishing written limits on the powers of Congress and the president if the courts could not enforce those limits, he asserted. Congress and the president are political actors, whose political motivations, Marshall apparently assumed, would predictably corrupt their judgments if it were left to them to determine the scope of their own constitutional powers. In a phrase from *Marbury* that has echoed through legal argumentation ever since, Marshall wrote that judicial review was necessary for the Constitution to establish "a government of laws, and not of men" and the separation of constitutional law from politics.[16]

The attraction of this logic is self-evident. But so is its deficiency. The problem is the ancient one of "Who will guard the guardians?" If the Constitution charges the courts with guarding Congress and the president, who will oversee the courts? To that question, *Marbury*'s implied answer seemed to be that among the branches of government, the courts are by far the least needful of guarding. As Hamilton had put it in *The Federalist No. 78*, the courts have "no influence over either the sword or the purse."[17] Nor are federal judges and justices political actors whose judgments are likely to be swayed or corrupted by political ambition. Because Article III of the Constitution guarantees the justices (along with other federal judges) life tenure and secures them against having their salaries reduced, they are as insulated from politics and its attendant temptations, and thus as enabled to act disinterestedly, as the lot of humanity permits.

Whatever one otherwise might think of this chain of reasoning, the facts of *Marbury* illustrate how fine the lines between law and politics and between myth and reality can be. *Marbury* grew out of a very political dispute. After the Federalist Party lost the election of 1800 but before the scheduled March inauguration of the new president, John Adams named his secretary of state, John Marshall, to become the new chief justice of the United States (as a substitute for John Jay, who was Adams's first choice for the post). During the same period, the outgoing Federalist Congress authorized the creation of thirteen new

---

[16] 5 U.S. (1 Cranch) 137, 163 (1803).
[17] Alexander Hamilton, "No. 78: The Judiciary Department," in *The Federalist Papers*, *supra*, 464.

federal judgeships, thereby doubling the size of the federal judiciary, and Adams swiftly named, and the Federalist-dominated Senate confirmed, Federalists to occupy all of the slots. Congress also created a number of more minor positions as justices of the peace that President Adams acted similarly quickly to fill.

In correspondence written during his retirement, Adams purported to see nothing discreditable in his party's rush to nominate and confirm "the midnight judges." As he noted, George Washington had continued to fill offices up to the moment of his departure from office, just as he had continued to conduct other presidential business. But Jefferson and the Democratic-Republicans viewed events through a less charitable lens. From their perspective, Adams and the Federalists had sought to capture the judiciary with partisan goals in mind and to maintain the lock-up well beyond the expiration of their terms in office. However one judges Adams's behavior, the episode not only set a precedent for future efforts by presidents and their congressional allies to stock the judiciary with supporters but also provoked a predictable tit-for-tat reaction.

Jefferson and the newly elected Democratic-Republican congressional majority struck back as soon as possible after taking office. Among other steps, Congress enacted, and the president signed into law, legislation abolishing the new federal judgeships that Adams and the Federalists had so recently filled. This was, to say the least, a constitutionally dubious step in light of the provision of Article III that "[t]he Judges, both of the supreme and inferior Courts, shall hold their Offices during good Behaviour."[18] The Jefferson administration also refused to deliver the "commissions" that were necessary to formalize the appointments of a few newly minted justices of the peace who had not yet received them.

Litigation predictably ensued. In *Marbury v. Madison*, William Marbury, who had been nominated by the outgoing President Adams and confirmed by the Senate to become a justice of the peace, asked the Supreme Court to order James Madison, the newly installed secretary of state, to deliver the "commission" formalizing his appointment. Another case – which history has mostly forgotten – challenged the constitutional validity of the highly consequential legislation abolishing the thirteen newly created federal judgeships.[19]

---

[18] U.S. Const., art. III, § 1.
[19] *Stuart v. Laird*, 5 U.S. (1 Cranch) 299 (1803).

In the context of the time, it was widely assumed that if the Supreme Court ruled in favor of either William Marbury or the challengers to the legislation abolishing the new judgeships, President Jefferson and Secretary Madison would adopt a departmentalist stance and defy the Court. If events had unfolded in that way, the prevailing balance of political power ensured that the executive branch would have prevailed in any standoff. The Democratic-Republican Congress stood squarely behind Jefferson and Madison. And the Court – lacking the power of either "the sword or the purse" – would have had no effective means of enforcing its judgment. Yet if the Supreme Court acquiesced to the administration in both cases, it would have appeared supine if not impotent.

Chief Justice Marshall's opinion in *Marbury* responded to the apparent dilemma with an ingeniously passive-aggressive strategy. In the opinion's aggressive aspect, Marshall claimed the power of judicial review and implied that the Supreme Court, in the name of the Constitution, could command action by a high official such as the secretary of state in a proper case. But Marshall then slipped into a passive mode, concluding that the Court, given the facts of the case, could award no relief to Marbury because it lacked the jurisdiction, or proper legal authorization, to decide the case at all.

Only in the Court's discussion of jurisdiction did the power of judicial review enter Marshall's analysis. Although Marshall concluded that a statute purported to grant the Supreme Court jurisdiction to rule in Marbury's case, that statute, Marshall held, contravened a specific constitutional limitation on the Court's authority involving a distinction between "appellate" and "original" jurisdiction. The Constitution, according to Marshall, would have allowed the Supreme Court to exercise appellate jurisdiction to review Marbury's case if he had sued first and lost in a lower court, but it would not permit the Supreme Court to exercise "original" jurisdiction over his case by being the first court to hear it. And the Court, having determined that the Constitution forbade it to act as a trial court in a case in which a law enacted by Congress directed it to do so, must enforce the Constitution by holding the jurisdiction-conferring statute invalid, Marshall held. With that ruling, Marshall set a precedent for the exercise of judicial review that was necessary to the decision in the case before the Court. And the ruling was one that it was impossible for Jefferson, Madison, and the Democratic-Republicans to exercise any departmentalist prerogative to defy since Madison, not Marbury, won the case of *Marbury v. Madison* in the Supreme Court.

The myth that *Marbury* decisively resolved any doubts about the Supreme Court's power to determine the constitutional validity of acts of Congress and laid the foundation for the modern regime of judicial supremacy is interesting for two reasons. First, the myth has an irony at its core. The Court claimed the necessity of judicial review in order to maintain the separation of law from politics. As the justices were all too painfully aware, however, the circumstances of the case left them with no choice but to accede to the political power of the Jefferson administration. The Court's decision to rule as it did in *Marbury* was thus, in one sense, very much a political one.

Second, the myth of *Marbury* as having established an enduring precedent for judicial review is interesting because it is so transparently false. A few decades after *Marbury*, when the Supreme Court issued a decision adverse to President Andrew Jackson's notorious "Indian removal" policy of uprooting Native American tribes from their native lands in eastern states and relocating them in the West, a possibly apocryphal report records Jackson as responding: "John Marshall has made his decision; now let him enforce it."[20] Whether or not Jackson actually uttered those words, it is well documented that occasional resistance to Supreme Court claims of ultimate authority in constitutional interpretation persisted throughout the antebellum era.[21] Widespread recognition of the Supreme Court as the ultimate arbiter of constitutional issues, whose decisions bind other institutions and officials including the president, would come in time. But *Marbury* was not causally responsible for that development.[22]

The Political Foundations of Judicial Review

Before judicial review could take root and judicial supremacy in constitutional interpretation could flourish, the Supreme Court had to define a role for itself that dominant political forces – including

---

[20] See, for example, Jon Meacham, *American Lion: Andrew Jackson in the White House* (New York, NY: Random House, 2008), 204.

[21] See Richard H. Fallon Jr. et al., *Hart & Wechsler's the Federal Courts and the Federal System*, 7th ed. (New York, NY: Foundation Press, 2015), 464–75.

[22] Keith Whittington, *Repugnant Laws: Judicial Review of Acts of Congress from the Founding to the Present* (Lawrence, KS: University Press of Kansas, 2019), 60–119.

high national officeholders and the major political parties – would find tolerable and even beneficial. As comparative work involving other democracies has shown, claims of courts to "supremacy" in constitutional interpretation will be accepted only where courts win sufficient trust and respect from various relevant constituencies, including the leaders of political parties who must anticipate that they will sometimes hold governing power but that sometimes they will not. In these circumstances, political leaders must think that the establishment and observance of a norm requiring them to acquiesce to judicial rulings will somehow serve their own long-term interests, even if it frustrates their short-term goals. It is easy, moreover, to imagine terms on which present, past, and future political leaders would agree to, and expect that they would benefit from, a regime of (constrained) judicial supremacy. If courts can achieve a reputation as evenhanded enforcers of constitutional norms, then courts with the power to rule authoritatively on legal and constitutional issues can provide checks against abuses of power by an incumbent regime, including through harassment and persecution of former officeholders from rival parties and other political opponents. An independent judiciary equipped with the power of judicial review can also provide a hedge against subsequent administrations ignoring laws that a prior regime successfully enacted. Furthermore, a powerful national judiciary, headed by a Supreme Court, can play a valuable role in enforcing the Constitution (provided that other national officials are prepared to back it up) against recalcitrant states.

Before there could be a bargain or equilibrium in which Congress and the president would accept the ultimate authority of the Supreme Court in constitutional matters, however, the Court would need to establish a reputation for relative evenhandedness. In other words, it would need to be seen as more than a collection of politicians in robes, put on the bench to do the bidding of one political party or another. And the public would need to trust the courts sufficiently to be ready to punish elected officials who refused to obey judicial decrees – for example, by demanding the impeachment of disobedient officials or voting them out of office.

In order to achieve the trust and prestige necessary for a regime of judicial supremacy to take root and ultimately flourish, the justices would need to accommodate themselves to what mainstream political leaders and most ordinary Americans will accept as correct, or at least reasonable, discharge of properly judicial functions. It is hard, perhaps impossible, to cash out this stricture in precise terms. Surely the Supreme Court does not need to – and indeed must not – calibrate its decisions to every uptick or downtick in public opinion. The greater the esteem that the Court possesses at any particular time, the broader the limits of the interpretive power that it can successfully assert in the name of the Constitution without triggering successful defiance by or retaliation from presidents or other political leaders. As the circumstances surrounding *Marbury* demonstrate, however, judicial power cannot simply be taken for granted. If the Court had ordered Secretary of State Madison to deliver William Marbury's commission to be a justice of the peace, it would have come out the loser in the ensuing confrontation.

Interestingly, moreover, the Court has learned that among the ways for it to inspire trust and cultivate prestige is to cast itself as carrying on in the tradition of hallowed forebears, including John Marshall, who by the end of the nineteenth century had attained near-legendary status as a great, visionary, above-the-political-fray chief justice. Only then did the Supreme Court begin to cite *Marbury v. Madison* as having settled authoritatively that it possessed the power of judicial review. And only later still, in the middle of the twentieth century, would the Court begin its modern practice of invoking *Marbury* – celebrated as the handiwork of the now-lionized Marshall – as the legal authority for the proposition that the Supreme Court is the ultimate expositor of the Constitution to whose interpretations all others must accede.

2 HISTORICAL OVERVIEW OF CONSTITUTIONAL ADJUDICATION BY THE SUPREME COURT

As Chief Justice Charles Evans Hughes gaveled the Supreme Court to order on April 12, 1937, the fate of the New Deal hung in the balance. So, potentially, did the future of the Court. The previous November, President Franklin Roosevelt had swept to one of the most conclusive electoral victories of the twentieth century. When Roosevelt won election the first time, with the country in the grip of the devastating Great Depression, he had promised "bold, persistent experimentation" in pursuit of remedies.[1] During his first term, Roosevelt had kept that pledge. He had proposed, and the Congress had enacted, economic regulatory legislation of unparalleled scope. He had also sponsored, and the Congress had passed, bills to assist the financially needy, including the Social Security Act. In seeking reelection, Roosevelt had committed to more of the same.

But his capacity to deliver was in doubt. The obstacle was the Supreme Court. The Court had long instructed that the government of the United States was designed to be one of "limited" or "enumerated," not plenary, powers.[2] To pass economic regulatory legislation that the Constitution's Framers would have found hard to imagine,

---

[1] Franklin D. Roosevelt, "Address at Oglethorpe University (May 22, 1932)," in 1 *The Public Papers and Address of Franklin D. Roosevelt*, ed. Samuel I. Rosenman (New York, NY: Harper & Brothers, 1938), 639, 646.
[2] As noted in Chapter 1, a few scholars have begun to question this understanding, but the Supreme Court so far has not.

Roosevelt and his New Deal lawyers had relied on a provision of Article I that empowers Congress "[t]o regulate Commerce ... among the several States." But in 1935, the Supreme Court held that the Commerce Clause granted Congress no authority to regulate economic activities, including manufacturing and farming, that occurred within the territorial boundaries of a single state.[3] As a source of power to provide direct financial assistance to the poor and the elderly, Roosevelt had pointed to the Taxing and Spending Clause, which authorizes Congress "to lay and collect Taxes ... to pay the Debts and provide for the common Defence and the general Welfare of the United States." Yet in 1936, the Supreme Court had ruled that Congress had no power, under the Spending Clause or otherwise, to provide pensions for coal miners.[4] In light of rulings such as these, Roosevelt had reason to fear that the Court might invalidate his cherished Social Security Act and more generally wreck his second term.

Without a better alternative, in February 1937 Roosevelt advanced a bill that would have permitted him to name six new justices to the Supreme Court from among the many able lawyers who shared his pragmatic constitutional philosophy. The Court-packing proposal, as it was called, represented a break from longstanding practice, but it accorded with the letter of the Constitution. Although the Supreme Court has had nine justices since 1869, the Constitution permits Congress to fix the number by statute. At earlier points in history, the Court had as few as six and as many as ten justices. In 1937, however, Roosevelt's plan was deeply controversial because it was viewed as a threat to judicial independence, to the system of constitutional checks and balances, and potentially to individual rights. As a result, Congress appeared closely divided over Roosevelt's scheme. Even so, many observers expected its passage.

Then came the thunderclap of April 12. By a vote of 5–4, the justices upheld an important piece of New Deal regulatory legislation governing the steel industry that Congress had enacted under the Commerce Clause.[5] That ruling highlighted the significance of a decision that the Court had handed down two weeks earlier when it withdrew the obstacles to state regulation of workers' wages and hours that

---

[3] *Railroad Retirement Board v. Alton Railroad Company*, 295 U.S. 330 (1935); *A. L. A. Schechter Poultry Corporation v. United States*, 295 U.S. 495 (1935).
[4] *Carter v. Carter Coal Company*, 298 U.S. 238 (1936).
[5] *National Labor Relations Board v. Jones & Laughlin Steel*, 301 U.S. 1 (1937).

it previously had interposed under the Due Process Clause.[6] The Court then ratified its stunning turnaround in May by upholding the Social Security Act as a valid exercise of Congress's powers under the Spending Clause.[7]

Following the Supreme Court's about-face, which appeared to reflect a dramatic change of position by two of the Court's members – Chief Justice Hughes and Justice Owen Roberts – the New Deal was safe. And so was the Court. Although Roosevelt continued to press his Court-packing proposal, it died in the Senate after what contemporary commentators dubbed "the switch in time that saved nine."[8] As a reluctant supporter observed, "Why run for a train after you've caught it?"[9]

The inflection point that occurred in 1937 was unusually dramatic, but it also illustrates a characteristic feature of the Supreme Court's history. Although obviously continuous in one respect, that history can be also be divided into eras, marked by the dominant judicial philosophies or outlooks that have prevailed at different times. Occasionally, moreover, the transition from one period to another has occurred quite suddenly. At the risk of some oversimplification, the remainder of this chapter describes five eras of Supreme Court history leading up to the one that we inhabit now.

The Marshall Era: 1801-1835

In retrospect, John Marshall was a great, indeed the greatest, chief justice – the judicial parallel to George Washington. In his own time, however, Marshall was a vastly more divisive figure, and the Supreme Court remained a vulnerable institution long after its tactical retreat in *Marbury v. Madison*[10] (1803) and a companion case that in effect acceded to the abolition of a number of judgeships occupied by members of Marshall's Federalist Party.[11] Following the realignment in national politics that brought Thomas Jefferson's

---

[6] *West Coast Hotel Company v. Parrish*, 300 U.S. 379 (1937).
[7] *Steward Machine Co. v. Davis*, 301 U.S. 548 (1937); *Helvering v. Davis*, 301 U.S. 619 (1937).
[8] Joseph Alsop and Turner Catledge, *The 168 Days* (Garden City, NY: Doubleday, Doran, & Co., 1938), 135.
[9] *Ibid.* at 152 (quoting Senator James Byrnes).
[10] 5 U.S. (1 Cranch) 137 (1803).
[11] See *Stuart v. Laird*, 5 U.S. 299 (1803).

Democratic-Republicans into a position of dominance beginning in 1800, the Court and its incumbent justices remained tainted by their association with the Federalist Party, including the justices' involvement in enforcing the Sedition Act. Enacted in 1798 by a Federalist Congress, the Sedition Act made it a criminal offense to "print, utter, or publish ... any false, scandalous, and malicious writing" about the government of the United States. When federal prosecutors filed charges under the Act, mostly against Democratic-Republicans, the task of charging juries fell to the mostly Federalist judiciary, including justices of the Supreme Court during those parts of the year when they acted as lower court judges "riding circuit." Republicans thought that a number of the jury charges delivered by the justices crossed the line into rank partisanship.

So alleging, in 1804, the House of Representatives voted articles of impeachment against Justice Samuel Chase, one of the Court's most outspoken members. If he had been convicted by the Senate, impeachments of more justices likely would have followed. Although the Senate failed to muster the requisite two-thirds vote to remove Chase, the justices appear to have absorbed a lesson from the episode. For the Supreme Court to survive as a stably independent institution, the justices needed to eschew overtly partisan judging, even if they sometimes could not avoid taking stands on issues with political implications.[12]

Within the boundaries loosely marked by the tolerance of national political leaders and ultimately the American public, John Marshall and the Court that surrounded him pursued two interconnected objectives that history – at least as written after the Civil War – has largely approved. The first was to establish the authority of the national judiciary, especially the Supreme Court. The second was nation-building through the establishment of broad congressional power to legislate in the national interest despite state objections.

With regard to assertions of judicial power, the most foundational decision of the Court subsequent to *Marbury v. Madison* came in *Martin v. Hunter's Lessee* (1816).[13] The central question in *Martin* was whether the Supreme Court could review and reverse a decision of

---

[12] Barry Friedman, *The Will of the People: How Public Opinion Has Influenced the Supreme Court and Shaped the Meaning of the Constitution* (New York, NY: Farrar, Straus and Giroux, 2010), 64–71.
[13] 14 U.S. 304 (1816).

the Virginia State Supreme Court on a question of federal law involving the rights of British subjects under a federal treaty. Today, the answer to that question is so obviously an affirmative one that it can be hard to comprehend the controversy. Framed in terms that sometimes haunt constitutional law even today, the issue seemed debatable in 1816 because of the implications of Virginia's claim that it was a "sovereign" state. What it meant to be a sovereign, according to Virginia, was to be answerable to no higher authority. And in light of this premise, Virginia contended, the highest court of the sovereign state of Virginia could not be subject to the appellate jurisdiction of the court of any other sovereign, including the Supreme Court of the United States. In an opinion by Justice Joseph Story, the Court patiently demonstrated the irreconcilability of that position with the language and history of the Constitution.

Today, *Martin v. Hunter's Lessee* occupies a prominent place in texts on constitutional law and the jurisdiction of the federal courts. It is regarded as fundamental in welding states and their courts into a single nation with a Supreme Court capable of enforcing the supremacy of federal over state law. And the Supreme Court, following *Martin v. Hunter's Lessee*, did not hesitate to review state court decisions and to hold that some of them violated rights – including property and contract rights – that the Constitution guarantees. Nonetheless, up until the Civil War, state supreme courts in some states continued occasionally to insist that decisions by the Supreme Court did not bind them.

Insofar as national power was concerned, the Marshall Court took an expansive view of Congress's regulatory authority as tested by the debated issues of the time. (During the Marshall years, the kinds of New Deal legislation that provoked the confrontation between the Court and President Roosevelt in 1937 – including national legislation protecting union organizing and creating a Social Security system – would have fallen outside the scope of anyone's imagining.) The most celebrated decision of the Marshall Court on the scope of national power came in *McCulloch v. Maryland* (1819),[14] which presented issues involving both the substantive reach of congressional power and proper methodologies of constitutional interpretation.

The first question in *McCulloch* was whether the Constitution authorized Congress to create a "Bank of the United States" (with

[14] 17 U.S. 316 (1819).

branches throughout the country) as a depository for federal funds and as a means of creating networks of commercial credit. Although all sides agreed that Congress possessed no powers beyond those conferred by the Constitution, and although Article I nowhere referred expressly to a congressional power to create a national bank, Marshall had no difficulty in upholding the Bank of the United States. He reasoned that the Constitution granted Congress a number of "great powers," including those "to lay and collect Taxes ...; To borrow Money ...; To regulate Commerce ...; To declare War ...; [and] To raise and support Armies."[15] All of those great powers being given, it would make no sense, he wrote, to read the Constitution as precluding the use of a means – in this case a national bank – that Congress reasonably thought necessary or appropriate in executing those powers: "[A] government, entrusted with such ample powers, on the due execution of which the happiness and prosperity of the nation so vitally depends, must also be entrusted with ample means for their execution."

Two sentences from *McCulloch* exemplify Marshall's approach to issues of congressional power. First, "[W]e must never forget that it is a *constitution* we are expounding." Second, the Court should interpret the Constitution, which does not "partake of the prolixity of a legal code," in such a way as to make it "adapt[able] to the various *crises* of human affairs."[16] Marshall also wrote that the Court should prefer interpretations that would promote prudent and otherwise desirable consequences.

With Congress's power to create the bank having been established, the next question was whether it was constitutionally permissible for Maryland to tax it. Marshall briskly ruled that it was not. No bit of constitutional language spoke to this issue, but Marshall again appealed to the Constitution's broadest purposes and its underlying assumptions. An "unlimited power to tax" the bank was, "necessarily," the "power to destroy" it, he wrote.[17] A constitution that empowered Congress to create a bank thus could not sensibly be read to leave the states with a potentially destructive power to eviscerate it though taxation.

---

[15] *Ibid.* at 407 (emphasis in original).
[16] *Ibid.* at 407, 415 (emphasis in original).
[17] *Ibid.* at 327.

Although Marshall wrote for a unanimous Court in *McCulloch*, his reasoning was controversial, especially among Democratic-Republicans who championed the cause of states' rights and looked askance at expansive claims of national power. As an intellectual matter, the difficulty with Marshall's argument in *McCulloch*, which he never confronted, is that different people will predictably, sometimes systematically, differ in their views of what would make the Constitution fairer or better or truer to its dominant purposes. Looking at the national bank at issue in *McCulloch*, Marshall emphasized the character of the Constitution in vesting Congress with "great powers," the full effectuation of which should not be frustrated. But an opponent of the bank might as easily have emphasized the constitutional design to give Congress only limited powers, as subsequently emphasized by the Tenth Amendment: "The powers not delegated to the United States by the Constitution, nor prohibited by it to the States, are reserved to the States respectively, or to the people."

In my judgment, it is impossible to interpret vague constitutional language sensibly except in light of its purposes, even though reasonable people will sometimes disagree about what those purposes are or how best to describe them. And it is for this reason, I believe, that Marshall's iconic opinion in *McCulloch* is widely upheld as a paradigm of compelling constitutional reasoning. Implicitly if not explicitly, it recognizes that courts should resolve constitutional ambiguities in just and prudent ways and that judgments of justice and prudence are in that sense integral to constitutional interpretation in some cases. At the same time, we should recognize that the central issue in *McCulloch* also helps to illustrate the possibility of reasonable, good faith constitutional disagreement by people with differing normative views.

In a highly influential commentary on the Marshall Court written in the early 1960s, Harvard political scientist Robert McCloskey wrote that "the cornerstones of American constitutionalism had been laid," and "securely" so, during Marshall's tenure and that "no court in world history had ever done so much to affect the destiny of a great nation."[18] Although this summation is probably accurate at one level, it is misleading on another. To put the Marshall Court in proper perspective, account needs to be taken of how Marshall's work achieved

---

[18] Robert G. McCloskey, *The American Supreme Court*, 6th ed. (Chicago, IL/London, UK: University of Chicago Press, 2016), 50, 52.

its effects. Even with *Marbury v. Madison* long behind, the House of Representatives passed a bill in 1831 (though it died in the Senate) that would have stripped the Supreme Court of appellate jurisdiction to review state court decisions such as the one the Court reviewed in *Martin v. Hunter's Lessee*. And in another famous episode in the 1830s, already noted in Chapter 1, President Andrew Jackson purportedly threatened to defy a Supreme Court ruling that was unfriendly to his "Indian removal" policy with the sneering observation, "John Marshall has made his decision; now let him enforce it."[19] Even more ominously, by the time of Marshall's retirement in 1835, deepening divisions over slavery raised doubts about whether the Union that he had worked to strengthen could survive at all. Insofar as our current constitutional order rests on foundations that Marshall laid, it is also the result of projects of construction and reconstruction conducted during and after the Civil War, including by the Union Army. I have never forgotten the admonition of my constitutional law professor, Charles Black, who used to tell his classes that legal historians who wrote admiringly of the Constitution's eighteenth-century Framers should not overlook the contributions of the "constitutional logicians" who fought and many of whom died on Civil War battlefields to preserve and strengthen the Union that their forebears had sought to forge.

The Taney Era: 1836–1864

Upon John Marshall's retirement, leadership of the Supreme Court passed to Roger Taney, a Jacksonian Democrat. In an era when the Democratic Party dominated national elections, the Taney Court generally skirted controversy and, by doing so, helped to foster trust in the Court as a nonpartisan enforcer of constitutional norms. As respect for the Court grew, so did the Court's authority. Then, in 1857, the justices took the most egregious misstep in the Court's history.

By the 1850s, the issue of slavery in the federal territories, many of them awaiting admission to the Union as states, was tearing the country apart. Northern antislavery states feared the emergence of a proslavery majority in Congress. The slave states were equally fearful of shifts in the congressional balance of power. As the country

---

[19] See, for example, Jon Meacham, *American Lion: Andrew Jackson in the White House* (New York, NY: Random House, 2008), 204.

awaited the inauguration of president-elect James Buchanan following the 1856 election, the case of *Dred Scott v. Sandford*[20] (1857) made its way to the Supreme Court. Among the issues was whether Scott, who had been held in slavery since birth, had achieved free status when he accompanied his purported "master" into the free territory of Wisconsin and thereby became a "citizen" capable of suing in the courts of the United States.

The Supreme Court could have decided the case on the narrow ground that Scott's status as either a citizen or a noncitizen was determined by the law of the state in which he resided. If the law of Missouri settled the issue, Scott, whom state law categorized as a slave, would not have been a "citizen" capable of suing in federal court, and the Court could have dismissed the case as one over which it lacked "jurisdiction" to render any further substantive ruling. But Buchanan and some other Democratic political leaders urged the justices to issue a broader pronouncement, technically unnecessary to resolve the case, that Congress lacked any power under the Constitution to prohibit slavery in Wisconsin or most if not all other federal territories. Such a ruling, some misguidedly dared to hope, might put an end to divisive debates about whether and how Congress should regulate slavery in the territories by establishing that Congress had no power under the Constitution to do so at all.

In *Dred Scott*, a majority of the justices ruled as Buchanan had hoped. There was a tangle of opinions in the case that make it difficult to speak of clear rulings by "the Court" on some points. But the lead opinion announcing the Court's judgment, which Chief Justice Taney authored, had three important components. First, the Court held that it had no jurisdiction over the case – and thus no power to rule on the merits of Scott's substantive claim to the status of a free person – because he, as a man of African descent, was incapable of being a "citizen" within the meaning of the Constitution. As characterized by today's standards, the Court's reasoning on this point was originalist (regardless of whether the chief justice's claims about the Constitution's original meaning were correct). Taney purported to determine as a historical matter that the Constitution's reference to "citizens" as a category of litigants entitled to sue "citizens" of other states in federal court did not include Black people. Taney's reasoning

---

[20] 60 U.S. 393 (1857).

to that conclusion rested on the premise that the Framers were "great men," not hypocrites – and hypocrites they would have been if they professed to believe that "all men are created equal" yet held Black men in bondage.[21] The hypocrisy, in the eyes of Roger Taney, disappeared only on the premise that Black people were not men in the relevant sense and were, accordingly, incapable of becoming citizens.

At this point the Court could have, and legally should have, stopped on the ground that it lacked jurisdiction to issue any further ruling. Instead, it plunged on. Scott's claim to freedom was further flawed, the chief justice held, by its reliance on the premise that he had traveled in a "free" territory. Congress, the Court's majority ruled, had no power to forbid slavery in the territories. Although Article IV of the Constitution authorizes Congress to "make all needful rules and regulations" for the territories, this language had no application to any territory – such as Wisconsin or other territories that were then eligible to become states – that had not belonged to the United States at the time when the Constitution was written and ratified, Taney wrote.

In support of this conclusion, which finds no support in the language of Article IV, the Court advanced a third, further argument based on the Due Process Clause of the Fifth Amendment, which provides that "no person shall ... be deprived of life, liberty, or property, without due process of law." An Act of Congress that purported to deprive a citizen of his property in a person held as a slave, merely because he "brought his property into a particular Territory of the United States, ... could hardly be dignified with the name of due process of law," Taney pronounced.[22] Taney's determination that the Due Process Clause not only was a guarantee of procedural fairness but also provided a basis for the judicial invalidation of legislation that the Court deemed substantively unfair represented the first example of what would later come to be called "substantive due process" reasoning in the Supreme Court – a matter to be discussed briefly in this chapter and explored more fully in Chapter 8.

In rendering a broad decision predicated on legally dubious reasoning, but one calculated to stop the country from splintering over slavery, the justices in the *Dred Scott* case may have thought that they acted in the statesmanlike tradition of John Marshall in *Marbury v.*

[21] *Ibid.* at 410, 418.
[22] *Ibid.* at 450.

Madison, which also had relied on shaky legal analysis to reach a result believed necessary to the long-term future of the country and the Court. But *Dred Scott*, unlike *Marbury*, was a fiasco. Besides taking the wrong side of a constitutional issue with profound moral implications, the justices quixotically overestimated the practical reach of judicial power.[23] The Court's ruling – which effectively held that the defining political aim of the nascent Republican Party to ban slavery in the territories was unconstitutional – provoked fierce and eloquent opposition from slavery's opponents. Debates about slavery in the territories continued unabated. And the flimsiness of the Court's reasoning plunged it into angry disrepute among those who opposed slavery or its spread.

After *Dred Scott*, as the bonds of constitutional government frayed, judicial power went into eclipse. During the Civil War, the Supreme Court generally acquiesced in actions by Congress, the president, and the Union Army that arguably overstepped constitutional bounds. In a relatively isolated case of judicial resistance to intrusions on civil liberties during wartime, President Abraham Lincoln actually defied a ruling by Chief Justice Taney – acting as a "circuit" judge rather than on behalf of the Supreme Court – denying the authority of military officials to detain suspected Confederate sympathizers without bringing them into court and proving them guilty of crimes.[24]

In a further show of disrespect for the judicial branch, Congress, during the remainder of the Civil War and the early Reconstruction era, repeatedly manipulated the size of the Supreme Court to expand opportunities for Republican Presidents Lincoln and Grant to appoint justices and to deny appointments to Democrat Andrew Johnson, who opposed the Republican Congress's Reconstruction policies. At that time, Court-packing encountered far fewer objections than it subsequently did in 1937.

From Reconstruction through the New Deal (or "the *Lochner* Era"): 1865–1937

As the nation regrouped following the Civil War, the Supreme Court slid into perhaps the most puzzling era in its history. That epoch

---

[23] For criticism of the decision by a later member of the Court, see Stephen G. Breyer, "A Look Back at the Dred Scott Decision," 35 *Journal of Supreme Court History* 110 (2010).
[24] *Ex parte Merryman*, 17 F. Cas. 144 (CCD Md. 1861).

began during Reconstruction, with Republican majorities holding the reins of power in Congress and with the Union Army occupying parts of the former Confederacy. Thereafter until the early years of the New Deal in the 1930s, the Republican Party continued to hold more sway than any other party in the nation's sometimes divided politics, and justices appointed by Republican presidents dominated the Supreme Court. The leading issues involved the proper interpretation of the Civil War Amendments and related matters involving the permissibility of regulation of an increasingly nationalized and industrialized economy.

Though the Republicans were "the party of Lincoln" and the sponsors of Reconstruction, political enthusiasm for prosecuting a Reconstruction agenda involving military occupation of the South waned rapidly in a country already exhausted by war. As it did so, the Supreme Court adopted interpretations of the Thirteenth, Fourteenth, and Fifteenth Amendments that substantially deprived them of effect in achieving equal basic rights for African Americans. The first of the important cases interpreting the Civil War Amendments, the *Slaughter-House Cases* (1873),[25] turned principally on the Privileges or Immunities Clause of the Fourteenth Amendment, which provides that "no State shall make or enforce any law which shall abridge the privileges or immunities of citizens of the United States." Much about the history of the Fourteenth Amendment is contested. But there is a widespread belief among historians that the congressional sponsors of the Fourteenth Amendment viewed the Privileges or Immunities Clause as the most important of its rights-conferring provisions. On one familiar account, it was broadly understood to forbid discrimination with respect to "fundamental" or "civil" rights that were viewed as basic to citizenship and constituted "the privileges or immunities of citizens of the United States."[26]

The *Slaughter-House Cases* presented a strange test case under a constitutional amendment with the predominant, but by no means necessarily exclusive, purpose of securing the rights of African Americans recently released from slavery. Whether for good or for corrupt purposes, the governing officials of New Orleans granted a slaughterhouse monopoly. It was challenged by a white resident who claimed that the

---

[25] 83 U.S. 36 (1873).
[26] Eric Foner, *The Second Founding: How the Civil War and Reconstruction Remade the Constitution* (New York, NY: W.W. Norton, 2019), 74–76, 133–34.

right to pursue a lawful trade – in this case, that of a butcher – numbered among the "privileges or immunities of citizens" and thus was entitled to protection by the federal courts. By a vote of 5–4, the Court rejected that argument by holding that nearly all of what were traditionally understood as the privileges or immunities of citizenship were privileges or immunities of *state* citizenship, not national citizenship, and that the Fourteenth Amendment had done nothing to change that state of affairs. As a result, butchers who were stopped from plying their trade in New Orleans might be able to bring complaints in state court alleging violations of rights under state law, but they had no federal constitutional claim under the Privileges or Immunities Clause. An alternative interpretation that took a broader view of "the privileges or immunities of citizens of the United States," the majority reasoned, would constitute the Supreme Court as "a perpetual censor" of state laws, including such mundane provisions as those licensing butchers.[27] With *Dred Scott* still a live memory, a majority of the justices shrank from that role. Although the immediately losing parties were white butchers, the implication of the Court's reasoning was to deprive Black people of what otherwise might have been an important constitutional protection against state laws denying them fundamental rights.

Following the *Slaughter-House Cases*, the most promising constitutional foundation for challenges to racial injustice lay in the Equal Protection Clause. By the late nineteenth century, however, the Supreme Court had also deprived that provision of any substantial effect in protecting racial minorities. In the notorious case of *Plessy v. Ferguson* (1896),[28] which Chapter 7 will discuss at length, the Court ruled that state-enforced segregation generally did not offend the equal protection guarantee as long as Black and white people were afforded "separate but equal" facilities. In nearly all instances, separate facilities were grossly unequal, but the Court resolutely looked the other way. The Court also refused to act as southern states stripped Blacks of voting rights that the Fifteenth Amendment had appeared to secure.

In a startling juxtaposition, at the same time that the Supreme Court was rendering the Fourteenth Amendment substantially ineffectual as a tool for protecting racial minorities, it increasingly deployed that Amendment as an instrument for protecting business interests.

[27] *Slaughter-House Cases*, 83 U.S. 36, 78 (1873).
[28] 163 U.S. 537 (1896).

During this period, Congress and a number of state legislatures began to enact various forms of "progressive" regulatory legislation, including measures to prohibit child labor, give workers the right to unionize, and establish minimum wages and maximum hours for laborers. The Supreme Court met these developments with constitutional objections on two fronts. First, in cases challenging federal legislation, the Court frequently held that Congress had exceeded the bounds of its power under Article I of the Constitution when, for example, it sought to regulate child labor.[29] Second, when the states enacted regulatory legislation, the Court's conservative majority began to hold that restrictions on "the freedom of contract" infringed on individual liberty and therefore triggered "substantive due process" review under the Due Process Clause of the Fourteenth Amendment.

The so-called *Lochner* era of "substantive due process review," which took its name from a notorious case in which the Supreme Court struck down a state law limiting the hours that could be worked by bakery employees,[30] stretched into the 1930s. By the latter part of this period, the Court made some gestures toward protecting civil liberties involving speech and religion. But most of its substantive due process cases engaged in review of what the Court took to be the fairness or reasonableness of restrictions on the capacity of businesses and their workers to enter into contractual relationships that both parties, the Court reasoned, must have adjudged to be in their best interests. If workers agreed to long hours, low wages, and hazardous conditions, it must be because they preferred the deals that they freely chose to the alternatives available to them, and it was unreasonable for the states to interfere with their freedom of contract, the Court often concluded.

Controversial from the outset, the Supreme Court's antiregulatory stance increasingly engendered outrage during the Great Depression, especially as majorities of the justices invalidated central elements of President Franklin Roosevelt's New Deal and threatened to scuttle others. The constitutional showdown that occurred in 1937, resulting in "the switch in time that saved nine," marked the beginning of a new era in Supreme Court history. That transition also illustrates a number of points that will be of recurring importance throughout the remainder of this book. First, the Supreme Court "is a 'they,' not

---

[29] See *Hammer v. Dagenhart*, 247 U.S. 251 (1918).
[30] *Lochner v. New York*, 198 U.S. 45 (1905).

an 'it.'"³¹ Before 1937, the justices had been deeply divided about the constitutionality of New Deal legislation. Even in the spring of 1937, at least seven of the nine justices remained wedded to their former positions. The decisions of one or two "swing" justices determined the outcome of the key cases marking the transition from the *Lochner* era to its successor period. With one or two different members, the Court might have upheld New Deal legislation from the beginning – or it might have continued to invalidate programs such as Social Security through 1937 and possibly beyond.

Second, like the events surrounding *Marbury v. Madison*, developments in 1937 illustrate that the Supreme Court operates within politically constructed bounds. In 1937, if the Supreme Court had persisted in invalidating popular New Deal legislation, President Roosevelt's Court-packing plan might well have succeeded. When a majority of the justices take positions that the public finds deeply objectionable, presidential candidates can run against the Court, promising to appoint justices with different philosophies and thereby pull the Court back in line with public opinion.

Third, presidential leadership can have a powerful role in shaping the constitutional views of the American people and reshaping the positions of the Supreme Court, typically through the nominations of new justices. Franklin Roosevelt had a constitutional vision of expansive government adequate to tame the business cycle, ensure a living wage to all who were willing to work, and provide a social safety net for the elderly and disabled. He successfully sold that vision to large majorities of the public. By winning elections, Roosevelt, over more than three presidential terms, was able to appoint eight justices to the Supreme Court, even without the aid of Court-packing. By the time of his death in 1945, the Supreme Court could fairly have been called "the Roosevelt Court." The old regime, defined by a judicial commitment to enforce traditional limits on government's power to regulate economic relations, was out. A new regime, defined by a set of constitutional assumptions that accepted sweeping economic regulation and redistributive programs such as Social Security, had taken its place and would reign largely unchallenged for roughly the next fifty years.

---

[31] See Adrian Vermeule, "The Judiciary Is a They, Not an It: Interpretive Theory and the Fallacy of Division," 14 *Journal of Contemporary Legal Issues* 549 (2005).

The Supreme Court of the New Deal Settlement and the Civil Rights Revolution: 1937–1969

At the risk of crude oversimplification, the constitutional regime that emerged from Franklin Roosevelt's reshaping of the Supreme Court – which ran roughly from 1937 to 1969, when Earl Warren retired as chief justice – included two main elements. The first, which represented Roosevelt's direct legacy, involved a broad acceptance of the regulatory and redistributive agenda of the New Deal. Historians sometimes refer to this acceptance by the Supreme Court, which represented a dramatic transformation from the *Lochner* era, as "the New Deal settlement." The second defining element of the post-*Lochner* regime involved an evolving judicial commitment to the identification and enforcement of constitutional rights of racial minorities, the poor, and politically disempowered groups of various kinds.

In remaking the Supreme Court, Franklin Roosevelt set out to appoint progressive or "liberal" justices. In the context of a time in which judicial "conservatives" had thwarted the enforcement of progressive legislation, judicial liberals were generally those who believed that the Court should give Congress and the state legislatures a relatively free hand. In other words, New Deal liberals preached judicial deference to the decisions of the political branches or what is sometimes characterized as "judicial restraint." Once liberals had acceded to a position of judicial dominance, however, reflection on the lessons of the *Lochner* era led some justices and commentators to the conclusion that the Court's prior error had not lain in its willingness to enforce constitutional rights, or even unwritten constitutional rights, but in its selection of the wrong kinds of rights to protect. According to a newly emerging line of liberal thought, the Court should almost never invalidate economic regulatory legislation, but it should not hesitate to protect civil rights and liberties, including freedom of speech. In particular, in light of the Fourteenth Amendment, the Court should give vigilant protection to the rights of racial and religious minorities. The Supreme Court first articulated that alternative vision of the judicial role in a famous footnote in the case of *United States v. Carolene Products* (1938),[32] which portentously reserved the question "whether prejudice against discrete and insular minorities may be a special

---

[32] 304 U.S. 144, 153 n.4 (1938).

condition, which tends seriously to curtail the operation of those political processes ordinarily to be relied upon to protect minorities, and which may call for a correspondingly more searching judicial inquiry."

The seeds planted in *Carolene Products* began to bear conspicuous fruit under the Warren Court, so called after Chief Justice Earl Warren, who was named to the bench in 1953. One of the early landmarks of his tenure came when the Court held in *Brown v. Board of Education*[33] (1954) that the Equal Protection Clause of the Fourteenth Amendment forbade race-based discrimination in public schools. As is discussed further in Chapter 7, this conclusion was fiercely controversial at the time. Today, however, nearly everyone regards *Brown* as among the triumphant moments of Supreme Court history. It served as a prelude to other Warren Court decisions that expanded the scope of the constitutional guarantee of equal protection of the laws, First Amendment freedoms of speech and religion, and a variety of rights of criminal suspects, including those emerging from the Court's revolutionary decision in *Miranda v. Arizona* (1966).[34]

Augmenting the significance of many of these doctrinal innovations were the Warren Court's holdings that most guarantees in the federal Bill of Rights – including those mandating fair procedures in criminal trials and investigations – applied against the states. The path to this result included a series of sometimes bizarre twists and turns. As noted in Chapter 1, the Bill of Rights did not initially create rights against the states. And although there is a serious historical argument that the Privileges or Immunities Clause of the Fourteenth Amendment was originally understood by most observers as encompassing some or all Bill of Rights guarantees among the "privileges or immunities" that it aimed to protect against the states,[35] the Supreme Court, as we have seen, held otherwise in the *Slaughter-House Cases*. But then, during the *Lochner* era, the Court began to rule that some of the rights enforceable against the federal government under the Bill of Rights – including the First Amendment right to freedom of speech – were part of the "liberty" that the Fourteenth Amendment's Due Process Clause

---

[33] 347 U.S. 483 (1954).
[34] 384 U.S. 436 (1966).
[35] See, for example, Foner, *Second Founding, supra,* at 26; Akhil Reed Amar, *The Bill of Rights: Creation and Reconstruction* (New Haven, CT: Yale University Press, 1998); William E. Nelson, *The Fourteenth Amendment: From Political Principle to Judicial Doctrine* (Cambridge, MA: Harvard University Press, 1988).

protects against state interference. And those decisions, which garnered a nod of approval in the iconic *Carolene Products* footnote, survived the rejection of *Lochner*-era rulings protecting economic liberties and provided a foundation on which subsequent cases built.

Questions involving which provisions of the Bill of Rights were "incorporated" by the Fourteenth Amendment and thus made applicable against the states represented a subject of intense controversy from the 1940s through the 1960s. But by the late 1960s, incorporation doctrine was nearing an equilibrium that had solidified by the early 1970s and has remained relatively stable ever since. The still-prevailing doctrine, largely constructed by the Warren Court, rests on three main premises: First, the Due Process Clause incorporates those guarantees of the Bill of Rights that the Supreme Court deems "fundamental." Second, in determining whether a particular right is fundamental, the Court will inquire whether it is "fundamental to the American scheme of justice" as it has existed historically.[36] Third, when a right is incorporated by the Fourteenth Amendment, it ordinarily applies to states in exactly the same way as it applies to the federal government.

Earl Warren was a warm, conspicuously decent man. A former governor of California, he had an easy charm and confident moral and political instincts. From the bench, Warren would sometimes ask counsel who had made technical legal points whether they thought that the results that they urged were fair – not whether they were supportable by legal argument but whether they were just or decent in a deeper sense. Often a majority of the justices followed where he led. Some thrilled to the approach of the Warren Court. Many law professors were perplexed, often sympathetic to the Court's results but skeptical of the soundness of its constitutional reasoning. And some, of course, were horrified by the Court's departures from precedent, especially in the domains of equal protection, free exercise of religion

---

[36] The Court adopted the formula that the Fourteenth Amendment incorporated the procedural rights included in the Bill of Rights that were "fundamental to the American scheme of justice" in *Duncan v. Louisiana*, 391 U.S. 145, 149 (1968). Before the 1960s, the Court had held some of the guarantees of the Bill of Rights to be applicable against the states but only insofar as they were "implicit in the concept of ordered liberty." *Palko v. Connecticut*, 302 U.S. 319, 324–25 (1937). Under this formula, the demands of due process were "less rigid and more fluid" than the more specific guarantees of the Bill of Rights, and "[t]hat which may, in one setting, constitute a denial of fundamental fairness ... may, in other circumstances, and in the light of other considerations, fall short of such denial." *Betts v. Brady*, 316 U.S. 455, 462 (1942).

(including a mandate to end prayer in the public schools), and constitutional criminal procedure. By any fair account, the Supreme Court was once again at the center of national political controversy through most of the Warren years.

The 1968 presidential election marked the end of the Warren era. During the latter half of the 1960s, as crime rates spiked and court-ordered busing to enforce the desegregation mandate of *Brown v. Board of Education* became deeply unpopular, a shift occurred in the politically constructed bounds within which the Supreme Court operates. In the 1968 presidential campaign, the Republican nominee, Richard Nixon, took clear aim at the Warren Court's decisions, especially those that had expanded the rights of criminal suspects. According to critics, the Warren Court's decisions repeatedly loosed dangerous criminals onto the streets on the basis of newly minted legal technicalities such as the rule requiring *Miranda* warnings. If elected, Nixon promised, he would appoint "law and order" justices with a "strict constructionist" philosophy. Nixon's appeal struck a resonant chord. He won. By 1972, he had appointed four new justices, and the Warren Court was no more.

The Post-Warren Court: 1969–2016

Surprisingly or not, the jurisprudential residue of the New Deal and Warren Courts had a long half-life. Warren Burger succeeded Earl Warren as chief justice in 1969, William Rehnquist became the chief in 1986, and John Roberts acceded to the chief justiceship in 2005. All were appointed by Republican presidents, and all presided over Courts with a majority of members who were conventionally classified as conservatives. But the Burger and Rehnquist Courts and the early Roberts Courts were dominated by justices who had come to legal maturity during the era of the New Deal settlement and who were conservatives in the traditionalist sense of that term. Majorities of the justices did not want to rip things up and start over. They also were mostly willing to accommodate changes in social mores – including those involving sexual morality and gender roles – that they thought they could not effectively resist.

These attitudes were perhaps most visible during the era of the Burger Court. It was during the Burger years that the Court began to hold for the first time that the Equal Protection Clause afforded women robust protections against sex-based discrimination. Albeit with more dissension and agonizing, the Burger Court lent its stamp of approval to limited forms of affirmative action, perhaps based on a sense that both elite educational institutions and big businesses had assimilated it into their modes of doing business. The most breathtaking decision of a purportedly conservative Court during the Burger years came in *Roe v. Wade* (1973),[37] which held that the Due Process Clause guaranteed a right to abortion by the remarkable margin of seven to two. For some of the justices, *Roe* may have registered as a women's rights issue. For others, it may have been an accommodation to changing norms of sexual morality and increasing numbers of out-of-wedlock births at a time when there was no longer an understanding, explicit or implicit, that an unwed pregnancy would result in a wedding.

Roe triggered shock waves along two related dimensions. First, in a development that clearly caught the predominantly secular justices of the Burger Court by surprise, *Roe* helped to provoke convulsions in politics, including the rise of the religious right. Second, *Roe* occasioned consternation among substantial numbers of law professors, especially but not exclusively on the political right, who were appalled by the inadequacy of the Court's legal reasoning. At the time of its decision and thereafter, *Roe*'s result – affirming a woman's right to choose to terminate an unwanted pregnancy – attracted many passionate defenders. But almost no one found the legal arguments that the Court offered in support of that conclusion to be persuasive. In one of the most influential critiques of Justice Harry Blackmun's *Roe* opinion, law professor John Hart Ely scornfully observed that it deviated so far from traditional norms of constitutional analysis that "it is *not* constitutional law and gives almost no sense of an obligation to try to be."[38]

By the late 1970s and early 1980s, there was a gathering sense among conservative legal thinkers outside the Supreme Court that the nation's constitutional law – as crafted and administered by the justices – had run dramatically off the rails and that the Burger Court had shown far too little disposition to right the situation. Not coincidentally, it was during the 1970s and 1980s that "originalism" emerged as a distinct theory of constitutional interpretation increasingly embraced

---

[37] 410 U.S. 113 (1973).
[38] John Hart Ely, "The Wages of Crying Wolf: A Comment on *Roe v. Wade*," 82 *Yale Law Journal* 920, 947 (1973).

by political and judicial conservatives. In the eyes of its proponents, originalism expressed the commonsense view that constitutional law ought to be the law laid down by the Constitution's Framers and ratifiers, not the invention of latter-day legal elites sitting on the Supreme Court in Washington, DC. It also provided a foundation for a conservative theory of constitutional interpretation that could justify the abandonment of liberal precedents that had proliferated since the New Deal. During the Reagan administration, Attorney General Edwin Meese began to call for a jurisprudence of "original intent." Justice Antonin Scalia, whom Reagan named to the Supreme Court in 1986, influentially proposed a refocusing of the originalist ideal to judicial decisions based on the Constitution's "original public meaning." What mattered, he argued, was not the possibly secret intentions of the Constitution's drafters but what reasonable members of the public understood the Constitution to mean when they voted to ratify it.

President Reagan achieved notable progress in pushing the Supreme Court to the right, including through his nomination of William Rehnquist – the most conservative of the then sitting justices – to succeed Warren Burger as chief justice. In another consequential development, President George H. W. Bush appointed the originalist Justice Clarence Thomas to the Court in 1991. Following Thomas's confirmation, Republican presidents had appointed seven of the nine justices. Among the Rehnquist Court's accomplishments was what some hailed as a "federalism revolution," recognizing various prerogatives of the states' status as "sovereign" entities and modestly limiting the regulatory powers of the federal government. During the Rehnquist era, however, leaders of conservative legal movements were nearly as dissatisfied with the Court's performance as were legal liberals. In the view of the former, several Republican presidents' Supreme Court appointees turned out to be bitter disappointments. (Many viewed Bush nominee David Souter as particularly traitorous.) And there were always "moderate" conservative "swing" justices – beginning with Nixon nominee Lewis Powell and later including Reagan nominees Sandra Day O'Connor and Anthony Kennedy – as a result of whose votes *Roe v. Wade* survived repeated attacks and affirmative action in higher education remained permissible through the time of Justice Scalia's death.

No major change of course ensued immediately after John Roberts replaced William Rehnquist as chief justice in 2005. The Court remained closely divided between conservatives and liberals and issued major rulings upholding gay rights. In the run-up to Justice Scalia's unanticipated death in 2016, Justices John Paul Stevens and David Souter, both appointed by Republican presidents but long counted as liberals, confirmed their apostasy by resigning during the presidency of Barack Obama, who got to appoint their successors. As President Obama's tenure in office neared its end, the Court thus had five conservative justices, all appointed by Republican presidents, and four liberals, all appointed by Democrats. As a result, Scalia's death, which occurred with Obama still in the White House, looked to many to mark the end of the era of the post-Warren Court and, potentially, the beginning of a new era with a narrow majority of liberal justices for the first time since early in the presidency of Richard Nixon. As noted in this book's Introduction, dramatic changes were indeed about to occur, though not of the kind for which liberals had hoped.

3 THE SUPREME COURT TODAY

In May 2022, a journalist at *Politico* published a draft Supreme Court opinion in the case of *Dobbs v. Jackson Women's Health Organization*[1] (2022) authored by Justice Samuel Alito. The draft, announcing the overruling of *Roe v. Wade* (1973),[2] stunned the legal and political worlds. For one thing, the leak represented a severe breach of the Court's internal norms – one that would prompt an unsuccessful investigation in which all of the justices' law clerks (though not the justices themselves) were required to surrender their laptop computers to Court investigators.[3] For another, the overturning of *Roe*, when it finally came a month later, was a constitutional decision of epic magnitude. For nearly fifty years, *Roe* had been the law of the land. As the Court's opinion in *Planned Parenthood v. Casey*[4] (1992) had remarked thirty years earlier, a generation of women had come to rely on the availability of abortion in organizing their professional and personal lives.

In Senate confirmation hearings, several of the justices who would constitute the *Dobbs* majority had pledged, though in hedged and guarded terms, that they had deep respect for the legal principle of stare decisis and that *Roe* was a settled precedent. As a final contributor

---

[1] 597 U.S. 215 (2022).
[2] 410 U.S. 113 (1973).
[3] "Marshall's Report of Findings & Recommendations," *Office of the Marshall, Supreme Court of the United States* 13 (2023).
[4] *Planned Parenthood v. Casey*, 505 U.S. 833, 856 (1992).

to the shock value of the leaked *Dobbs* draft and then the ultimate Court opinion, the Court's language was scathing in its treatment of *Roe* and subsequent cases that had relied on it. "*Roe*," Justice Alito wrote, "was egregiously wrong from the start."[5] Part of the difficulty, he maintained, was that it was inconsistent with the original meaning of the constitutional provision on which it was based, the Due Process Clause of the Fourteenth Amendment, and that it lacked deep roots in the American tradition. But *Roe* was shoddy in other ways as well, he insisted. If a majority of the justices felt ready not merely to overrule *Roe v. Wade* but also to mock and savage it, many observers – from the most informed to the more episodic – wondered aloud what else the Court might do.

By nearly all accounts, the current Supreme Court is the most conservative Court since the New Deal "switch in time" in 1937. Also by nearly all accounts, it consists of six conservative justices, some or all of whom are often characterized as originalists, and three liberals. But the labels "conservative" and "liberal" have different connotations from those that they carried in 1937, when the *Lochner* era ended, or in 1973, when *Roe* was decided, or even when the Reagan administration began to call for a constitutional jurisprudence based on "the intent of the Framers."

This chapter aims to provide a foundation for the efforts of subsequent chapters to understand current constitutional law and to anticipate some of the ways in which the Supreme Court seems likely to change it. The chapter unfolds in three parts. The first describes the political climate in which the most recently appointed justices were named to the Court and in which they now function. The second discusses constitutional originalism and its relationship to long-established norms of legal argumentation and ideals of the judicial role in which even the originalist justices are steeped. The third offers brief biographical sketches of each of the current justices, highlighting hallmarks of their distinctive judicial philosophies.

Polarized Legal Culture

Before their appointments to the Supreme Court, today's conservative justices, all of whom were nominated by Republican presidents, were more thoroughly vetted than any comparable cohort of

---

[5] *Dobbs v. Jackson Women's Health Organization*, 597 U.S. 215, 231 (2022).

justices in the Court's history. During the period in which every current member of the Supreme Court except for Clarence Thomas was appointed, the rallying cry in conservative circles has been "No more David Souters."

David Souter, who served on the Court from 1990 until 2009, was appointed by President George H. W. Bush. In naming Souter, Bush expected to get a reliable conservative. But Souter, who had spent most of his professional career in New Hampshire, was little known outside the state. At the time of his appointment, his lack of prominence had seemed more an asset than a drawback. In 1987, the Democrat-controlled Senate had refused to confirm Reagan nominee Robert Bork, an intellectually iconoclastic conservative whose prior government service and scholarship had left a provocative paper trail that allowed opponents to characterize him as racially insensitive and otherwise hard-hearted. By contrast, Souter had written almost nothing that could make him vulnerable to attack. In nominating him, Bush relied heavily on the advice of a trusted New Hampshire Republican senator, Warren Rudman. By the time Souter had served on the Supreme Court for a few years, commentators regularly listed him among the Court's liberals.

The experience with Souter was not unprecedented. When President Gerald Ford needed a Supreme Court nominee in 1975, he largely outsourced the responsibility of selection to his independent-minded attorney general, Edward Levi, who had been named to his post to restore the Department of Justice's reputation for nonpartisanship following the Watergate scandals. Levi recommended John Paul Stevens, a respected judge on the Seventh Circuit Court of Appeals in Chicago who had spent most of his career in private practice and never attracted much of a stir. Early in his career on the High Court bench, Stevens, like Levi, acquired the reputation of an independent-minded moderate conservative. By the end of his career, however, Stevens was the acknowledged leader of the Court's liberal wing. He claimed that he had not changed but, rather, that the Court had moved to the right around him. Although it is undoubtedly true that the Court had grown more conservative, most close observers would agree that Stevens had grown more liberal, too.

Among the current crop of Republican-nominated justices, there are no analogues to Souter or Stevens, nor are there likely to be any in the foreseeable future. The days in which a candidate without well-known legal and political views could be successfully nominated to the Supreme Court, at least by a Republican president, are gone. Too much information about too many able candidates is now available. Since the 1990s, conservative lawyers, law professors, and law students in the United States tend to be tightly networked. An organization called the Federalist Society has played an outsized role in organizing and facilitating the networking.[6]

The Federalist Society was originally formed in 1982 as an organization for conservative law students at the Yale, Harvard, and University of Chicago Law Schools who felt the need for a mutual support network within the predominantly liberal legal academy. Over time, it has grown into a potently influential national organizing force, richly supported by wealthy conservative backers. On the campuses of individual law schools, the Federalist Society brings conservative students together to hear speakers and enjoy each other's fellowship. There are Federalist Society chapters for conservative lawyers in most major cities. Annual conferences now attract thousands of lawyers, hundreds of judges, and law students from around the country. As a result of the Federalist Society, conservative law students and young conservative lawyers are well known to each other from the early days of their budding careers. The Federalist Society network helps young conservatives to get matched with conservative judges, who disproportionately choose them as law clerks, and with other conservative mentors. Equally important, the members of the Federalist Society become acquainted with and observe and interrogate each other on a continual basis as their careers unfold. By the time a conservative lawyer is at a stage for nomination to a lower court judgeship, and certainly for a position as a Supreme Court justice, he or she is well known. The lawyers who rise to the top are almost invariably highly able, and they are also highly reliable in their basic conservative orientations.

The power of the networked conservative legal elite manifested itself in 2005, when President George W. Bush nominated White House lawyer Harriet Miers, whose professional experience was mostly in Texas and who was little known to leading national legal conservatives, to fill a Supreme Court vacancy. Howls of protest immediately arose

---

[6] See generally Amanda Hollis-Brusky, *Ideas with Consequences: The Federalist Society and the Conservative Counterrevolution* (New York, NY: Oxford University Press, 2015); see also Steven M. Teles, *The Rise of the Conservative Legal Movement: The Battle for Control of the Law* (Princeton, NJ: Princeton University Press, 2012), 135–180.

among congressional conservatives and conservative legal elites in part because Miers was not a sufficiently known quantity. The Miers nomination failed as a result of conservative, rather than liberal Democratic, opposition. The vacant seat on the Court went instead to Samuel Alito, who would author the *Dobbs* opinion roughly twenty years later.

Some of the same social and political currents that enabled the rise of the Federalist Society also shape the culture that the justices inhabit once they are on the Supreme Court. At one time, conservatives who were disappointed by the Court's decisions complained that justices who came to the Court initially touted as conservatives too often fell under the spell of Washington media and social elites who disproportionately held liberal views, especially regarding social issues. The Georgetown dinner party circuit was widely mocked as a source of temptation and corruption. Some conservatives also grumbled that initially conservative justices were swayed by the predictably favorable coverage in elite national media when they adopted liberal positions on issues such as abortion, affirmative action, and gay rights.

Today, the media environment is much more polarized. Justices who take staunchly conservative positions can be assured of adulatory audiences at Federalist Society and other conservative conclaves. In offering these observations, I do not mean to accuse any justice of any era, including the current one, of succumbing to illicit influences of any kind. Nonetheless, today's conservative justices emerged from and function in different professional, social, and political environments than did their predecessors.

Constitutional Originalism and the Conventional Norms of Constitutional Argument

Among conservative legal elites, the most favored theory of constitutional interpretation, at least since the 1980s, has been originalism. But originalism turns out to be surprisingly difficult to define. Whereas early leaders in the movement asserted that the touchstone for constitutional interpretation should be "the intent of the Framers," most current originalists seek to identify not the Framers' psychological intentions but the Constitution's "original public meaning."[7] Some

---

[7] Lawrence B. Solum, "The Public Meaning Thesis: An Originalist Theory of Constitutional Meaning," 101 *Boston University Law Review* 1953, 1964–67 (2021).

others argue for interpreting the Constitution in light of "original interpretive methods" or the background "law of interpretation" that prevailed at the time of the Founding.

Originalists often profess that their theories are politically neutral: They say that disputed cases should be resolved based on disinterested historical inquiries and call for letting the chips fall where they may. But the brands of originalism that justices of the Supreme Court have been prepared to practice have always enjoyed a complicated relationship with political conservatism. It is no accident that most originalists are conservatives.[8] As noted in Chapter 2, part of originalism's attractiveness to the conservative legal intellectuals who pioneered its development in the 1970s was that it provided a principled theoretical basis for overthrowing liberal judicial precedents that had proliferated since the New Deal.

But originalism, as professed and practiced by justices of the Supreme Court, does not demand that all constitutional cases should be decided on the basis of the Constitution's original meaning. Even today, when many observers characterize the Court as dominated by originalists, important areas of constitutional law remain mostly untouched by originalist reasoning.[9] To take just one example, modern free speech doctrine, as will be discussed in detail in Chapter 5, has developed with scant reference to the original meaning of the relevant constitutional language. When two research assistants and I looked at all of the Supreme Court's constitutional decisions during the term that began in October 2021 and ended in June 2022 – the year in which the Court decided *Dobbs* – we counted only five cases in which the Court relied directly on evidence of the Constitution's original meaning as the basis for its ruling.[10] Moreover, among the decisions in which Court majorities rested their holdings on other grounds, we found only three in which any of the originalist justices argued that the Court should have ruled based on originalist evidence instead.

In light of this pattern, nonoriginalist critics of Supreme Court decision-making see selectivity and even hypocrisy in the purportedly originalist justices' demand for originalist analysis in the cases

---

[8] See, for example, Keith E. Whittington, "The New Originalism," 2 *Georgetown Journal of Law & Public Policy* 599, 601–02 (2004).

[9] See generally Richard H. Fallon Jr., "Selective Originalism and Judicial Role Morality," 102 *Texas Law Review* 222 (2023).

[10] Ibid. at 264.

in which those justices deploy it. Rarely do the originalist justices follow originalist evidence to reach conclusions that conservatives would find objectionable. Their appeals to originalist premises occur most noticeably in cases in which they want to overrule nonoriginalist precedents or criticize nonoriginalist justices for reaching liberal conclusions unsupported by the Constitution's original meaning.

Justice Elena Kagan is among those who have leveled criticisms along these lines. A press account of a talk she gave at Northwestern Law School in September 2022 reported as follows:

> Kagan said the use of originalism has been flexible in recent opinions – a critique that has also come from many legal experts following rulings this term. "My thinking about originalism is, I'm not sure what it means given that it seems to be sort of fluctuating over time and over cases in ways that, again, makes you concerned that the rules change as the desired outcomes change," Kagan said.[11]

A few academic originalists also believe that the conservative justices' patterns of selective reliance and nonreliance on originalism are indefensible. They advocate a purer brand of originalism than the ostensibly originalist justices practice. But the originalist justices, who are mostly not defensive about their only sometime insistence on deciding cases based on original constitutional meanings, embrace brands of originalism that are tempered by two longstanding conventions of legal analysis. Once these tempering doctrines are introduced, originalism becomes a much more complex and flexible theory than one might imagine when hearing originalists avow – as they often do – that the only alternative to decisions based on the Constitution's original meaning is a regime in which nonoriginalist justices get to decide cases based on their subjective preferences.

The first legal doctrine that dilutes the conservative justices' constitutional originalism is "the party presentation principle."[12] A premise of this country's adversarial system of justice is that courts

---

[11] Kelsey Reichmann, "With Jabs at Her Colleagues, Justice Kagan Warns the Court 'Needs to Act Like a Court,'" *Courthouse News Service* (Sept. 14, 2022), www.courthousenews.com/with-jabs-at-her-colleagues-justice-kagan-warns-the-court-needs-to-act-like-a-court.

[12] See, for example, *N.Y. State Rifle & Pistol Ass'n v. Bruen*, 142 S. Ct. 2111, 2130 n.6 (2022) ("[I]n our adversarial system of adjudication, we follow the principle of party presentation" [quoting *United States v. Sineneng-Smith*, 140 S. Ct. 1575, 1579 (2020)]).

should normally address those questions and arguments, and only those questions and arguments, that are framed for them by the parties to a particular case. Even in constitutional litigation in the Supreme Court, both sides often claim that they are entitled to prevail based on the proper application of prior judicial precedents. When arguing their cases in the lower courts, the parties naturally focus on prior cases' implications because the lower courts are bound by Supreme Court rulings, even when they think that the High Court was mistaken, including on originalist grounds. Perhaps surprisingly often, arguments based on precedent continue to occupy center stage in appeals to the Supreme Court.

The party presentation principle is not absolute. The justices occasionally ask the parties to address issues that neither side had raised independently. To take a famous example, in *Brown v. Board of Education* (1954),[13] the justices requested that the parties discuss whether the Fourteenth Amendment was originally intended or understood to forbid racial segregation in public schooling.[14] But *Brown* was an exception. Most often the Supreme Court leaves the framing of issues to the parties, and even the originalist justices feel justified in overlooking issues, including ones involving the Constitution's original meaning, that the parties do not raise on their own.

Working hand in hand with the party principle is the much better known principle of stare decisis or adherence to precedent. Originalism's relationship to stare decisis is complex. In an aspiration to principled consistency, some originalist law professors believe that nonoriginalist precedent should never prevail over the Constitution's original meaning in a constitutional case in the Supreme Court. But most originalists, including the conservative originalist justices, accept some version of stare decisis. If challenged to reconcile this acceptance with their originalism, originalists offer different explanations. Justice Scalia used to say that allowance for stare decisis was an exception to his originalist philosophy, not an element of it.[15] Others say that the

---

[13] 347 U.S. 483 (1954).
[14] See *Brown v. Bd. of Educ.*, 345 U.S. 972, 972 (1953) (per curiam) (restoring the case to the calendar for reargument and directing the parties to focus, in part, on how the "Congress which submitted and the State legislatures and conventions which ratified the Fourteenth Amendment contemplated or did not contemplate, understood or did not understand, that it would abolish segregation in public schools").
[15] See Antonin Scalia, "Response," in *A Matter of Interpretation: Federal Courts and the Law*, ed. Amy Gutmann (Princeton, NJ: Princeton University Press, 1997), 129, 140.

principle of stare decisis was presupposed by, and thus was part of the original meaning of, "the judicial power" that the Supreme Court possesses under Article III of the Constitution.

From the perspective of originalist theory, the crucial feature of the doctrine of stare decisis – which makes it acceptable and even attractive to the originalist justices – is that it is not absolute or categorical. By nearly all accounts, the doctrine of stare decisis is a principle of policy, capable of being overcome when there is a sufficiently good reason to overrule a precedent in a particular case.[16] In cases in which arguments to overturn precedent are made, the justices sometimes quibble about the best articulation of the criteria that should be used to determine whether sufficiently good reasons exist to abandon a precedent. But when the justices disagree, the nub of their disputes often involve whether a prior decision was, as Justice Alito put it in *Dobbs*, "egregiously wrong."

Understood as a principle of policy rather than an absolute command, stare decisis has the practical effect of giving justices who profess to be originalists a choice in cases in which they believe that prior Court precedents have deviated from the Constitution's original meaning. Stare decisis gives the justices legally sufficient reason to adhere to precedent if they think it wise or prudent to do so, but it rarely requires the justices to follow a precedent that they think seriously misguided. The resulting range of choice is considerable. Nearly all would agree that the justices should not upset too much precedent all at once. But no one thinks that the justices should adhere to all decisions that they view as mistakes. When attention thus gets focused on only a relatively few questionable precedents at any one time, judgments about whether overruling a particular past decision would be wise or prudent are almost inescapably ideologically inflected. A conservative Court can, and should be expected to, apply or not apply the doctrine of stare decisis in ways that typically yield conservative results. (If we had a liberal majority, we could similarly expect liberal results.)

It is also familiar that, regardless of whether the justices decide a particular case based on precedent or on evidence of original constitutional meaning, their ideological outlooks will often influence their interpretation of the legal materials on which they are focused. As

---

[16] See, for example, *Payne v. Tennessee*, 501 U.S. 808, 828 (1991) (quoting *Helvering v. Hallock*, 309 U.S. 106, 119 [1940]).

this book's Introduction explained, legal interpretation is inherently forward-looking as well as backward-looking. Interpretation is inherently backward-looking because it seeks to recover the meaning of past words or events. Justices who did not relate their conclusions to the words of texts written in the past would be engaged in invention, not interpretation. But when the justices consider candidate interpretations, they are, and ought to be, concerned about the present and future implications of the determinations that they reach – as Chief Justice John Marshall's opinion in *McCulloch v. Maryland* (1819),[17] which Chapter 2 discussed, famously recognized. In judging which interpretation would be best, as it is the justices' job to do, they make partly normative judgments. This, after all, is why we have so little difficulty in sorting justices into "conservative" and "liberal" camps and why nominations to the Supreme Court have grown so highly contested.

The Current Justices

As I have emphasized, the Supreme Court is "a 'they,' not an 'it.'" When the sophisticated lawyers who litigate regularly before the Court plot their strategy, they begin by disaggregating "the Court" into nine individual justices and asking, "Which arguments can I make that will give me the best chance of winning the votes of five of them, considered one-by-one?" For lawyers arguing for conservative causes, the prospects of getting to five are generally better than for lawyers on the liberal side of contested, high-profile issues. But different justices in both the conservative and liberal camps have different judicial philosophies, concerns, and styles.

In offering thumbnail sketches of the nine justices, I break them into three groups of three: the three conservative justices who were already sitting on the Supreme Court before Donald Trump named three more, the three Trump-nominated justices, and the three liberals.

The Pre-Trump Conservative Justices

Chief Justice John Roberts was nominated by President George W. Bush and confirmed to serve as the seventeenth chief justice of the United States in 2005. He was fifty years old at the time and had an

---

[17] 17 U.S. 316 (1819).

impeccable resume. A graduate of Harvard College and Harvard Law School, Roberts had served as a law clerk to then Associate Justice William Rehnquist, argued numerous cases before the Supreme Court both as the principal deputy solicitor general of the United States and as a lawyer in private practice, and spent roughly two years as a judge on the United States Court of Appeals for the District of Columbia Circuit. At the time of his nomination, Roberts had deep and longstanding connections to the Republican legal establishment. During the Reagan administration, he had served not only as the principal deputy solicitor general but also as a special assistant to Attorney General William French Smith and then as an associate White House counsel.[18]

By all accounts, Roberts is a brilliant lawyer. Perhaps partly as a result of his temperament and partly as a result of his position as chief justice, Roberts plainly cares about the Court's reputation for nonpartisanship. Although always a member of the Court's conservative bloc, Roberts sometimes shows more hesitancy than some of his colleagues to overrule liberal precedents. His preferred style is to chip away at liberal decisions that he disapproves by narrowing their scope of application. Consistent with this preference, Roberts refused to join Justice Alito's *Dobbs* opinion overruling *Roe v. Wade*, even though he would have permitted the state of Mississippi to ban abortions after fifteen weeks of pregnancy. According to press reports, Roberts angered his conservative colleagues in 2012 by shifting his vote late in the Court's deliberations about the constitutionality of the Affordable Care Act's individual mandate to buy health insurance – a development to be discussed at length in Chapter 9. As reported by some, Roberts disliked the optics of the Court's five conservative justices, all appointed by Republican presidents, voting to invalidate the defining achievement of the Obama administration over the dissent of four justices appointed by Democratic presidents. Instead, Roberts voted with the Court's four liberals to uphold the individual mandate (albeit not on the grounds that the liberals would have preferred).

Following Justice Anthony Kennedy's resignation from the Court in 2018, Roberts for a few years was the so-called swing justice – the conservative who stood closest along the ideological spectrum to the four liberals then on the Court. But his capacity to determine

---

[18] A valuable biography of Roberts is Joan Biskupic, *The Chief: The Life and Turbulent Times of Chief Justice John Roberts* (New York, NY: Hachette Book Group, 2019).

outcomes has diminished, since the replacement of Justice Ginsburg by Justice Barrett created a 6–3 conservative majority. If the other five conservatives stick together, they do not need Roberts's vote in order to prevail. Nevertheless, Roberts retains disproportionate influence. In his role as chief justice, he determines which justice will write the Court's majority opinion in any case in which he is on the winning side. In exercising this power, he often either assigns the opinions in the most complex and important cases to himself or chooses a justice whose thinking closely aligns with his own.

Clarence Thomas, who joined the Court in 1991, is the longest serving justice now on the Court and by most measures its most unbending conservative originalist. Thomas was born in 1948 near Savannah, Georgia, and had an impoverished and difficult early childhood. His mother and father split up while he was still a toddler, and a judge awarded custody of the young Clarence and his siblings to his mother's aunt. A few years later, when he was about seven, he was sent to live with his grandfather, whom he has described as the most powerful formative influence on his early life.[19] Thomas attended Catholic schools that were segregated during his early years. Having become very religiously devout, he briefly attended a Catholic seminary before earning a BA degree from the College of the Holy Cross in 1971 and a JD from Yale Law School in 1974.

During Thomas's college years, he was attracted to the Black Power movement. But after law school, he took a job working for Missouri's Republican Attorney General John Danforth and later, after a stint in private practice, followed then Senator Danforth to Washington as a legislative assistant from 1979 to 1981. Further cementing his ties to Republican politics during the Reagan administration, Thomas served as the assistant secretary for civil rights in the Department of Education and as the chair of the US Equal Employment Opportunity Commission (EEOC). President George H. W. Bush nominated him to the District of Columbia Circuit in 1990 and then to the Supreme Court, to succeed the Court's first Black justice, the civil rights icon Thurgood Marshall, in 1991.

Thomas joined the Court amid bombshell allegations during his confirmation hearings that he had sexually harassed a subordinate

---

[19] See generally Clarence Thomas, *My Grandfather's Son: A Memoir* (New York, NY: HarperCollins, 2007).

while at the EEOC. Responding in sworn testimony on national television, he angrily denounced his accuser and the senators who sponsored her testimony as perpetrators of "a high-tech lynching." In recent years, Thomas has again found himself the target of accusations of ethical misconduct, this time involving his receipt of expensive and undisclosed gifts from wealthy conservative businessmen. Some critics have also argued that Thomas should recuse himself from cases involving matters to which his wife, a right-wing activist who has served on the boards of a number of conservative organizations, has had direct or indirect connections. So far, he has not done so.

When a majority of the justices decide a case on nonoriginalist grounds, Thomas often writes separately to call for reexamining decisions that he believes to be doubtful in a future case. When Justice Scalia was once asked how Thomas's originalist philosophy compared with his own, Scalia reportedly replied, "I am an originalist [but] I am not a nut."[20]

Samuel Alito, who wrote the *Dobbs* decision, joined the Court in 2006 after conservative opposition sank President George W. Bush's nomination of Harriet Miers. There was no risk that Alito would turn out to be "another David Souter." A graduate of Princeton and Yale Law School, Alito did a postgraduation clerkship for a lower court judge, then served as a government lawyer in the Republican presidential administrations of Ronald Reagan and George H. W. Bush from 1981 to 1990. When seeking a promotion in the Reagan administration Justice Department in 1985, Alito described himself as being "particularly proud" of his work on cases in which the administration argued "that racial and ethnic quotas should not be allowed and that the Constitution does not protect a right to abortion."[21] In 1990, President Bush appointed Alito to the United States Court of Appeals for the Third Circuit.

Since joining the Supreme Court, Alito has described himself as "a practical originalist,"[22] by which he apparently means that he views

---

[20] "Scalia Vigorously Defends a 'Dead' Constitution," *NPR* (Apr. 28, 2008), www.npr.org/templates/story/story.php?storyId=90011526.

[21] Amy Goldstein and Jo Becker, "Alito Helped Craft Reagan-Era Move to Restrict 'Roe,'" *Washington Post* (Dec. 1, 2005), www.washingtonpost.com/archive/politics/2005/12/01/alito-helped-craft-reagan-era-move-to-restrict-roe/1b8e180f-47dc-4d92-a554-14b5e8c7c874/.

[22] Matthew Walther, "Sam Alito: A Civil Man," *American Spectator* (Apr. 21, 2014), https://spectator.org/sam-alito-a-civil-man.

decisions in accord with the Constitution's original meaning as an ideal but not necessarily one that the Court should seek to attain all at once. Critics accuse him of being opportunistic in his invocation of originalist premises. Defenders praise him for exhibiting prudent judgment in his respect for stare decisis.[23] During Alito's early years on the Supreme Court, he frequently formed a voting bloc with John Roberts as a more moderate, step-at-a-time conservative than Justices Scalia and Thomas. Since then, however, Alito has drifted into a harder right-wing posture.

In public speeches and even in his Court opinions, Justice Alito sometimes expresses grievances that adherents of traditional and Christian beliefs are disrespected and marginalized by elite institutions and popular culture. Dissenting in *Obergefell v. Hodges* (2015),[24] which upheld a constitutional right to gay marriage, Alito protested that the decision "will be used to vilify Americans who are unwilling to assent to the new orthodoxy" and that defenders of traditional marriage "will risk being labeled as bigots and treated as such by governments, employers, and schools."

The Trump-Appointed Conservatives

Neil Gorsuch, Donald Trump's first nominee to the Supreme Court, was confirmed by the Senate and took the seat once held by Antonin Scalia a little more than a year after Scalia's death. During the 2016 presidential campaign, Trump had included Gorsuch's name on a list of potential conservative nominees, many of them reportedly supplied by sources connected to the Federalist Society.

Gorsuch comes from an elite background. He was educated at Columbia University and Harvard Law School and holds a DPhil degree (the equivalent of a doctorate) in legal philosophy from Oxford University. His mother, Anne Gorsuch Burford, was the administrator of the Environmental Protection Agency during the Reagan administration. Gorsuch himself served as a law clerk to two Supreme Court justices, Byron White and Anthony Kennedy. He practiced law in the private sector for roughly ten years before becoming the principal deputy associate attorney general for one year during the presidency of

---

[23] See, for example, J. Joel Alicea, "The Originalist Jurisprudence of Justice Samuel Alito," 46 *Harvard Journal of Law & Public Policy* 653 (2023).
[24] 576 U.S. 644, 741 (2015) (Alito J., dissenting).

George W. Bush, who appointed him to serve on the United States Court of Appeals for the Tenth Circuit in 2006. His decisions during his roughly ten years on that court were reliably conservative.

Having been born in Denver, Colorado, and having lived there during his time on the Tenth Circuit, Gorsuch styles himself as a westerner. He is also a legal intellectual, who has written books about legal theory,[25] and a self-identified originalist.[26] Although Gorsuch is a staunch conservative, he occasionally breaks with his conservative colleagues on issues involving the claimed legal entitlements of Native American tribes. In matters of statutory interpretation, he is an avowed textualist, as Scalia was before him. In a purported application of textualist premises, Gorsuch astonished and disappointed many conservatives when he wrote a Court opinion holding that the provision of the 1964 Civil Rights Act barring discrimination on the basis of sex encompasses a prohibition against discrimination on the basis of sexual orientation.[27] Chief Justice Roberts joined him in that opinion, as did the Court's liberal justices. The other conservatives dissented sharply. In most appraisals of the justices, however, Gorsuch ranks either with or just behind Justices Thomas and Alito as one of the Court's three most conservative members.

Brett Kavanaugh joined the Court in 2018 as the successor to Justice Kennedy, for whom he had clerked. Kavanaugh was fifty-three years old at the time. After graduating from Yale College and Yale Law School, he clerked for two conservative judges prior to his year with Kennedy, which happened to coincide with Neil Gorsuch's clerkship. Kavanaugh worked for Independent Counsel Kenneth Starr in two related investigations of President Bill Clinton, the second involving his sexual relationship with a White House intern. After two stints in private practice, Kavanaugh worked for five years in the White House of President George W. Bush before Bush named him to the District of Columbia Circuit in 2006.

Many of the cases on the docket of the D.C. Circuit involve administrative law or the powers and prerogatives of federal

---

[25] Neil M. Gorsuch, *A Republic, If You Can Keep It* (New York, NY: Crown Forum, 2019).
[26] Ibid. at 116–27 (advancing a defense of originalism); *Oil States Energy Services, LLC v. Greene's Energy Group, LLC*, 138 S. Ct. 1365, 1381 (2018) (Gorsuch, J., dissenting) (contending that "[t]he Constitution's original public meaning supplies the key" to its interpretation).
[27] *Bostock v. Clayton County*, 140 S. Ct. 1731 (2020).

administrative agencies. During Kavanaugh's service on the D.C. Circuit, he acquired a reputation as a champion of presidential power and a skeptic of the constitutional validity of statutes, enacted by Congress, that walled off ostensibly independent agencies from presidential control. A law review article that Kavanaugh wrote on this topic was said to have drawn the approving attention of President Donald Trump when he was vetting potential Supreme Court nominees.[28]

Kavanaugh's Supreme Court confirmation hearings, like those of Clarence Thomas, included late-breaking allegations of sexual misconduct, in his case arising from events during his high school and college years. Like Thomas, Kavanaugh replied with fiery denials and recriminations that were widely credited with saving his nomination from defeat. Also important to his confirmation was a pledge to moderate Republican Senator Susan Collins, among others, that he believed in the importance of adherence to precedent and that he regarded *Roe v. Wade* as settled law. Collins reportedly felt "misled" when Kavanaugh subsequently joined Justice Alito's opinion overruling *Roe*.[29]

On the Court, Kavanaugh is a consistent conservative, but he is less ardent than some of his colleagues in championing originalist theory. He often votes with Chief Justice Roberts in cases in which a divide opens between the more and the less unyieldingly conservative members of the Court – though, according to press reports, Kavanaugh resisted multiple entreaties from Roberts to join him in a concurring opinion in *Dobbs* that would have narrowed, rather than wholly overruled, *Roe v. Wade*. Kavanaugh did, however, write separately in *Dobbs* (in addition to joining the majority opinion) to emphasize that nothing in the Court's ruling should be read to "threaten or cast doubt" on apparently nonoriginalist decisions concerning other rights, including rights of access to contraceptives and interracial and same-sex marriage.

Amy Coney Barrett replaced Ruth Bader Ginsburg on October 27, 2020, just days before the November election that Donald Trump lost to Joseph Biden. Barrett had served on the Seventh Circuit Court of Appeals, to which she was also nominated by Trump, since 2017. Unlike the other Trump nominees, Barrett had never served in a Republican political administration, but she had clerked for a very

---

[28] See generally Brett M. Kavanaugh, "Separation of Powers during the Forty-Fourth Presidency and Beyond," 93 *Minnesota Law Review* 1454 (2009).

[29] Carl Hulse, "Kavanaugh Gave Private Assurances. Collins Says He 'Misled' Her," *New York Times* (June 24, 2022), www.nytimes.com/2022/06/24/.

conservative federal appellate judge and for Justice Scalia, who was an enthusiastic admirer. At the time of her nomination, which was announced at a White House ceremony at the height of the COVID-19 pandemic at which several guests appear to have contracted COVID, Barrett said that Scalia's judicial philosophy was her judicial philosophy.[30]

Among the current justices, Barrett is the only one not to have attended Harvard or Yale Law School. She graduated first in her class from Notre Dame Law School, after receiving her BA from Rhodes College. She practiced law in Washington, DC, for two years after her clerkship with Justice Scalia, then joined the faculty of Notre Dame Law School on which she served from 2002 to 2017. Barrett is the mother of seven children, two of whom are adopted from Haiti and one of whom has Down syndrome. As a law professor, Barrett, who is a Catholic, once coauthored a law review article suggesting that Catholic judges might be unable to enforce the death penalty.[31] On the bench, she has proved reliably conservative on nearly all issues, but she is conspicuously analytically punctilious and sometimes breaks with her conservative colleagues when she thinks that they have cut intellectual corners on the path to a preferred result. Her style both in her opinions and on the bench is to eschew flamboyant gestures and rhetoric.

The Liberal Justices

Sonia Sotomayor was nominated to the Court by Barack Obama in 2009 following her service as a federal district court judge and as an appellate judge on the Second Circuit in New York. Sotomayor was born in 1954 in the South Bronx and mostly spoke Spanish at home during her childhood. Her father died when she was only nine, not long after she had been diagnosed with diabetes.[32]

---

[30] See "Full Transcript: Read Judge Amy Coney Barrett's Remarks," *New York Times* (Sept. 26, 2020), www.nytimes.com/2020/09/26/us/politics/full-transcript-amy-coney-barrett.html ("I clerked for Justice Scalia more than 20 years ago, but the lessons I learned still resonate. His judicial philosophy is mine, too.").

[31] John H. Garvey and Amy V. Coney, "Catholic Judges in Capital Cases," 81 *Marquette Law Review* 303 (1998).

[32] Sotomayor has written about her early life in Sonia Sotomayor, *My Beloved World* (New York, NY: Alfred A. Knopf, 2013).

Sotomayor graduated in 1976 from Princeton, where she was a star student and a well-known campus activist for liberal causes, and from Yale Law School three years later. She married in 1976 while still at Princeton but was divorced after seven years and has not remarried. Following her law school graduation, Sotomayor was a criminal prosecutor in New York from 1979 to 1984 and a lawyer for private clients from 1984 to 1992, when President George H. W. Bush named her to be a district court judge. Bill Clinton elevated her to the Second Circuit Court of Appeals in 1998.

While in private practice, Sotomayor was active in civic and charitable activities. As a lower court judge, she continued to speak out about matters of public policy, including racial justice. In a comment that drew sustained attention during her Supreme Court confirmation hearings, she once said in a speech that "I would hope that a wise Latina woman with the richness of her experiences would more often than not reach a better conclusion than a white male who hasn't lived that life."[33] Since becoming a justice, Sotomayor has earned a reputation as an aggressive questioner during oral argument. By most measures, she is the Court's most consistent liberal. When in dissent, she sometimes writes passionate opinions and has strongly decried the Court's most notable movements to the right.

Elena Kagan was appointed by President Obama in 2010, a year after Justice Sotomayor. She graduated from Princeton in 1981, Oxford University in 1983, and Harvard Law School in 1986. She clerked for Justice Thurgood Marshall and briefly worked in private practice before becoming a law professor at the University of Chicago, where she specialized in free speech issues, beginning in 1991. She served for four years in the Clinton administration at the conclusion of which she moved to Harvard Law School, where she became the dean a few years later in 2003. Kagan, who has never married, moved back into the government when President Obama named her as the first female solicitor general – the principal lawyer representing the government in cases before the Supreme Court – in 2009. She ascended to the Supreme Court seat previously occupied by Justice John Paul Stevens in 2010.[34]

---

[33] Sonia Sotomayor, "A Latina Judge's Voice," 13 *Berkeley La Raza Law Journal* 87 (2002).
[34] A biography is Meg Greene, *Elena Kagan: A Biography* (Santa Barbara, CA: Greenwood, 2013).

Kagan possesses an acute analytical mind and is a brilliant stylist, rivaling the late Justice Scalia in that respect. She also has the temperament of a politician and a dealmaker. Sometimes willing to narrow the terms of an unavoidable legal defeat through negotiation, she occasionally joins opinions that fail to realize liberals' hopes but that also forestall the broad conservative rulings that those on the right had hoped to achieve.

Ketanji Brown Jackson, who was born in 1970, was nominated by President Biden to succeed Stephen Breyer, for whom she had clerked, in 2022. She graduated from Harvard College in 1992 and Harvard Law School in 1996, then worked briefly in private practice both before and after her clerkship with Justice Breyer. She then served as an assistant special counsel to the United States Sentencing Commission and, from 2005 to 2007, as a federal public defender. Her varied professional career subsequently included more private sector law practice, tenure as vice chair of the United States Sentencing Commission, service as a district court judge in the District of Columbia from 2013 to 2021, and a brief stint on the court of appeals for the D.C. Circuit beginning in 2021.

As a justice of the Supreme Court, Jackson has aligned herself with the Court's liberal wing. In her opinions, she tends to seize opportunities to present originalist arguments for liberal conclusions. During her confirmation hearings, Jackson said that she "believe[s] the Constitution is fixed in its meaning" and that "it is appropriate to look at the original intent, original public meaning of the words" as "a limitation on my authority to import my own policy views."

The Difference That Six Makes

During the many years when conventional counts had conservative justices outnumbering the liberals by 5–4, conservative commentators complained that the liberals succeeded frustratingly often in garnering the vote of one or another conservative justice to produce 5–4 liberal decisions in high-profile cases. Sometimes the swing justice was Sandra Day O'Connor, who voted to save abortion rights and affirmative action. Sometimes it was Justice Anthony Kennedy, who followed in O'Connor's footsteps regarding those issues and who cast the decisive votes upholding gay rights in several pathbreaking cases as well. When the fate of the Affordable Care Act was on the line in 2012, John Roberts uncharacteristically joined with the liberals to save the individual mandate to buy health insurance.

Since the appointment of Amy Coney Barrett to succeed Ruth Ginsburg created a 6–3 conservative majority in the fall of 2020, the situation has changed. Some deviations by conservative justices from conservative preferences have occurred, and more will undoubtedly happen going forward. But it is much harder for a lawyer for a liberal cause who is trying to "count to five" to capture two conservative votes than it was to pick off one. And lawyers for conservative causes have less reason to worry that the time may not yet be right to push for major rightward shifts in constitutional doctrine. Overall, past generalizations about what "the Court" has tended to do historically – such as the once-conventional wisdom that the Court seldom deviates very far from mainstream public opinion – look like much less reliable guides to the future than they did a few years ago. Although constitutional change is by no means inherently exceptional, we inhabit an era in which doctrinal shifts – almost always in a conservative direction – have come with unusual rapidity and seem more likely to accelerate than to diminish in the years to come.

4 FREEDOM OF RELIGION
The Crumbling "Wall of Separation" between Church and State

The First Amendment contains two clauses dealing with religion. The first, the Establishment Clause, provides that "Congress shall make no law respecting an establishment of religion." The second, the Free Exercise Clause, adds that neither may Congress "prohibit[] the free exercise thereof." It is easy to identify paradigmatic violations of both provisions. Congress would violate the Establishment Clause if it designated one institution as the official church of the United States or appropriated tax revenues for a single church's benefit. It would just as clearly transgress the Free Exercise Clause if it forbade the wearing of yarmulkes or head scarves.

But agreed paradigm violations do not resolve hard modern cases under either of the Religion Clauses. Nor do they rule out the possibility that there could be tensions between the values that the two clauses reflect. During the time when the United States relied on a draft to staff the military, debates about whether the government should or must provide draft exemptions for people whose religious beliefs forbade them to fight in wars exemplified the potential. On the one hand, drafting religious conscientious objectors (and punishing them if they failed to report for duty) could be viewed as abridging their free exercise rights. On the other hand, granting draft exemptions to religiously motivated conscientious objectors could be characterized as a religion-based preference that violated the Establishment Clause, including by making those with non-preferred beliefs more likely to be drafted than they would be otherwise.

For now, the draft is gone, and there is no precise analogue to the debates about the Religion Clauses that it once provoked. But questions involving possible tensions between the two clauses remain. The recent case of *Carson v. Makin*[1] (2022) not only exhibits the possibility of conflict but also provides a window into the current Court's interpretive stance toward both the Establishment and Free Exercise Clauses. Not coincidentally, it illustrates a number of the remarkable changes that have occurred in the Religion Clause doctrine in the twenty-first century.

Carson arose from a Maine statute providing educational vouchers for children living in rural areas. Most of the state's school-aged students attended local public schools. But those growing up in parts of the state that were too sparsely populated to support secondary schools received vouchers from the state. Under the scheme at issue in *Carson*, students could cash their vouchers in nearby public school districts or at secular private schools but not at private schools affiliated with churches. Maine had excluded parochial schools from eligibility based partly on the legal advice of a former state attorney general that for it to provide financial subsidies for sectarian education would violate the Establishment Clause.

That former attorney general's interpretation presents a view of the Establishment Clause that could be aptly described as "strict separationist." Under this approach, the Establishment Clause requires states to refrain from giving either material or symbolic support to religion, religious practice, and religious institutions. Strict separationism posits that the underlying ideal of the two Religion Clauses, interpreted in conjunction, is religious *voluntarism*. On this view, the Free Exercise Clause affords protections to voluntarily adopted religious beliefs, while the Establishment Clause prevents the government from supporting or promoting religion in ways that might skew those convictions. In particular, the Establishment Clause forbids the deployment of governmental power and resources – including funds extracted from taxpayers with divergent religious views – to assist religious institutions. According to strict separationists, government financial support for sectarian education, even via a voucher scheme, would too closely approximate the kind of taxing and spending to promote religion that the Establishment Clause was historically understood to forbid.

---

[1] 596 U.S. 767 (2022).

On the other side of *Carson v. Makin* stood religiously devout parents who wished to send their child to a school that integrates religious and secular instruction. From their perspective, the state's withholding of an educational voucher from them and their child, solely because they wished to cash it at a religiously affiliated rather than a secular private school, was a form of discrimination against religious belief and believers that infringed their right to the free exercise of their religion. For heuristic purposes, we can think of the Carsons' position as embodying a "strong free exercise" view of the proper interpretation of the First Amendment. The strong free exercise interpretation reflects an understanding of the two Religion Clauses as seeking to advance religious *liberty*, understood as a value potentially different in subtle respects from religious voluntarism. From the perspective of the Carsons and their supporters, the Establishment Clause should not be read so broadly as to bar the state of Maine from facilitating the Carsons' exercise of their religious liberty to send their child to a religiously affiliated school – at least as long as it did not transgress relatively clear, historically marked lines such as the one barring governmental taxing and spending to support a single, favored, church. And if the Establishment Clause does not require the state to deny funding to families seeking religious education for their children, the Carsons and other advocates of a strong free exercise interpretation maintained, then the Free Exercise Clause forbade those families' discriminatory exclusion from the Maine voucher scheme.

There was, of course, a third possible view of how the two Religion Clauses fit together. One could hold that the Establishment Clause did not forbid Maine to allow the use of its educational vouchers at sectarian schools but that neither did the Free Exercise Clause require the state to subsidize religious education on the same basis as secular education. In fact, the Supreme Court had taken substantially that position in *Locke v. Davey*[2] (2004) a little less than two decades earlier. In *Locke*, Chief Justice William Rehnquist had written for the Court's majority in reasoning that the two Religion Clauses leave some room for "play in the joints." On the play-in-the-joints view, the Establishment Clause does not mandate strict separationism, but neither does the Free Exercise Clause require the strong conclusion that

---

[2] 540 U.S. 712, 718–19 (2004).

the government must provide material support for religious practices on the same terms as for otherwise similar secular practices.

In *Carson v. Makin*, the Supreme Court, by a vote of 6–3, embraced the strong interpretation of the Free Exercise Clause that the Carsons advanced. That clause, the Court held, forbade Maine from discriminating against religious schools in its provision of subsidies for private education. In ruling as it did, the Court necessarily rejected the strict separationist interpretation of the Establishment Clause that the prior state attorney general had advanced and that a majority of the justices had frequently embraced during the 1960s and 1970s. The Court also moved on from the version of the play-in-the-joints position concerning the relationship of the Establishment and Free Exercise Clauses that had prevailed as recently as *Locke*.

As of now, *Carson* represents the most recent turn in a history that has exhibited more than one previous shift of direction in the Supreme Court's interpretation of both the Establishment and the Free Exercise Clauses. As *Carson* signals, six justices appear committed to a relatively weak (as distinguished from a strict separationist) interpretation of the Establishment Clause that allows the government new latitude to support or facilitate religious practice. Correspondingly, the conservative supermajority has adopted an interpretation of the Free Exercise Clause that emphasizes the importance of religious liberty and forbids discriminations against religious practice and religious institutions, including in the distribution of government funds. At least in the short term, the central questions going forward are how much further from strict separationism the Court will travel and how robustly expansive an interpretation of the Free Exercise Clause a majority of the justices will embrace.

Although it is impossible to think coherently about how to interpret just one of the Religion Clauses without considering how it relates to the other, the remainder of this chapter mostly addresses them sequentially in the order in which they appear in the First Amendment. I begin with a series of issues under the Establishment Clause, then consider the central strands of the Free Exercise doctrine. A short section near the end then picks up two important loose ends. It returns to Establishment Clause issues that arise when the government specifically attempts to facilitate the practice of religion in ways that the Free Exercise Clause does not require, including by compelling private employers to accommodate their employees' wishes to exercise their faiths. The same section also deals briefly with questions involving how to define "God" and specify what counts as "religion" under both Religion Clauses.

Introduction to the Establishment Clause: Material Support for Religion

Disputes about the proper interpretation of the Establishment Clause, like those involving most constitutional provisions, begin (though they do not necessarily end) with efforts to understand the clause's originally understood meaning. The historical record abounds with statements by members of the Founding generation, including James Madison and Thomas Jefferson, demanding strict separation of church and state. Yet the federal government had barely begun operation when both Houses of Congress hired chaplains to be paid out of public funds and President George Washington designated a national day of prayer and thanksgiving.

The Supreme Court did not hear any early cases requiring interpretations of the Religion Clauses. Indeed, only two Establishment Clause cases received significant consideration by the justices before 1947. In that year, in *Everson v. Board of Education* (1947),[3] the Court held for the first time that the Fourteenth Amendment had "incorporated" the Establishment Clause, which begins with the words "Congress shall make no law ...," and thus made it applicable against state and local governments. Recognition that the states are subject to the Religion Clauses vastly magnified the significance of those clauses in American law, culture, and politics.

The substantive dispute in *Everson* concerned whether a New Jersey township violated the Establishment Clause by affording free bus transportation to students attending parochial as well as public schools. Like many Establishment Clause issues, including the one in *Carson*, that question called for line-drawing. On one side of the line that the justices had to mark, all sides concurred that the government could not provide financial support solely to a favored church or to students attending a single church's schools. On the other side, the Establishment Clause just as plainly does not preclude public authorities from providing police and fire protection to churches on the same

---

[3] 330 U.S. 1, 8 (1947).

terms that it furnishes those services to others. (Among other things, for the government not to put out fires or punish crimes at churches would put the safety of the broader public at risk.) In *Everson*, a narrow majority of the justices located bus transportation for children going to parochial schools on the same, permitted, side of the line as the services of police and fire departments. A dissenting opinion, joined by four justices, disagreed vehemently. "Public money devoted to payment of religious costs, educational or other, brings the quest for more," they warned. "It brings too the struggle of sect against sect."[4]

The dissenting justices in *Everson* offered their ominous forecast based more on generalizations about human nature and extrapolation from world history than on specific American experience. Through most of US history, it was uncommon for the government to give money or other items of value directly to religious institutions (with the exceptions of broadly shared public services and tax breaks – a topic about which I shall say more shortly). But the permissibility of direct governmental aid emerged as a divisive political issue in the 1960s. Parochial schools, nearly all operated by the Roman Catholic Church, sparked the controversy.[5] Citing a desire to promote effective education, local and national governments began to furnish aid to sectarian schools or to parents who wished to utilize them. On the other side, opponents of public support for parochial schooling deplored provisions for it as special-interest legislation enacted for the benefit of Catholics.

Starting in the 1960s and through the middle of the 1980s, the Warren and Burger Courts mostly took the position – borrowed from Thomas Jefferson, and more in line with the dissenting than the majority opinion in *Everson* – that the Establishment Clause required a "wall of separation" between church and state.[6] In defense of that figurative divide, the Court of that era frequently applied a test first articulated in *Lemon v. Kurtzman* (1971),[7] which invalidated a governmental

---

[4] *Ibid.* at 53.
[5] For social, political, and legal analysis of the history of the debate about the constitutionality of public funding for parochial schools, see John C. Jeffries Jr. and James E. Ryan, "A Political History of the Establishment Clause," 100 *Michigan Law Review* 279 (2001).
[6] *Everson v. Board of Education of Ewing Township*, 330 U.S. 1, 16 (1947) (quoting Letter from Thomas Jefferson to a Committee of the Danbury Baptist Ass'n (Jan. 1, 1802), in 16 *The Writings of Thomas Jefferson*, ed. A. Lipscomb (privately printed, 1903), 281, 281–82).
[7] 403 U.S. 602, 612–13 (1971).

subsidy for the teaching of secular subjects in parochial schools. Under "the *Lemon* test," as it was called, a government program would be deemed invalid if (1) it had the purpose of promoting religion, (2) its principal or primary effect was either to promote or inhibit religion, or (3) it promoted entanglement between church and state.

Although *Lemon* epitomized a commitment to strict separationism, the justices found it difficult to sustain that commitment consistently. The Warren and Burger Courts invalidated numerous government programs aiding parochial schools, but they also upheld some. And, in a bow to historical practice, *Walz v. Tax Commission*[8] (1970) sustained a state's grant of tax exemptions for "property used exclusively for religious, educational, or charitable purposes" on the theory that the inclusion of other charities in the subsidy showed that its purpose was "neither the advancement nor the inhibition of religion." Even constitutional scholars had a hard time making sense of the Burger Court's overall pattern of decisions as exhibiting a consistent, coherent application of the *Lemon* test.

Then, in the 1980s and 1990s, strict separationism began to fall out of favor, both in American culture and politics and among the justices of the Supreme Court. Since the 1960s, conservative Protestant denominations had begun to operate church schools in growing numbers. As they did so, the issue of aid to parochial schools increasingly affected Protestants as well as Catholics. As a further contributor to changed attitudes about governmental assistance to parochial schools and other religious institutions that provided secular services, political conservatives of the Reagan era believed that the private sector could deliver a variety of services more efficiently than government bureaucracies. From that perspective, it made good sense for the government to subsidize private service organizations, including churches and affiliated organizations, as an alternative to direct public provision of education and other services such as treatment for drug and alcohol abuse.

Against the background of these trends, a Supreme Court that grew increasingly conservative as a result of appointments by Presidents Ronald Reagan and George H. W. Bush gradually relaxed the Establishment Clause restrictions on governmental aid to religious

---

[8] 397 U.S. 664, 672 (1970).

institutions. In *Zelman v. Simmons-Harris* (2002),[9] the Rehnquist Court gave a constitutional green light to voucher-style funding programs in which the government allows the ultimate consumers of goods and services – including the parents of children seeking education – to choose between secular and religious providers. According to Chief Justice Rehnquist, such programs' most constitutionally salient characteristic was that they were "neutral" as between religion and nonreligion. If aid flowed into the coffers of religious institutions, its arrival resulted from the private choice of voucher recipients, not the government, he reasoned.

Since the Rehnquist years, the strict separationist stance that the Warren and Burger Courts had tried to uphold in cases involving material support for religion and religious institutions, albeit with only partial success, has crumbled even further. In *Kennedy v. Bremerton School District* (2022),[10] the Supreme Court, by a 6–3 vote – with Justice Neil Gorsuch writing for the Court and the other two Trump nominees joining the majority – announced definitively that the *Lemon* test for Establishment Clause violations, which forbade governmental actions with the principal or primary effect of aiding religion, was mistaken from the outset and no longer governed. Henceforth, Justice Gorsuch wrote, decisions under the Establishment Clause must "faithfully reflect the understanding of the Founding Fathers."[11] Although the Court did not pause in *Kennedy* to provide a detailed portrayal of what that understanding was, the justices in the majority plainly assumed that it did not require the uncompromising "wall of separation" between the state and religion that a predecessor Court had devised the *Lemon* test to enforce.

A more specific indicator of when the Supreme Court will now uphold programs that provide material support to religious institutions and practices came, as we have seen, in *Carson v. Makin*. So long as government programs that disburse material benefits do so on religiously "neutral" terms, they do not violate the Establishment Clause even when their practical effect is to benefit religion or religious institutions. Other recent decisions establish that direct government distributions of assistance to religious along with nonreligious institutions

---

[9] 536 U.S. 639 (2002).
[10] 597 U.S. 507 (2022).
[11] *Ibid.* at 536.

are equally permissible even in the absence of intervening choices by "private benefit recipients" such as the Carsons.[12]

To summarize, in matters involving material support for religious institutions under the Establishment Clause, the Roberts Court frequently relies on the concept of "neutrality" as a measuring gauge. More particularly, provisions of material aid to religious institutions and those wishing to engage in religious practices are constitutionally permissible as long as the government delivers them on a nondiscriminatory basis to the religious and nonreligious alike.

Government Sponsorship of Religious Symbols and Exercises

Although the Supreme Court interprets the Religion Clauses as requiring governmental neutrality between religion and nonreligion with regard to some matters, it does not insist that the Establishment Clause requires neutrality with regard to all. The Court's tolerance for nonneutrality under the Establishment Clause is most evident in cases involving what I shall describe as "symbolic" support for religion through such practices as inscription of "In God We Trust" on the currency, presidential proclamations of national days of prayer, and designation of Christmas as a national holiday. To cite just one more example, the Supreme Court begins its own sessions with a summons by the Court's marshal that includes the words "God save the United States and this honorable Court."

Even justices who otherwise have embraced strict separationist interpretations of the Establishment Clause have not challenged practices such as these. In cases decided by the Warren, Burger, and Rehnquist Courts, a common explanatory trope involved "ceremonial deism" – the idea, roughly, that some governmental references and appeals to God have gone on for so long that their rote recitation has lost its religious significance in most minds. The justices' reluctance to challenge symbolic recognitions of God, religion, and religiosity likely reflected a mix of considerations. Both before and after originalism's rise to prominence in the 1980s, nearly everyone has believed that historical understandings and practices should matter to constitutional

---

[12] See, for example, *Espinoza v. Montana Department of Revenue*, 591 U.S. 464 (2020); *Trinity Lutheran Church v. Comer*, 582 U.S. 449 (2017).

interpretation. It is therefore difficult (though perhaps not impossible) to maintain that the Founding Fathers misunderstood the Constitution when they proclaimed days of prayer and thanksgiving and began sessions of Congress with prayers led by chaplains or that Abraham Lincoln behaved culpably when he approved the inscription of "In God We Trust" on the currency. Another factor that may influence even justices otherwise committed to strict separationism is anxiety about triggering an angry public backlash. A judicial ruling that required the root-and-branch removal of all references to God in all public practices and displays would have sparked outrage at any moment in constitutional history – including in the heyday of the Warren Court – that the justices were misusing their position to impose their own elitist, secular preferences on the American people.

Although no justice has ever demanded an end to all governmental sponsorship of religious symbols and displays, the Supreme Court has not yet explicitly embraced an anything-goes approach, either. In the not-too-distant past, the Court held in a few notable cases that the prominent display of a creche at Christmastime and some exhibitions of the Ten Commandments violated the Establishment Clause.[13] But the justices were sharply divided in those cases. During the years of the Burger and Rehnquist Courts, the justices most committed to strict separationism adhered to the *Lemon* test, which would have barred all governmental references to religion that have either the purpose or the primary effect of promoting religion.[14] Another coterie of justices, who denounced strict separationism as historically insupportable, advanced the much more tolerant view that symbolic governmental support for religion (not involving children in the public schools) did not offend the Establishment Clause unless it rose to the level of coercion or sustained one-sect proselytization.[15] And for two decades or more, the controlling votes within the Court belonged

---

[13] See, for example, *County of Allegheny v. ACLU*, 492 U.S. 573 (1989) (invalidating the display of a creche but upholding display of a Chanukah menorah); *McCreary County v. ACLU*, 545 U.S. 844 (2005) (invalidating display of the Ten Commandments). But the Court of this era was prone to drawing very fine lines. See, for example, *Van Orden v. Perry*, 545 U.S. 677 (2005) (upholding display of the Ten Commandments on the same day that the *McCreary County* decision invalidated another Ten Commandments display); see also *Lynch v. Donnelly*, 465 U.S. 668 (1984) (upholding display of a creche).

[14] See *County of Allegheny*, 492 U.S. at 637–38 (Brennan J., concurring in part and dissenting in part).

[15] *County of Allegheny*, 492 U.S. at 659–60 (Kennedy, J., concurring in the judgment in part and dissenting in part).

to centrist justices who employed a test, initially proposed by Justice Sandra Day O'Connor, that identified Establishment Clause violations in cases arguably involving symbolic support for religion by asking whether a "reasonable observer" would view particular religious displays as constituting "endorsements" of religion.[16]

Under the Roberts Court, the second of those positions appears ascendant, but with the test now reframed to emphasize the significance of historical understandings of what the Establishment Clause allows and disallows. *Kennedy v. Bremerton School District*, as noted earlier, rejected the *Lemon* test. Equally importantly for current purposes, *Kennedy* also repudiated judicial inquiries into whether a "reasonable observer" might perceive religious images or invocations as constituting governmental "endorsements" of religion. Instead, the Court held, the exclusive marker of Establishment Clause violations was "the understanding of the Founding Fathers." *Kennedy* was an unusually divisive case, even by current standards, because its facts involved publicly visible prayer by a public high school football coach. As will be discussed later in the chapter, the Supreme Court, in the past, frequently manifested special apprehensions about religious displays and practices in the context of public school activities. For present purposes, however, the significance of *Kennedy* lies in its adoption of an exclusively originalist or history-based test for the identification of Establishment Clause violations.

Kennedy's reliance on a historical test to gauge Establishment Clause violations in cases involving symbolic support for religion largely echoed the position that a majority of the justices had previously embraced in *Greece v. Galloway* (2014).[17] In *Greece*, the Court, by 5–4, upheld the practice of Greece, New York, of beginning the meetings of its town board with prayers. The Court opinion by Justice Anthony Kennedy relied on an earlier decision that had allowed a state legislature to initiate its sessions with invocations by a chaplain. But Justice Kennedy also wrote, more generally, that "the Establishment Clause must be interpreted by reference to historical practices and understandings,"[18] and he took prayers at official events, including sessions of Congress and state legislatures, to have been commonplace

---

[16] See *McCreary County*, 545 U.S. at 883 (O'Connor, J., concurring); *County of Allegheny*, 492 U.S. at 630–32 (O'Connor, J., concurring in part and concurring in the judgment).
[17] 572 U.S. 565 (2014).
[18] Ibid. at 576.

historically. The dissenting opinion by Justice Elena Kagan saw a distinction between the prayers by a legislative chaplain that the Court had upheld previously and prayers at meetings attended by "ordinary citizens," some of whom had no choice but to be present in order to obtain land-use permits and licenses. Justice Kagan worried that such attendees might construe invocations and benedictions by religious leaders as signaling the outsider status of those with nonconforming views.

Between the decision in *Greece* and that in *Kennedy, American Legion v. American Humanist Association*[19] (2019) rejected an Establishment Clause challenge to the maintenance on public land of a Latin cross that had originally been erected nearly a hundred years before as a monument to soldiers killed in World War I. Although divided in some of their reasoning, a majority of the justices agreed that "retaining established, religiously expressive monuments symbols, and practices is quite different from erecting or adopting new ones" and that "[t]he passage of time gives rise to a strong presumption of constitutionality."[20]

Following the prescription of *Greece* and *Kennedy* that challenges to symbolic governmental support for religion must now be assessed in light of "historical practices and understandings" and "the understanding of the Founding Fathers," the outstanding question appears to be whether, and if so when, the Court will overrule a few decisions by the Warren, Burger, and Rehnquist Courts that reflect more nearly strict separationist stances, such as one from 1989 that forbade a county to erect a creche display in a prominent place in a courthouse. Lower courts will be bound by that ruling in *County of Allegheny v. American Civil Liberties Union* (1989)[21] unless and until the Supreme Court overrules it. But the Court's more recent emphasis on the controlling importance of history and tradition as gauges of constitutional permissibility provides a basis for reconsidering *County of Allegheny* if the conservative supermajority wishes to do so.

Religion in the Public Schools

It also remains to be seen whether the Roberts Court may reconsider decisions beginning in the 1960s and continuing through the Rehnquist Court that barred the intrusion of state-sponsored

---

[19] 588 U.S. 29 (2019).
[20] *Greece*, 572 U.S. at 590.
[21] 492 U.S. 573 (1989).

religious practice and symbols into public schools. In pathbreaking decisions in the 1960s, the Supreme Court held that officially organized school prayer and Bible readings violated the Establishment Clause.[22] The school prayer decisions stirred intense controversy. Their historical foundations were doubtful. There was little public schooling at the Founding, but nondenominational Protestant prayer and Bible reading were staples of the common school curriculum that spread in the nineteenth century. As arrayed against that tradition, the Warren Court's school prayer rulings upheld an ideal of religious voluntarism under which the government should not proselytize in support of religious views, especially to children.

Residues of that stance persisted in the Rehnquist Court's decision in *Lee v. Weisman* (1992),[23] which ruled that religious invocations and benedictions at public school graduation ceremonies crossed a forbidden line. The author of the Court's decision in *Lee* was Justice Kennedy, who later wrote for the majority in *Greece v. Galloway*, which allowed prayers at the beginning of town board meetings. But Kennedy, who cast the decisive vote in both cases, viewed the issues as different. Students attending graduation exercises were more likely than adults to feel "public pressure, as well as peer pressure," to participate in government-sponsored prayers, he concluded.

As we have seen, however, *Kennedy v. Bremerton School District*, decided by a more recent Court including the three justices appointed by President Trump, drew no distinction between the gauge of Establishment Clause violations that applies in the context of public schools and related activities and the test that governs in more predominantly adult settings. In affirming that "the understanding of the Founding Fathers" governs, Justice Gorsuch's opinion for a six-justice majority dismissively rejected suggestions that members of a high school football team might have experienced coercive pressures – which he may have assumed that the Founding Fathers would have objected to if they had existed – to join one of their coaches in postgame prayers.

Kennedy's renunciation of the *Lemon* test also raises questions about other precedents that have long barred governmental promotion of religion within the public schools. These include *Epperson*

---

[22] See *Engel v. Vitale*, 370 U.S. 421 (1962) (concerning prayer); *Abington School District v. Schempp*, 374 U.S. 203 (1963) (concerning Bible reading).
[23] 505 U.S. 577 (1992).

v. Arkansas (1968),[24] which struck down a statute forbidding public school teachers to teach the theory of evolution, and *Stone v. Graham* (1980),[25] which invalidated a Kentucky statute that mandated posting the Ten Commandments on classroom walls. Also potentially vulnerable to overruling are the signal precedents involving religion in the public schools: the Warren Court's decisions banning school prayer. Perhaps out of a desire to avoid too much unwanted controversy, some of the less aggressively conservative and originalist members of the current conservative supermajority could imaginably choose to leave the school prayer decisions untouched, at least for the time being. As noted in Chapter 3, most originalists aver that their theories include an exception for stare decisis, or adherence to precedent, in some (though not all) cases. Clearly, however, the winds of change are blowing, as evidenced perhaps most notably by *Kennedy v. Bremerton School District*.

The Free Exercise Clause

Although some elements of the Free Exercise Clause doctrine are also in flux, there is clarity about two important points. First, it is firmly established that free exercise principles forbid the government either to compel or to prohibit religious practices based on their religious character unless doing so is somehow necessary to a compelling governmental interest. A leading case is *Church of the Lukumi Babalu Aye, Inc. v. City of Hialeah* (1993),[26] which grew out of a Hialeah ordinance that forbade the ritual killing of small animals. The language of the statute revealed its aim or purposes. It did not forbid all killings of small animals but instead targeted those occurring in the context of a "ritual," such as those conducted in the City of Hialeah by members of the Santeria religion, some of whom apparently left the remains of their sacrifices in public spaces. The Free Exercise Clause, the Court unanimously held, precluded Hialeah from taking deliberate aim at "ritual" killings of animals that could lawfully be killed in other, including equally painful, ways.

Second, as we have seen, *Carson v. Makin* extends the principle that the government may not single out religious institutions and practices for disfavored treatment (absent a "compelling" justification

---

[24] 393 U.S. 97 (1968).
[25] 449 U.S. 39 (1980).
[26] 508 U.S. 520 (1993).

for doing so) to the more controversial domain of governmental disbursal of funds and other benefits. As noted earlier, *Carson*'s holding that the selective denial of financial subsidies to religious institutions and activities constitutes discrimination forbidden by the Free Exercise Clause marks a substantial and controversial change in the governing law. At one point in the past, the Court had held that the channeling of material aid to religious institutions even on a neutral basis violated the Establishment Clause if it had the principal or primary effect of advancing religion or if it promoted undue "entanglement" between the government and religion. And as recently as 2004, in *Locke v. Davey*, the Rehnquist Court had allowed the government to make discretionary choices about whether to extend funding to religious institutions and activities on the same basis as to their secular counterparts. Although *Carson* purported to distinguish *Locke*, not overrule it, the majority opinion appeared to limit *Locke*'s continuing vitality to the special case of a state's withholding funds that otherwise would be used to train students specifically for the ministry. "*Locke*'s reasoning expressly turned on what it identified as the 'historic and substantial state interest' against using 'taxpayer funds to support church leaders,'" the Court said.[27] Otherwise, the Free Exercise Clause now forbids nonneutral exclusions of religious entities and activities from government funding programs.

The most salient flux in free exercise doctrine involves the issue of whether, and if so when, the Free Exercise Clause requires the government to make exceptions to generally valid laws for people who have religiously motivated reasons to engage in conduct that those laws prohibit or substantially burden. The Supreme Court's first major decision interpreting the Free Exercise Clause, *Reynolds v. United States* (1878),[28] posed a version of that question, which has remained a subject of chronic dispute. At issue in *Reynolds* was whether the Free Exercise Clause precluded the enforcement of an antipolygamy statute against religious Mormons at a time when the Mormon Church considered polygamy a religious duty. The Court answered in the negative. In doing so, it distinguished between religious belief, which the Free Exercise Clause immunizes from regulation, and religiously motivated conduct. "Congress was deprived of all legislative power over mere

---

[27] *Carson*, 596 U.S. at 788.
[28] 98 U.S. 145 (1878).

opinion, but it was left free to reach actions which were in violation of social duties or subversive of good order," the Court reasoned.[29] This is a plausible position but also arguably a harsh one. The government confronts its citizens with what Justice Potter Stewart once termed "a cruel choice" when it demands that they either breach their religious duties or violate secular law.[30]

During the 1930s and 1940s, the Supreme Court gradually softened the stance it had adopted in *Reynolds* and began to hold that the Free Exercise Clause sometimes protects religiously motivated conduct, especially when it is coupled with speech (as, e.g., in the distribution of religious literature). The Warren and Burger Courts pushed even further, moved by a sense that a broad interpretation of the Free Exercise Clause was necessary to protect religious minorities. Statutes have rarely put members of mainstream religions to a choice between violating the secular law and breaching what they take to be God's commands. During Prohibition, for example, bans on the possession and use of alcohol exempted Communion wine. In light of the Warren Court's more general concern with protecting "discrete and insular minorities," interpreting the Free Exercise Clause to mandate protections for those who wished to practice minority religions was an integral aspect of a broader agenda.

The Warren Court's most iconic interpretation of the Free Exercise Clause came in *Sherbert v. Verner* (1963).[31] *Sherbert* involved a claim to unemployment benefits by a Seventh-Day Adventist who lost her job because she refused to work on Saturday. (When she was hired, the work week was five days, but her employer subsequently added mandatory Saturday shifts.) Government officials concluded that Sherbert's unemployment was voluntary and denied her claim under a rule that barred benefits for those who willingly gave up their jobs. The Supreme Court overturned that decision. In an opinion by Justice William Brennan, the Court held Sherbert had a right under the Free Exercise Clause to be exempted from the normal rule denying unemployment benefits to those who lost their jobs for refusing to comply with the jobs' requirements. Under a close facsimile of what later came to be called the "strict judicial scrutiny" test, *Sherbert* held

---

[29] *Ibid.* at 164.
[30] *Braunfeld v. Braun*, 366 U.S. 599, 616 (1961) (Stewart, J., dissenting).
[31] 374 U.S. 398 (1963).

that people claiming to act on the basis of religious duties were entitled to exemptions from otherwise applicable laws unless the government had a "compelling state interest" in denying them.[32]

If *Reynolds* represented a narrow interpretation of the Free Exercise Clause, *Sherbert* articulated a far-reaching one. The strict scrutiny test that *Sherbert* prescribed for determining when the Free Exercise Clause required exceptions to generally applicable laws also proved difficult to administer. Seemingly sensibly, the Supreme Court required a "substantial" burden on religious practice to trigger strict scrutiny. But judging the significance of burdens on religion threatened to involve the judiciary in religious inquiries. The Court responded by crediting any good-faith claim about what an individual's personal religious beliefs required. In addition, the normally stringent strict judicial scrutiny formula, which the Court also applies to enforce a number of other constitutional guarantees including under the Free Speech and Equal Protection Clauses, created difficulties and occasional embarrassments in its application to free exercise cases. In one leading decision,[33] members of the Old Order Amish asserted a religious objection to paying Social Security taxes. A judicial mandate to allow religious exemptions from ordinary tax obligations would have been an administrative nightmare for the government. The Court therefore rejected the claim. But if the result was reasonable, the Court's effort to justify it in doctrinal terms was more troublesome. If the convenience of officials in administering a law or policy counts as a "compelling" governmental interest, then that stringent-looking standard has been diluted quite considerably.

Two other cases involving free exercise claims by members of Native American tribes further perplexed and divided the Court during the 1980s. In one, Native American parents objected that a state law requiring their children to have Social Security numbers to receive state benefits would rob the children's spirits and thus impair their free exercise of religion.[34] In another, tribal members sought to block the government's construction of a road and its authorization of timber harvesting on government property that would substantially impair their ability to worship at a sacred site.[35] Fractured Courts rejected

---

[32] *Ibid.* at 403.
[33] *United States v. Lee*, 455 U.S. 252 (1982).
[34] *Bowen v. Roy*, 476 U.S. 693 (1986).
[35] *Lyng v. Northwest Indian Cemetery Protective Association*, 485 U.S. 439 (1988).

both claims. Meantime, criticisms of the Court's free exercise jurisprudence proliferated among some on the secular left. According to them, if the government grants exemptions from otherwise applicable laws and policies for the benefit of religious believers, but not for nonbelievers, it effectively promotes religion and should therefore be viewed as violating the Establishment Clause.[36]

In light of concerns occasioned by experience with the application of strict judicial scrutiny to enforce claims to religious exceptions from generally applicable laws, the Rehnquist Court effected a sharp change of direction in *Employment Division v. Smith* (1990).[37] *Smith*, which held that a state that criminalized possession of the mildly hallucinogenic drug peyote need not make an exception for those who wished to use the drug for Native American religious rituals, refused to apply the strict judicial scrutiny that *Sherbert* was most naturally read to require. As interpreted or reinterpreted by *Smith*, the Free Exercise Clause does not mandate any exemptions from "neutral, generally applicable law[s]" such as a bar against peyote use.[38]

The Supreme Court that decided *Smith* was bitterly divided. Justice Antonin Scalia wrote for the five-justice majority. Joining him were three other conservative justices and the liberal John Paul Stevens. Although Justice Scalia labeled himself an originalist, his opinion in *Smith* paid scant attention to evidence of the Free Exercise Clause's original meaning.[39] "As a textual matter," he observed, the Clause might be read either to require special protections for religious practice or merely to prohibit the singling out of religiously motivated conduct for disfavored treatment. "Our decisions," he continued, "reveal that the latter reading is the correct one."[40] In support of that tendentious conclusion, which required him to treat *Sherbert* as aberrational and a number of other decisions as involving a hybrid mix of free exercise and other rights, Justice Scalia cited what he regarded as urgent policy concerns. It

---

[36] See generally, for example, Christopher L. Eisgruber and Lawrence G. Sager, "The Vulnerability of Conscience: The Constitutional Basis for Protecting Religious Conduct," 61 *University of Chicago Law Review* 1245 (1994).

[37] 494 U.S. 872 (1990).

[38] *Ibid.* at 888.

[39] For originalist criticism of the *Smith* decision, see, for example, Michael W. McConnell, "The Origins and Historical Understanding of Free Exercise of Religion," 103 *Harvard Law Review* 1409 (1990). For originalist support, see, for example, Philip A. Hamburger, "A Constitutional Right of Religious Exemption: An Historical Perspective," 60 *George Washington Law Review* 915, 916 (1992).

[40] *Smith*, 494 U.S. at 878–79.

would court "anarchy," he wrote, "[t]o make an individual's obligation to obey ... a law contingent upon the law's coincidence with his religious beliefs, except where the State's interest is 'compelling' – permitting him, by virtue of his beliefs, 'to become a law unto himself.'"[41]

The four justices who rejected *Smith*'s narrow interpretation of the Free Exercise Clause included three readily identifiable liberals and the moderate conservative Justice O'Connor. All worried that the Court's decision gave short shrift to the interests of "those whose religious practices are not shared by the majority and may be viewed with hostility."[42] To the ears of most liberals in 1990, Justice Scalia's reply on behalf of the Court's conservatives sounded callous: "It may fairly be said that leaving accommodation [of the religious practices of minorities] to the political process will place at a relative disadvantage those religious practices that are not widely engaged in; but that unavoidable consequence of democratic government must be preferred to a system in which each conscience is a law unto itself or in which judges weigh the social importance of all laws" against competing free exercise interests.[43]

Although the Supreme Court has never overruled *Smith*, the moral, political, and cultural ground has shifted dramatically underneath it. Increasingly, demands for exemptions from otherwise valid laws have come not from the kinds of religious minorities whose interests seemed most salient in 1990 but from conservative Christians who have objected to being compelled to sponsor employee health insurance that includes coverage of contraception and abortion,[44] to facilitate adoptions by same-sex couples,[45] and to provide goods and services for same-sex weddings.[46] As the incidence of pleas for religious accommodation has migrated from minority religions to the Christian right, the political valence of support for religious exemptions under the Free Exercise Clause has also shifted, with perhaps predictable consequences for decision-making within the Supreme Court.

The most dramatic changes to date have involved the narrowing of the set of cases to which *Smith*'s holding that the Free

---

[41] Ibid. at 885.
[42] Ibid. at 902.
[43] Ibid. at 890.
[44] See *Burwell v. Hobby Lobby Stores, Inc.*, 573 U.S. 682 (2014).
[45] See *Fulton v. City of Philadelphia*, 593 U.S. 522 (2021).
[46] See *Masterpiece Cakeshop v. Colorado Civil Rights Commission*, 584 U.S. 617 (2018).

Exercise Clause requires no exceptions to generally applicable laws applies. Increasingly, exceptions to *Smith* are swallowing the rule that it appeared to have established. In *Hosanna-Tabor Evangelical Lutheran Church and School v. Equal Employment Opportunity Commission* (2012),[47] the justices ruled unanimously that the Free Exercise Clause mandates an exception to laws forbidding employment discrimination for cases involving religious organizations' choice of clergy. *Smith*'s rule that generally applicable statutes require no religious exceptions does not extend to cases involving governmental interference with "an internal church decision that affects the faith and mission of the church itself," the Court concluded. "By imposing an unwanted minister, the state infringes the Free Exercise Clause, which protects a religious group's right to shape its own faith and mission through its appointments," Chief Justice Roberts wrote.

More recently, the Court has further narrowed what once was widely understood to be *Smith*'s reach through its interpretation of what constitutes a "neutral, generally applicable law[]" to which the Free Exercise Clause mandates no exceptions. *Fulton v. City of Philadelphia*[48] (2021) involved a claim by a Catholic agency to an exemption under the Free Exercise Clause from a requirement that city contractors place children with same-sex foster couples on a nondiscriminatory basis. In an opinion by Chief Justice Roberts, the Court held that a provision allowing exceptions to the nondiscrimination requirement at the "sole discretion" of a city official rendered that requirement less than generally applicable. The city's failure to grant a religiously based exemption therefore triggered strict judicial scrutiny, which it could not survive.

Also indicative of the Court's recent disposition to narrow *Smith* and expand entitlements to exemptions from statutes and other rules that burden religious exercise is *Tandon v. Newsom* (2021).[49] In *Tandon*, the Court held, by 5–4, that California could not enforce an emergency pandemic rule limiting the size of gatherings in private homes against those wishing to congregate for religious purposes. Because the state allowed similarly sized or larger gatherings in a variety of commercial spaces, *Smith* did not control; strict scrutiny applied to the state's failure to make an exception for at-home religious

---

[47] 565 U.S. 171 (2012).
[48] 593 U.S. 522 (2021).
[49] 593 U.S. 61 (2021) (per curiam).

gatherings; and the state, the Court ruled, had failed to demonstrate that denial of a religious exception was necessary to a compelling governmental interest. Four dissenting justices complained that the majority should not have second-guessed the determination by the state of California that at-home religious gatherings were likely to occur in spaces that were not well ventilated and that it was reasonable to think they posed larger health risks than the congregations of people in commercial spaces that the state allowed.

Commentators have described *Fulton* and *Tandon* as applying a "most favored nation" approach to claims under the Free Exercise Clause based on a term familiar in treaties governing international trade: If exemptions from otherwise applicable statutory requirements are granted to any parties or analogous activities, then parties wishing to engage in religiously motivated conduct must be treated as least as favorably absent a showing that the denial of religious exceptions is necessary to a compelling governmental interest.[50] This approach looks like a compromise between the rule of *Sherbert v. Verner*, under which all substantial burdens on religion trigger strict judicial scrutiny, and the apparent ambition of Justice Scalia in *Employment Division v. Smith* to reject claims to religious exemptions under the Free Exercise Clause except in narrow circumstances.

In practice, however, the Supreme Court's recent decisions mandate the recognition of a very broad swathe of exceptions to otherwise valid laws. In addition to narrowing the category of "neutral, generally applicable laws" to which no exceptions are required, the Court has made the strict scrutiny test nearly impossible to satisfy in cases to which it now applies. The Court has done so by reasoning that if the government has created any exceptions to a rule, as in *Fulton* or *Tandon*, it cannot credibly argue that it has a compelling interest in denying further exceptions for religious groups or practices. If an interest in denying exceptions were truly compelling, the Court insists, then the government would not allow any exemptions at all.

Despite the considerable erosion of the rule of *Employment Division v. Smith* that has occurred already, the three justices who are normally counted as the most conservative – Thomas, Alito, and

---

[50] See, for example, Douglas Laycock, "The Remnants of Free Exercise," 1990 *Supreme Court Review* 1, 49 (suggesting religion and religious claims should be accorded the equivalent of most-favored status).

Gorsuch – have argued that the Court should take the further step of overruling *Smith* altogether.[51] Their position is noteworthy partly because of the pivot that it reflects from what was almost universally understood to be the "conservative" view about the proper interpretation of the Free Exercise Clause at the time when Justice Scalia authored the Court opinion in *Smith*. Many liberals have undergone a parallel change of position at a time when Christian conservatives have increasingly sought exceptions from statutes enacted to ensure women's access to contraception and reproductive health care and to forbid discrimination against members of the LGBTQ community. In the legal academy and among advocacy groups, many former critics of *Smith*, who once derided its insensitivity to the interests of minority religions, have now become defenders.

Amid these shifting currents, two justices sometimes classed as among the more "moderate" of the conservatives, although enthusiastically embracing the most-favored-nation approach to religious exemptions, have hesitated about overruling *Smith* entirely. In *Fulton*, Justice Barrett, joined by Justice Kavanaugh (and the liberal Justice Stephen Breyer), expressed reservations about mandating a "categorical strict scrutiny regime" for identifying constitutionally mandated exceptions under the Free Exercise Clause "when this Court's resolution of conflicts between generally applicable laws and other First Amendment rights – like speech and assembly – has been much more nuanced."[52] It is not yet clear what a "more nuanced" approach to claims to religious exceptions from otherwise valid laws under the Free Exercise Clause might look like. Meantime, Court majorities continue to read *Smith* narrowly, and strict judicial scrutiny of denials of religious exceptions is increasingly common.

Voluntary Governmental Efforts to Accommodate Religious Practices

Two final topics that have not attracted much recent attention from the Supreme Court deserve at least brief mention in a survey of the Religion Clause doctrine. The first involves the permissibility under

---

[51] See *Fulton*, 593 U.S. at 545 (Alito, J., joined by Thomas and Gorsuch, JJ., concurring in the judgment).
[52] *Fulton*, 593 U.S. at 543.

the Establishment Clause of governmental efforts to accommodate religious practice in ways that the Free Exercise Clause does not require. The cases within this category are diverse. Some involve exemptions of religious institutions from generally applicable laws, including tax laws that make religiously motivated practices more expensive.[53] Another kind of example comes from state and federal laws compelling private employers to accommodate their employees' religious beliefs by, for example, adjusting their work schedules to permit prayer or religious observances.

Only a few Supreme Court cases directly address issues of this kind, and some are difficult to square with others. Although it is unclear how the current Court would resolve some issues that may sometime come before the justices again, the Court's commitment to two general principles would almost certainly structure its approach.

First, any governmental effort to accommodate religious beliefs by facilitating religious practice must be neutral among faiths. For example, the government could not expressly designate Christians or those who wish to engage in Christian rituals as entitled to accommodations not available to Jews or Muslims. To be clear, the government can establish Christmas Day as a holiday for all with no similar designation for any Jewish or Muslim holy day. But it could not make adherence to Christianity or any other faith a formal condition of entitlement to a benefit or opportunity.

Second, religious accommodations for some must not impose unreasonably substantial hardships on others. The leading case of this kind remains *Thornton v. Caldor* (1985),[54] which invalidated a state statute that categorically required private employers to allow time off to employees who asserted religious duties to participate in religious services without regard to resulting hardships to others. The modern Court almost surely would adhere to the view that the Establishment Clause forbids the government to mandate religious accommodations that impose unreasonable burdens on others, even if the current justices might draw the line between permissible and excessive impositions in a different place than the justices who sat on the Court in 1985.[55]

---

[53] See, for example, *Texas Monthly, Inc. v. Bullock*, 489 U.S. 1 (1989) (invalidating a sales-tax exemption for religious periodicals).

[54] 472 U.S. 703 (1985).

[55] See *Cutter v. Wilkinson*, 544 U.S. 709, 720 (2005) (upholding a statute requiring state and local governments to relax rules that otherwise would stop institutionalized persons from

The second dangling thread of a topic without which a discussion of the Religion Clauses would not be complete is, simply, what is "religion" in the constitutionally relevant sense? Although that question can come up in many guises, the Supreme Court has never had occasion to provide a comprehensive answer. Back when the United States had a military draft and Congress had provided exemptions for those "who, by reason of religious training and belief ... opposed ... participation in war in any form," the Court interpreted the statute as granting conscientious objector status to people whose opposition to war rested on moral beliefs that did not include the existence of a "Supreme Being,"[56] but occupied a place in the claimants' lives "parallel to that filled [by] God in traditionally religious persons."[57] The Court did not say, however, that religion and religious belief had to be defined similarly broadly for all constitutional purposes. Indeed, if that were the case, an argument could be made that any teaching about ethics in the public schools that included no reference to a traditional God impermissibly promotes nontheistic over theistic "religion" in violation of the Establishment Clause. Although scholars have expressed radically diverse views about how best to define the concept of "religion" to which the Religion Clauses refer, the modern Court would likely begin any consideration of the question with an inquiry into the original constitutional understanding of that term.

Conclusion

Constitutional doctrine under the Religion Clauses has recently experienced not just change but upheaval. The strict separationist principles that the Warren and Burger Courts sought to enforce under the Establishment Clause are mostly relics of the past. Today's justices look much less askance at religious invocations and symbols in the public square than did their predecessors of a few decades ago. Nonetheless, Warren-era decisions banning prayer in the public schools continue in force for now. Under the Free Exercise Clause, the supermajority of conservative justices on the Roberts Court has nearly, but not yet

---

practicing their religions and emphasizing that the law does not impose excessive burdens "on nonbeneficiaries").
[56] *United States v. Seeger*, 380 U.S. 163, 165–66 (1965).
[57] *Welsh v. United States*, 398 U.S. 333, 340 (1970) (internal quotations omitted).

completely, abandoned the holding of *Employment Division v. Smith* that the government need not grant religious exceptions to otherwise valid, generally applicable laws. In the increasingly ascendant view, the Free Exercise Clause provides expansive protections for religious liberty. Among other developments, if the government subsidizes education in private secular schools, the Court now classifies the withholding of similar assistance to parochial schools as a form of constitutionally forbidden discrimination.

Commitments to originalism have undoubtedly driven a number of recent revisionist decisions, but they cannot explain everything that the Court has done or everything that it has so far failed to do. Practical concerns about the impacts of decisions on different segments of the public – which conservative and liberal justices often appraise differently – have also loomed large. For now, the central pending question is how many rulings of the Warren and Burger Courts and even the Rehnquist Court remain to be toppled.

5 THE FREEDOM OF SPEECH
The Ascent of "The Persuasion Principle"

The United States gives more robust protection to freedom of speech and expression than any other nation in the world. A stark example involves speech calculated to arouse racial or religious hatred. Every other major liberal democracy has pledged to outlaw such speech. The United States has not. To the contrary, when the United States otherwise agreed to the International Covenant on Civil and Political Rights in 1992, its ratification included a reservation disavowing any commitment to bar speech inciting racial and religious hatred. The reason for the reservation: As interpreted by the Supreme Court, the First Amendment's Free Speech Clause protects much, though not necessarily all, racial and religious vilification. In other examples of the extraordinarily broad protections that the First Amendment's guarantee of "the freedom of speech" confers, the Supreme Court has invalidated restrictions on campaign advertising by corporations, on films depicting illegal cruelty to animals, and on deliberate lies by people falsely claiming to have earned military honors.

As late as the middle of the twentieth century, the Supreme Court interpreted the Free Speech Clause much more narrowly. The leading elements of free speech doctrine, nearly all of which began to emerge after 1960, have all been shaped or reshaped during the twenty-first century by Supreme Court justices who are widely counted as conservatives. Yet the doctrine is not originalist. Nor is it conservative in traditional ways. Political scientists seeking to rank individual justices' votes in constitutional cases as either "liberal" or "conservative" have traditionally coded all decisions upholding free speech claims as liberal and those denying speech rights as conservative.[1] This categorization made sense in an era in which the central free speech issues involved asserted rights to disseminate allegedly obscene books, magazines, and films and governmental efforts to suppress the speech of Communists, anarchists, and related subversive organizations. In that period, conservatives widely favored restrictions on speech as a means of protecting or conserving traditional values and established political structures. Since the Reagan years, however, judicial conservatism, like political conservatism, has evolved to encompass more libertarian commitments, which the Supreme Court's interpretations of the Free Speech Clause now exemplify.

Modern free speech doctrine is complex and multipartite. Grouping cases into categories requires potentially controversial judgments. There are untidy exceptions to nearly every generalization. For heuristic purposes, this chapter divides current free speech doctrine into four parts, of which the first is the most extensive and important.

The first, central element of the doctrine establishes that nearly all efforts by the government to regulate speech on the basis of its content – including racial vilification and advocacy of unlawful violence – are constitutionally suspect. Content-based regulation normally triggers strict judicial scrutiny, under which a challenged regulation is unconstitutional unless "necessary" or "narrowly tailored" to a "compelling" governmental interest, or some comparably exacting test. This aspect of the doctrine is best explained by what David Strauss has labeled "the persuasion principle": The government should not be able to regulate speech based on an apprehension that readers or listeners might find it persuasive and, as a result, come to hold what the government views as false or dangerous beliefs.[2]

The second strand of the doctrine involves a few categories of speech that the Supreme Court, based largely on traditional understandings, deems to lie outside the coverage of the First Amendment and that the government is free to prohibit for nearly any reason. These include "obscenity," "fighting words," and speech that is inextricably connected to criminal activity, such as "conspiracy" to fix prices or commit fraud or theft.

---

[1] See Harold J. Spaeth et al., 2020 *Supreme Court Database*, Version 2020, Release 1, 50–51.
[2] David A. Strauss, "Persuasion, Autonomy, and Freedom of Expression," 91 *Columbia Law Review* 334, 334 (1991).

The third branch of judicial doctrine under the Free Speech Clause consists of cases in which the Supreme Court has held that the free speech guarantee implicitly creates rights to freedom of association. Although the justices have all agreed that a right to freedom of association exists, they have disagreed, sometimes sharply, about its content.

The fourth component of free speech doctrine applies in contexts in which the government's primary role involves functions other than regulating the speech of private individuals. Examples include providing public services such as police and fire protection, administering welfare bureaucracies, and furnishing public education. In performing missions such as these, the government needs to be able to enforce regulations – including ones dictating what its employees can and must say in order to do their jobs effectively – that cannot be content neutral. In a famous dictum, the Supreme Court once said that "[n]either students [n]or teachers shed their constitutional rights to freedom of speech or expression at the schoolhouse gate."[3] Even so, their rights are necessarily different from and more circumscribed than those of ordinary citizens who can claim rights against content-based censorship in other contexts. To take a plain example, public school teachers have no protected right to opine about politics during a mathematics class.

This chapter describes the historical emergence of the four parts of modern doctrine under the Free Speech Clause in a corresponding four-part sequence. Especially in discussing the first part, the chapter includes multiple subdivisions, reflecting the doctrine's complexity. When one stands back from the intricacies, however, a clear trend line cuts across the most important doctrinal subcategories: The modern "conservative" Court has outdone predecessor Courts, just as it has outdone other countries, in expanding recognized rights to freedom of speech and expressive association.

Content-Based Regulation of Speech

Remote Origins of Modern Doctrine: Historical Debates

The Free Speech Clause of the First Amendment enjoins that "Congress shall make no law ... abridging the freedom of speech, or of the press." Justice Hugo Black used to insist that "no law" meant

---

[3] *Tinker v. Des Moines Independent Community School District*, 393 U.S. 503, 506 (1969).

no law and that freedom to speak was "absolute." But when the Free Speech Clause is read in its entirety, it does not say that Congress shall make no law abridging "speech" but instead that it shall make no law abridging "*the freedom of speech*." In light of that phrase, the relevant question is not "What is speech?" but "What is the freedom of speech?"

In exploring the original meaning of "the freedom of speech," historians have largely concluded that the Founding generation would have been astonished by the scope of the protections that the Supreme Court enforces today. Leading historians once maintained that the Framers viewed "the freedom of speech" as embracing protections only against administrative licensing schemes, referred to as "prior restraints," that required speakers and publishers to preclear commentary on certain matters and possibly against prosecutions for criticizing the government and its officials.[4] More recent scholars have reached different conclusions. According to their research, the originally understood meaning of the freedom of speech included a broad presumptive right to speak freely but one that was subject to reasonable regulation by the legislature.[5] On neither view, and contrary to the position that Justice Black once espoused, was the freedom of speech "absolute."

The first major national debate about the First Amendment freedom of speech took shape in 1798, when a Federalist-dominated Congress enacted the Sedition Act, which, as recounted in Chapter 2, made it a crime to "utter or publish ... any false, scandalous[,] and malicious" criticism of the national government. Opponents from the Democratic-Republican Party protested that the statute infringed the freedom of speech. On the other side, Federalist leaders defended it as a reasonable and therefore permissible regulation necessary to protect domestic harmony and respect for government.

After the presidential election of 1800, the newly elected Democratic-Republican Thomas Jefferson issued pardons to all those who had been convicted under the Sedition Act, which he denounced as unconstitutional. But the question of the Act's constitutionality

---

[4] See, for example, Leonard W. Levy, *Emergence of a Free Press* (New York, NY: Oxford University Press, 1985), xii–xv.
[5] See Genevieve Lakier, "The Invention of Low-Value Speech," 128 *Harvard Law Review* 2166, 2195 (2015); see also Jud Campbell, "Natural Rights and the First Amendment," 127 *Yale Law Journal* 246, 257 (2017).

never reached the Supreme Court, largely because of the pardons that Jefferson issued. In a 1964 decision limiting the capacity of public officials to recover damages based on false allegations of official misconduct, the Court wrote that "although the Sedition Act was never tested in this Court, the attack upon its validity has carried the day in the court of history."[6]

More Proximate Origins of Modern Doctrine

The origins of modern free speech doctrine can be traced to Supreme Court decisions addressing the constitutionality of the Espionage Act that Congress adopted during the early days of World War I. Before then, Congress had enacted little legislation restricting speech, and the Court's discussions of freedom of expression had consisted largely of sweeping, mostly unsympathetic, generalities. Nor had the Supreme Court applied the First Amendment to strike down state laws. As noted in Chapter 1, the Bill of Rights did not initially apply to the states, and only during the 1920s did the Court begin to enforce the First Amendment against the states on the theory that it had been made applicable to them by the Fourteenth Amendment. In assessing whether the Espionage Act violated the First Amendment, the Court thus found itself with a relatively blank page on which to write.[7]

Enacted as a war measure, the Espionage Act made it a crime to cause, attempt to cause, or conspire to cause insubordination in the armed forces or obstruction of military recruiting. The Supreme Court first encountered a question of the statute's validity under the First Amendment in *Schenck v. United States* (1919).[8] Charles Schenck, the general secretary of a Socialist party, and some companions had mailed leaflets to roughly 15,000 men drafted for military service. On one side, the leaflets compared the draft with slavery; on the other, they implored recipients to "Assert Your Rights." Justice Holmes, who would later emerge as a champion of speech rights, wrote the unanimous opinion upholding the defendants' convictions for attempting to cause and conspiring to cause interferences with the American war effort.

---

[6] *New York Times Co. v. Sullivan*, 376 U.S. 254, 276 (1964) (footnote omitted).
[7] On the earlier history of First Amendment litigation, see generally David M. Rabban, "The First Amendment in Its Forgotten Years," 90 *Yale Law Journal* 514 (1981).
[8] 249 U.S. 47 (1919).

Holmes dealt brusquely with a tangle of issues. First, he rejected suggestions that the force of the Free Speech Clause might extend no further than to prohibit prepublication licensing schemes or prior restraints. "We admit that in many places and in ordinary times the defendants in saying all that [they] said ... would have been within their constitutional rights," he wrote. Second, he emphasized that speech can cause harm. "The most stringent protection of free speech would not protect a man in falsely shouting fire in a theatre and causing a panic," Holmes ruled. With that premise in place, Holmes reasoned next that speech encouraging resistance to the draft in a time of war would prove harmful if it produced its intended consequences: "[T]he document would not have been sent unless it had been intended to have some effect, and we do not see what effect it could be expected to have upon persons subject to the draft except to influence them to obstruct the carrying of it out." Taking account of that risk, Holmes concluded that the values advanced by protecting speech must be weighed against the harms that speech could cause pursuant to a still-famous test: "The question in every case is whether the words used are used in such circumstances and are of such a nature as to create a clear and present danger that they will bring about substantive evils that Congress has a right to prevent."[9]

The "clear and present danger" test sounds as if it might protect a lot of speech – and Holmes would later insist that it did. In *Schenck*, however, he and the other justices seemed to think it sufficient to justify a prohibition that speech might make substantive evils such as resistance to the draft more likely to occur than they would have been otherwise. Certainly the Court did not require any proof that Schenck's leaflets had led to any change in anyone's behavior, even short of actual draft resistance, in order for him to be convicted. Holmes took a similar stance in authoring the Supreme Court's unanimous opinion in *Debs v. United States* (1919),[10] which upheld the conviction under the Sedition Act of a prominent left-wing politician and third-party presidential candidate for making a political speech at a Socialist convention. In the centerpiece of that address, Debs enjoined young men to "know that you are fit for something better than slavery and cannon fodder."[11]

---

[9] Ibid. at 52.
[10] 249 U.S. 211 (1919).
[11] Ibid. at 214.

Today, Debs's conviction for having made a political speech opposing war in which he never explicitly called for anyone to violate any law appears to be a mockery of free speech principles: A central function of the Free Speech Clause is, or at least should be, to protect political debate and dissent. And after *Schenck* and *Debs*, Justice Holmes appears to have had a change of heart, even though he continued to profess his belief that *Schenck*, at least, was rightly decided under the "clear and present danger" test. The proper approach, he now began to maintain, was for courts to look searchingly and even skeptically at claims that speech that the government sought to punish really did pose a clear and present danger. He dissented on that basis in *Abrams v. United States* (1919),[12] in which he offered a stirring defense of expansive free speech rights rooted in the imagined benefit of a marketplace of ideas:

> [W]hen men have realized that time has upset many fighting faiths, they may come to believe even more than they believe the very foundations of their own conduct that the ultimate good desired is better reached by free trade in ideas – that the best test of truth is the power of the thought to get itself accepted in the competition of the market, and that truth is the only ground upon which their wishes safely can be carried out.[13]

A few years later, Justice Louis Brandeis made a further, enduring, contribution to free speech debates in a much-quoted concurring opinion in *Whitney v. California* (1927).[14] "[F]reedom to think as you will and to speak as you think are means indispensable to the discovery and spread of political truth," Brandeis argued.[15]

For more than a decade, Holmes and Brandeis wrote mostly in dissent as Supreme Court majority opinions continued to uphold convictions of left-wing radicals who advocated unlawful action to promote political goals – resistance to the draft, or mass strikes that would cripple wartime production, or the overthrow of industrial capitalism. Nonetheless, the power of their arguments rallied opinion gradually to their side, as they personally became heroes of American constitutional culture. Among the shades of conservative gray that defined

---

[12] 250 U.S. 616 (1919).
[13] *Ibid.* at 630 (Holmes, J., dissenting).
[14] 274 U.S. 357 (1927).
[15] *Ibid.* at 375 (Brandeis, J., concurring).

most Supreme Court justices of the era, Holmes stood out as a handsome patrician with a gift for eloquence and an infectious desire to meet and know the young as well as the famous. Brandeis possessed an equal capacity to inspire. The first Jew ever to serve on the Supreme Court, he had championed causes of the poor and disadvantaged before his appointment. He too wrote with unusual flair. By the 1930s and 1940s, the Supreme Court frequently applied the "clear and present danger" test in the searching way that Holmes and Brandeis had said that it should be applied to protect radical dissenters from mainstream opinion.

But then came *Dennis v. United States* (1951).[16] *Dennis* arose at the height of Cold War anxiety about militant, subversive Communism. It involved prosecutions of American Communist Party leaders for advocating the overthrow of the government of the United States by force, not immediately but when the time grew ripe. A divided Supreme Court upheld the convictions entered by a lower court. Although the evil of a Communist insurrection seemed remote, the Court determined that "imminent" threats were not needed to justify conviction under the "clear and present danger" test. Rather, courts "must ask whether the gravity of the 'evil,' discounted by its improbability, justifies such invasion of free speech as is necessary to avoid the danger."[17]

Like *Schenck* and *Debs*, which were decided in the flush of fear and patriotism accompanying American entry into World War I, *Dennis* was the product of its fearful time in the McCarthy era, so-called after the bullying Senator Joseph McCarthy who briefly mesmerized the nation with chilling but mostly baseless allegations of Communist infiltration into the highest levels of government. Seen in that context, the Court's decision in *Dennis* was "quite understandable," according to legal scholar John Ely, because judges, in frightening times, may be as prone or nearly as prone as others to overestimate the risks that speech poses.

Before little more than another decade had passed – and after vigorously protected rights of speech and assembly had proved vital to the success of the civil rights movement of the 1950s and 1960s – the Supreme Court adopted a corrective strategy in *Brandenburg v. Ohio*

---

[16] 341 U.S. 494 (1951).
[17] *Ibid.* at 868.

(1969).[18] Brandenburg, a Ku Klux Klan (KKK) leader, was prosecuted and convicted under a state statute that made it a crime to advocate criminal activity as a means of political reform. By a unanimous vote, the Court reversed his conviction on First Amendment grounds. The Court's opinion made no reference to the "clear and present danger" test, which it effectively abandoned. Instead, the Court purported to extract from prior decisions "the principle" that a state may never punish the mere advancement of ideas, as opposed to express calls for violation of the law. Earlier cases, the justices asserted, had recognized that the government may not "forbid or proscribe advocacy of the use of force or of law violation except where such advocacy is directed to inciting or producing imminent lawless action and is likely to incite or produce such action."[19]

Despite *Brandenburg*'s suggestion to the contrary, a majority of the justices had never previously endorsed any "principle" affording so much protection to free speech. Although earlier cases had suggested that only advocacy of violence can be punished, and not the promulgation of abstract political ideas, the Court had never before held that even the express advocacy of violence was protected by the First Amendment unless it was likely to produce "imminent lawless action." Had the *Brandenburg* test been applied in previous cases, the speakers in *Schenck*, *Debs*, and *Dennis* would all have gone free. In *Schenck* and *Debs*, it is at least arguable that the defendants did not expressly advocate violation of the law, and neither in those cases nor in *Dennis* had the government proved that the speech at issue was likely to incite "imminent," or nearly immediate, violence. Far from merely making explicit a principle already reflected in prior decisions, *Brandenburg* gave broader protection to speech encouraging or advocating violation of the law than either Holmes or Brandeis had ever defended. To fall outside the protective reach of *Brandenburg*, speech must expressly advocate law violation, not merely create a clear and present danger that such violation may occur, and it must be likely to produce its effects imminently.

One measure of *Brandenburg*'s protective reach may come from reactions to President Donald Trump's speech to his supporters on the National Mall in Washington on January 6, 2021. In the view of many observers, the assault on the Capitol that occurred a few hours

---

[18] 395 U.S. 444 (1969) (per curiam).
[19] *Ibid.* at 447.

later would not have taken place in the absence of Trump's oration. Even so, special prosecutor Jack Smith, although charging Trump with other crimes, chose not to seek an indictment against him for "incitement" of lawless action. Smith may well have concluded that Trump's remarks did not clearly advocate unlawful action, as distinguished from peaceful demonstration, or that the time necessary for the march to the Capitol rendered the lawless action that occurred there insufficiently imminent to fall outside the scope of First Amendment protection under *Brandenburg*.

It may or may not be ironic that the first beneficiary of the *Brandenburg* rule was a member of the KKK preaching hatred of racial and religious minorities. As noted in the introduction to this chapter, most other liberal democracies have put speech inciting racial and religious hatred into a category of its own and have prohibited it. The Supreme Court might have followed a parallel course, treating racially and religiously bigoted speech as unprotected by the First Amendment because it is incompatible with an underlying constitutional assumption of human equality. *Brandenburg*, however, drew no such lines. Possibly, the Court considered Brandenburg's speech to be loosely political and deserving of protection on that ground. Possibly the justices recalled, though they did not refer to, Justice Brandeis's assertion in *Whitney v. California* "that fear breeds repression; that repression breeds hate; [and] that hate menaces stable government."[20] Better to let the hatemongers talk openly, the Court may have thought, than to drive them out of the public square and into unseen cauldrons. If so, the Court was making an empirical and predictive judgment, quite possibly correct but also contestable. Whatever *Brandenburg*'s motivating concerns may have been, the case vividly symbolizes the extent to which the First Amendment currently protects freedom to express what Holmes once termed "the thought that we hate."[21]

The Rise of the Demand for Content Neutrality

As late as the early 1960s, First Amendment debates among the justices of the Supreme Court lacked an agreed structure. Justices Black and William O. Douglas sometimes claimed that the First Amendment's

---

[20] 274 U.S. at 375.
[21] *United States v. Schwimmer*, 279 U.S. 644, 655 (1929) (Holmes, J., dissenting).

free speech guarantee was absolute. Justice Felix Frankfurter championed relatively ad hoc balancing of competing individual and governmental interests. Other justices adopted the view that free speech claims enjoyed a "preferred position" in the constitutional hierarchy but without coming to agreement about the test or tests that the Court should employ to implement that premise.

Against that background, *Brandenburg* numbered among a series of decisions during the 1960s and 1970s in which the Supreme Court adopted a categorical or "definitional balancing" approach to a number of First Amendment issues.[22] Rather than asking on a case-by-case basis whether particular utterances, such as those of KKK leader Clarence Brandenburg, posed a sufficient danger to be deemed unprotected by the Free Speech Clause, the Court picked out an entire category of speech – speech encouraging unlawful action to promote political goals – and held it to be protected unless the stringent conditions specified by the *Brandenburg* test were satisfied.

More or less contemporaneously with *Brandenburg*, another, even larger, shift in First Amendment methodology was under way. This shift can be described in different ways with different emphases. But the core insight of the emerging analytical paradigm was that the government may regulate speech for two distinct kinds of reasons that, the Court began to insist, should trigger disparate forms of judicial scrutiny under the Free Speech Clause.

First, the government may regulate speech based on its objections to the message that a speaker wishes to communicate. A prohibition against speech criticizing public officials would occupy this category, as would a law outlawing verbal attacks on religious beliefs. Content-based regulation, the Supreme Court now maintains, should almost invariably be viewed as suspect and subjected to searching judicial scrutiny, most often pursuant to the strict scrutiny formula. It is at least presumptively objectionable under modern doctrine for the government to silence speakers because it does not trust listeners to decide for themselves what to believe and disbelieve.

Second, the government sometimes may regulate speech or expression to avert harms that are unrelated to the content of a

---

[22] See Melville B. Nimmer, "The Right to Speak from Times to Time: First Amendment Theory Applied to Libel and Misapplied to Privacy," 56 *California Law Review* 935 (1968), 944–45.

speaker's message.[23] To take a trivial but usefully illustrative example, shouting in a cardiac ward is likely to cause harm regardless of the particular views that a shouting speaker might happen to express. Since the 1960s, when the government restricts speech in order to prevent harms unrelated to speakers' messages, the Supreme Court normally subjects challenged regulations to a much less searching form of First Amendment scrutiny than it applies to content-based regulations.

One of the first articulations of this two-track approach to the definition of free speech rights came in *United States v. O'Brien* (1968),[24] a case involving a claimed First Amendment right to engage in expressive conduct (rather than pure speech).[25] David O'Brien, who had publicly burned his draft card to protest the Vietnam War, was convicted under a federal statute making it a crime to knowingly mutilate or destroy a draft certificate. In assessing a claim that the prosecution infringed a free speech right, the Court began by denying "that an apparently limitless variety of conduct can be labeled 'speech' whenever the person engaging in the conduct intends thereby to express an idea." Nonetheless, without saying more about this issue, the Court accepted that O'Brien had raised a First Amendment argument worthy of judicial solicitude. Proceeding on that assumption, it continued its analysis by focusing on whether the government's reason for prohibiting the destruction of draft cards was related or "unrelated to the suppression of free expression." If the statute's only purpose was to stifle critics of the Vietnam War, the Court suggested that it would be invalid. But that was not the case, the Court determined: The challenged regulation "further[ed] an important or substantial governmental interest" in stopping the destruction of items necessary for the efficient operation of the draft, and its "incidental restriction on alleged First Amendment freedoms [was] no greater than is essential to the furtherance of that interest."[26] On that understanding of the law and facts, the Supreme Court upheld O'Brien's conviction.

---

[23] Among the most influential early commentaries to develop the distinction of alternative bases on which the government might regulate speech was John Hart Ely, "Flag Desecration: A Case Study in the Roles of Categorization and Balancing in First Amendment Analysis," 88 *Harvard Law Review* 1482 (1975).

[24] 391 U.S. 367 (1968).

[25] The use of the terminology of "tracks" to describe the Supreme Court's approach was developed by Laurence Tribe. See, for example, Laurence H. Tribe, *American Constitutional Law*, 2nd ed. (Mineola, NY: Foundation Press, 1988), 789–94.

[26] *Ibid.* at 377.

Although the result in *O'Brien* was controversial, largely because some evidence suggested that the Congress had enacted the law at issue in order to thwart displays of antiwar sentiment, the analytical framework that the Court applied to resolve it continues to govern First Amendment cases involving a mixture of speech and conduct. If the government bars a form of conduct as a means of stifling messages, the courts will almost invariably find a constitutional violation. To cite a once highly fraught example, a closely divided Supreme Court invalidated prohibitions against flag burning in *Texas v. Johnson*[27] (1989) and *United States v. Eichman* (1990).[28] The justices ruled that the government's interest in prohibiting this conduct related to the message that flag burning conveyed and to the offense that it generated. The Court found no compelling justification for governmental suppression of symbolically expressed criticisms of the United States or of policies pursued in its name.

As *O'Brien* expressly held, however, a governmental regulation of expressive conduct will be allowed "if it furthers an important or substantial governmental interest ... unrelated to the suppression of free expression" and extends no further than necessary to protect that interest. Finding the government's purposes to be unrelated to suppression of ideas, the Court has upheld a ban against sleeping on the National Mall in Washington even as it applied to protestors who wished to dramatize "the plight of the homeless."[29] The Court concluded that interests in maintaining the beauty of the mall justified an across-the-board ban on sleeping and camping there, even when enforcing it thwarted expressive conduct.

Over time, *O'Brien* has proved among the Supreme Court's most influential free speech decisions. Although initially framed as providing a test for the permissibility of regulations of expressive conduct, *O'Brien* both anticipates and helps to illustrate the influence of the persuasion principle (as formulated in the introduction to this chapter). When the government bans either conduct or speech based on harms unrelated to the message being conveyed, the likelihood that it is trying to manipulate its citizens' beliefs by depriving them of access to ideas or information is small. By contrast, if the government's regulatory

---

[27] 491 U.S. 397 (1989).
[28] 496 U.S. 310 (1990).
[29] See *Clark v. Community for Creative Non-violence*, 468 U.S. 288 (1984).

purpose is related to the suppression of ideas, strict judicial scrutiny should apply. By emphasizing that not all regulations of speech and expressive conduct necessarily embody censorial purposes, *O'Brien* helped to crystallize the presumptive offensiveness of those that do. Over time, the premises underlying *O'Brien*'s approach to appraising free speech rights in cases of expressive conduct have helped to support a more general presumption that all content-based regulations of speech should elicit strict judicial scrutiny.

Shocking and Offensive Speech

Another important step in the development of modern First Amendment law came in *Cohen v. California* (1971).[30] Like *O'Brien*, *Cohen* made its way to the Supreme Court during the era of protests against the Vietnam War. The case originated when Paul Robert Cohen walked into a courthouse wearing a jacket bearing the words "Fuck the Draft." The State of California prosecuted and convicted him under a statute that forbade disturbing the peace. In defending Cohen's conviction, the state argued that it had no intent to censor his antiwar message: He was free to express that message however he liked, as long as he did not disturb the peace of his fellow citizens by employing shocking and offensive words. The Court rejected this argument. It deemed Cohen's message inseparable from the words that he employed to express it. Linguistic expression, the Court wrote, has "emotive" as well as "cognitive force," and Cohen's chosen words conveyed a depth of emotion that other formulations might not have communicated. "[W]e cannot indulge the facile assumption that one can forbid particular words without also running a substantial risk of suppressing ideas in the process," the Court said.[31]

Cohen's reasoning is compelling, even if its conclusion was jarring in light of prevailing social norms in 1971: The First Amendment protects a right to shock and offend as inseparable from the right to express opinions. A more recent example of the Supreme Court's commitment to the protection of shocking and offensive messages comes from *Snyder v. Phelps* (2011),[32] which ordered the dismissal

---

[30] 403 U.S. 15 (1971).
[31] *Ibid.* at 26.
[32] 562 U.S. 443 (2011).

of a suit seeking damages from a group of antigay activists who had intentionally inflicted emotional distress on a grieving father by hurling antigay slurs outside the funeral of his son, who had been a member of the US armed services at the time of his death. While invalidating a content-based prohibition against speech calculated to inflict emotional distress, the Court suggested that a state or local government might permissibly enact a content-neutral prohibition against all noisy or disruptive picketing within the near proximity of funerals.

A Note on "Hate Speech"

In common parlance, people often refer to "hate speech" as a category of speech that they think is, or should be, prohibitable under the First Amendment. But the Supreme Court has never recognized such a category. To the contrary, when the Village of Skokie, Illinois, sought to ban a march by Nazis targeting a heavily Jewish population that included a substantial number of Holocaust survivors, the lower court found the Nazis demonstration of hatred protected by the Free Speech Clause, and the Supreme Court declined to hear the case.[33] The lower court's result reflected principles traceable to *Brandenburg v. Ohio*, which involved racist speech by a member of the KKK, and to *Cohen v. California*.

Following the Hamas assault on Israeli civilians of October 7, 2023, and the ensuing Israeli military attacks in Gaza, protest demonstrations and counterdemonstrations broke out on many American college campuses. After some protestors employed antisemitic language, presidents of leading universities were summoned before a congressional committee and questioned about whether they tolerated antisemitic hate speech and advocacy of genocide on their campuses. One of the presidents, Claudine Gay of Harvard, answered, "It depends." Although she was roundly denounced for that response, she was correct in her evident apprehension about the protection for "the freedom of speech" that the First Amendment, as construed by the Supreme Court, requires.

As interpreted by the Court, the First Amendment does not protect threats of physical violence. Nor does it protect what the Court has termed "fighting words." Roughly speaking, these are one-on-one

---

[33] *Collin v. Smith*, 578 F. 2d 1197 (7th Cir. 1978), *cert. denied*, 439 U.S. 916 (1978).

face-to-face epithets that the Court, back in the 1940s, characterized as immediate incitements to brawl.[34] But the line between speech in these categories and protected expressions of hateful opinion is sometimes hard to draw. Moreover, much of what would colloquially be called "hate speech" often lies on the protected side of the line. As we have seen, *Cohen* teaches that there is often no distinction between a constitutionally protected substantive message and the form, however shocking or hateful, in which the message is expressed. And *Brandenburg* affirms that advocacy of violence to achieve political goals is constitutionally protected unless it is both calculated to incite and likely to incite imminent lawless action.

Commercial Speech

Before the 1970s, the Supreme Court accorded no First Amendment protection to commercial advertising.[35] It began to change course in *Virginia State Board of Pharmacy v. Virginia Citizens Consumer Council* (1976).[36] The Virginia Board of Pharmacy forbade pharmacists to advertise the prices that they charged for prescription drugs. The board had adopted its policy to preserve the competitive position of small drug stores, which often needed to charge higher prices than large chains because their costs were higher. According to the board, small neighborhood pharmacies were likely to be more knowledgeable about their individual customers, and thus to give better service and advice, than chain stores. In striking down the Virginia regulation, the Supreme Court majority emphasized the interest of consumers in having access to price information so that they could decide for themselves what to buy and where to buy it. The Court declined to articulate a clear test governing when the regulation of advertising might be permissible. It doubted, however, that the government could ever be justified in barring the dissemination of truthful information simply for the purpose of keeping consumers in the dark.

At the time of *Virginia Pharmacy Board*, the Supreme Court's most "liberal" justices were those most eager to extend First Amendment protection to commercial advertising. William Rehnquist, who was then the Court's most conservative associate justice (before

---

[34] See *Chaplinsky v. New Hampshire*, 315 U.S. 568, 573 (1942).
[35] See, for example, *Valentine v. Chrestensen*, 316 U.S. 52 (1942).
[36] 425 U.S. 748 (1976).

becoming chief justice a decade later), dissented. As a policy matter, he worried that "[u]nder the Court's opinion the way will be open not only for dissemination of price information but for active promotion of prescription drugs, liquor, cigarettes, and other products the use of which it has previously been thought desirable to discourage." Rehnquist dissented again from the Court's ruling in *Central Hudson Gas & Electric Corp. v. Public Service Commission* (1981),[37] which established a test for the permissibility of restrictions on commercial advertising that the Supreme Court has never abandoned. Under that test, for commercial speech to be entitled to First Amendment protection at all, it "must concern lawful activity and not be misleading." If that threshold is crossed, government may regulate commercial advertising only if the regulation directly promotes a "substantial" governmental interest and "is not more extensive than is necessary to serve that interest."[38]

As subsequent developments have revealed, the justices in *Virginia Pharmacy Board* and *Central Hudson* might easily have seemed misaligned in a way not much noticed at the time. In both cases, the challenged restrictions on speech were parts of a broad framework of economic regulation. The state of Virginia licensed pharmacies such as those involved in the *Virginia Pharmacy Board* case and closely regulated their business practices. Similarly, the party claiming free speech rights in *Central Hudson* was a highly regulated electric power company – indeed, a licensed monopolist – challenging a restriction on the promotional aspect of its business. As the Nobel Prize–winning economist Ronald Coase pointed out, in the decades following the New Deal, liberals generally championed broad regulation of economic markets but maintained that the government had no business regulating speech under the First Amendment.[39] During the same period, conservatives protested governmental intervention in economic markets but tended to support the regulation of speech in a variety of contexts (including the prohibition of obscenity and the suppression of speech by "subversive" organizations such as the Communist Party). According to Coase, both positions were inconsistent. On the one hand, if the government was good at regulating economic markets (as liberals thought), it was unlikely to be much worse at regulating

---

[37] 447 U.S. 557 (1980).
[38] *Ibid.* at 566.
[39] See generally Ronald H. Coase, "Advertising and Free Speech," 6 *Journal of Legal Studies* 1 (1977).

speech markets or, at least, at regulating the advertising of economic transactions. On the other hand, if government intervention into economic markets tended to bring adverse consequences (as conservatives maintained), the government was unlikely to perform better when it regulated speech.

Since Coase offered his comment, the position of judicial liberals has changed some, while that of judicial conservatives has shifted a great deal. In subsequent decades, the justices regularly classified as conservatives have emerged as enthusiastic champions of commercial speech rights for reasons captured by the persuasion principle: The government should not be permitted to deny consumers information that might affect their thinking about which goods to purchase. In *Lorillard Tobacco Co. v. Reilly* (2001),[40] the five most conservative justices then sitting on the Court thus outvoted four typically more liberal dissenters to invalidate a Massachusetts statute barring billboard advertising of tobacco products within 1,000 feet of a school or playground. Without disputing the state's claims that tobacco advertising helps attract children to addictive and deadly products, the Court's majority ruled that the burdens on speech imposed by the state law were too "onerous" to survive constitutional scrutiny.

Subsequent cases have often revealed similar voting patterns. An important example comes from *Sorrell v. IMS Health, Inc.* (2011).[41] In *Sorrell*, in an opinion by Justice Kennedy that all of the conservative justices joined, the Court invalidated a state law that forbade the sale, transmission, or use of pharmacy records that revealed individual doctors' prescribing practices. The statute impermissibly restricted speech, the Court reasoned, because it imposed "content- and speaker-based burden[s]" on protected expression, including by drug companies seeking to advertise their products to physicians. Three liberal justices dissented, protesting that the statute regulated a commercial activity for the purpose of protecting the privacy and wellbeing of patients undergoing medical care. Echoing a concern voiced by the conservative Justice William Rehnquist in *Virginia Pharmacy Board*, the liberal Justice Stephen Breyer objected that the Court had misguidedly relied on the Free Speech Clause to replicate judicial practice during the *Lochner* era, when "it was common practice for this Court to strike

[40] 533 U.S. 525 (2001).
[41] 564 U.S. 552 (2011).

down economic regulations ... based on the Court's own notions" of sound regulatory policy.[42]

However one judges that argument, modern cases protecting commercial advertising under the Free Speech Clause exemplify the dynamic development of free speech doctrine over the past fifty years, the ascendency of the persuasion principle, and the sometimes-shifting stances of judicial liberals and conservatives alike.

Political Campaign Advertising

If commercial speech cases involve a fusion of economic markets with what Justice Holmes called the "marketplace of ideas," the same might be said of cases arising from efforts to regulate the expenditure of money in political campaigns. To a large extent, political campaigns are exercises in speech, as candidates and their supporters try to persuade others to embrace their positions. And for campaign speech to be effective in the modern world takes money. Campaign organizations need staff, phone lists, email addresses, websites, bumper stickers, signs, and the like. In addition, advertising in the media, which can be enormously expensive, is hugely important. Although regulations of campaign advertising should surely be subject to scrutiny under the First Amendment, donations and expenditures of money to generate political speech can also threaten the integrity of American political democracy. In the crudest example of corruption, monied interests can trade cash with dishonest politicians for specific, expressly requested political favors. More insidiously, big donors can effectively buy access to politicians, and access – possibly coupled with implicit promises of more donations to future campaigns or tacit threats to support other candidates – often translates into influence. Some find it antithetical to democratic ideals that economic power should translate so readily into political power.

Since the early years of the twentieth century, Congress has enacted a variety of measures aimed at protecting American politics from the corrupting influence of money. Because these measures and the judicial decisions evaluating them have included innumerable complexities, any short summary must oversimplify some points. Roughly speaking, however, attempted regulations fall into two main

---

[42] *Ibid.* at 585 (Breyer, J., dissenting).

categories. One deals with *contributions*, or gifts of money by individuals or corporations to candidates or candidates' political committees, for the candidates – not the donors – to use to generate political speech. Other regulations have attempted to limit direct *expenditures* of money by individuals or organizations to create and disseminate political advertising of their own. By way of illustration, if the Acme Corporation gives a check for $100,000 to a candidate for public office or the candidate's campaign committee, it has made a contribution. By contrast, if Acme itself spends $100,000 to place an Acme-produced advertisement supporting a candidate on a local television station, it has made a direct expenditure.

The Supreme Court's first major encounter with the constitutional issues raised by campaign finance regulation came in *Buckley v. Valeo* (1976).[43] *Buckley* drew a sharp First Amendment line between regulations of campaign contributions and regulations of direct expenditures. *Buckley* upheld the contribution limitations that Congress had imposed. According to the Court's majority, direct gifts to candidates posed a risk of corruption, by which the Court appeared to mean something very close to bribery (which no one thinks is protected by the First Amendment), or the appearance of corruption. By contrast, *Buckley* invalidated restrictions on expenditures by candidates and, of equal importance, on "independent" expenditures by a candidate's supporters on campaign advertising. In the Court's view, independent expenditures – which, by definition, could not be coordinated with a candidate or a candidate's campaign committee – pose a much lesser risk of corruption than do gifts of money directly to a candidate's campaign. In response to the argument that the government has an interest in stopping wealthy individuals from achieving undue political influence as a result of their expenditures, the Court took the position – consistent with the persuasion principle – that restriction of some speakers on the ground that their speech might prove too influential was antithetical to the First Amendment.

In the years following *Buckley*, money continued to pour ever more voluminously into political campaigns, with more spent in each election cycle than in the one that preceded it. Much of the influx came through purportedly "independent" expenditures by corporations and labor unions, often to broadcast "attack" ads targeting candidates

[43] 424 U.S. 1 (1976).

whom they wished to defeat. Spurred by the crusading efforts of Senators John McCain and Russell Feingold, Congress responded in 2002 by enacting the Bipartisan Campaign Reform Act (BCRA), which barred corporations and labor unions from running advertisements that refer by name to any candidate for federal office within thirty days of a primary or caucus or within sixty days of a general election.

In 2003, in *McConnell v. Federal Election Commission*,[44] the Supreme Court upheld all of BCRA's main elements by a 5–4 vote. To do so, it essentially put corporations and labor unions in a class by themselves. Although Congress could not stop individuals from running political advertisements because of a concern that their speech would give them undue influence, it was permissible, the Court said, for the government to restrict spending by corporations and labor unions. Corporations were distinctive, the majority reasoned, in light of the compelling interest in avoiding "the corrosive and distorting effects [on our politics] of immense aggregations of wealth that are accumulated with the help of the corporate form and that have little or no correlation to the public's support for the corporation's political ideas."[45] The four dissenting justices, all from the Court's conservative wing, registered their disagreement in especially caustic opinions. In their view, the Court's decision violated the premise that the government may not silence speakers based on a concern that the speakers might persuade their audiences. But the moderate conservative Justice Sandra Day O'Connor – the only member of the Court at that time who had ever held elective office (as an Arizona state senator) – thought that corporate spending on political advertisements was sufficiently harmful to justify governmental regulation. In *McConnell*, Justice O'Connor coauthored the most important sections of the majority opinion.

Three years later, after Justice O'Connor retired from the Court and the more ardently conservative Justice Samuel Alito took her place, the Court overruled *McConnell* and held that the provision of BCRA that limits campaign advertising by corporations and labor unions violates the First Amendment. It is as objectionable for the government to stifle political speech by corporations as it is to stifle political speech by individuals, the majority held in *Citizens United v.*

---

[44] 540 U.S. 93 (2003).
[45] *Ibid.* at 205.

Federal Election Commission (2010),[46] because corporations are ultimately just collections of individuals and because the voters should be able to decide for themselves whether or not to be persuaded by corporate speech. No one believes that the government should be able to regulate the political speech of media corporations on the editorial pages of their newspapers, regardless of how much influence a media corporation might achieve. In the view of the *Citizens United* majority, there is no principled ground for treating other kinds of corporations differently.

Four outraged liberal dissenters lambasted the majority's decision as conservative judicial "activism" at its worst. The *Citizens United* majority had invalidated an act of Congress rather than deferring to Congress's judgment about the urgent practical need for regulation. In overruling the recent decision in *McConnell v. FEC*, the Court showed no respect for precedent. And with corporations historically having been subject to a host of regulations not applicable to individuals, the majority could find no firm anchor for its ruling in the original understanding of the First Amendment, the dissenters maintained. To the contrary, Justice Stevens argued, the Founding generation viewed corporations as pervasively subject to governmental regulations and as possessing no powers other than those that government specifically gave them. Although the majority opinion offered no direct response, Justice Scalia concurred separately to argue that Justice Stevens had advanced no evidence that the Founding generation would not have thought that citizens who joined together for expressive purposes would not retain free speech rights that they possessed as individuals. Beyond their attacks on the *Citizens United* majority's treatment of relevant precedent and history, the dissenting liberals denounced the decision as among the most ruinous judicial rulings in the history of American democracy. In their view, it threatened to turn the political marketplace of ideas into an economic market, dominated not by those who have the best ideas but by those with the most money.

Citizens United is another of the decisions that marks the United States as affording broader free speech rights than any other liberal democracy. It also illustrates the development of modern free speech doctrine as the working out of a normative commitment to the

---

[46] 558 U.S. 310 (2010).

persuasion principle or similar ideas, largely driven by conservative justices, with little direct reliance by Supreme Court majorities on evidence of the First Amendment's original meaning.

The Right Not to Be Compelled to Speak

The Supreme Court has long held that the First Amendment freedom of speech implies a right not to be compelled to speak. The leading case is *West Virginia State Board of Education v. Barnette* (1943),[47] which held that school children could not be required to salute the flag. The Court had approved a compulsory flag salute just three years earlier, but in *Barnette*, with the country at war against the Third Reich, two justices switched their votes. In condemning a requirement that children utter a pledge of allegiance, Justice Robert Jackson wrote for the Court: "If there is any fixed star in our constitutional constellation, it is that no official, high or petty, can prescribe what shall be orthodox in politics, nationalism, religion, or other matters of opinion, or force citizens to confess by word or act their faith therein."[48] Today there is a broad consensus that *Barnette* was correct in holding that the Free Speech Clause creates a right not to be compelled to affirm ideological beliefs. It is also widely agreed that the Court reached the proper conclusion in *Miami Herald Publishing Co. v. Tornillo* (1974),[49] which invalidated a Florida statute that required newspapers to publish responses to their criticisms of candidates for public office if the candidates wished to reply. Just as the First Amendment forbade the government from censoring the press, it barred the government from compelling newspapers to publish material that they did not wish to include in their pages, the Court held.

Nonetheless, the justices' efforts to define and apply the First Amendment right not to speak have divided the Court as often as they have united it. To begin with, there are many contexts in which the government can undoubtedly require people to speak against their wills. For example, the Free Speech Clause affords no protection against demands to disclose information in tax returns and to testify in court proceedings. The overall pattern of decisions suggests that the right not to speak is most clearly implicated in cases, such as *Barnette*, in which

[47] 319 U.S. 624 (1943).
[48] *Ibid.* at 642.
[49] 418 U.S. 241 (1974).

the government seeks to force citizens to utter or support propositions contrary to their conscientious moral or political beliefs.

An important testing case for the scope of the judicially defined right not to speak has involved governmental mandates that public sector employees must pay "agency fees" to support the collective bargaining activities of union representatives. In *Janus v. American Federation of State, County, & Municipal Employees, Council 31* (2018),[50] the five conservative justices then on the Supreme Court overruled an earlier decision and held that mandates to pay agency fees violate the Free Speech Clause. Union representatives might adopt positions in labor negotiations to which some employees object, Justice Alito's majority opinion reasoned, and by compelling support for union speech, the government violates the objecting employees' rights not to be compelled to speak or to support speech with which they disagree. Writing in dissent, Justice Kagan accused the Court of "weaponizing" the First Amendment to upset schemes of economic regulation long accepted under the New Deal settlement that ended the *Lochner* era – a refrain that liberal dissenting justices have also sounded in cases upsetting restrictions on commercial advertising.

Conflicts between Rights Not to Speak and Antidiscrimination Laws

The Supreme Court has occasionally found regulatory statutes that incur strict judicial scrutiny to be narrowly tailored to compelling governmental interests. It did so in *McConnell v. FEC*, for example. Although *McConnell* has now been overruled, the Court also upheld the enforcement of what it viewed as a content-based regulation in *Holder v. Humanitarian Law Project* (2010).[51] *Holder* allowed the enforcement of a statute that barred the provision of "material support or resources" to foreign terrorist organizations to be applied to a group whose support consisted solely of speech providing training in techniques of peaceful advocacy and dispute resolution. Because the provision of free training of any kind might permit a terrorist organization to allocate more resources to unlawful activities, the Court found the challenged prohibition to be narrowly tailored to an urgent interest in combating terrorism.

---

[50] 585 U.S. 878 (2018).
[51] 561 U.S. 1 (2010).

In recent years, the question whether compelling government interests might override claims of free speech rights, including rights not to speak, has cropped up in cases involving attempted applications of antidiscrimination laws. An important example came in *303 Creative LLC v. Elenis* (2023).[52] *303 Creative* arose when a website designer claimed that constructing websites for same-sex weddings would be inherently expressive conduct, communicating a message of celebration contrary to her moral beliefs, and that she should therefore be exempted from a state antidiscrimination law that apparently would have required her to create such websites at clients' behest. By a vote of 6–3, the Supreme Court accepted the website designer's argument. In ruling for the challenger, the Court did not pause to consider whether the state had a compelling interest in barring discrimination that might justify an infringement of the website designer's free speech interest. Rather, without reference to the original meaning of the Free Speech Clause, the majority treated the right of a person not to engage in symbolic speech contrary to her conscientious views as enjoying a form of absolute, categorical protection under the First Amendment. *303 Creative* thus demonstrates the view of the Supreme Court's current conservative majority that the right not to be compelled to speak occupies a privileged status in the hierarchy of constitutional values and can override even highly important governmental interests.

Platforms and the Question of Who Is a Speaker with First Amendment Rights

Although it is usually obvious whether a party claiming free speech rights is a speaker entitled to First Amendment protections, disputes occasionally arise, as in *Moody v. NetChoice, LLC* (2024).[53] In 2021, both Florida and Texas enacted statutes restricting the ability of large social media companies and internet platforms to engage in content moderation of third-party posts by, for example, filtering, prioritizing, labeling, and occasionally removing them. The states' asserted aim was to counteract the platforms' liberal biases and to ensure audience access to a broader range of perspectives and ideas. Prior cases, including *Miami Herald v. Tornillo*, had established a nearly categorical right of newspapers, book publishers, and other acknowledged

---

[52] 600 U.S. 570 (2023).
[53] 144 S. Ct. 2383 (2024).

speakers to make editorial decisions about which third-party speech to include or not to include with their own. Among the questions in *NetChoice* and a companion case was whether social media companies and internet platforms could claim speakers' and editors' rights on the same basis as newspapers and book publishers.

By a vote of 6–3, the Supreme Court answered in the affirmative with regard to the central content moderation functions performed by social media companies and platforms such as Facebook and YouTube. The consolidated case in which the Court addressed both the Florida and the Texas statutes presented multiple issues, some of which the majority opinion labored to disentangle so that the lower courts could properly address them on remand. But Justice Elena Kagan wrote for six justices in holding that entities compiling and curating speech into an expressive product enjoy robust First Amendment protections against governmental interference with their editorial functions, even if "a compiler includes most items and excludes just a few."

Justice Alito, joined by Justices Thomas and Gorsuch, agreed that the cases should be returned to the lower courts. But he, unlike the majority, would have postponed decision about which of the challengers could claim speakers' rights pending further clarification of the affected entities' actual practices in curating third-party speech. According to Justice Alito, various platforms' protections under the Free Speech Clause might depend on whether their content moderation decisions were made by actual human beings or by algorithms.

Unprotected Categories of Speech

The Supreme Court's strong presumption that it is impermissible for the government to regulate speech on the basis of its content, which I have emphasized thus far, does not apply to restrictions on all categories of speech. In *Chaplinsky v. New Hampshire* (1942),[54] the Supreme Court offered the much-quoted observation that "[t]here are certain well-defined and narrowly limited classes of speech, the prevention and punishment of which has never been thought to raise any Constitutional problem." The Court continued: "These include the lewd and obscene, the profane, the libelous, and the insulting or 'fighting' words – those which by their very utterance inflict injury or tend to

[54] 315 U.S. 568, 571–72 (1942).

incite an immediate breach of the peace." In *Schenck v. United States*, Justice Holmes asserted casually but unassailably that the freedom of speech could not reasonably encompass a right to falsely cry "Fire!" in a crowded theater. The Supreme Court also regularly treats some speech that is integral to criminal conduct, such as threats and communications demanding bribes and planning illegal acts, as outside the coverage of the Free Speech Clause.

As illustrated by cases such as *Cohen v. California*, which effectively rejected *Chaplinsky*'s characterization of profanity as unprotected by the First Amendment, the list of excluded categories has proved historically variable. "Libelous" or defamatory speech, another category that *Chaplinsky* listed as outside the First Amendment, has also received an important measure of protection since the 1964 decision in *New York Times Co. v. Sullivan*.[55] In that case, the Court held that public officials could not recover damages for the harms that false and defamatory speech does to their reputations unless they can demonstrate by clear and convincing evidence that the defendant knew his or her statements to be false or acted with "reckless disregard" for the truth. Nevertheless, the idea that there are some categories of speech to which the First Amendment affords little or no protection seems too rooted in history and common sense to be discarded. Almost no one contends that the First Amendment should protect threats, solicitations of bribes, or verbal agreements to fix prices any more than it protects false cries of fire in a crowded theater. Even so, disputes have often flared about whether particular categories of speech should be deemed unprotected and, if so, how precisely those categories should be defined.

The longest-running controversies have swirled around the category of "obscenity" to which *Chaplinsky* passingly referred. Obscenity cases occupied an inordinate amount of the Supreme Court's attention during the 1950s and 1960s, probably due to changes in social mores that led to a proliferation of sexually explicit materials in magazines and films. In the context of the time, judicial conservatives defended anti-obscenity statutes by citing government interests in "order and morality." Liberals derided obscenity laws as illicit interference with the marketplace of ideas concerning sex and sexuality. For a time, running through most of the decade of the 1960s, a majority of the justices

[55] 376 U.S. 254 (1964).

agreed that the First Amendment afforded no protection to obscenity, as properly defined, but could not agree on how to define it. To determine whether particular films were obscene, the justices sometimes felt obliged to gather in a screening room in the basement of the Supreme Court building to watch for themselves. Justice Potter Stewart famously stated in one case that although he was unsure how to define constitutionally prohibitable obscenity, "I know it when I see it."[56]

Miller v. California[57] (1973) broke the definitional impasse. In it, a narrow majority of the justices, all viewed as conservatives, laid down a test for identifying the obscenity that receives no protection from the First Amendment. As defined by the Court, a material is obscene if it (1) "taken as a whole, appeals to the prurient interest," (2) "depicts or describes, in a patently offensive way, sexual conduct specifically defined by ... applicable state law," and (3) "taken as a whole, lacks serious literary, artistic, political, or scientific value." Although all of the Court's liberal justices dissented in *Miller*, the case's still-controlling definition of obscenity is narrow. As a result, *Miller* has done little to stem a mounting flood of sexually explicit materials into American popular culture.

Roughly a decade later, the Court identified a further unprotected category of sexually explicit material. By unanimous vote, *New York v. Ferber*[58] (1982) upheld a state law prohibiting the production, distribution, and sale of "child pornography," defined to include the presentation or depiction of live "sexual conduct" by a child under sixteen years old. A state court had held the statute unconstitutional because it applied to all materials showing children engaged in sexual conduct, without regard to whether the material satisfied the obscenity test of *Miller v. California*. Emphasizing the severe harm to children forced to engage in sexual performances, the Court found child pornography to be a separately prohibitable category of speech.

Since *Ferber*, as support for broadly speech-protective interpretations of the First Amendment has migrated rightward along the political and judicial spectrums, the Supreme Court has not formally recognized any new unprotected categories of speech. *United States v. Stevens*[59] (2010) reflects the now-prevailing judicial stance. *Stevens*

[56] *Jacobellis v. Ohio*, 378 U.S. 184, 197 (1964) (Stewart, J., concurring).
[57] 413 U.S. 15, 24 (1973).
[58] 458 U.S. 747 (1982).
[59] 559 U.S. 460 (2010).

involved a federal statute barring the creation, sale, or possession of depictions of animal cruelty, defined to include filmed images "in which a living animal is intentionally maimed, mutilated, tortured, wounded, or killed" in violation of state or federal law. The government acknowledged that the statute lay outside of any previously defined category of unprotected speech but argued that "'depictions of animal cruelty' should be added to the list." More generally, the government posited that "[w]hether a given category of speech enjoys First Amendment protection depends upon a categorical balancing of the value of the speech against societal costs."[60]

In contrast with the approach that the Court had taken in the 1960s and 1970s and as recently as 1982 in *New York v. Ferber*, Chief Justice John Roberts's opinion for the Court responded to this suggestion with shock and horror. "The First Amendment's guarantee of free speech does not extend only to categories of speech that survive an ad hoc balancing of relative social costs and benefits," he wrote. In order for a category of speech to be unprotected, Roberts maintained, it must be one that has been historically recognized as unprotected. The Court reiterated that stance a year later in *Brown v. Entertainment Merchants Association* (2011),[61] in which it invalidated a California statute that prohibited the sale or rental of violent video games to minors. Justice Scalia's majority opinion explained: "[W]ithout persuasive evidence that a novel restriction is part of a long (if heretofore unrecognized) tradition of proscription, a legislature may not revise the 'judgment [of] the American people,' embodied in the First Amendment, 'that the benefits of its restrictions on the Government outweigh the costs.'"

Taken in conjunction, *Stevens* and *Brown* represent both a substantive and a methodological statement on the part of the Supreme Court's conservative majority. Substantively, the decisions reveal the Court's commitment to a strong presumption that content-based regulation of speech should be impermissible even with regard to categories of speech that might, on the surface, appear to have little or no social value and to pose significant threats of palpable harm. Methodologically, *Stevens* and *Brown* embrace history and tradition as gauges that the Court will sometimes employ to identify permissible and impermissible regulation under the Free Speech Clause.

---

[60] *Ibid.* at 460–61.
[61] 564 U.S. 786, 792 (2011).

The theoretical justification for that methodological approach is not clear. Neither *Stevens* nor *Brown*, in which the self-avowedly originalist Justice Antonin Scalia wrote the majority opinion, was framed as an originalist decision. The Court did not maintain that the First Amendment, as originally understood, would have precluded the government from outlawing depictions of illegal animal cruelty or the sale of violent video games to minors. Rather, the Court relied on a presumption, which it did not attempt to trace to the Founding era, that the First Amendment affords strong protection against content-based restrictions to all categories of speech unless the government can demonstrate an affirmative historical tradition of subjecting a type of speech to regulation. This approach would accord with originalist premises if history and tradition were consulted solely as evidence of original constitutional meanings but not if history and tradition are viewed – as they appeared to be in *Stevens* and *Brown* – as furnishing an alternative basis for judicial decision-making.

The Court's reliance on a test of history and tradition to protect depictions of animal cruelty in *Stevens* and violent video games in *Brown* may thus be a reminder that some if not all of the conservative originalist justices are more conservative than they are originalist. Also deserving of note is the course of historical events that brought about a situation in which the championing of robust protection for depictions of animal cruelty and violent video games – apparently pursuant to the persuasion principle or some libertarian analogue – counts as a "conservative" position.

Freedom of Association

The First Amendment contains no explicit reference to freedom to associate for expressive purposes. Nonetheless, the Supreme Court has held that such a right exists, largely because of the role that association plays in helping to promote speech: People often join groups in order to advocate for their causes more effectively. A generative case in the development of the doctrine was *NAACP v. Alabama* (1958),[62] in which the state had demanded that the local chapter of the National Association for the Advancement of Colored People (NAACP), a civil rights organization, disclose its membership lists. In Alabama in 1958,

[62] 357 U.S. 449 (1958).

public identification of NAACP members almost certainly would have subjected them to widespread hostility if not violence. In addition, the threat of future identification would have discouraged membership in civil rights organizations. Confronted with these facts, the Court held that the Constitution protects a right to associate for expressive purposes. It then ruled that for Alabama to force public disclosure of the NAACP's membership rolls would impose a burden on that right and that the Constitution forbade the imposition of such a burden in the absence of a powerful reason, which the state had not demonstrated. A subsequent decision in *Brown v. Socialist Workers '74 Campaign Committee*[63] (1982) held that a statute mandating disclosure of campaign contributions and expenditures could not validly be applied to a minor party whose members might face threats or harassment if their identities were revealed.

Once recognized, the right to freedom of association for expressive purposes implies a right not to associate, just as the freedom of speech implies a right not to be compelled to speak in some contexts. For example, the NAACP should not have to admit white racists, nor should the KKK have to admit African Americans. At the same time, the right not to associate should not be defined too broadly. Otherwise, it would threaten the government's power to bar discrimination on the basis of race, religion, and gender whenever an affected group or business claims an expressive purpose.

Roberts v. U.S. Jaycees[64] (1984) presented a question about the right of expressive organizations, as distinguished from for-profit sellers of goods and services, to discriminate on the basis of sex. The Jaycees, an organization with a national bylaw that restricted regular membership to men between the ages of eighteen and thirty-five, fit into the former category. They were a nonprofit corporation organized to promote educational, charitable, and civic purposes. In a case with complicated facts, the national Jaycees claimed that a Minnesota statute that barred chapters within the state from discriminating on the basis of sex abridged their right to freedom of expressive association. The Supreme Court disagreed. It rested its conclusion on two considerations without making clear whether either alone would have sufficed. First, the government had a "compelling" interest in preventing discrimination on

---

[63] 459 U.S. 87 (1982).
[64] 468 U.S. 609 (1984).

the basis of sex. Second, the Jaycees had failed to establish that the challenged statute impeded their ability to communicate their "preferred views" because they had presented no evidence that "women might have a different attitude" from men concerning the political, economic, and charitable issues on which the group sometimes spoke.

By contrast, a sharply divided Supreme Court upheld a claimed right not to be compelled to associate in *Boy Scouts of America v. Dale* (2000).[65] The Scouts removed Dale as an assistant scoutmaster upon learning that he was gay, was the copresident of the Rutgers University Lesbian/Gay Alliance, and had been quoted in the press on the need for gay role models. After a New Jersey court found the removal to be unlawful under a state antidiscrimination law, the Scouts pressed a freedom of association claim in the Supreme Court. By a 5-4 vote, with the most conservative justices joining an opinion by Chief Justice Rehnquist, the Court ruled for the Scouts. The majority found that the Scouts were an expressive organization, seeking to instill moral values. It also accepted the Scouts' claim, vigorously contested by the dissenting opinion, that the Scouts had a longstanding position that acts of same-sex sexual intimacy were morally inappropriate. Building on these premises, the Court then held in essence that Dale's continued presence in the Scouts would have sent a progay message at odds with the message that the Scouts wished to communicate. The Court distinguished *Roberts* on the ground that forcing the Jaycees to admit women did not "materially interfere with the ideas" that the Jaycees aimed to express. In the view of the majority, it was as if Dale were a walking progay billboard, and the Scouts, as an expressive association, could not be forced into an association that would dilute their message by commingling it with his.

Managerial Domains in Which the Demand for Content Neutrality Does Not Apply

In all of the cases and doctrinal domains discussed thus far, the government has sought to regulate speech by one private party to one or more other private parties or has imposed burdens on interests in freedom of association in order to preserve the peace, maintain public order, or protect its citizens from harm by others. But sometimes the government performs more affirmative functions such as educating

[65] 530 U.S. 640 (2000).

students in public schools, providing municipal services such as fire protection and trash collection, and encouraging citizens to pursue healthy lifestyles. The government could not perform roles such as these effectively if it were required to adhere to a presumptive First Amendment demand for content neutrality in all of its expressive and managerial activities.

Employing vocabulary developed by Robert Post, I shall refer to exercises of governmental authority to regulate speech incidentally to the provision of public services such as those listed earlier as occurring within "managerial" domains.[66] But I caution that this terminology is inexact. The set of topics that I am about to discuss is in some ways a hodge-podge. The common, uniting element may simply be a recognition that it would be impossible, or at least unreasonable, to insist that the First Amendment requires the government to adhere to an ideal of content neutrality in all contexts in which it endeavors to communicate with its citizens or to provide public services other than regulating private conduct. If that premise is granted, two questions follow: When does the requirement of content neutrality not apply, and what alternative limits on governmental action, if any, does the Free Speech Clause then impose?

Government Speech

The Supreme Court has recognized repeatedly that the government is entitled to speak on its own behalf and to take positions, including controversial ones. It can condemn some foreign governments, discourage smoking and promote the consumption of fruits and vegetables, and include quirky messages on roadside signs and license plates. In *Johanns v. Livestock Marketing Association* (2005),[67] the Court held that the government could use compulsory payments from livestock producers to propound messages encouraging people to eat beef. (By contrast, *Janus v. American Federation of State, County, & Municipal Employees, Council 31*, as discussed earlier, ruled that the government cannot compel its employees to support speech by labor unions or other private entities with which they disagree.)

---

[66] See Robert C. Post, *Constitutional Domains: Democracy, Community, Management* (Cambridge, MA/London, UK: Harvard University Press, 1995).
[67] 544 U.S. 550 (2005).

The Establishment Clause would bar the government from endorsing any single religion (though not, as we have seen, from proclaiming "In God We Trust" on the currency). But the Free Speech Clause has been held to impose few if any further constraints on the government's discretion in choosing messages to propound in the government's own name.

Regulation of Government Employees' Speech

Because the government typically can speak only through the utterances of its officials and employees, government employees generally can be required to speak as the government directs when executing their official responsibilities, and they can be disciplined or even fired if they go off script.[68] As I noted passingly earlier, no one doubts that public school teachers can be required to speak about mathematics, and not to opine about politics, during algebra classes. The free speech issues can grow more challenging when government employees speak on their own time but convey messages that might reasonably be thought to disrupt relations in the workplace. When public employees speak out on matters of public concern, *Pickering v. Board of Education*[69] (1968) and *Connick v. Myers*[70] (1983) hold that a balancing test applies to determine whether their speech ultimately enjoys First Amendment protection. But if an employee speaks on a matter of purely private concern, the First Amendment furnishes no immunity against employment sanctions up to and including dismissal. In that situation, the Court has held, the government's managerial interests take precedence over its employees' speech interests.

It can sometimes be difficult to determine whether employee speech occurs in the discharge of governmental functions and is therefore subject to governmental direction. In *Kennedy v. Bremerton School District* (2022),[71] which is discussed at greater length in Chapter 5, the Supreme Court, by 6–3, held that a football coach acted on his own time when he chose to pray at the fifty-yard line following the conclusion of football games. Under those circumstances, the Court found, the coach's prayers did not violate the Establishment Clause,

---

[68] See, for example, *Garcetti v. Ceballos*, 547 U.S. 410 (2006).
[69] 391 U.S. 563 (1968).
[70] 461 U.S. 138 (1983).
[71] 597 U.S. 507 (2022).

and, absent an Establishment Clause violation, were protected by the Free Speech as well as the Free Exercise Clause.

Speech in the Public Schools

In a celebrated decision that I quoted earlier, *Tinker v. Des Moines Independent Community School District* (1969),[72] the Supreme Court held that neither students nor teachers "shed their constitutional rights to freedom of speech or expression at the schoolhouse gate." On its facts, *Tinker* found that school officials violated the Free Speech Clause when they disciplined students for wearing black arm bands in silent protest of the Vietnam war. The protest was akin to "pure speech," the Court reasoned, and was constitutionally protected because it did not invade the rights of others or cause a "material and substantial interference" with school activities. Subsequent decisions have clarified that teachers and school administrators have more capacity to control and discipline students' speech, and that students correspondingly enjoy less protection under the Free Speech Clause, when they are engaged in school-sponsored activities, such as speaking at an assembly or writing for a school newspaper.[73]

Recent cases in the lower courts have often involved students' off-campus speech, frequently over the internet, that has allegedly had disruptive on-campus effects. In *Mahanoy Area School District v. BL* (2021),[74] the Supreme Court ruled that school officials violated the First Amendment when they disciplined a high schooler for posting a profane Snapchat message protesting her rejection for a spot on the cheerleading squad. But the decision was narrowly written. It left many unanswered questions about schools' capacity to regulate various other kinds of off-campus speech by students that have disruptive on-campus reverberations.

Selective Subsidization of Private Speech and the Public Forum Doctrine

Just as the government need not be content neutral when speaking on its own behalf and in prescribing its employees' communicative

---

[72] 393 U.S. 503 (1969).
[73] See, for example, *Hazelwood School District v. Kuhlmeier*, 484 U.S. 260 (1988).
[74] 594 U.S. 180 (2021).

duties, the government can sometimes engage in selective, content-based subsidization of private speech. The Supreme Court has held, for example, that the government can subsidize private entities' conveyance of messages of support for some forms of family planning but not for abortion.[75] Nonetheless, governmental subsidies for private speech often pose hard issues, in part because selective funding of private speakers carries risks that the government might wield its power of the purse to distort the messages that private speakers otherwise would communicate.

Although the cases do not all fit together easily, one clear line stands out in this contested terrain. The Supreme Court has consistently held that the government cannot leverage its ownership of streets, parks, and sidewalks to exclude speakers with messages that it dislikes while offering access to speakers whose messages it approves. In decisions running back to the 1930s, the Court has reasoned that streets, parks, and sidewalks constitute "public fora" that the government has maintained "immemorially" as sites for the free exchange of ideas and that it must therefore continue to hold open for expressive purposes.[76] Under what is known as the "public forum doctrine," the government can enforce reasonable "time, place, and manner" regulations on the use of public streets and parks for expressive activity, but any such restrictions must be content neutral. For example, the government can bar all parades on busy city streets, but it cannot permit parades by those wishing to communicate preferred messages while forbidding parades by others.

"Forum doctrine," as it is sometimes called, includes myriad complications, chiefly because not all governmental property falls within the "public forum" category. Military bases do not, nor does the White House Rose Garden, nor do courthouses, including the Supreme Court building. The web of precedents elaborating the diverse First Amendment rules for subcategories of government property can prove confounding. Even so, the Court's insistence that most if not all public streets and parks must be open for expressive activity, and that any regulation of their uses for such purposes must be content neutral, is a cornerstone of free speech doctrine in the United States.

---

[75] See *Rust v. Sullivan*, 500 U.S. 173 (1991).
[76] See, for example, *Hague v. Committee for Industrial Organization*, 307 U.S. 496 (1939).

Regulation of the Broadcast Media

Surprisingly or unsurprisingly, the Supreme Court has long regarded governmental regulation of the broadcast media as lying within a managerial domain, due to the government's ownership of the airwaves. To prevent a chaos of competing voices attempting to broadcast over the same frequencies, the Federal Communications Commission (FCC) licenses use of the broadcast spectrum, and the Supreme Court has held that the FCC may wield its licensing power to demand programming in the public interest. For example, the FCC can require that the broadcast media provide news coverage. In *Red Lion Broadcasting Co. v. FCC* (1969),[77] the Court also upheld the constitutionality of the commission's now-abandoned "fairness doctrine," which once required balanced treatment of public issues.

In *FCC v. Pacifica Foundation* (1978),[78] the Supreme Court went further in holding that the FCC may enforce regulations prohibiting broadcast over the public airwaves of speech that the Commission deems "indecent," even if it is not "obscene" under the test of *Miller v. California*, at least during times when children may be listening. The *Pacifica* case arose when a San Francisco radio station played a recorded monologue by the comedian George Carlin titled "Filthy Words," featuring seven words that Carlin himself described as barred from the public airwaves – "the ones that will curve your spine, grow hair on your hands and ... maybe, even bring us ... peace without honor ... and a bourbon." The monologue repeatedly used the seven "filthy" words to comic effect but not to the amusement of the FCC. When the FCC threatened to enforce a regulation barring the broadcast of "indecent" material, Pacifica claimed a violation of its rights under the First Amendment. The Supreme Court disagreed. Although Carlin could not have been punished for delivering his monologue in a theater or a nightclub (because it was not "obscene" under the *Miller* test), a majority of the justices concluded that Pacifica could be penalized for broadcasting it over the public airwaves. Relying on different arguments from those they had advanced in *Red Lion*, the justices emphasized two considerations in holding that the First Amendment gives less protection to the

---

[77] 395 U.S. 367 (1969).
[78] 438 U.S. 726 (1978).

broadcast media than to other kinds of speakers: Radio and television broadcasts come directly into the home, and they are uniquely accessible to children.

The narrow anomalousness of the First Amendment doctrine involving the broadcast media needs to be stressed. The rules applicable to over-the-air broadcasters do not apply to cable television. Like the over-the-airwaves media, cable television comes directly into the home and is widely accessible to children. But unlike the traditional broadcast media, cable operators deliver their signals through privately owned wires, not publicly owned and licensed airwaves. That difference in mode of transmission results in very disparate rights: Context-based regulation of cable companies would trigger strict judicial scrutiny.[79]

The same is true of speech over the internet. In *Reno v. American Civil Liberties Union* (1997),[80] the Court struck down a federal statutory provision barring the sending or display of "patently offensive" (but not necessarily "obscene") material in a manner available to anyone younger than eighteen years of age. As the Court noted, this prohibition effectively restricted the messages that could be sent to chat rooms or newsgroups, and it would have imposed prohibitively expensive burdens on speakers with websites to verify that all of their users are adults. The Court thus ruled that the prohibition swept too broadly and thereby violated the First Amendment, despite serious concerns about children's access to inappropriate materials. It is not impossible to image the Court reaching a different conclusion in a future case if technological advances should make it more feasible for websites to verify the ages of their users.

Conclusion

With the emergence of a widespread insistence that any governmental restriction of speech should be content neutral, free speech doctrine has undergone vast transformations since the 1960s and early 1970s. The historical surprise, and to some extent the causal explanation, is that what we now know as judicial conservatism includes substantial elements of free speech libertarianism. Free speech doctrine is

---

[79] See, for example, *United States v. Playboy Entertainment Group*, 529 U.S. 803 (2000).
[80] 521 U.S. 844 (1997).

not originalist, even though justices who are often originalist in other contexts have endorsed nearly all of its central elements. For better or for worse, the Supreme Court interprets the First Amendment, which was ratified in 1791, as creating broader freedoms of speech than exist in any other country in the world. Some think the rest of the world should learn from us. Others think we could learn lessons from the rest of the world.

6 THE EXPANDING AND CONTESTED "RIGHT TO KEEP AND BEAR ARMS"

As a special police officer in the District of Columbia, Dick Heller was authorized to carry a gun while working. But the district's gun control laws, which were among the strictest in the country, forbade him to keep a handgun at home for self-defense. To D.C. officials, stringent restrictions on the possession of firearms in an urban environment made sense. The District of Columbia had a high incidence of crime-related gun violence. Its congested neighborhoods left no space for hunting, and a stray bullet was all too likely to hit an unintended target. The best way to keep the population safe was to exclude guns from the district to the greatest extent possible, officials believed. Other jurisdictions might have good reason to have looser restrictions or even no restrictions at all. But D.C., its officials thought, had done what was best for a city population terrorized by gun violence.

Heller saw things differently. He believed he would be safer if he could have a weapon in his home. Moreover, he thought that the Second Amendment to the Constitution gave him, along with any other law-abiding citizen, a right to keep a handgun in his house if he wanted one.

During a long period in US constitutional history, legal experts would have scoffed at Heller's argument. The Second Amendment reads: "A well regulated Militia, being necessary to the security of a free State, the right of the people to keep and bear Arms, shall not be infringed." Heller's wish to keep a handgun for self-defense had nothing to do with a "well regulated Militia." And prior to 2008, the Supreme Court had never held that the Second Amendment protects a right to possess "Arms" for personal use. During a 1991 television interview, retired Chief Justice Warren Burger – who had been appointed as a law-and-order conservative and whose career justified his conservative billing – had dismissed claims by "the gun lobby" that the Second Amendment protects the possession of weapons by the civilian population as "one of the greatest pieces of fraud ... on the American people by special interest groups that I have ever seen." By the time that Heller filed suit to challenge D.C.'s gun laws a little more than a decade later, however, the cultural and political landscape had changed. And a majority of the justices of the Supreme Court stood ready to take seriously arguments that their predecessors would have dismissed.

In *District of Columbia v. Heller* (2008),[1] the Court ruled for the first time that the Second Amendment confers a personal right to keep and bear arms for purposes unrelated to militia service. The author of the Court's opinion was Justice Antonin Scalia, who defended the decision on originalist grounds. By many accounts, Scalia was extraordinarily proud of his opinion, which he viewed as an exemplar of originalist analysis. But Scalia's was not the only originalism-based opinion in the case. There were two dissents in *Heller*, one of which, by Justice John Paul Stevens, vehemently contested Scalia's conclusions on originalist and textualist grounds of his own. In Stevens's view, the Second Amendment was written and originally intended to protect a right to keep and bear arms for militia service, not for other personal uses. In another dissenting opinion, Justice Stephen Breyer insisted that even if there were a right to possess guns for personal use, that right should be subject to reasonable regulation to protect public safety. The D.C. ordinance ought to pass muster on that basis, he maintained.

The Supreme Court decision in *Heller* was a watershed event in constitutional law. It was simultaneously a culmination of developments that overran once unassailable interpretive assumptions about the meaning of the Second Amendment and the beginning of a new, still-unfolding effort by the justices to define a constitutional right to gun possession that, as Justice Scalia acknowledged, "[l]ike most rights, ... is not unlimited." Many questions remain to be answered.

[1] 554 U.S. 570 (2008).

In order to describe the doctrine as it exists today, this chapter begins by sketching relevant historical background. It then discusses the leading modern cases, including the important decision that the Second Amendment applies to the states as well as to the federal government. The chapter also elaborates the framework for analyzing modern restrictions on gun ownership and carriage – based almost exclusively on the Second Amendment's text and the country's "history and tradition" – that those cases have developed.

Historical Background to Current Issues

Uniquely among provisions of the US Constitution, the Second Amendment begins with its own preamble: "A well regulated Militia, being necessary to the security of a free State ...." During the debates that preceded the Constitution's ratification, critics complained about its failure to guarantee a right to keep and bear arms based largely on worries that the proposed new national government might abolish or disable state militias. In eighteenth-century parlance, the term "militia" encompassed both the "general" militia, consisting of the able-bodied white men of a community, and the "special" or "select" militia, made up of males trained for military service. State militias, many believed, would function as an indispensable safeguard against both foreign invasion and a potentially tyrannical national government.

In response to anxieties expressed during the state ratification debates, the first Congress drafted and proposed the Second Amendment, the two clauses of which have framed subsequent interpretive debates. The first clause highlights the purpose of the Amendment to enable or ensure the existence of "a well regulated Militia." The second clause states its operative guarantee: "[T]he right of the people to keep and bear Arms shall not be infringed." Both in 1791 and thereafter, there have been at least two plausible interpretations. On the first, the right to keep and bear arms is a right linked to membership in the kind of well-regulated militia necessary to the security of a free state and is subject to regulation accordingly. As the historian Garry Wills once put it, "To bear arms is, in itself, a military term. One does not bear arms against a rabbit."[2] On the second interpretation, the

---

[2] Garry Wills, "To Keep and Bear Arms," *New York Review of Books*, September 21, 1995, 62, 64.

first clause states the animating reason for the enactment of the Second Amendment, but the second clause then guarantees a right to keep and bear arms that sweeps more broadly. More specifically, it refers and gives expressly constitutional status to a preexisting natural or common law right, widely understood to be among the longstanding prerogatives of free citizens in both England and America, that includes but is not limited to the possession of weapons for militia service. As so interpreted, the Second Amendment might indeed enshrine a right to keep and bear arms for rabbit-hunting.

The Supreme Court's most relevant discussion of the meaning of the Second Amendment prior to *Heller* came in *United States v. Miller* (1939),[3] a case involving a federal statute that prohibited transporting unregistered sawed-off shotguns (among other firearms) across state lines. In *Miller*, the justices concluded unanimously that the statute did not offend the Constitution. The Court's opinion repeatedly emphasized the textual and historical linkage between the Second Amendment and the needs of "a well regulated Militia." Miller's claim under the Second Amendment failed, the Court concluded, because sawed-off shotguns had no plausible military usage.

With *Miller* on the books, several generations of constitutional lawyers largely took it for granted that both the federal government and the states could ban the private possession and use of firearms. During that period, "gun control" legislation grew progressively stricter in some parts of the country, including the District of Columbia, partly in response to an alarming rise in violent crime in the 1960s and 1970s. At that time, restrictions on gun possession and use fit with an anti-crime agenda that political conservatives favored as much as liberals. Chief Justice Burger, as quoted earlier, expressed a view of the Second Amendment that many if not most other law-and-order conservatives shared as late as 1991.

The politics of gun control changed substantially during the latter decades of the twentieth century, however, as many conservatives began to perceive restrictions on gun ownership as threats to the lifestyles of hunters, outdoors people, and those who cherished traditional prerogatives of self-defense. Over this period, the National Rifle Association became a zealous defender of rights to handguns as well as rifles. As gun control became a partisan political issue,

---

[3] 307 U.S. 174 (1939).

opponents increasingly wrapped themselves in the mantle of the Second Amendment.[4] And amid renewed interest in the Second Amendment, historians and law professors directed more attention to evidence of the Amendment's original meaning. Perhaps predictably, they disagreed in their conclusions.

The Origins of Modern Doctrine: *District of Columbia v. Heller*

It was in this climate that the Supreme Court agreed to hear Dick Heller's claim that he had a personal right to keep a gun at home for self-defense. The D.C. gun laws at issue in *District of Columbia v. Heller* were among the most restrictive in the nation. In addition to banning virtually all handguns, the District of Columbia required that other firearms, including rifles, be kept under conditions that would render them useless for defense against sudden threats, including home invasions. By a 5–4 vote, the Court invalidated the challenged statutory provisions, which the majority thought so extreme that they posed few of the potentially difficult issues that other gun control laws might present. The Court did, however, clearly hold that the Second Amendment protects a right to keep and bear arms for purposes unrelated to militia service, most especially for self-defense in the home.

As Justice Scalia's majority opinion in *Heller* illustrates, modern disputes about the Second Amendment include three analytically distinct issues. The first involves the *nature* of the right to keep and bear arms. Is it a right to keep and bear arms solely in connection with service in a militia, or is it a broader, personal, right to possess and use firearms for other purposes? The second issue is the *scope* or breadth of the right. For example, does it encompass sawed-off shotguns (as in *Miller*) or assault rifles? And are there places to which it does not extend such as schools, courthouses, bars, or airplanes? The third issue concerns the *strength* of the Second Amendment right. Is it absolute, or is it subject to override in cases in which the government can assert a sufficiently weighty regulatory interest (as is often the case with First Amendment rights under, for example, the strict judicial scrutiny formula or the *O'Brien* test)?

---

[4] See Reva B. Siegel, "Dead or Alive: Originalism as Popular Constitutionalism in Heller," 122 *Harvard Law Review* 191 (2008).

The majority and dissenting opinions in *Heller* clashed at greatest length about the nature of the Second Amendment right. Although acknowledging that the Amendment's preamble avers a purpose of protecting arms for militia service, Justice Scalia's opinion differentiated sharply between the purpose that inspired the Second Amendment and the meaning of the guarantee that it enshrines in the Constitution. Even if the central purpose was to protect state militias from being disarmed by the national government, Scalia maintained, the guarantee of "the right of the people to keep and bear Arms" referred to and codified a traditional right of free citizens that was already widely recognized in the states of the United States as well as in England. That aim of giving express constitutional protection to a pre-existing right is evident, Scalia maintained, in the Second Amendment's reference to "*the* right to keep and bear arms" as what it guarantees. And that right, Scalia labored to establish, minimally included an entitlement to possess guns in the home for self-defense.

Writing in dissent, Justice Stevens examined many of the same historical materials as Justice Scalia but came to a starkly different conclusion about their import. On his reading, both the Second Amendment's text and the historical evidence surrounding its ratification demonstrated that it was intended to create a right to the kinds of arms necessary to a well-regulated militia, not a right to keep handguns for personal use. Even if there were room for doubt on that point, Justice Stevens further argued, the doctrine of stare decisis should have required the Court to adhere to the militia-focused interpretation of the Second Amendment that the Court had embraced in *United States v. Miller*. All of the Court's liberal justices agreed with Justice Stevens's appraisal of the historical and textual evidence.

Having devoted dozens of pages to establishing the originally understood nature of the Second Amendment right as a personal right not necessarily linked to militia service, Justice Scalia's majority opinion in *Heller* said less about the right's scope. It sufficed for purposes of deciding the case before the Court, he wrote, that the personal right to keep and bear arms included a right to possess weapons adequate for the defense of self and family in the home. Nonetheless, without much more elaboration or citation to original historical sources, Justice Scalia added – somewhat cryptically but highly significantly – that "nothing in our opinion should be taken to cast doubt on longstanding prohibitions on the possession of firearms by felons and the mentally ill, or laws forbidding the carrying of firearms in sensitive places such as schools and government buildings, or laws imposing conditions and qualifications on the commercial sale of arms."[5] Further, Justice Scalia embraced the Court's formulation in *United States v. Miller* describing the scope of Second Amendment rights as limited to weapons "in common use." Based on Justice Scalia's qualifying language about the scope of the right to keep and bear arms, a number of commentators emphasized what they described as *Heller*'s ultimately moderate holding, which they thought would allow a fair amount of, although surely not all, gun control legislation to survive.

With regard to the strength of the personal right to keep and bear arms, or its capacity to resist competing governmental interests, *Heller* said relatively little except to respond to Justice Breyer's dissenting opinion. Besides joining Justice Stevens's dissent, Breyer argued separately that even if the Second Amendment creates a personal right, that right should be subject to reasonable regulation and that the Court should uphold the challenged D.C. regulation based on an "interest-balancing" analysis. In reply, Justice Scalia brusquely rejected the notion that Second Amendment rights might be subject to override based on judicial interest-balancing. That approach was no more appropriate in a case involving Second Amendment rights than it would be in a case involving free speech rights, he reasoned. Nevertheless, Justice Scalia did not explicitly rule out the possibility that one of "the traditionally expressed levels" of judicial scrutiny such as strict scrutiny or intermediate scrutiny might have a role in some Second Amendment cases just as they do in some cases under the First Amendment.

The Supreme Court's decision in *Heller* merits five brief comments that will help both to illuminate its significance and to explain some continuing debates and uncertainties. First, *Heller* was a revolutionary decision that upended traditional judicial understandings of the Second Amendment. Its methodology exhibits the modern justices' sometime reliance on originalist analysis as a propellant of constitutional change.

Second, although all nine justices in *Heller* either wrote or joined opinions that purported to rest on the Second Amendment's original meaning, the Court nevertheless divided 5–4 in its conclusion concerning that question and, strikingly, did so along what commentators

---

[5] *Heller*, 554 U.S. at 626–27.

had no difficulty identifying as ideological lines. The Court's other most conservative justices joined Justice Scalia in reaching a historical conclusion that most political conservatives undoubtedly welcomed: The Second Amendment guarantees a right to keep and bear arms for personal purposes, including self-defense. Correspondingly, the Court's four more liberal justices as of 2008 arrived at a historical determination that most liberals would have applauded for policy reasons, whatever the history might have been.

Third, despite its revolutionary intimations, *Heller* exhibited a counterbalancing moderation through its assurances that the Court's decision posed no threat to a variety of "longstanding" restrictions on the possession, sale, and use of firearms. In this aspect, the opinion displayed a willingness to temper originalist analysis with other traditional considerations in constitutional analysis such as reliance on historical practice and precedent. Some commentators believe that Justice Anthony Kennedy may have insisted on the inclusion of some of the moderating language as a necessary condition for his signing onto Justice Scalia's majority opinion.

Fourth, *Heller*'s mix of originalist with precedent-based reasoning in defining the scope of the Second Amendment right produced a quasi-paradoxical conclusion on a key point. The Court's holding that the Second Amendment protects rights to possess and bear only weapons that are "in common use" means that "the Militia" could not today perform the functions that the first clause of the Second Amendment contemplated. Without highly sophisticated weapons, a modern militia could neither defend "a free state" against foreign invasion nor fight off a tyrannical national government. "But the fact that modern developments have limited the degree of fit between the prefatory clause and the protected right cannot change our interpretation of the right," Justice Scalia wrote. The upshot is that, under *Heller*, Second Amendment rights are almost wholly disjoined from what Justice Scalia acknowledged to have been the Founders' central, animating purpose of preserving a well-regulated militia. On the one hand, the right to "bear arms" extends to the use of nonmilitary weapons for sport and self-defense. On the other, it bestows no right to the kind of weapons that a militia would need to discharge "a well regulated Militia['s]" historical functions.

Finally, although *Heller* settled the crucial threshold issue of the nature of Second Amendment rights – by determining that they include entitlements to keep and bear arms for personal purposes unrelated to militia service – it left open a number of further questions about those rights' scope and strength. Nearly two decades later, lower courts, commentators, and the justices themselves are still struggling to work out *Heller*'s implications.

The "Incorporation" of the Second Amendment against the States

Two years after *Heller*, the Supreme Court's next major Second Amendment decision of the modern era came in *McDonald v. City of Chicago* (2010).[6] *McDonald* arose from a Chicago ordinance that paralleled the District of Columbia law at issue in *Heller* by banning possession of handguns in the home. Chicago did not deny the similarity of its ban to the one that *Heller* had invalidated. Instead, it argued that *Heller* did not control because the Second Amendment applies only to the federal government and does not preclude firearms regulation by cities and states.

As a technical legal matter, the central question in *McDonald* thus was whether the Second Amendment was "incorporated," and thus made applicable against the states, by the Fourteenth Amendment. By a vote of 5–4, replicating the division among the justices that *Heller* exhibited, the Court held that it was. As noted in Chapter 1, the Bill of Rights, including the Second Amendment, did not initially apply to the states. As summarized in Chapter 2, however, during the twentieth century the Supreme Court began to hold that some provisions of the Bill of Rights were incorporated by the Due Process Clause. Under the formula on which the Court ultimately converged, the test for incorporation is whether a right listed in the Bill of Rights is "fundamental to the American scheme of justice" as it has existed historically. By the time of *McDonald*, the Court had held that nearly all of the provisions of the Bill of Rights are fundamental but that a few – such as the Seventh Amendment right to trial by a jury (rather than a judge) in civil suits for money damages – are not.

Justice Samuel Alito wrote the principal opinion in *McDonald*. Joined by three other conservative justices, he concluded that the right to possess guns for self-defense, which *Heller* had found to be "the central component of the Second Amendment right," was "deeply

[6] 561 U.S. 742 (2010).

rooted in this Nation's history and tradition" and that it was therefore incorporated against cities and states. Justice Thomas wrote a separate opinion concurring in the judgment based on what he took to be the original meaning of the Fourteenth Amendment and, in particular, of the Privileges or Immunities Clause. In his opinion, Thomas rejected the premise that the Due Process Clause protects any substantive rights, including the right to bear arms. In his view, however, the right to keep and bear arms is one of the privileges or immunities of citizenship that Privileges or Immunities Clause protects. On that basis, he reached the same bottom-line conclusion as Justice Alito that the Second Amendment applies against the states.

The four liberal justices dissented. Justice Stevens began with the premise that the primary function of substantive due process analysis is to protect personal "liberty." Given that premise, he argued that gun rights should not be accorded recognition as fundamental. Their relation to liberty is too "ambivalent," he maintained, since recognition of one person's right to possess a weapon can increase the level of threat to others. Justice Breyer argued that in light of what he viewed as mixed historical evidence, it should matter to the "fundamental rights" analysis that "every State regulates firearms extensively, and public opinion is sharply divided on the appropriate level of regulation." In light of public divisions and varied circumstances in different parts of the country, Breyer, joined by two other liberals, thought that the Court should not embrace a conclusion that would frustrate local choice regarding gun regulation.

As was true of *Heller*, *McDonald* displayed the Supreme Court's proclivity to mix originalist and nonoriginalist reasoning in its development of Second Amendment doctrine. Under *Heller*, the substantive content of the Second Amendment right as a right to possess guns for nonmilitia purposes depends on what the Court takes to be the Amendment's original meaning. By contrast, the Court's determination in *McDonald* that the Second Amendment applies to the states because it is "incorporated" by the Fourteenth Amendment's Due Process Clause makes no pretense of reflecting the Due Process Clause's originally understood meaning. *McDonald* and subsequent cases in which the Court's conservative justices have applied the Second Amendment to the states are thus methodologically originalist in one respect, involving their specification of the substantive content of the right to keep and bear arms. But they rely on judicial precedent running back to the *Lochner* era, not evidence of original constitutional meaning, to justify their determination that the Due Process Clause of the Fourteenth Amendment incorporates the Second Amendment and makes it applicable against the states.

Defining Rights by History and Tradition

After *McDonald* in 2010, the Supreme Court did not decide another major Second Amendment case on the merits until 2022, when it invalidated a New York law that forbade possession of a gun without a license and conditioned the award of "unrestricted" licenses that would allow carriage outside the home on a demonstration of special need. Since *McDonald*, as the originalist Justice Clarence Thomas pointedly noted in his majority opinion in *New York Rifle & Pistol Association v. Bruen* (2022),[7] the lower federal courts had converged on a two-step approach to determining the *strength* of Second Amendment rights:

> The Courts of Appeals [first] ascertain the original scope of the right based on its historical meaning .... [I]f the historical evidence at this step is "inconclusive or suggests that the regulated activity is *not* categorically protected," the courts generally proceed to step two. At the second step, ... [i]f a "core" Second Amendment right [such as the right to possess a gun in the home for self-defense] is burdened, the courts apply "strict scrutiny" and ask whether the Government can prove that the law is "narrowly tailored to a compelling governmental interest." Otherwise, they apply intermediate scrutiny and consider whether the Government can show that the regulation is "substantially related to an important governmental interest."

Under this two-step framework, the lower courts had upheld far more restrictions on the sale, possession, and display of firearms than they invalidated. In particular, they had mostly approved restrictions on what many took to be "noncore rights," such as asserted rights to possess automatic weapons or carry handguns in public places, pursuant to the "intermediate scrutiny" test. The lower courts' pattern of decisions at least partly vindicated the assessment of some commentators

[7] 597 U.S. 1 (2022), 18.

that *Heller* was a generally moderate decision that left a fair amount of regulatory authority in the hands of Congress and the state legislatures.

Justice Thomas's *Bruen* opinion rejected that view by holding that the lower courts had misunderstood *Heller*. With the Supreme Court now comprising a strong conservative supermajority, Justice Thomas dismissed the lower courts' two-step approach to the identification of Second Amendment rights as involving "one step too many." "If the last decade of Second Amendment litigation has taught this Court anything, it is that federal courts tasked with making ... difficult empirical judgments" regarding whether firearms regulations are sufficiently closely tailored to sufficiently important state interests "often defer to the judgments of legislatures," Justice Thomas wrote in an opinion for the six conservative justices. Making Second Amendment rights turn on judgments about such matters as the closeness of laws' tailoring to governmental interests with weights that require judicial appraisal was error, he continued: "The Second Amendment 'is the very *product* of an interest balancing by the people' and it 'surely elevates above all other interests the right of law-abiding, responsible citizens to use arms' for self-defense. It is this balance – struck by the traditions of the American people – that demands our unqualified deference."[8]

Viewing the Second Amendment as the "product of an interest balancing" that left no room for either legislatures or courts to perform any further kind of balancing analysis, the Court concluded that judges should ascertain the *scope* of the Second Amendment by asking whether a claimed right came within its "text, as informed by history." If so, any infringement would be invalid under the Second Amendment unless the government can "prove that its firearms regulation is part of the historical tradition that delimits the outer bounds of the right to keep and bear arms." "[T]he lack of a distinctly similar historical regulation ... is relevant evidence" that a modern restriction is invalid, Justice Thomas added. He also pointedly affirmed that judges and justices have no authority to engage in "means-ends scrutiny" or interest-balancing to determine whether the party challenging a firearms restriction was ultimately entitled to prevail.

In thrusting onto the government the obligation to prove that a challenged firearm regulation has "distinctly similar" historical

---

[8] *Ibid.* at 26.

analogues, *Bruen* acknowledged that many modern regulations might have been "unimaginable at the founding." In such cases, Justice Thomas explained, courts would need to "reason[] by analogy – a commonplace task for any lawyer or judge." Although Thomas declined to venture "an exhaustive survey of the features that render regulations relevantly similar under the Second Amendment," he had no difficulty in invalidating the New York regulations at issue in *Bruen*, which forbade carrying a gun outside the owner's home or place of business without a license and required anyone seeking a license to "demonstrate a special need for self-protection distinguishable from that of the general community." "The ... plain text" of the Second Amendment's reference to a right to bear arms "presumptively guarantees" a right to bear arms "in public for self-defense," the majority reasoned. And while some regulations of gun sales, ownership, and carriage had long existed, none of the specific analogies that New York offered in support of its rules was close enough. In particular, there was no "historical tradition limiting public carry only to those law-abiding citizens who demonstrate a special need for self-defense."[9]

Four of the other conservative justices, though signing onto the majority opinion, also either wrote or joined concurring opinions that commented on some aspect of Justice Thomas's interpretive methodology. Justice Kavanaugh, joined by Chief Justice Roberts, emphasized *Bruen*'s continuity with earlier Second Amendment cases. "The Court employs and elaborates on the text, history, and tradition test that *Heller* and *McDonald* require for evaluating whether a government regulation infringes on the Second Amendment right to possess and carry guns for self-defense," he wrote. Justice Barrett, meanwhile, noted two ambiguities in the "text, history, and tradition" approach that Justice Thomas's opinion had no occasion to resolve. First, writing as an originalist, Justice Barrett noted that although the Court had cited post-ratification history and tradition in support of its holding, it did "not conclusively determine the manner and circumstances in which post-ratification practice may bear on the original meaning of the Constitution." Justice Barrett also pointed out that the Court had not determined whether the proper reference point for determining the original meaning of the Second Amendment in its application to the

---

[9] *Ibid.* at 38.

states was 1791, when the Second Amendment was originally ratified, or 1868, when it was incorporated by the Fourteenth Amendment.

Justice Breyer wrote an emphatic dissenting opinion, in which the liberal Justices Sotomayor and Kagan joined, that highlighted a deeper methodological and ultimately practical division within the Supreme Court. "In 2020," he began, "45,222 Americans were killed by firearms." The problems posed by gun violence were acute and complex, he argued, and the Court should afford legislatures reasonable flexibility to craft solutions suited to local conditions. In addition, Justice Breyer maintained, "the Court's application of its history-only test" demonstrated the subjectivity and pitfalls of trying to pick out relevant and irrelevant historical analogies to modern regulations of modern weapons. Laws "regulating the public carriage of firearms in general, and concealed firearms in particular," had existed for 700 years or more. In resisting all of the proffered analogies, the Court, Justice Breyer argued, had taken "either an unnecessarily cramped view of the relevant historical record or a needlessly rigid approach to analogical reasoning."[10] In a concurring opinion that further emphasized differences among the justices about the proper approach to Second Amendment issues, Justice Alito dismissed Justice Breyer's lengthy disquisition on the ravages of gun violence in the United States, and especially its cities, as irrelevant to the constitutional issue before the Court.

As the proliferation of opinions in *Bruen* might suggest, its demand for a methodology that relies exclusively on text, history, and tradition to identify rights under the Second Amendment marked a bold innovation. In support of the Court's call for an exclusively historical measure of both the scope and the strength of Second Amendment rights, Justice Thomas cited the Court's practice in determining whether categories of speech lie outside the coverage of the First Amendment. As discussed in Chapter 5, *United States v. Stevens*[11] (2010) rebuffed a suggestion that the Court should resolve that question via a balancing analysis. The exclusive test for whether a category of speech should be deemed unprotected, *Stevens* proclaimed, is whether it has been historically recognized as unprotected. But the question whether a category of speech is wholly unprotected is different from questions involving the strength of speech rights in cases to which the First Amendment

---

[10] *Ibid.* at 130 (Breyer, J., dissenting).
[11] 559 U.S. 460 (2010).

applies. It is more nearly the norm than the exception that burdens on speech within the coverage of the Free Speech Clause will be assessed pursuant to the *O'Brien* test, strict judicial scrutiny, or some other framework that takes account of the nature and weight of competing governmental interests to determine the validity of challenged statutes. In mandating a one-step historical test for the validity of restrictions on the possession, purchase, and use of firearms, *Bruen* thus put Second Amendment doctrine onto a new course on which courts would be unaided by some of their most tried and trusted navigational devices. The Court's plain intent was to ensure more robust protection of the right to keep and bear arms than lower courts had previously afforded it under what many commentators had adjudged to be the "moderate" decision in *Heller*.

A Partial Modification of the History-and-Tradition Approach

By nearly all accounts, *Bruen*'s instruction that Second Amendment cases should turn solely on whether modern regulations have sufficiently close historical analogues produced uncertainty, inconsistency, and confusion in the lower courts. Lawyers' briefs and judicial opinions abounded with references to historical gun regulation, both before and after the ratification of the Second Amendment and of the Fourteenth Amendment, which made the Second Amendment applicable to the states for the first time. But no agreed approach emerged for identifying the comparative significance of diverse historical data points or for judging relevant similarities between past and modern regulations.

United States v. Rahimi[12] (2024) arrived at the Court in this context. Zackey Rahimi was arrested and charged under a federal statute that makes it a crime for a person subject to a domestic violence restraining order to possess a firearm if the order includes a finding that the person poses a credible threat of future violence. A Texas judge had issued a restraining order against Rahimi after he dragged his former girlfriend by the hair during an argument, slammed her head against his car's dashboard, brandished and fired a gun during the same incident, and telephoned the victim of his assault to warn that he would

[12] 144 S. Ct. 1889 (2024).

shoot her if she reported it. Rahimi repeatedly violated the restraining order, which, among other things, forbade him from possessing a firearm for two years. When police subsequently arrested him for multiple violent crimes, some involving the use of deadly weapons, they discovered guns and ammunition in his possession along with a copy of the restraining order.

Rahimi would have had no plausible constitutional defense against charges that he had committed crimes of violence punishable under Texas law. But the federal indictment for possessing a firearm while subject to a domestic violence restraining order, he argued, abridged his Second Amendment right "to keep and bear Arms." The lower court that heard Rahimi's case agreed. Seeking to apply *Bruen*'s text-history-and-tradition methodology, it found no sufficiently precise eighteenth- or nineteenth-century analogue to the statute under which the government sought to punish Rahimi for possessing a weapon. Many constitutional experts thought the Supreme Court might agree.

Instead, by the surprisingly wide vote of 8–1, the justices not only overturned the lower court's decision but also appeared to adjust the test for the permissibility of gun regulation under the Second Amendment that courts should apply going forward. "Some courts have misunderstood the methodology of our recent Second Amendment cases," Chief Justice Roberts wrote for the majority. The Court's "precedents were not meant to suggest a law trapped in amber," he continued. Where *Bruen* had suggested that modern gun regulations should be struck down unless a "distinctly similar historical regulation" had been upheld or accepted, *Rahimi* demanded only that past restrictions be "relevantly similar." "The Second Amendment permits more than just those regulations identical to ones that could be found in 1791," the Court said.[13]

The decisive consideration, Chief Justice Roberts elaborated, was not necessarily the degree of factual similarity of a modern statute to a historical analogue but whether a challenged modern regulation is "consistent with the *principles* that underpin our regulatory tradition." In applying that subtly reformulated historical test to uphold a statute prohibiting possession of a firearm by a person subject to a domestic violence restraining order, the *Rahimi* majority primarily relied on two partial historical parallels. The first, surety laws, authorized magistrates

---

[13] Ibid. at 691–92.

to require persons likely to engage in illegal conduct, including spousal abuse and misuse of firearms, to post a bond (or sum of money) that they would forfeit if they subsequently broke the law. The second relevant analogue, "affray" laws, forbade "riding or going armed, with dangerous or unusual weapons, [to] terrify[] the good people of the land." Although those historical precursors were "by no means identical" to the federal statute that Rahimi challenged, they did "not need to be." "Taken together," the chief justice concluded, "the surety and going armed laws confirm what common sense suggests: When an individual poses a clear threat of physical violence to another, the threatening individual may be disarmed."[14]

For observers seeking to discern how *Rahimi* fits together with *Bruen*, its reference to "common sense" as a relevant consideration seems notable. So does the identity of the sole dissenter in *Rahimi*: Justice Thomas, the Court's most nearly uncompromising originalist, who had written the Court's opinion in *Bruen* two years earlier. Thomas's *Rahimi* dissent noted the obvious dissimilarities between the law at issue in *Rahimi* and the historical predecessors that the majority cited. Neither surety laws nor affray laws outlawed the mere possession of a gun by a person merely believed to be dangerous. In addition, both imposed punishments for the possession of a gun only after a separate criminal infraction had occurred. In the view of Justice Thomas, the historical analogies were therefore not close enough to justify a statute barring Rahimi from possessing a gun before he had been convicted of any crime.

With *Rahimi* apparently having determined that decisions of future cases should be based on the "principles" that underlay historically accepted gun regulations rather than on the existence of "distinctly similar" historical antecedents, a central challenge for courts going forward will be to discern what the relevant principles were. Although the justices endorsed the reliance on principles rather than precise analogues by a vote of 8–1, experience has taught judges and lawyers the difficulty of extracting principles from historical traditions. A recurrent source of disagreement involves the "level of generality" at which the legally controlling principles should be framed. In *Rahimi*, Chief Justice Roberts said the relevant principle was that "[w]hen an individual poses a clear threat of physical violence to another, the

[14] *Ibid.* at 698.

threatening individual may be disarmed." But why should the principle not be a broader or more general one, such as, "the government may impose restrictions on the possession and use of dangerous weapons on terms reasonably necessary to keep the community safe from violence"? And Justice Thomas, of course, could have argued that the relevant principle underlying the cited historical analogies was a much narrower one, more along the lines of "when individuals brandish weapons to terrorize others, they may be punished for doing so after the fact, but not deprived of their arms on suspicion of dangerousness before they have committed any crime." The chief justice's opinion gave little guidance concerning how a court should judge.

Nor did the *Rahimi* majority address an important methodological issue that Justice Barrett has raised concerning why "tradition" should matter to constitutional interpretation insofar as the events that constitute a tradition occurred after the ratification of a constitutional amendment. As Barrett pointed out in a case decided at roughly the same time as *Rahimi*, following up on a comment that she had made in *Bruen*, her fellow conservative justices might view post-ratification history and tradition as relevant to constitutional adjudication for either of two purposes.[15] History and tradition might be relevant only insofar as they constitute persuasive evidence of a constitutional provision's originally understood meaning. If so, however, it seems precarious to assume that the historical absence of a particular type of weapons regulation reflected a belief among legislators that a restriction would have violated the Second Amendment. Legislatures often refrain from passing the most stringent laws that they think the Constitution would permit them to enact. Alternatively, the conservative justices might think that traditional patterns of regulation furnish a freestanding limit on the government's authority to restrict the possession and carriage of firearms. If so, however, the justification for that limitation would also call for explanation. If a form of firearms regulation would not violate the Constitution's original meaning, why should subsequent historical patterns of nonregulation restrict the discretion of legislatures to enact what they take to be prudent gun safety laws today?

Acknowledging some of the difficulties that the interpretive approach laid out in *Bruen* and subsequently adjusted in *Rahimi*

---

[15] See *Vidal v. Elster*, 602 U.S. 286, 322–25 (2024) (Barrett, J., concurring in part).

must surmount, Justice Kavanaugh authored a concurring opinion in *Rahimi* in which he sought to furnish guidelines for conducting constitutional analysis by historical analogy. In it, he also offered a general defense of a method of constitutional analysis based solely on text, history, tradition, and occasionally precedent. "[H]istory is far less subjective than policy," Kavanaugh maintained, and "reliance on history is more consistent with the properly neutral judicial role than an approach where judges subtly (or not so subtly) impose their policy views on the American people." It was imperative, he asserted, for courts to eschew approaches to constitutional adjudication that "require[] judges to weigh the benefits or burdens of a law" to determine whether, "in the judge's view, the law is sufficiently reasonable or important."[16] Justice Kavanaugh said he did not mean to suggest that the Court should overrule cases in which it has previously applied such means-ends scrutiny in enforcing other constitutional provisions – as it has, for example, in applying tests such as strict or intermediate judicial scrutiny to resolve cases under the Free Speech, Free Exercise, and Equal Protection Clauses. But he insisted that the Court should not extend such "tests to new areas, including the Second Amendment."

Although the liberal justices voted with the Court's majority to uphold the statute challenged in *Rahimi*, they expressed sharp disagreement with some of the opinion's premises, which they accepted only for purposes of clarifying how the *Bruen* framework, which rejects judicial means-ends scrutiny of legislation, should be interpreted and applied. In a concurring opinion in *Rahimi*, Justice Sotomayor, joined by Justices Kagan and Jackson, maintained that the Court had taken a wrong turn in *Bruen* when it made the validity of gun regulations depend exclusively on historical analogues without regard to whether they serve important or compelling governmental interests.

Concluding Observations and Pending Issues

United States v. Rahimi exhibits Second Amendment doctrine in a state of evolution that has not yet reached a stable equilibrium. Among the vital substantive questions that the Court's Second Amendment cases have not settled so far are these: Which types of weapons are subject to restriction on the ground that they are

---

[16] *Rahimi.* 144 S. Ct. at 731 (Kavanaugh, J., concurring).

unusually dangerous? Which kinds of places fall within the category of especially sensitive locations from which firearms can be excluded? And which individuals' possession of guns would pose sufficient danger to the community for their access to firearms to be restricted based on which historical analogues?

Even in the absence of answers to those questions, *Rahimi* clarifies the implications of *New York Rifle & Pistol Association v. Bruen* by affirming that "the Second Amendment permits more than just those regulations identical to ones that could be found in 1791." Instead, courts must assess whether modern restrictions are consistent with the "principles" that underlay historical predecessors.

Although that gloss on the test for identifying Second Amendment rights is undoubtedly important, the significance of *Rahimi*'s continuity with *Bruen* deserves equal emphasis. Like *Bruen*, *Rahimi* signals the current majority's eagerness to develop an interpretive methodology that eschews means-ends tests such as strict and intermediate judicial scrutiny. As the Supreme Court's decision to clarify or revise *Bruen* in *Rahimi* shows, the emerging approach is still in the experimental stage. But if the conservative majority should view the ongoing experiment as a success, it is easy to imagine their expanding it into other areas of constitutional law, potentially including the equal protection and substantive due process doctrines that Chapters 7 and 8 address.

7 THE EQUAL PROTECTION OF THE LAWS
What It Once Meant and Now Means

In June 2023, the Supreme Court effectively held that race-based affirmative action in higher education – even when practiced on terms that the Court had blessed for nearly fifty years – violates the Equal Protection Clause of the Fourteenth Amendment. The Court's decision, in *Students for Fair Admissions (SFFA) v. Harvard*,[1] emblematized the legal vision and self-confidence of the current Court's conservative majority in matters involving race and the Constitution.

That the case involved the admissions policies of Harvard College contributed to its significance as a study in constitutional change. In the Court's first important decision involving affirmative action, in *Regents of the University of California v. Bakke* (1978),[2] the controlling opinion by Justice Lewis Powell had quoted at length from Harvard's admissions policy and held it up as a model for how affirmative action could be practiced without affront to constitutional norms. In *SFFA*, with Harvard's policy once again in the spotlight, the majority, by 6–3, ruled that it violated the rights of white and Asian applicants not to be discriminated against on the basis of race.

Viewed in retrospect, the *Bakke* decision was a characteristic decision of the Burger Court in addressing a vexing and divisive constitutional issue. It was a messy compromise, arrived at partly by accident

---

[1] 600 U.S. 181 (2023).
[2] 438 U.S. 265 (1978).

and partly by design. The accident involved the conflicting and sometimes idiosyncratic views of the Court's nine justices. The design came from Justice Powell, who announced the Court's decision and who alone among the justices endorsed every aspect of *Bakke*'s complex holding. Four of his colleagues would have held that a federal statute forbade educational institutions that accept federal funds to take race into account at all in making admissions decisions – a position very close to that which the *SFFA* majority ascribed to the Equal Protection Clause. Four others – including Justice Thurgood Marshall, who had been one of the lead lawyers in the Supreme Court's landmark decision in *Brown v. Board of Education* (1954)[3] – would have upheld affirmative action by virtually any educational institution in the United States as a remedy for past, race-based, societal discrimination. For the eight justices who took one of the other of those two positions, *Bakke*, which permitted affirmative action but only on very restricted terms, was wrong about some things, even if right about others.

With different coalitions of justices aligning with him on different points, Justice Powell held that colleges and universities – as apparently distinguished from other governmental entities such as police and sanitation departments – have a distinctively "compelling" interest in being able to take race into account in order to achieve "diversity" in their student bodies. The "[a]cademic freedom" of universities, Powell reasoned, "though not a specifically enumerated constitutional right, long has been viewed as a special concern of the First Amendment," and it encompasses the prerogative of a university to make judgments concerning "the selection of its student body." Because students learn from classmates as well as their teachers, having students with a broad mix of backgrounds and experiences permits colleges to provide better education to all, including whites as well as nonwhites. In some cases, Powell therefore thought, a student's racial background might enhance his or her capacity to enrich the educationally valuable diversity and thus the overall quality of a school's student body. Nonetheless, any reliance on race was constitutionally disfavored or "suspect" under the Equal Protection Clause, Powell further posited, and could enter admissions decisions only as part of a holistic appraisal in which every candidate received individualized consideration of his or her capacity to contribute to the overall excellence of an educational institution's

[3] 347 U.S. 483 (1954).

entering class. Under these circumstances, Powell opined, an "applicant who loses out [to] another candidate receiving a 'plus' on the basis of ethnic background" would have "his qualifications ... weighed fairly and competitively" and "would have no basis to complain of unequal treatment under the Fourteenth Amendment."[4]

Critics on both sides of the affirmative action debate scoffed at Powell's *Bakke* opinion. Champions of affirmative action complained that the Court should have allowed race to be considered more transparently as a remedy for past and continuing societal discrimination and that colleges should be free to adopt racial quotas if they chose. Critics on the other side viewed the Court as having wrongly authorized race-based classifications that mocked the constitutional ideal of racial equality that the Equal Protection Clause embodies. Nevertheless, Powell's compromise position – which allowed colleges and universities to take some account of race but only as one aspect of a candidate's overall capacity to contribute to the excellence and diversity of a school's student body – survived repeated challenges over more than forty years.

When the Supreme Court invalidated Harvard's affirmative action policy in the *SFFA* case, its decision was as characteristic of the Roberts Court as *Bakke* was of the Burger Court. As I shall explain, the *SFFA* decision was not and did not purport to be "originalist." Nor did it rest on the close textual analysis that the Roberts Court sometimes deploys. The six justices in the *SFFA* majority plainly viewed themselves as enforcing an important principle of colorblindness that they believed their more compromising predecessors had allowed to be corrupted, not only in *Bakke* but also in a string of subsequent decisions. But if the history of equal protection doctrine teaches anything, it is that the path of principle often lies in the eye of the beholder.

Equal Protection and the Constitution

Despite the reference in the Declaration of Independence to "all men" being "created equal," the original Constitution contained no guarantee of equal rights. To the contrary, it included protections for slavery and tolerated the subjection of women to myriad legal disabilities. After the Civil War, the Thirteenth Amendment abolished slavery but said nothing explicit about broader entitlements to equal

---

[4] *Bakke*, 438 U.S. at 318 (opinion of Powell, J.).

treatment. The Fourteenth Amendment, which was proposed in 1866 and ratified in 1868, clearly sought to go further, though in ways that appear to have embodied ambiguous compromises and that have perplexed subsequent interpreters. The relevant language of Section One of the Fourteenth Amendment bears quoting:

> [1] No State shall make or enforce any law which shall abridge the privileges or immunities of citizens of the United States; [2] nor shall any State deprive any person of life, liberty, or property, without due process of law; [3] nor deny to any person within its jurisdiction the equal protection of the laws.

In efforts to discern the meaning of the Fourteenth Amendment, including the Equal Protection Clause, the Fifteenth Amendment also merits attention. Added to the Constitution two years after the Fourteenth, it provides that "the right of citizens of the United States to vote shall not be denied or abridged by the United States or by any state on account of race, color, or previous condition of servitude." With the Fourteenth Amendment already having included a guarantee of "the equal protection of the laws," why, a modern reader might ask, was a further amendment needed to bar race discrimination with regard to voting rights? Indeed, why wouldn't race discrimination in voting "abridge the privileges or immunities of citizens of the United States" and thus violate the Fourteenth Amendment's Privileges or Immunities Clause as well as the Equal Protection Clause? An additional data point is that relatively few Americans in 1868 or during the remainder of the nineteenth century appear to have thought that the Fourteenth Amendment barred state and local governments from operating racially segregated public schools or from prohibiting interracial marriages. Among the states then operating segregated schools, none changed its practices upon the Fourteenth Amendment's ratification.

In attempting to explain the original meaning of the Fourteenth Amendment, historians have emphasized that the generation that drafted and ratified it drew distinctions among categories of "rights" that modern parlance no longer recognizes. More specifically, many nineteenth-century Americans differentiated among what they called "civil," "political," and "social" rights.[5] Within this

---

[5] See, for example, Eric Foner, *The Second Founding: How the Civil War and Reconstruction Remade the Constitution* (New York, NY: W.W. Norton & Company, 2019), 6–7.

categorical scheme, civil rights were those that nineteenth-century lawyers viewed as fundamental or basic and "included legal entitlements essential to pursuing a livelihood and protecting one's personal security – the right to own property, go to court, ... sign contracts, and move about freely." According to many if not most legal historians, the principal drafters of the Fourteenth Amendment intended the Privileges or Immunities Clause to guarantee the equal *civil* rights of all citizens, white and Black alike. In the minds of many nineteenth-century lawyers, however, the civil rights that were widely understood to constitute the privileges or immunities of citizenship did not encompass political rights such as the right to vote. On this understanding, the distinction between civil and political rights would explain the need for the Fifteenth Amendment to prohibit racial discrimination in voting.

Nor, in the view of leading historians, did the nineteenth-century category of civil rights, as protected by the Privileges or Immunities Clause, embrace a further, amorphous, set of "social" rights "that included personal and business relationships of many kinds" and that "lay outside the realm of governmental supervision."[6] Against the background of this conceptual framework, a number of authors maintain, the principal, anticipated function of the Equal Protection Clause was not to demand equality in the distribution of all categories of rights but, rather, to require that states must enforce their laws – including prohibitions against physical violence – for the equal benefit of all citizens.[7]

Although the account that I have just offered is accepted by many constitutional historians, there are influential dissenters,[8] and I do not mean to press it dogmatically. No more with the Fourteenth Amendment than with other constitutional provisions did the framers and ratifiers reach consensus on their expectations and write those

---

[6] Ibid. at 7.
[7] Randy E. Barnett and Evan D. Bernick, *The Original Meaning of the Fourteenth Amendment: Its Letter and Spirit* (Cambridge, MA: Belknap Press of Harvard University Press, 2021), 320–21; John Harrison, "Reconstructing the Privileges or Immunities Clause," 101 *Yale Law Journal* 1385, 1450 (1992).
[8] See, for example, William Baude, Jud Campbell, and Stephen E. Sachs, "General Law and the Fourteenth Amendment," 76 *Stanford Law Review* 1185, 1188, 1190 (2024), which offers a different account of nineteenth-century categorizations of rights. The authors conclude that the Privileges or Immunities Clause was understood by its congressional sponsors to authorize Congress and the federal courts to enforce preexisting "general law" rights that were widely recognized by all free governments and were not, strictly speaking, distinctively rights of either federal law or of state law.

expectations into law. On many points, they undoubtedly disagreed among themselves. On some, they appear to have preferred ambiguity to clarity. They also worked against the background of a moral tradition opposing slavery and celebrating the ideal of "natural" rights, which constituted yet another category, that were shared by all human beings even if not explicitly written into positive law. Some historians and constitutional theorists thus maintain that the Equal Protection Clause constitutionalizes a moral right to equality of respect or concern and that it is this moral right, not the framers' interpretive expectations, that ultimately ought to matter in constitutional adjudication.[9] Even granting that interpretive possibility, however, virtually no one contends that a majority of the framers and ratifiers specifically expected the Fourteenth Amendment to outlaw all forms of race-based discrimination.

As discussed more extensively in Chapter 8, the Supreme Court dashed what many view as the framers' expectations concerning the significance of the Privileges or Immunities Clause in the *Slaughter-House Cases* (1873),[10] which construed that provision so narrowly as to be almost meaningless. And with the Privileges or Immunities Clause out of the picture, disputes about equal rights under the Constitution, which the Fourteenth Amendment clearly was intended to protect at least in some contexts, migrated to the Equal Protection Clause.

The ensuing pattern of decisions has exhibited extraordinary twists and turns, nearly always driven by considerations other than close analysis of constitutional language or evidence of its original meaning. In the remainder of this chapter, I first examine cases in which the Supreme Court has considered the permissibility of different kinds of governmental classifications – such as those based on race and sex – under the Equal Protection Clause. I then turn, more briefly, to a lesser-known component of equal protection doctrine involving rights that are deemed "fundamental" under the Equal Protection Clause. Voting rights provide a paradigmatic example. Inequalities in the

---

[9] See, for example, William E. Nelson, *The Fourteenth Amendment: From Political Principle to Judicial Doctrine* (Cambridge, MA: Harvard University Press, 1988), 80 (arguing that the framers and ratifiers were mostly concerned with general moral ideals and did not attempt to reach clear understandings with respect to many specific applications); Ronald Dworkin, *Freedom's Law* (Cambridge, MA: Harvard University Press, 1996), 8–10 (arguing that whatever the framers' specific expectations, the Equal Protection Clause embodies a moral principle, which must be interpreted in light of its ultimate moral meaning).

[10] 83 U.S. 36 (1873).

distribution of rights that are characterized as fundamental for equal protection purposes sometimes receive elevated scrutiny even in cases not involving discrimination on the basis of race, religion, sex, or similar characteristics.

Issues Involving Race

Invidious Discrimination

Application of the Equal Protection Clause to practices of race discrimination began with *Strauder v. West Virginia* (1880),[11] in which the Supreme Court invalidated a state law excluding Blacks from jury service. In *Strauder*, the Court cited indiscriminately to the various rights-conferring provisions of the Fourteenth Amendment, including the Equal Protection Clause, and asked rhetorically: "What is this but declaring that the law in the States shall be the same for the black as for the white ... and, in regard to the colored race, for whose protection the amendment was primarily designed, that no discrimination shall be made against them by law because of their color?"[12] *Strauder* thus provides evidence, if it were needed, that not all informed nineteenth-century lawyers interpreted the Equal Protection Clause in the same way or viewed it as having only the narrow scope suggested by the historical account that I laid out earlier.

But *Strauder*'s broad promise of nondiscrimination proved short-lived. Less than two decades later, in the notorious case of *Plessy v. Ferguson* (1896),[13] the Supreme Court upheld a Louisiana law requiring that passenger railroads provide "equal but separate accommodations for the white, and coloured races." After being excluded from the "white" car on a Louisiana train, Homer Plessy argued first that he carried only a small proportion of Black blood and thus was white, not Black. That claim failing, he argued next that Louisiana's race-based classification violated the Equal Protection Clause. By a vote of 7–1, the Court disagreed. Asserting that the Fourteenth Amendment was not "intended to abolish [all] distinctions based upon color, or to enforce social, as distinguished from political, equality," the Court held that the legislature had the power to enact race-based

---

[11] 100 U.S. 303 (1880).
[12] *Ibid.* at 307.
[13] 163 U.S. 537 (1896).

classifications – at least within the domain of "social" rights – as long as those classifications were "reasonable."[14]

In this aspect of its ruling, *Plessy* appears to have accorded with what many believe to be the historically understood meaning of the Equal Protection Clause: It did not mandate equality in the distribution of "social rights." Almost immediately, however, the Court encountered a complication. It assumed that all governmentally mandated discriminations – whether based on race, age, educational background, or any other trait – must at least be "reasonable" to be legally permissible and must be "enacted in good faith for the promotion of the public good, and not for the annoyance or oppression of a particular class." Applying this requirement, the Court readily accepted that it was reasonable for Louisiana to accommodate prevailing social attitudes by mandating "separate but equal" railroad cars for whites and Blacks. The difficulty for the Court's majority involved whether the separate accommodations involved in *Plessy* could be adjudged equal. As a matter of fact, the white cars were nearly invariably more comfortable than the Black cars. Increasing the awkwardness was that whites were in fact permitted to sit in the Black cars, which often doubled as smoking cars, if they so chose, while Blacks were wholly excluded from the white cars. The Court dealt curtly with objections such as these: "We consider the underlying fallacy of the plaintiff's argument to consist in the assumption that the enforced separation of the two races stamps the colored race with a badge of inferiority. If this be so, it is not by reason of anything found in the act, but solely because the colored race chooses to put that construction upon it."[15]

From a modern perspective, that assertion is hard to take seriously. Among all the opinions of the Supreme Court, the law professor Charles Black once wrote, this may be the point at which "[t]he curves of callousness and stupidity intersect at their respective maxima."[16] At the time of its decision, however, *Plessy v. Ferguson* attracted no stir. During the last two decades of the nineteenth century, race relations in the United States sank toward an abysmal low, especially in the South. For most of the country, as for most of the justices, it may have seemed almost unimaginable that the Constitution could mandate

---

[14] *Ibid.* at 544, 550.
[15] *Ibid.* at 551.
[16] Charles L. Black Jr., "The Lawfulness of the Segregation Decisions," 69 *Yale Law Journal* 421, 422 n.8 (1960).

what the Court described as the enforced "commingling" of the races. For people who perceived racial discrimination as natural, not invidious, it may even have been possible to believe that the accommodation of white preferences for separation conveyed no message of Black inferiority.

But it was also possible to perceive the reality of the situation. "The thin disguise of 'equal' accommodations for passengers in railroad coaches will not mislead any one," Justice John Marshall Harlan wrote in a solitary dissenting opinion. "[I]n view of the Constitution," he maintained, "there is in this country no superior, dominant, ruling class of citizens .... Our Constitution is color-blind."[17] That last resonant phrase, though widely ignored at the time, would later become a touchstone of disagreement in affirmative action debates beginning nearly a century later.

Meantime, despite Justice Harlan's protest, *Plessy*'s regime of "separate but equal" endured for more than fifty years. Over time, its morally shameful character grew apparent to increasing numbers of Americans, including those sitting on the Supreme Court. For the justices, a testing case involving race-based discrimination came in *Korematsu v. United States* (1944),[18] in which a military order had excluded all persons of Japanese ancestry from designated areas of the West Coast and effectively required them to submit to detention in "relocation centers." Confronted with a challenge to the exclusion order, the Court began its opinion by announcing that "all legal restrictions which curtail the civil rights of a single racial group are immediately suspect" and subject to "the most rigid scrutiny." This assertion was in one way remarkable. The Equal Protection Clause applies only to the states, not the federal government, and the Court was still a decade away from holding explicitly – as it later would, wholly without originalist pretensions – that the Due Process Clause of the Fifth Amendment establishes antidiscrimination norms binding on the government of the United States.

In *Korematsu*, however, the analysis that the Court conducted and the conclusion that it reached belied the egalitarian rhetoric with which the opinion commenced. The majority upheld the race-based exclusion based on scanty evidence contained in what a dissenting justice termed an

---

[17] *Ibid.* at 559 (Harlan, J., dissenting).
[18] 323 U.S. 214 (1944).

"unsworn, self-serving statement, untested by any cross-examination," offered by the general who had issued the exclusion order.[19] Writing for the Court, Justice Hugo Black insisted that "[t]o cast this case into outlines of racial prejudice ... merely confuses the issue."

Today, *Korematsu* is frequently grouped with *Dred Scott v. Sandford*, *Plessy v. Ferguson*, and *Lochner v. New York* as part of the constitutional "anticanon" of cases that illustrate egregiously misguided constitutional analysis from which lessons now have been learned and that the Supreme Court should never repeat. The Court acknowledged as much in 2018 in an opinion by Chief Justice Roberts: "*Korematsu* was gravely wrong the day it was decided, has been overruled in the court of history, and – to be clear – 'has no place in law under the Constitution.'"[20]

In the aftermath of *Korematsu*, predominant American social attitudes concerning race continued to evolve. In 1948, President Harry Truman ordered the integration of the armed forces, which had remained segregated throughout World War II. Increasing numbers of Blacks rose to national prominence. The 1948 platform of the Democratic Party included a strong civil rights plank for the first time. During roughly the same period, lawyers for the National Association for the Advancement of Colored People (NAACP) had begun a brilliant legal campaign attacking segregation in public education.[21] For tactical reasons, NAACP lawyers initially accepted the "separate but equal" framework traceable to *Plessy v. Ferguson*. Having done so, they then demonstrated in one setting after another that the separate educational facilities maintained for racial minorities were not at all equal to those that whites enjoyed. After winning a number of victories with this strategy, they prepared to argue that racially discriminatory education was inherently unequal and thus unconstitutional.

---

[19] *Korematsu*, 323 U.S. at 245 (Jackson, J., dissenting).

[20] *Trump v. Hawaii*, 585 U.S. 667, 710 (2018) (quoting *Korematsu*, 323 U.S. at 248 (Jackson, J., dissenting)). Chief Justice Roberts offered his observation in response to the argument of Justice Sotomayor's dissenting opinion that the majority had repeated the error of *Korematsu* by upholding a presidential proclamation that restricted entry into the United States by nationals of six predominantly Muslim countries. According to Justice Sotomayor, the proclamation, like the exclusion order in *Korematsu*, rested on "dangerous stereotypes" and "animus." In response, Roberts replied that the order upheld in *Trump v. Hawaii* was "facially neutral" and involved no discrimination against US citizens.

[21] See Mark V. Tushnet, *The NAACP's Legal Strategy against Segregated Education, 1925–50* (Chapel Hill, NC/London, UK: University of North Carolina Press, 1987).

The NAACP pressed this contention in *Brown v. Board of Education* (1954).[22] In the justices' initial deliberations, they found themselves troubled and divided. However wrong segregation might be, some worried that they lacked an adequate legal basis to upset the rule that had prevailed for more than fifty years under *Plessy*. They also fretted that it might lie beyond the proper reach of judicial power to decree a revolutionary change in racial relations in a significant portion of the United States. With early discussions "indicat[ing] a vote somewhere between five to four for sustaining school segregation and six to three for striking it down,"[23] the justices took the unusual step of asking for a second round of arguments in the case. Prior to the reargument, Chief Justice Fred M. Vinson – who was generally unsympathetic to the challengers' case – died. To replace Vinson, President Dwight Eisenhower nominated the far more progressive Earl Warren, a former governor of California. Justice Felix Frankfurter is said to have remarked, "[T]his is the first solid piece of evidence I've ever had that there really is a God."[24]

Under the leadership of the new chief justice, the Court decided *Brown* by the astonishing vote of 9–0, ruling that legally mandated segregation in public education violated the Equal Protection Clause. Historical inquiries, conducted by the parties at the Court's request, gave the justices little help in reaching that conclusion. Nevertheless, the Court refused to be deterred. "In approaching this problem, we cannot turn the clock back to 1868 when the [Fourteenth] Amendment was adopted, or even to 1896 when *Plessy v. Ferguson* was written," Warren wrote. Focusing on the present day, he emphasized that education had become "perhaps the most important function of state and local governments" and that segregation, as a matter of social and psychological fact, communicated a message of race-based inferiority. In an opinion lacking further rhetorical flourishes, the Court held that "in the field of public education the doctrine of 'separate but equal' has no place."[25]

On the day that the Court decided *Brown*, it paid even less heed to evidence of the Constitution's originally understood meaning

---

[22] 347 U.S. 483 (1954).
[23] Michael J. Klarman, "An Interpretive History of Modern Equal Protection," 90 *Michigan Law Review* 213, 242 (1991).
[24] Phillip Elman and Norman Silber, "The Solicitor General's Office, Justice Frankfurter, and Civil Rights Litigation, 1946–1960: An Oral History," 100 *Harvard Law Review* 817, 840 (1987).
[25] *Brown*, 347 U.S. at 492, 495.

in a ruling that mandated an end to discrimination in the District of Columbia schools, to which the Equal Protection Clause did not apply. *Bolling v. Sharpe* (1954)[26] reasoned that segregation in the District of Columbia schools "constitutes an arbitrary deprivation of [Black children's] liberty in violation of the Due Process Clause" of the Fifth Amendment, which was added to the Constitution in 1791 and was widely viewed as compatible with slavery at that time. In support of its holding, the Court cited *Korematsu* as having established that "[c]lassifications based solely upon race must be scrutinized with particular care, since they are contrary to our traditions and hence constitutionally suspect."

Although *Brown* mandated a revolutionary change in the organization of Southern education, the Supreme Court did not insist that the revolution begin immediately. Instead of ordering that schools must desegregate forthwith, the Court called for yet a third argument in the case, devoted solely to the issue of remedies.[27] Nearly a year later, the Court pronounced that responsibility for school desegregation rested in the first instance with state and local officials, not the federal courts. Such officials, it said, must proceed, not necessarily immediately, but with "all deliberate speed." As I shall explain more fully later, the Supreme Court did not begin to insist firmly on effective desegregation of the public schools until the mid-1960s, after Congress had shown its commitment to racial equality by enacting the 1964 Civil Rights Act, the most sweeping civil rights legislation since Reconstruction. (A few courageous judges on the lower federal courts took firmer stands, sometimes at considerable personal risk to themselves and their families.)

To some extent, the Supreme Court appears to have been waiting, attempting to create as few waves as possible, hoping for public opinion to rally to its side. Among its temporizing steps, the Court went out of its way to avoid ruling on the constitutionality of state prohibitions against interracial marriage. In *Naim v. Naim* (1955),[28] the Court essentially refused to decide a case challenging a Virginia statute that forbade whites to marry nonwhites (except, bizarrely, the descendants of Pocahontas). Justice Frankfurter, a former Harvard

---

[26] *Bolling v. Sharpe*, 347 U.S. 497, 500 (1954).
[27] See *Brown v. Board of Education* (II), 349 U.S. 294 (1955).
[28] 350 U.S. 891 (1955).

Law School professor who had also been a close advisor to Franklin Roosevelt and who had as much confidence in his political as his legal judgment, apparently persuaded his fellow justices that interracial marriage aroused such "deep" and hostile feeling that a Court pronouncement would undermine support for *Brown* and school desegregation.[29] On a pretext, the Court dismissed the appeal and permitted the statute to be enforced.

By 1967, the Court at last stood ready to condemn statutes barring interracial marriage. In *Loving v. Virginia*,[30] the justices ruled unanimously that such prohibitions violated the Equal Protection Clause. Within a few more years, the Court had formulated the still-applicable "strict judicial scrutiny" test under which it will invalidate all laws that discriminate on the basis of race unless they are "necessary to promote a compelling government interest."

Since *Loving*, the Court has not backslid. *Palmore v. Sidoti*[31] (1984) reflects its insistence that classifications rooted in attitudes of racial hostility are deeply suspect and virtually never permissible. *Palmore* arose from the efforts of a divorced white father to have his daughter removed from the custody of his ex-wife after she married a Black man. A state court held in favor of the father on the ground that the transfer of custody would promote the best interests of the child – the usual legal standard in child custody matters – because if the daughter remained in a biracial household, "social stigmatization ... is sure to come." The Supreme Court rejected this reasoning. By a unanimous vote, the Court ruled that even if private prejudices might lead to "social stigmatization," such attitudes could not be permitted to influence a child custody decision: "The Constitution cannot control such prejudices but neither can it tolerate them. Private biases may be outside the reach of the law, but the law cannot, directly or indirectly, give them effect."[32]

Although *Palmore* did not employ the language of "strict scrutiny," its approach helps to illustrate what strict judicial scrutiny means. In some minimal way, it might have been "rational" for a court to consider whether a child is likely to suffer social stigmatization from living in a biracial household as one among many factors relevant to

---

[29] See Klarman, "An Interpretive History of Modern Equal Protection," *supra*, at 243.
[30] See *Loving v. Virginia*, 388 U.S. 1 (1967).
[31] 466 U.S. 429 (1984).
[32] *Ibid.* at 433.

determining the child's best interests. Under strict scrutiny, however, the mere fact that it would be rational (in some minimal sense) to take race into account will not suffice to justify governmental decisions based on race.

When social and doctrinal developments from Reconstruction through *Brown* and *Loving* are viewed in hindsight, it is remarkable how fast a national consensus emerged that publicly enforced race discrimination, which had been a feature of American life from the beginning, was morally and constitutionally intolerable. In the 1950s, the correctness of *Brown v. Board of Education* was much debated. By the 1970s, *Brown* enjoyed almost unanimous support in the legal community. Today, anyone who maintained that the case was wrongly decided would be disqualified from service on the Supreme Court. The president would not nominate, and the Senate would not confirm, a person who took that view.

If we pause to probe why *Brown* enjoys such iconic status, the answer, as we have seen, has nothing to do with fidelity to the original understanding of constitutional language. It has much more to do with *Brown*'s capacity to symbolize what nearly all now view with pride as a towering moral and political achievement in our national history: the rejection of state-sponsored race-based segregation as an accepted feature of American life in many institutions throughout the country.

Also contributing to *Brown*'s iconic status, perhaps ironically, is its capacity to stand for different principles in the minds of different people. That capacity was on display in *SFFA v. Harvard*, discussed at the beginning of this chapter, as it is in surrounding debates about race-based affirmative action. The majority opinion in *SFFA*, which contained almost no discussion of the Fourteenth Amendment's originally understood meaning, relied heavily on an interpretation of *Brown* as committed to a constitutional ideal of colorblindness. (Some commentators refer to the conservative justices' centering of *Brown* in their analysis of the constitutionality affirmative action as "*Brown* originalism,"[33] substituting the original meaning of *Brown* for the original meaning of the Fourteenth Amendment as the foundation for their arguments.) As we shall see, the dissenting justices in *SFFA* read *Brown* quite differently. In their view, *Brown* should be read as a case recognizing the

---

[33] Pamela S. Karlan, "What Can Brown® Do for You?: Neutral Principles and the Struggle over the Equal Protection Clause," 58 *Duke Law Journal* 1049, 1052 (2009).

urgent importance of racial integration to ensure the equal rights and status of minorities, and especially Blacks, in American society.

From Invidious Discrimination to Affirmative Action

When the Supreme Court began to treat race-based discrimination as constitutionally suspect in the middle of the twentieth century, it did so in cases in which the government employed racial classifications to promote white supremacy. Not immediately obvious, at least to everyone, was whether race-based decision-making would be appraised in the same way when used for such purposes as fostering integration and enhanced opportunities for racial minorities. An initial reliance on race to promote integration came when the Court began to insist that previously segregated school districts must make race-based school assignments in order to dismantle previously segregated regimes. In *Brown*, the Court had apparently assumed that it would suffice for segregated school systems merely to end expressly race-based assignments of whites to all-white schools and of Blacks to all-Black schools. By the late 1960s and early 1970s, however, the Court began to demand meaningful integration, with substantial numbers of white and Black students actually attending the same schools. In order to achieve that result, the Court – in a highly controversial development – upheld lower court orders requiring the busing of some students from the schools closest to their homes to schools in other neighborhoods.

In these cases, the Supreme Court treated race-based school assignments as a necessary remedy for historic and continuing racial segregation. Nevertheless, its position invited (though it did not require) the inference that race-based classifications of school students were constitutionally acceptable, not suspect, when employed to integrate racial minorities into traditionally white environments. The Court's relevant decisions all involved school districts that had been ordered to redress previously discriminatory practices. On at least one occasion, however, the Court encouraged voluntary steps by school officials (not required as remedies for past unlawful actions) to take account of students' races in order to achieve integrated school environments. In *Swann v. Charlotte-Mecklenburg Board of Education* (1971),[34] Chief Justice Warren Burger wrote: "School authorities ...

---

[34] 402 U.S. 1, 16 (1971).

might well conclude ... that in order to prepare students to live in a pluralistic society each school should have a prescribed ration of Negro to white students reflecting the proportion for the district as a whole."

Thirty-six years later, a bitterly divided Roberts Court, by a vote of 5–4, repudiated that position. In *Parents Involved in Community Schools v. Seattle School District No. 1* (2007),[35] the Court held that local school districts in Seattle, Washington, and Louisville, Kentucky, had violated the Equal Protection Clause when they voluntarily took race into account in assigning students to public schools for the purpose of promoting integration. In the lead opinion announcing the Court's decision, Chief Justice John Roberts dismissed what the Court had said in *Swann* as ill-considered "dicta" that was not necessary to the Court's actual holding about the rights and obligations of the parties before it. According to Roberts, the touchstone for considering governmental classifications based on race was *Brown*, and *Brown* was best read as deeply suspicious, if not flatly condemning, of all race-based school assignments, even for the purpose of bringing about more integration. "The way to stop discrimination on the basis of race is to stop discriminating on the basis of race," he wrote. In a short, unusually personal dissenting opinion, Justice John Paul Stevens, who had served on the Court for more than thirty years, observed: "It is my firm conviction that no Member of the Court that I joined in 1975 would have agreed with today's decision."[36] No other justice disputed that assessment.

As in the movement from *Plessy* to *Brown*, constitutional change was underway. Chief Justice Roberts's opinion in *Parents Involved* prefigured the opinion he would later write for six justices in *SFFA v. Harvard*, involving affirmative action not only by Harvard but also by the University of North Carolina and other traditionally selective state colleges and universities (which, unlike primary and secondary schools that educate everyone within a school district, admit some students while denying admission to others).

In the social climate that existed prior to *Brown* and the civil rights revolution of the 1950s and 1960s, voluntarily adopted policies of race-conscious admissions that aimed at benefitting racial minorities would have been politically unimaginable. And when selective colleges began to practice affirmative action in the aftermath of *Brown*, their

---

[35] 551 U.S. 701 (2007).
[36] *Ibid.* at 803 (Stevens, J., dissenting).

efforts predictably drew challenges by whites claiming to be the victims of constitutionally intolerable "reverse discrimination." But the issues raised by uses of race to promote integration arguably differ from those posed cases involving reliance on race to exclude and demean disfavored minorities. Under the theory inspired by the *Carolene Products* case[37] (which I briefly discussed in Chapter 2) that the aim of searching judicial scrutiny of legislative decisions should be to protect "discrete and insular" minority groups from "prejudice" in the political process, affirmative action programs would trigger no alarms. Such programs are designed to benefit members of minority groups rather than harm them, and they are not likely to be motivated by prejudice against the white majority. Colleges and universities routinely, and mostly without objection, prefer some students over others based on such considerations as their grades, test scores, athletic ability, and state of residence. On a *Carolene Products* theory, preferences based on minority status would be no more objectionable than a preference based on one of these criteria.

In the *Bakke* case, Justice Powell had of course adopted a somewhat different view, centering interests in fairness to what he called "innocent" whites who had no complicity in past societal injustices. Still, he laid out a framework for constitutionally permissible affirmative action designed to promote the anticipated benefits of diversity in higher education. In *Grutter v. Bollinger* (2003),[38] Justice Sandra Day O'Connor, who like Powell was a moderate conservative sometimes prone to difference-splitting, not only reaffirmed the core elements of the *Bakke* compromise but also cited the importance of diversity in arenas beyond university classrooms:

> [M]ajor American businesses have made clear that the skills needed in today's increasingly global marketplace can only be developed through exposure to widely diverse people, cultures, ideas, and viewpoints. What is more, high-ranking retired officers and civilian leaders of the United States military assert that, "[b]ased on [their] decades of experience," a "highly qualified, racially diverse officer corps ... is essential to the military's ability to fulfill its princip[al] mission to provide national security." ... At present, "the military cannot achieve an officer

---

[37] *United States v. Carolene Products Company*, 304 U.S. 144 (1938).
[38] 539 U.S. 306, 330–31 (2003).

corps that is *both* highly qualified *and* racially diverse unless the service academies and [other officer training programs] use[] limited race-conscious recruiting and admissions policies."

At the same time, however, Justice O'Connor took the unusual step of observing in a majority opinion that judicial tolerance of race-based affirmative action might be subject to a temporal limit: "We expect that 25 years from now, the use of racial preferences will no longer be necessary to further the [diversity] interest approved today."

Meanwhile, the opposition to affirmative action – including on constitutional grounds – never waned. In *Grutter* and then in subsequent cases, conservative justices kept up a drumbeat of criticism denouncing affirmative action as both invidiously discriminatory against whites and as implicitly stigmatizing of its intended beneficiaries. The achievements of talented minority students would inevitably be tainted by doubts about whether they could have earned their credentials without a racial preference, Justice Clarence Thomas argued.[39] The Court's last major decision upholding an affirmative action program came in 2016, written by the moderate conservative Justice Anthony Kennedy and joined only by justices counted as "liberals."[40] When the Court agreed to hear the *SFFA* case following President Trump's nomination of the three new justices who established a conservative supermajority, there was not much doubt about the outcome.

Although Chief Justice Roberts did not formally announce the overruling of any prior cases, he construed and applied the strict scrutiny formula in such a way that no affirmative action program, including Harvard's, could satisfy it. Harvard, Roberts reasoned, had refused to specify the number of minority students necessary to achieve the diversity that it sought, and, absent such a specification, it could not demonstrate that its practices were narrowly tailored to the attainment of its avowed educational goal. Taken in isolation, the Court's demand that Harvard specify a target number of minority students might seem reasonable. But the Court's interpretation of the strict formula confronted Harvard with a Catch-22 that no affirmative action program could escape. As Roberts surely recognized, if Harvard had articulated how many minority students were necessary to achieve the diversity

---

[39] Ibid. at 373 (Thomas, J., concurring in part and dissenting in part); *Fisher v. University of Texas*, 570 U.S. 297, 333–34 (2013) (Thomas, J., concurring).
[40] *Fisher v. University of Texas*, 579 U.S. 365 (2016).

that it sought, the Court would have condemned it for maintaining a de facto racial quota rather than giving every applicant the individualized consideration that the Court's precedents required.

Notably absent from Chief Justice Roberts's *SFFA* opinion, which all of the conservative justices joined, was any serious reliance on the originally understood meaning of the Equal Protection Clause. In an interesting inversion of a more typical division among the justices, the opinion in *SFFA* that rested most heavily on evidence of the Fourteenth Amendment's originally understood meaning was Justice Sonia Sotomayor's dissent, in which the two other liberal justices, Kagan and Jackson, joined. Justice Sotomayor cited several pieces of Reconstruction legislation adopted by the same Congress that sponsored the Fourteenth Amendment that included race-based appropriations distinctively for categories of "colored" citizens.[41] Based partly on that evidence, she argued that "[t]he text and history of the Fourteenth Amendment make clear that the Equal Protection Clause permits race-conscious measures" intended to aid racial minorities.

Chief Justice Roberts chose not to respond to the evidence on which Justice Sotomayor relied. Without citation to any specific opinion of the Court in any prior case, the chief justice offered only the cryptic and enigmatic comment that "[t]he dissents ... fail to mention that the entirety of their analysis of the Equal Protection Clause – the statistics, the cases, the history – has been considered and rejected before."[42] Although Justice Thomas filed a concurring opinion maintaining that the original meaning of the Fourteenth Amendment forbade racial preferences that are not necessary to a compelling governmental interest, none of the other ostensibly originalist justices joined him, possibly because the historical support for his position was so weak. If one turns to *SFFA* to draw lessons about the current Supreme Court's governing philosophy of constitutional interpretation, one conclusion should be that in this context as in some others, originalism takes a backseat to conservatism at least as often as the reverse occurs.[43]

---

[41] See *SFFA*, 600 U.S. at 325 (Sotomayor, J., dissenting) (citing statutes providing funds for "'the relief of destitute colored women and children,' without regard to prior enslavement," Act of July 28, 1866, 14 Stat. 317, and for "colored soldiers and sailors" who had served in the Union Army, Act of June 15, 1866, 14 Stat. 357; Act of Mar. 3, 1869, ch. 122, 15 Stat. 301; Act of Mar. 3, 1873, 17 Stat. 528).

[42] *Ibid.* at 227.

[43] In a footnote, the Court reserved the question of whether its reasoning would apply to the admissions policies of the US military academies. See 600 U.S. at 213 n.4.

Rational Basis Review

In *SFFA v. Harvard*, the parties challenging the admissions practices of Harvard and the University of North Carolina trained their complaints on the use of race as a consideration. But what if they had complained about admissions preferences for students with good grades or high test scores, for recruited athletes, for applicants from particular states – a common concern of many state universities – or for the children of alumni? How would the Supreme Court have assessed their objections to criteria such as these?

Within the judicially devised structure of equal protection doctrine, the strict scrutiny that applies to race-based classifications (as well as those based on religion and national origin) is a rarity. Normally, in determining whether challenged statutes or policies pass muster under the Equal Protection Clause, courts apply "rational basis review." Under this formula, nearly all of the classifications that governments sometimes employ – including those based on age, experience, education, and income – are routinely upheld as long as they are "rationally related" to a "legitimate" governmental interest. As with much else about equal protection doctrine, an understanding of this standard, which the Court has described as a "paradigm of judicial restraint,"[44] requires an awareness of its history.

In its first encounter with the Fourteenth Amendment in the *Slaughter-House Cases* (1873),[45] the Supreme Court said, "We doubt very much whether any action of the State not directed ... against the negroes as a class, or on account of their race, will ever be held to come within the purview of" the Equal Protection Clause. During the so-called *Lochner* era that ran from the late nineteenth century through 1937, however, the Court began to insist that for a statutory classification to afford equal protection, it must be "reasonable" or, in a later formulation, not "arbitrary." Throughout that period, formulae such as these paralleled similar tests that the Court deployed under the Due Process Clause to review and not infrequently invalidate economic regulatory legislation. When the Court abandoned *Lochner*-style substantive due process review, it simultaneously relaxed its scrutiny of economic regulatory legislation under the Equal Protection Clause.

---

[44] *FCC v. Beach Communications, Inc.*, 508 U.S. 307, 313–14 (1993).
[45] 83 U.S. 36, 81 (1873).

Since the New Deal, the appropriateness of the "rational basis" formula for the vast bulk of equal protection cases has not engendered much controversy. All agree that the requirement that states afford everyone "the equal protection of the laws" cannot mean that the government must treat everyone "the same." Nearly all accept the dictates of common sense that the very young can be denied drivers' licenses, as can the blind, and that admissions to state universities can be based on high school grades and test scores. In explanation of how the rational basis formula reflects a guarantee of "equal protection," it is often said that the Equal Protection Clause requires that like cases be treated alike but that it allows cases to be treated as unlike as long as there is a rational reason for the government to classify people differently. For example, rules classifying some people as eligible to drive automobiles and others as ineligible – based, for instance, on their age, eyesight, and performance on a driving test – are permissible if they plausibly promote highway safety. Similarly, criteria for admission to public colleges differentiate like from unlike cases if they are designed to separate those with more academic ability and grit from those with less and if they serve any "legitimate" purpose such as distributing educational opportunities to those most likely to benefit from them. Further relaxing the demands of rational basis review, the Court normally takes the word of government lawyers for what a law's purportedly legitimate purpose is or was. If a state government taxes one type of business at a higher rate than another, the Court will ask only whether there is any imaginably rational basis for the differential treatment, such as a belief that one is more beneficial to the state's economy or culture than the other.[46]

Although the Supreme Court almost always upholds legislative judgments in applying rational basis review, there are occasional exceptions. A revealing study identified 110 cases in which the Court applied the rational basis test during the 25-year period from 1971 to 1996.[47] In 100 of those cases, the Court upheld the challenged law, but in 10, or about 9 percent of the total, it found a constitutional violation. In some of the outlier cases in the sample and in a few more that have arisen subsequently, commentators apprehend that the justices in the majority are not really applying the traditional rational basis

---

[46] See *Fitzgerald v. Racing Ass'n of Central Iowa*, 539 U.S. 103 (2003).
[47] See Robert C. Farrell, "Successful Rational Basis Claims in the Supreme Court from the 1971 Term through Romer v. Evans," 32 *Indiana Law Review* 357, 370 (1999).

test even if they purport to do so. In the 1970s, invalidation of a statute that discriminated against women, although nominally pursuant to rational basis review, prefigured the Court's announcement a few years later that sex-based classifications should be subject to a formally identified mode of heightened scrutiny. More recently, the Court has sometimes appeared to apply more than normally stringent standards in scrutinizing classifications that discriminate against gays and lesbians, even though it has not said explicitly that it is doing so. I shall discuss both sex discrimination cases and gay rights cases later in the chapter.

In some cases, however, the Court's surprisingly searching applications of rational basis review seem more ad hoc. A now-dated but perhaps still representative example comes from *United States Department of Agriculture v. Moreno* (1973).[48] *Moreno* held that a federal statute offended equal protection principles by denying food stamps to "any household containing an individual who is unrelated to any other member of the household." The Court might easily have upheld the statute by ruling that Congress could permissibly choose to subsidize only households that resemble traditional families. In determining eligibility for spending programs, Congress generally enjoys great flexibility to protect the public treasury by drawing lines, and lines that give preferences to families and family members are permissible in many contexts. Instead, despite its frequent assertions that legislation will be upheld if there is any imaginable basis on which it might be supported, the Court focused on what it said was the statute's real purpose – to exclude "hippie" communes from achieving eligibility. Pronouncing that "a bare congressional desire to harm a politically unpopular group cannot constitute a *legitimate* governmental interest," the Court invalidated the challenged statutory exclusion.[49]

Plainly implicit in *Moreno* and a few similar cases is an assumption that not all governmental purposes are legitimate and that not all means even to legitimate purposes meet the minimal demands of rationality. It bears emphasis, however, that the morally judgmental disposition reflected in *Moreno* rarely manifests itself in rational basis cases. Where rational basis review applies, the Court's dominant tendency is to uphold any classification that a legislature may adopt. Sometimes, the justices recognize, the government just needs to be

[48] 413 U.S. 528 (1973).
[49] *Ibid.* at 534.

able to draw lines – as when it says that those who are sixteen are eligible to drive but those who are fifteen years and eleven months old are not. And sometimes the effort to enforce norms of fairness when the government gives benefits to some but not others – for example, to apple growers but not cranberry growers, or vice versa – may seem to risk intruding the judiciary too deeply into the familiar horse-trading of the political process. So far, the justices in Supreme Court's current conservative supermajority have shown no disposition to upset the Court's traditional commitment to highly deferential rational basis review in nearly all cases.

Racially Disparate Impact

The dichotomous pairing of strict judicial scrutiny for race-based classifications with rational basis review of almost all others can pose testing issues of categorization in cases of "racially disparate impact." *Washington v. Davis*[50] (1976) exemplifies the phenomenon. Under a rule adopted by the District of Columbia, candidates to become police officers had to record a minimum score on a test designed to measure verbal ability and reading comprehension. On its face, that hiring criterion had nothing to do with race, and normally it would pass muster easily under rational basis review (as is the case with the use of standardized test scores as a basis for college admissions). The complicating factor was that Black candidates failed the police exam in *Washington v. Davis* at four times the rate of whites. Citing the test's skewed impact, challengers argued that it was racially discriminatory in effect, even if not in form, and that it should therefore trigger heightened scrutiny analogous if not identical to the strict scrutiny that the Supreme Court applies to explicitly race-based classifications.

The Court rejected that argument. Racially disparate impact, such as that resulting from the civil service test in *Washington v. Davis*, does not by itself constitute forbidden race discrimination, the justices held. Nor do such statutes ordinarily call for heightened judicial scrutiny. Rather, under *Washington v. Davis*, rational basis review applies to statutes and policies with racially disparate impacts unless a challenger can prove that the statute or policy in question was enacted for the discriminatory purpose of harming a racial minority group.

---

[50] 426 U.S. 229 (1976).

The Court's reasoning in *Washington v. Davis* was blunt. In American society, there are likely to be many rules and policies under which Blacks on average fare less well than whites. If all governmental classifications with racially disparate impacts were invalid absent a compelling governmental justification, courts could expect challenges to "a whole range of tax, welfare, public service, regulatory, and licensing statutes that may be more burdensome to the poor and [thus] to the average black [who is more likely to be poor] than to the more affluent white."[51] What is more, governmental bodies (for better or for worse) would feel a subtle pressure to pay attention to race in order to avoid racially disparate impacts that could cause them to be sued. In light of this assessment of the costs and benefits, the Supreme Court made racially discriminatory intent, rather than racially discriminatory effects, the measure of constitutional permissibility in cases alleging race-based discrimination under the Equal Protection Clause.

Although the complaining parties in the cases in which Supreme Court devised its disparate impact jurisprudence were members of minority groups, classifications that are race-neutral on their faces can sometimes have disparate impacts that adversely affect whites. To take a topical example, in the aftermath of *SFFA v. Harvard*, some public school systems and colleges have adopted admissions preferences for students who are economically disadvantaged or who reside in zip codes that they know to be predominantly inhabited by members of racial minority groups. If the purpose for reliance on these criteria is to increase representation of students who have grown up in poverty without regard to their races, they should easily survive rational basis review. Expanding opportunities for the poor or those who grew up in impoverished neighborhoods is a legitimate governmental aim to which admissions preferences are rationally related. But if the purpose motivating a facially race-neutral policy is to increase representation of racial minorities, matters grow more complicated.

If the government gave preferences to those within certain zip codes with the aim of excluding racial minorities, that discriminatory purpose would trigger strict judicial scrutiny under *Washington v. Davis*. But should the same test apply if a nonracial criterion is employed for the purpose of increasing, rather than decreasing, opportunities for racial minorities? The pursuit of a racially defined goal

[51] *Ibid.* at 248.

(such as diversity) by race-neutral means (such as a preference based on zip code or low income) does not require government bodies to explicitly classify anyone on the basis of race. And in cases in which decision-makers act for mixed motives – for example, by granting a preference to applicants from impoverished backgrounds partly to benefit those who have had to overcome economic hardship but partly to enhance racial diversity – which of those purposes should determine the applicable level of judicial scrutiny under the Equal Protection Clause? The Supreme Court is likely to confront questions such as these sooner rather than later following its outlawing of explicitly race-based affirmative action in *SFFA v. Harvard* and its earlier decision forbidding consideration of race in making public school assignments in *Parents Involved v. Seattle School District*.[52]

Sex Discrimination

Through most of constitutional history, discrimination against women was accepted as a matter of course. In an 1873 case upholding a statute that denied women the right to practice law, the Court observed that "[t]he natural and proper timidity and delicacy which belongs to the female sex evidently unfits it for many of the occupations of civil life."[53] The Court's tone had not changed notably by 1948, when it sustained a law barring most women from obtaining bartenders' licenses: "The fact that women may now have achieved the virtues that men long claimed as their prerogatives and now indulge in vices that men have long practiced, does not preclude the States from drawing a sharp line between the sexes."[54]

The first decision invalidating a statute that discriminated on the basis of sex came in 1971.[55] The timing reveals much. By 1971 cultural attitudes about women's roles had shifted unmistakably. Shortly afterward, in a case challenging the military's policy of automatically providing "dependency" or spousal-support allowances to married male but not to married female members of the armed forces, Ruth Bader Ginsburg – later to be named a Supreme Court justice herself – argued

---

[52] For a helpful discussion of the legal issues, see Sonja Starr, "The Magnet School Wars and the Future of Colorblindness," 76 *Stanford Law Review* 161 (2024).
[53] *Bradwell v. Illinois*, 83 U.S. (16 Wall.) 130, 141 (1873).
[54] *Goesaert v. Cleary*, 335 U.S. 464, 465 (1948).
[55] See *Reed v. Reed*, 404 U.S. 71 (1971).

that sex-based classifications should be deemed constitutionally "suspect," and subjected to strict judicial scrutiny, just like those based on race. Ginsburg maintained that sex, like race, was an immutable trait, crucial to self-identity, "which the dominant culture views as a badge of inferiority justifying disadvantaged treatment." Ginsburg won the case, *Frontiero v. Richardson* (1973),[56] with eight of the nine justices agreeing that women were treated unfairly. But she could persuade only four justices, one short of a majority, that statutes that discriminate on the basis of sex should be analyzed the same way as statutes that discriminate based on race.

Whether ultimately justified or not, the Court's hesitation was understandable. Sex, like race, is a highly salient characteristic. People almost always notice the sex of those with whom they interact. Justice Ginsburg was also right that women have historically been disadvantaged on the basis of sex and that the disadvantages remained palpable in 1973: Women on average earned lower incomes than men, continued to confront formal and informal employment discrimination, and had achieved comparatively few positions of political and professional leadership. But if the struggle for sex equality has obvious parallels to the struggle for racial equality, there are important differences as well. First, although the distinction between males and females is not always binary, the physiological differences between men and women are typically more than skin deep. Prior to modern medical interventions, only women could get pregnant; men on average are stronger and heavier than women; and so forth. Second, whereas race would likely be irrelevant in an ideal world, sexual attraction would remain, as might sex-linked desires for privacy (e.g., in separate restrooms and showers). A third complicating factor is that women are a (small) majority of the American population, not a "discrete and insular minority." None of these considerations suggests that sex discrimination is not a problem of constitutional dimension – only that issues of sex-based discrimination present distinctive complexities.

With respect to the standard for judicial review, the Supreme Court ultimately decided to split the difference between the strict scrutiny applied to race-based classifications and the rational basis review used in most other cases. *Craig v. Boren*[57] (1976) held that

---

[56] 411 U.S. 677 (1973).
[57] 429 U.S. 190, 197 (1976).

sex-based discriminations should be deemed invalid unless they "serve important governmental objectives" and are "substantially related to achievement of those objectives." To this "intermediate scrutiny" formula the Court later added the gloss that sex-based discriminations are impermissible unless supported by "an 'exceedingly persuasive justification.'"[58]

At issue in *Craig* was an Oklahoma statute that forbade men between the ages of eighteen and twenty-one, but not women of the same age, to buy low-alcohol beer. The state defended the statute as a means of stopping drunk driving, to which it said that young men were more prone than young women. The Court, however, found the supporting evidence insufficient to justify the differential treatment. Its decision illumines a good deal about the "intermediate" scrutiny to which sex-based discriminations are subject.

Although many of the arguments for treating sex-based classifications as suspect involve historic discrimination against women, *Craig* applied elevated scrutiny to invalidate a statute that discriminated against men. In insisting on parallel treatment, the Supreme Court may have believed statutes that discriminate against men to be as presumptively unfair as those that discriminate against women. It may also have believed that sex stereotypes are the mirror images of one another. If so, a statute based on a stereotype of males as prone to engage in risky behavior such as drinking and driving may tend to reinforce a parallel stereotype of women as cautious and risk averse. In the long run, sex-based stereotypes probably tend to limit the opportunities open to men and women alike.

It also bears notice that although the statute involved in *Craig* failed intermediate scrutiny, it almost certainly would have passed the rational basis test. The state had a legitimate interest in reducing drunk driving, and the state actually adduced evidence that while men between the ages of eighteen and twenty-one displayed at least a modest tendency to drive while drunk, women of the same age almost never did. Nevertheless, the Court refused to permit the discrimination between men and women. Even when sex-based discrimination is otherwise rational, the Court apparently concluded, it can impose costs – possibly, once again, by reinforcing cultural stereotypes.

---

[58] See *United States v. Virginia*, 518 U.S. 515, 524 (1996) (quoting *Mississippi University for Women v. Hogan*, 458 U.S. 718, 724 [1982]).

Although *Craig* both established a test for the constitutionality of statutes that discriminate on the basis of sex and highlighted the Supreme Court's concern with sex-based stereotypes, subsequent decisions do not exhibit an entirely uniform approach to its application. For the most part, however, the cases manifest a diminishing tolerance for sex-based classifications over time. The most cited precedent is *United States v. Virginia* (1996),[59] in which the Court held that a state violated the Equal Protection Clause by excluding women from a prestigious college offering a distinctive educational program, at least without offering a comparably excellent program exclusively for women. The opinion's author was Ruth Bader Ginsburg, the trail-blazing lawyer for the plaintiff in *Frontiero* who became the second woman ever to serve on the Supreme Court when she was nominated by President Bill Clinton in 1993. In *United States v. Virginia*, Ginsburg emphasized that states may not discriminate between men and women based on stereotypes or overbroad generalizations. "Parties who seek to defend gender-based government action must demonstrate an 'exceedingly persuasive justification' for that action," she wrote. "The burden of justification is demanding and it rests entirely on the State."[60]

Nonetheless, *United States v. Virginia* pointedly stopped short of terming sex-based classifications as suspect as those based on race. To the contrary, the Court said in a footnote that it did not mean to decide whether separate classes for men and women in otherwise coeducational institutions would be permissible as long as equally good opportunities existed for both. The difficulty, of course, is that stereotypes and overbroad generalizations can be hard to distinguish from the reasoned awareness of "real differences" that can sometimes justify sex-based classifications. On the one hand, the lower courts have overwhelmingly assumed that real physiological differences between men and women justify single-sex athletic teams (although the Supreme Court has not had occasion to say so expressly). On the other hand, *United States v. Virginia* found that the state relied on an impermissible stereotype in concluding that women could not profit from the physically and psychologically arduous educational methods employed at Virginia Military Institute.

---

[59] 518 U.S. 515 (1996).
[60] *Ibid.* at 532, 533.

Although the Supreme Court appears committed to its intermediate scrutiny test for the permissibility of sex-based classifications, an important assumption that has long underlain the doctrine is coming under increasing pressure. This is the assumption that sex is both fixed at birth and binary and defines people's life-long identities: Everyone is born either male or female and stays that way. As one reflection of that assumption, the leading cases on sex-based discrimination under the Constitution have mostly used the terms "sex" and "gender" interchangeably.

Today, although usage is in flux and purportedly empirical claims are sometimes contested, it is much more common to treat "sex" and "gender" as distinguishable concepts. When that distinction is drawn, sex depends on physiology. Gender, by contrast, is a matter of presentation and self-identification. As a further complication, neither sex nor gender is necessarily strictly binary, and medical interventions can make sex subject to change.

As the concepts of sex and gender become more complex and contested, the lower courts have increasingly needed to resolve disputes about who is a male and who is a female. A recurring issue is whether, and if so when, a governmental decision-maker's rejection of an individual's self-categorization – for example, to exclude a person from a female swim team or bathroom based on "sex assigned at birth" – constitutes constitutionally forbidden sex or gender discrimination.[61]

When questions of this kind come before the Supreme Court, as they inevitably will, the justices may be able to extract some guidance from decisions crafted to resolve other issues involving sex and gender discrimination, but the prior cases could all be viewed as distinguishable. The decisions to date involve the permissibility of differential treatment for males and females once they have been sorted into those categories, not the prior question of how males and females can be distinguished permissibly. The language and original history of the Fourteenth Amendment will provide no help. In circumstances such as these, the current Court, as we have seen in prior chapters, sometimes appeals to "history and tradition" as sources of authority. Since the 1970s, however, the Court's cases dealing with sex- and gender-based classifications have largely dismissed historical practices as indefensibly discriminatory and confining. Like it or not, the justices will need

---

[61] See Jessica A. Clarke, "Sex Assigned at Birth," 122 *Columbia Law Review* 1821 (2022).

to adjudicate challenges to governmental practices in categorizing people as male or female based on assessments of what, in their view, fairness and good sense require.

Discrimination against Gays and Lesbians

Recent decades have witnessed continuing, often-heated debates about the constitutionality of statutes that discriminate against gays and lesbians. At one level, these debates have involved a relatively straightforward clash of moral and social outlooks. From the perspective of gay rights advocates, gays and lesbians are a classic discrete and insular minority that is the victim of prejudice. To them, traditional taboos against same-sex attraction and intimacy lack reasoned justifications. By contrast, cultural conservatives believe that open gay sexuality and gay marriage threaten traditional moral values built around the monogamous two-parent family, defined to include one father and one mother. In their view, gay sex reflects a perversion of the order of nature (and, in the eyes of many, the order ordained by God). For those who hold this position, many exclusions of gays and lesbians from benefits and opportunities available to others seem natural and appropriate, whether to show moral disapproval or to protect society from corruption.

As occurred with equal protection doctrine involving discriminations based on both race and sex, the Supreme Court's approach to discriminations against gays and lesbian has shifted over time, at least partly in response to changing social attitudes. In the middle of the twentieth century, the American Psychiatric Association classified homosexuality as a personality disorder. It withdrew that designation in 1973. When President Bill Clinton attempted to end the military's ban on service by gays and lesbians in 1993, he met a blizzard of opposition in Congress and had to back down. A "don't ask, don't tell" policy emerged as a compromise. By 2010, Congress authorized the abolition of "don't ask, don't tell" and the substitution of a nondiscrimination policy. The Supreme Court upheld a right to same-sex marriage five years later in *Obergefell v. Hodges* (2015).[62]

Even today, however, it remains difficult to state the applicable doctrine under the Equal Protection Clause. Among the impediments,

---

[62] 576 U.S. 644 (2015).

the loose category of gay rights litigation has involved challenges to at least three analytically distinct kinds of laws: (1) those involving explicit discriminations against gays and lesbians – for example, barring them from certain jobs or opportunities, such as service in the military; (2) prohibitions that apply only to same-sex behavior (such as ones against same-sex sodomy) but do not formally classify people based on their sexual orientation; and (3) statutes with a discriminatory effect on gays, such as those that limit marriage to one man and one woman (but, again, do not formally refer to anyone's sexual orientation as a basis for limiting marriage rights). The Supreme Court has mostly dealt with cases in the second and third categories under the Due Process Clause, though it has occasionally suggested, in doing so, that equal protection principles also matter. In this chapter, I deal only with gay rights issues that the Court has explicitly decided under the Equal Protection Clause. Although this division is not wholly satisfactory, I postpone the book's principal consideration of gay rights cases decided under the Due Process Clause until Chapter 8.

The Supreme Court's first decision marking the advent of a new era of protection of gay rights under the Equal Protection Clause came in *Romer v. Evans* (1996).[63] *Romer* arose when Colorado voters amended the state's constitution to forbid state or local legislation affording gays "any minority status, quota preferences, protected status or claim of discrimination." That Colorado voters would have been asked to approve such an amendment showed that cultural attitudes were in a state of flux and contest: The proposed amendment reflected a reaction by cultural conservatives against an emerging tendency by state and local governments not only to repeal statutes that previously had discriminated against gays but also to pass legislation affording gays some affirmative protections, including against private sector discrimination. By any standard, however, the Colorado amendment was poorly written and unclear. At a minimum, it prohibited the enactment within Colorado of legislation specifically protecting gays and lesbians against public or private discrimination (in the way that civil rights legislation frequently bars discriminations on the basis of race and sex, for example). It arguably, but only arguably, took the further step of leaving gay people without legal redress under Colorado law if they were discriminatorily denied rights otherwise conferred on all Colorado citizens,

[63] 517 U.S. 620 (1996).

such as the right to ride on public transportation (after tendering the fare) or to receive protection from the police and fire departments.

In a decision that surprised many observers, the Supreme Court held by 6–3 that the Colorado amendment violated the Equal Protection Clause. In so ruling, the Court appeared to assume that discriminations against members of the LGBTQ community are subject only to rational basis review, not strict or formally intermediate judicial scrutiny (such as that applied to discrimination based on sex). Even today, the Court has never formally held that discriminations against gays incur any elevated level of scrutiny under the Equal Protection Clause. Nevertheless, Justice Anthony Kennedy's majority opinion in *Romer* found that the Colorado amendment failed rational basis review because it was "at once too narrow and too broad":

> It identifies persons by a single trait and then denies them protection across the board.... A law declaring that in general it shall be more difficult for one group of citizens than for all others to seek aid from the government is itself a denial of equal protection of the laws in the most literal sense.[64]

The only explanation for such a law, Justice Kennedy wrote, was that it was "born of animosity toward the class of persons affected" and thus lacked the kind of legitimate purpose that rational basis review requires.

Following *Romer*, *Lawrence v. Texas* (2003),[65] which I discuss in Chapter 8, formally rested on the Due Process Clause in invalidating a state law prohibiting same-sex sodomy, but Justice Kennedy's opinion for the Court also observed, in passing, that there was a "tenable argument" that *Romer* dictated the same result under the Equal Protection Clause. Justice Kennedy again referred glancingly to equal protection in upholding a right to same-sex marriage under the Due Process Clause in *Obergefell v. Hodges* in 2015.[66] Although the challenged statute did not classify anyone on the basis of sexual orientation, Justice Kennedy suggested that it discriminated against "same-sex couples."

Where are we left today? In both *Lawrence* and *Obergefell*, Justice Kennedy wrote majority opinions in which four "liberal" justices, but no other conservatives, joined him. He also authored the

---

[64] *Ibid.* at 633.
[65] 539 U.S. 558 (2003).
[66] 576 U.S. 644 (2003).

Court opinion in *Romer*. Following Kennedy's retirement in 2018 and the installation of a robust conservative supermajority, the generative capacity of the Court's pro–gay rights precedents under the Equal Protection Clause is not clear – especially since, as noted earlier, no majority opinion has ever formally held that discrimination against gays and lesbians triggers more than rational basis review.

Bostock v. Clayton County[67] (2020) illumines one possible future, but by no means guarantees it. In *Bostock*, the conservative Justice Neil Gorsuch ruled for a 6–3 majority that an employer's firing of an employee "simply for being homosexual or transgender" constituted forbidden discrimination on the basis of "sex" under the 1964 Civil Rights Act. In other words, Justice Gorsuch effectively treated discrimination based on sexual orientation as a form of sex discrimination. If an employer fires a male employee for exhibiting attraction to men, but would not have fired a female employee for showing attraction to men, the employer discriminates against the male on the basis of his sex, Gorsuch reasoned.

It remains to be seen whether a majority of the justices would apply that reasoning in a case challenging discrimination against gays under the Fourteenth Amendment, both the language and history of which differ from those of the statute involved in *Bostock*. Among other differences, the Equal Protection Clause does not expressly prohibit discrimination based on "sex," as the 1964 Civil Rights Act does. It would therefore be possible for the Court to predicate a decision about the constitutional permissibility of discrimination based on sexual orientation on the Clause's original history and subsequent traditional practice. Or the Court could apply rational basis review as the presumptively applicable standard in equal protection challenges. But it would also be possible for the Court, citing *Bostock*, to rule based on equal protection precedents involving sex discrimination.

Judicial Review of Governmental Classifications under the Equal Protection Clause: Concluding Observations

For nearly a century after the ratification of the Fourteenth Amendment, the Supreme Court tolerated discrimination against racial minorities behind the façade of "separate but equal." It also acquiesced

---

[67] 590 U.S. 644 (2020).

in discrimination against women. An interlude of change ensued under the Warren and Burger Courts. In a eulogy for the Warren Court, John Hart Ely characterized its equal protection agenda as drawn from the *Carolene Products* footnote: The Court strove to protect "discrete and insular minorities." Subsequent developments have often pursued a different path. *SFFA v. Harvard* bars affirmative action for racial minorities in order to protect whites, among others, against race-based disadvantage. A parallel doctrinal structure affords men – hardly anyone's idea of a "discrete and insular minority" – the same protection against discrimination that it provides to women. Meanwhile, statutes with racially disparate impacts on minority groups incur only rational basis review, which they almost invariably survive.

As discussed in an earlier section of this chapter, modern doctrine seems equally divorced from what leading historians believe that most nineteenth-century Americans understood the Fourteenth Amendment to establish. Overall, recent changes in equal protection doctrine's evolutionary course reflect prevailing views among the justices about what fairness requires. The current justices who often hold themselves out as originalist and textualists would likely resist that description. But it is hard if not impossible to account for the turns that equal protection doctrine has taken, or to predict those that it is likely to take in the years ahead, on any other basis.

Fundamental Rights under the Equal Protection Clause: A Further Basis for Searching Judicial Review

In the types of equal protection cases discussed in this chapter thus far, the applicable standard of judicial review has depended on the basis on which the government draws classificatory lines. Strict judicial scrutiny applies to all classifications based on race or religion, regardless of the nature of the benefit or burden at issue. By contrast, statutes that classify on other bases – such as age, test scores, and educational attainments – ordinarily incur only rational basis review. That classification-based framework constitutes the core of equal protection doctrine.

But equal protection law also includes a second strand that furnishes an alternative basis for triggering strict judicial scrutiny. That second strand grows from the Supreme Court's identification of some rights as "fundamental" under the Equal Protection Clause.

When the government distributes fundamental rights to some but not to others, or selectively burdens the exercise of fundamental rights, strict scrutiny applies.

The fundamental rights branch of equal protection doctrine took shape during the 1950s and 1960s in pioneering decisions by the Warren Court, the most generative of which concerned voting rights. At one or another time, rights that the Court designated as fundamental under the Equal Protection Clause included the right to travel,[68] the right to procreate,[69] the right to marry,[70] and the right to litigate.[71] In the years since the Warren Court, the Supreme Court has constricted the fundamental rights branch of equal protection law in most respects. In a particularly important decision in 1973, the Burger Court refused to designate education as a fundamental equal protection right.[72] In this chapter, I shall therefore limit the discussion to voting rights – the domain in which equal protection fundamental rights have remained most important.

Before going forward, I should also offer a preliminary clarification. Equal protection fundamental rights stand in a confusing relationship, both methodologically and substantively, to another set of fundamental rights that the Supreme Court has recognized as existing under the Fourteenth Amendment's Due Process Clause. For nearly fifty years, the most famous fundamental right under the Due Process Clause was the abortion right proclaimed in *Roe v. Wade*[73] (1973) and renounced by *Dobbs v. Jackson Women's Health Organization* (2022).[74] In both equal protection and due process cases, the justices have frequently divided about the methods, if any, by which the courts properly identify fundamental rights. The principal conceptual difference between due process and equal protection fundamental rights appears to be this: Due process fundamental rights are rights that the states are obliged to recognize whether they wish to recognize them or not, as once was the case with abortion rights. By contrast, equal protection fundamental rights can be ones that state and

---

[68] For example, *Shapiro v. Thompson*, 394 U.S. 618 (1969).
[69] For example, *Skinner v. Oklahoma*, 316 U.S. 535 (1942).
[70] For example, *Loving v. Virginia*, 388 U.S. 1 (1967).
[71] For example, *Griffin v. Illinois*, 351 U.S. 12 (1956).
[72] *San Antonio Independent School District v. Rodriguez*, 411 U.S. 1 (1973).
[73] 410 U.S. 113 (1973).
[74] 597 U.S. 215 (2022).

local governments need not create in the first place, yet must distribute equally if they do create them. For example, a town does not need to have an elected school board. It could choose to have a mayor or other officials appoint those responsible for school policy. But if a town has a school board and allows anyone to vote in school board elections, then limitations on who can vote will elicit judicial scrutiny under the fundamental rights branch of equal protection doctrine – as the Supreme Court held in a case to be discussed shortly.

Voting Rights under the Equal Protection Clause: A Historical and Conceptual Introduction

Harper v. Virginia Board of Elections[75] (1966) presented an equal protection challenge to provisions of the Virginia state constitution that required payment of a $1.50 "poll tax" as a prerequisite to voting. If the Court had applied equal protection principles of the kind laid out in earlier parts of this chapter, one might have expected the poll tax to survive judicial review. The state of Virginia had a legitimate interest in promoting an informed electorate. If so, willingness to pay a poll tax furnished a crude but arguably rational measure of a citizen's interest in public affairs. But the Supreme Court, without directly appraising the legitimacy of the state's asserted interest, insisted that the distinctive constitutional significance of voting rights, which are "preservative of all rights," required more robust judicial protection than rational basis review would provide. "We have long been mindful that where fundamental rights and liberties are asserted under the Equal Protection Clause, classifications which might invade or restrain them must be closely scrutinized and carefully confined," Justice William O. Douglas wrote.[76]

Three years later, in *Kramer v. Union Free School District* (1969),[77] the Court similarly invalidated a scheme that limited the right to vote in school district elections to property owners, parents of school children, and a few others. "[I]f a challenged state statute grants the right to vote to some bona fide residents of requisite age and citizenship and denies the franchise to others, the Court must determine

---

[75] 383 U.S. 663 (1966).
[76] *Ibid.* at 667, 670.
[77] 395 U.S. 621 (1969).

whether the exclusions are necessary to promote a compelling state interest," Chief Justice Warren pronounced.

One could imagine that the Supreme Court might have developed a doctrine of fundamental rights under the Fourteenth Amendment rooted in an originalist interpretive methodology. As we have seen, a number of historians believe that leading members of the Congress that proposed the Fourteenth Amendment understood the Privileges or Immunities Clause as a guarantee of "civil" or "fundamental" rights. Yet available evidence also suggests that those who wrote and ratified the Fourteenth Amendment would have characterized the right to vote as a "political" rather than a fundamental or civil right. If so, voting rights would need to be protected by a different provision to be protected at all. The Fifteenth Amendment, it should be remembered, specifically provides that "the right of citizens of the United States to vote shall not be denied or abridged by the United States or by any state on account of race, color, or previous condition of servitude." The Nineteenth Amendment subsequently forbade sex discrimination in voting: "The right of citizens of the United States to vote shall not be denied or abridged by the United States or by any State on account of sex." The Twenty-Sixth Amendment furnishes an additional guarantee of voting rights: "The right of citizens of the United States, who are eighteen years of age or older, to vote shall not be denied or abridged by the United States or by any State on account of age."

In identifying other aspects or dimensions of the right to vote as fundamental without specific reliance on the original understanding of the Fourteenth Amendment, the Supreme Court of the era that coincided roughly with Earl Warren's tenure as chief justice relied instead on an inference from the Constitution's overall structure. Although the Court's opinion in *Harper* acknowledged that "the right to vote in state elections is nowhere expressly mentioned," it reasoned persuasively that voting rights are central to political democracy. In doing so, the Warren Court echoed the suggestion of the *Carolene Products* footnote that "legislation which restricts those political processes which can ordinarily be expected to bring about repeal of undesirable legislation" might "be subjected to more exacting judicial scrutiny under the general prohibitions of the Fourteenth Amendment than are most other types of legislation."[78] Laws restricting the voting rights are

---

[78] *Carolene Products*, 304 U.S. at 153 n. 4.

paradigmatic examples of "legislation which restricts those political processes" on which the promise of political democracy to empower "government of the people, by the people, for the people" depends.[79]

Decisions demarcating voting rights as fundamental, and burdens on such rights as calling for strict judicial scrutiny, were characteristic of the Warren Court in at least three ways. First, a number of the Court's voting rights decisions were precedent-shattering. In *Harper*, for example, the Court overruled an earlier precedent that had upheld the constitutionality of a poll tax.[80]

Second, as became clearer in retrospect, *Harper* and other voting rights cases reflected a Warren Court agenda not only to open channels of political change but also to provide equality of opportunity for the poor and disadvantaged. To well-off Virginians, a poll tax of $1.50 was at most a minor obstacle to voting. To the poor, it posed a major deterrent.

Third, the methodology of designating a right as fundamental as a basis for affording it heightened protection under the Equal Protection Clause was one that the Warren Court deployed repeatedly in cases involving statutes that did not explicitly discriminate on the basis of poverty but nonetheless burdened the poor more than the better-off. Its leading decisions finding impermissible discriminations in states' distributions of the rights to travel, to procreate, to marry, and to litigate all had the effect and probably the purpose of ensuring opportunities for members of impoverished groups. Perhaps needless to say, the agenda reflected in the Warren Court's development of equal protection fundamental rights doctrine has not remained unaltered over time.

The One-Person, One-Vote Cases

The Warren Court's largest innovation with regard to voting rights came in the bombshell one-person, one-vote cases, symbolized by *Reynolds v. Sims* (1964).[81] *Reynolds* involved a challenge to legislative districting in the state of Alabama. When the Court decided

---

[79] Abraham Lincoln, The Gettysburg Address (Nov. 19, 1863), in Abraham Lincoln, *Speeches and Writings 1859–1865* (New York, NY: The Library of America, 1989), 536.
[80] See *Breedlove v. Suttles*, 302 U.S. 277 (1937).
[81] 377 U.S. 533 (1964).

Reynolds, the Alabama legislature had not once "reapportioned" itself since 1901. Over the intervening sixty-three years, shifts in population had made it possible for voters in districts that included only about 25 percent of the state's citizens to elect a majority of the members in both the state Senate and state House of Representatives. Cities, which had grown larger, were underrepresented. Rural areas had disproportionate influence. Nor was the Alabama legislature likely to fix the problem. Fair reapportionment would have required many legislators to vote themselves out of jobs. Similar situations existed in other states.

Although voting arrangements that let minorities dominate state politics seemed inherently unfair, it was far from obvious that the Constitution empowered the Supreme Court to rectify the problem. Even apart from questions about the original meaning of the Fourteenth Amendment, the design of the United States Senate, in which each state has two senators, might suggest that disparities in voting powers are not inconsistent with the Constitution's overall design. In addition, many observers shared a concern to which Justice Frankfurter had given passionate voice in an earlier decision: that judicial oversight of legislative districting would plunge the Court into a dangerous "political thicket."[82] In Alabama or any other state, there are many ways that lines might be drawn to create voting districts of roughly equal population. As a result, any selection was likely to advantage either Democrats or Republicans. For Justice Frankfurter, electoral districting questions were political to the core. He thought that courts should treat them as coming within the so-called political question doctrine, which holds that some constitutional issues, including those that the courts would lack "judicially manageable standards" to resolve, are committed entirely to the "political branches" of government.[83] (I shall soon discuss the Court's subsequent holding that challenges to partisan gerrymanders of legislative districting scheme present nonjusticiable political questions.)

In *Reynolds v. Sims* and other one-person, one-vote cases during the 1960s, however, the Supreme Court dismissed these concerns and held that "seats in both houses of a bicameral state legislature must be apportioned on a population basis" following each decennial census.[84]

---

[82] *Colegrove v. Green*, 328 U.S. 549, 556 (1946).
[83] *Baker v. Carr*, 369 U.S. 186, 211, 226 (1962).
[84] *Reynolds*, 377 U.S. at 568.

Although the one-person, one-vote cases provoked sharp controversy at the time, within as little as a decade they – like *Brown v. Board of Education* – had won nearly universal acceptance. A rule demanding approximately equal populations in electoral districts turned out to pose few problems in implementation: Legislatures know the standard that they must meet to achieve judicial acceptance of their plans. When tempers had cooled, the idea that everyone's vote should have equal proportional weight also accorded with almost everybody's notion of basic fairness – as, apparently, did the idea that in a political democracy the right to vote should be regarded as "fundamental." From that conclusion, a majority of the justices have never looked back, though Justice Clarence Thomas has recently expressed some disposition to reconsider the issue on originalist grounds.[85]

Vote Dilution: Race Discrimination and Majority-Minority Districts

In conceptual terms, the one-person, one-vote cases involved not outright denials of the right to vote but vote dilution, or the diminishment of the voting power of some people and groups relative to others. Another form of vote dilution occurs when voting schemes are deliberately designed to minimize the chance that racial minorities will be able to elect representatives of their choice. In *Mobile v. Bolden* (1980),[86] the Burger Court assumed, and in *Rogers v. Lodge* it held,[87] that intentional racial vote dilution violates the Equal Protection Clause.

Since the 1990s, the Supreme Court has also held that state attempts to create "majority-minority" districts – in which statewide racial minorities (such as African Americans) enjoy majority status – elicit the same strict judicial scrutiny as schemes designed to dilute minority votes. States might set out to create majority-minority districts for a number of reasons, but perhaps the most common has involved the need to comply with a federal statute, the Voting Rights Act (VRA). Congress originally enacted the VRA in 1965 to stop states, especially in the South, from deliberately drawing district lines

---

[85] See *Alexander v. South Carolina State Conference of the NAACP*, 144 S. Ct. 1221 (2024) (Thomas, J., concurring in part).
[86] 446 U.S. 55 (1980).
[87] 458 U.S. 613 (1982).

that disadvantage racial minorities. It later amended and toughened the VRA when it thought that the Supreme Court had done too little to ensure that racial minorities were treated fairly. As interpreted by the Supreme Court, the amended VRA requires states to create majority-minority districts when (1) a minority community is large and compact enough to constitute the majority in a properly drawn district, (2) the minority community is politically cohesive, and (3) the majority has itself engaged in racially polarized voting.[88]

In the view of some critics, including some conservative justices, the VRA should be deemed unconstitutional insofar as it requires states to take race into account in their districting decisions and thus deviates from the principle of colorblindness that the Supreme Court enforces in other contexts. So far, however, no majority opinion has ever embraced that view, including in the current era of a conservative supermajority. Instead, the justices have held that it is constitutionally permissible for states to consider race as one factor among others in designing voting districts, including to comply with the VRA, as long as they do not act with the "predominant intent" of achieving a racially defined end (such as that of creating a majority-minority district). Complying with the VRA is a compelling governmental interest, the justices have reasoned, but the VRA does not require the states to subordinate all other districting principles – such as a preference for geographically compact voting districts – to interests in empowering racial minorities to elect their preferred representatives. The predominant intent test that the Court uses to gauge the permissibility of majority-minority voting districts emerged gradually from cases involving oddly shaped districts, the strange contours of which defied explanation on grounds other than race-based decision-making. Such districts, the Court wrote in *Shaw v. Reno* (1993),[89] "reinforce[] the perception that members of the same racial group – regardless of their age, education, economic status, or the community in which they live – think alike, share the same political interests, and will prefer the same candidates at the polls."

Dissenting justices have emphasized that legislatures can and sometimes do create oddly shaped districts to benefit groups other than racial minorities. For example, Justice John Stevens, who grew up

---

[88] See *Thornburg v. Gingles*, 478 U.S. 30 (1986).
[89] 509 U.S. 630, 647 (1993).

in the politically tribal Chicago of the 1920s and 1930s, sharply disagreed with the majority's analysis in *Shaw v. Reno*. Writing in dissent, he protested: "If it is permissible to draw boundaries to provide adequate representation for rural voters, for union members, for Hasidic Jews, for Polish Americans, or for Republicans" – as it generally is, as long as the districts observe one-person, one-vote principles – "it necessarily follows that it is permissible to do the same thing for members of the very minority group whose history in the United States gave birth to the Equal Protection Clause. A contrary conclusion could only be described as perverse."[90]

But the justices in the majority, now as much as then, reject that reasoning. In their eyes, race is different because it is peculiarly divisive and unfair as a basis for governmental decision-making, especially when it is plainly the predominant factor in producing oddly shaped voting districts.

Vote Dilution: Political Gerrymanders

In the view of many observers, among the deepest threats to the integrity of American political democracy is partisan gerrymandering. In a political or partisan gerrymander, the majority party in a state legislature uses its control over the districting process to draw district lines that maximally advantage it. The technique normally begins with the deliberate "packing" of as many members of the opposing party as possible into a relatively small number of districts. The packing ensures that many of the opposing party's votes will be "wasted" in districts where they are not necessary to elect a candidate. Then the mapmakers systematically split up concentrations of the other party's voters to divide them among voting districts where they will be an electoral minority.

Rucho v. Common Cause[91] (2019) illustrates how the process works. Although North Carolina is a relatively closely divided state, in which Democratic congressional candidates received more votes than Republican congressional candidates in 2012, the Republicans who controlled the state legislature following the 2010 census adopted a districting scheme designed to make it likely that Republicans would

---

[90] *Ibid.* at 679 (Stevens, J., dissenting).
[91] 588 U.S. 684 (2019).

win ten of the state's thirteen congressional seats in the next election. In a companion case from Maryland, the Democratic governor testified about his efforts to "flip" a Republican seat to the Democrats so that Maryland would elect seven rather than six Democratic House members and the number of Republican seats would diminish from two to one.

In a sequence of cases prior to *Rucho*, the Supreme Court had divided about whether there were "judicially manageable standards" by which the Court could judge the constitutional permissibility of partisan gerrymanders. If not, all agreed, cases challenging political gerrymanders would pose "political questions" beyond the constitutional authority of federal courts to decide under Article III of the Constitution. The peculiar difficulty in finding judicially manageable standards by which to determine the permissibility of partisan gerrymanders, Chief Justice John Roberts maintained in *Rucho*, was that, "while it is illegal for a [state] to depart from the one-person, one-vote rule, or to engage in racial discrimination in districting," the Constitution does not flatly bar political gerrymandering. Political gerrymandering has gone on from earliest constitutional history, albeit not to the degree or with the sophistication that modern, computer-based, technology permits. Nor could one reasonably expect the politicians who sit in state legislatures wholly to ignore considerations of partisan advantage when making districting decisions. The question, the chief justice wrote, thus "is one of degree: How to 'provid[e] a standard for deciding how much partisan dominance is too much.'"[92]

According to Roberts – whose opinion was joined by the four other justices who had been appointed by Republican presidents at the time of the Court's decision – the question of when partisan advantage-taking crossed the line into constitutionally forbidden territory was not one that the Court was competent to answer. The Constitution's language and history provided no "judicially manageable standard" for resolving it. And the Court could devise none, the chief justice maintained. Although the Court routinely develops tests of various kinds to implement the vague language of the Equal Protection Clause and other constitutional provisions – including, for example, the strict judicial scrutiny formula, the one-person, one vote

[92] *Ibid.* at 704.

rule, and the "predominant intent" measure of the permissibility of majority-minority voting districts – it could not do so to determine when partisan gerrymanders go too far. Questions about how to allocate power between political parties were inherently "political," not "legal," the chief justice reasoned.

Justice Elena Kagan, writing for the three liberal justices then serving on the Supreme Court besides herself – all of whom had been appointed by Democratic presidents – filed an impassioned dissent. Partisan gerrymanders, which permit parties that control districting processes to consolidate their position even when a majority of voters support their rivals, flout basic democratic principles and are inherently unfair, she emphasized. In her view, "when political actors have a specific and predominant intent to entrench themselves in power by manipulating district lines," a form of exacting scrutiny should apply: States should be required to articulate the districting criteria apart from partisan gain that they used in drawing voting districts – geographical compactness, leaving geographical subdivisions intact, and so forth. Once those criteria were specified, voting rights experts had demonstrated that computers could be used "to randomly generate a large collection of districting plans" that satisfy the state's own desiderata. And the computer-generated maps could then be arrayed along a continuum from those most favorable to Republicans to those most favorable to Democrats. Any extreme outlier in either direction, Justice Kagan argued, could justly be deemed to have gone "too far." Applying this approach, one expert produced 3,000 possible districting maps for the state of North Carolina, "[e]very single one of [which] would have produced at least one more Democratic House Member" than the state's "actual map, and 77% would have elected three or four more."[93]

For the majority, Chief Justice Roberts retorted that Justice Kagan's proposed framework for analysis failed to answer the fundamental question of "How much political motivation and effect is too much?" How many safe Republican seats should the North Carolina legislature be permitted to craft? In reply, Justice Kagan saw no need to answer that question in order to resolve the case before the Court. In this case, Justice Kagan argued, there was no plausible explanation for the lines that North Carolina and Maryland had drawn other than

[93] *Ibid.* at 738 (Jagan, J., joined by Ginsburg, Breyer, and Sotomayor, J.J., dissenting).

naked partisanship. It sufficed to say that "[t]his much is too much," she wrote. "The practices challenged in this case imperil our system of government," she argued. "Part of the Court's role in that system is to defend its foundations."[94]

At the time of the *Rucho* decision, most politically informed Americans appear to have believed that partisan gerrymandering tends to benefit Republicans more than Democrats. Against that background, many observers took note that the *Rucho* Court divided along a line that correlated with the Republican political affiliations of the presidents who had appointed the justices in the majority and the Democratic affiliations of the presidents who had nominated the justices who dissented. The division, as Justice Kagan remarked, had nothing to do with originalism. The Supreme Court's voting rights cases under the Equal Protection Clause have never purported to be originalist, and none of the justices argued in *Rucho* that the Court should seek to put the doctrine on originalist foundations. Rather, in explaining the divergent conclusions that they reached, the justices framed their division as one about the proper role of the judiciary, and in particular of the Supreme Court, in a case involving paired threats to the scheme of government that the Constitution sets up.

According to Chief Justice Roberts and the *Rucho* majority, the paramount consideration involved preserving the appearance and reality that the federal courts, and especially the Supreme Court itself, are nonpartisan institutions. As the chief justice viewed the case, *Rucho* pitted partisans scheming for political advantage against other equally partisan schemers and presented a demand for the Court to choose a winner by determining that the partisans on one side either had or had not gone too far. According to the majority, acceptance of a responsibility to rule either way would put public respect for the Court as a nonpolitical institution dangerously at risk. By contrast, the dissenters assigned a higher priority to maintaining what they viewed as the integrity of democratic elections. In their view, it was imperative for the Court to intervene to ensure that entrenched minorities cannot allocate voters to electoral districts in ways that predictably and designedly thwart majority rule. Reasonable justices could disagree about how to weigh these competing concerns. Still, the question would persist: Why did the justices divide along the lines that they did

---

[94] *Ibid.* at 751.

in answering it? To pose that question is not to answer it, I hasten to add – and it is as fairly posed about the liberal justices as it is about the conservatives.

Burdens on the Right to Vote: Voter Identification Laws

Discomfiting as it can be to recognize, modern Supreme Court decisions in other voting rights cases under the Equal Protection Clause have also exhibited conservative versus liberal divisions that correlate with the competing interests of the two major parties. An example comes from cases presenting challenges to state statutes that require voters to present government-issued photo identification (ID) as a condition of voting. Voter ID requirements are structurally similar to the poll tax that the Supreme Court struck down in *Harper v. Virginia Board of Elections*. Although they have the ostensible purpose of promoting election integrity, they impose disproportionate burdens on poor, elderly, and disabled voters who do not have drivers' licenses and who may experience the requirement to obtain a photo ID as daunting. In state legislatures, a political scientist has explained, "Republicans strongly favor voter ID laws as a way to prevent voter fraud while Democrats oppose them as a crass partisan tactic to suppress turnout among their strongest supporters."[95]

In *Crawford v. Marion County Election Board* (2008),[96] the Supreme Court sustained an Indiana voter ID statute by a vote of 6–3, with the Court's five conservative justices and a solitary liberal, Justice Stevens, constituting the majority. (Reflecting on the cases after his retirement, Stevens described the Indiana legislation as "partisan" and concluded that it "did not really serve the public interest."[97]) There can be little doubt that constitutional analysis of voter ID laws requires a normative trade-off. Requirements that voters present government-issued picture IDs prevent some fraud, though there is little evidence that much fraud occurs, but they also deter some otherwise eligible voters from casting ballots. Many constitutional issues similarly require the justices to weigh competing

---

[95] Terri Peretti, "Judicial Partisanship in Voter Identification Litigation," 15 *Election Law Journal* 214, 215 (2016).
[96] 553 U.S. 181 (2008).
[97] John Paul Stevens, *The Making of a Justice: Reflections on My First 94 Years* (New York, NY: Little, Brown and Company, 2019).

normative considerations, but the stakes are not typically measurable in such plain terms of partisan electoral advantage.

Equality in the Counting of Votes: *Bush v. Gore*

No account of equal protection voting rights case would be complete without a reference to *Bush v. Gore* (2000).[98] Of the justices who sat on the Supreme Court in *Bush v. Gore*, only Clarence Thomas remains. Even so, the case continues to color perceptions of the Supreme Court in some eyes.

Bush v. Gore emerged in the messy aftermath of the 2000 presidential election. Following a close vote nationwide, the outcome in the electoral college depended on which candidate had carried Florida. After a machine count and recount of ballots left the Democrat Al Gore trailing the Republican George Bush by fewer than 1,000 votes, a series of legal battles developed about whether there could be a manual recount of ballots on which the machine tabulation had failed to reflect any presidential choice. Many of the ballots were punch cards on which voters using a stylus had apparently left "hanging chads" or produced "dimples" but made no full perforation. In a highly controversial ruling, a narrow majority of the Florida Supreme Court ordered a recount in which they directed election officials and lower courts to attempt to discern "the intent of the voter" in determining which ballots to count. But the state supreme court gave no further specification of precisely how to identify what the intent of the voter was. The court's ruling kept the hopes of Gore and his supporters temporarily alive.

Opposing a recount, the Bush legal team rushed to the Supreme Court of the United States. As a preliminary matter, they asked the justices to "stay" or halt the recount while the parties prepared and filed their legal briefs and awaited a Supreme Court ruling on whether allowing a recount would violate the Constitution. By a vote of 5–4, with the Court's five most conservative justices constituting the majority, the Court granted the stay. Proceeding on a fast-paced, emergency basis, the Court then heard arguments in the case and announced its decision within just a few days. On the merits, the Court held that a recount conducted under the vague "intent of the voter" standard would have violated the "fundamental" right of Florida voters to have

---

[98] 531 U.S. 98 (2000).

their votes valued equally: "[T]he standards for accepting or rejecting contested ballots might vary not only from county to county but indeed within a single county from one recount team to another." Then, in an even more controversial ruling, the Court determined that it was too late for the Florida Supreme Court to fix the problem by giving further instructions framed to ensure reasonable consistency. The time for Florida to certify its electors to vote in the electoral college was too close at hand, the Court ruled.

The Supreme Court's opinion in *Bush v. Gore* had no identified author. It was issued "per curiam" or "by the Court." But the Court was far from unanimous. Justices Stevens, Ginsburg, and Breyer – all of whom were generally counted as "liberals" – wrote or joined opinions flatly denying that an equal protection violation had occurred. Justice David Souter agreed with them in protesting that even if a constitutional problem existed, the Florida Supreme Court should be given a chance to fix it by issuing clearer vote-counting instructions, rather than having the recount simply halted in its tracks.

When the dissenting votes were tallied and identified, it became clear that the Court's five most conservative justices made up the majority. In other cases under the Equal Protection Clause, the conservatives are those who are usually least likely to find rights violations (except in cases challenging affirmative action). Yet they adjudged the case before them to be unique, as the majority opinion made starkly clear, even if they did not fully explain their reason for thinking so: "Our consideration is limited to the present" facts involving "the special instance of a statewide recount under the authority of a single state judicial officer" who had the authority to prescribe uniform vote-counting standards but had failed to do so.

Equal Protection Voting Rights, the Supreme Court, and the Judicial Role

During the decades of the Warren and the Burger Courts, the premise that the Supreme Court has a special role to play in ensuring the fair operation of the political process, including through the allocation of voting rights in cases including *Reynolds v. Sims*, occupied the status of a constitutional truism. But as times change, so do perceptions of and expectations concerning the Supreme Court. As politics in the United States has become more acutely partisan, it has grown progressively harder to identify neutral ground from which to judge disputes about fairness in the definition and distribution of voting rights, both for observers of the Supreme Court and possibly for the justices themselves. In a politically polarized climate, it is perhaps to be expected that the justices would increasingly be portrayed as playing political roles by repeatedly favoring the interests of one political party over those of another – especially when some of the Court's decisions in high-profile cases are consistent with, even if they did not conclusively prove the accuracy of, that portrayal.

8 SUBSTANTIVE DUE PROCESS AND UNENUMERATED FUNDAMENTAL RIGHTS AFTER THE OVERRULING OF *ROE V. WADE*

One of the major constitutional earthquakes of the twentieth century came in 1973, when the Supreme Court decided *Roe v. Wade*.[1] *Roe* was stunning and consequential for lots of reasons, as was the *Dobbs* decision that overruled it roughly fifty years later.[2] To some, *Roe* was an Emancipation Proclamation for women carrying unwanted fetuses or fearful or unplanned pregnancies. To others, it was a Court-issued license for murder. If there was one thing everyone could agree on, it was that *Roe* had sweeping implications, upsetting the abortion laws of a large majority of the states. Attitudes toward abortion were changing rapidly in 1973. Antiabortion laws, which had mostly been enacted in the nineteenth century, might soon have been revised anyway, at least in many states. But *Roe* undoubtedly speeded the arrival of legal abortion and mandated broader abortion rights – up to the point of fetal viability – than most states' political processes might have produced otherwise.

Apart from its practical impact, *Roe* was shocking in its interpretive methodology. It relied on three sets of premises that have often divided judicial liberals from judicial conservatives – though, as we shall see, the liberal and conservative positions have not remained stable over time. Those three sets of premises are not only complex in their own right but also complexly related to one another.

---

[1] 410 U.S. 113 (1973).
[2] *Dobbs v. Jackson Women's Health Organization*, 597 U.S. 215 (2022).

The first involves the Due Process Clause of the Fourteenth Amendment. *Roe* rested on the long-contested postulate that the Due Process Clause – which says that no state shall "deprive any person of life, liberty, or property, without due process of law" – confers substantive protection on some "liberty" rights. Some commentators, judges, and justices have long mocked the concept of "substantive due process," or the idea that the Due Process Clause confers substantive rights, as a contradiction in terms – "sort of like 'green pastel redness.'"[3] According to those who take this line, the Due Process Clause is obviously a guarantee of fair process or procedures, not substantive rights, and it was a flat-out mistake for the Supreme Court to use this clause to invalidate legislation on the ground that it infringes a substantively protected liberty.

As all recognized, however, *Roe*'s reliance on the concept of substantive due process was not unprecedented. Some prior examples of substantive due process adjudication were ignominious. *Dred Scott v. Sandford* (1857),[4] in which Chief Justice Taney reasoned that a law depriving a slaveholder of legal authority over people whom he held as slaves "merely because he ... brought his property into a [free] Territory ... could hardly be dignified with the name of due process of law," was perhaps the most inglorious. And still vivid in memory in 1973 was the *Lochner* era, during which judicial "conservatives" embraced substantive due process in order to protect property and contract rights from governmental regulation. Liberals detested *Lochner* and, during the period to which it gave its name, denounced its reliance on the Due Process Clause as a basis for upsetting substantive legislation. But the idea of substantive due process also had roots in the antislavery tradition. A number of prominent abolitionists argued that slavery deprived those held in bondage of liberty and property without due process of law. More recently, too, the judicial liberals of the Warren Court had begun to recognize the existence of unenumerated yet "fundamental" substantive rights protected under the Equal Protection Clause of the Fourteenth Amendment, as discussed in Chapter 7.

If we think about *Roe* in light of the antislavery tradition and the broader idea that people possess natural or fundamental moral

---

[3] John Hart Ely, *Democracy and Distrust: A Theory of Judicial Review* (Cambridge, MA: Belknap Press of Harvard University Press, 1980), 18.
[4] 60 U.S. 393 (1857).

rights that all governments are obliged to respect, the second set of complex premises that *Roe* implicated begins to come into focus. This is a set of premises involving the relationship between constitutional law and interpretation, on the one hand, and background moral principles, or principles of natural or moral right, on the other hand. According to one view, which the Court in *Roe* adopted, the Constitution presupposes the existence of certain basic or fundamental rights that it does not necessarily enumerate, and otherwise vague constitutional language ought to be interpreted in light of them. By tradition or convention, the Supreme Court has often cited the Due Process Clause as the textual basis for protecting otherwise unlisted liberties. But from the perspective of those who see the Constitution as tacitly assuming the existence of some such liberties, little would be lost or gained if the Court were to enforce fundamental moral rights that the Constitution does not specifically list under some other constitutional provision such as the Fourteenth Amendment's Privileges or Immunities Clause or the Ninth Amendment, which provides that "[t]he enumeration in the Constitution, of certain rights, shall not be construed to deny or disparage others retained by the people." The crucial point is that we should think of the Constitution as presupposing, and interpret it in light of, background moral rights and principles.

The third set of principles underlying *Roe* involves the role of evolving moral and legal understandings in assigning content to background fundamental rights. According to a loosely defined interpretive tradition sometimes called "living constitutionalism," there is no embarrassment in affirming that the Constitution is properly read to protect a fundamental right or liberty in the modern era even if virtually no one would have believed that such a right existed at the time when relevant constitutional language was adopted.[5] In one way or another, living constitutionalists believe that current generations can sometimes achieve moral or political insights not available to earlier generations. Equally importantly and perhaps more controversially, they also believe that judges and especially the justices of the Supreme Court should, over time, revise prevailing interpretations of the Constitution to reflect advancing moral discernment.

---

[5] See, for example, David A. Strauss, *The Living Constitution* (Oxford/New York, NY: Oxford University Press, 2010).

Whether substantive due process adjudication is better viewed as an important engine for the realization of justice or a recipe for moral and constitutional disaster depends heavily on one's appraisal of who the justices of the Supreme Court are likely to be. With the right justices, all might turn out splendidly. With the wrong ones, substantive due process may be as likely to saddle the nation with decisions such as *Dred Scott* and *Lochner* as to realize the enlightened results that champions of a "living" Constitution hopefully anticipate. There are those who viewed *Roe* as exemplifying both of these antithetical possibilities.

Today, *Roe* is gone, with its overruling reflecting one of the most defining achievements of the conservative, supermajority-charged Roberts Court. Perhaps surprisingly, however, *Dobbs* neither rejects the concept of substantive due process nor denies the existence of unwritten or unenumerated constitutional rights. Instead, the *Dobbs* majority – in an interpretive move characteristic of the current Court – seeks to rely on history and tradition to identify, as well as to define the scope of, substantive rights that it holds to be protected by the Due Process Clause.

As we shall see, the future of substantive due process adjudication is difficult to predict in important respects. What is clear is that it is impossible to understand current law, and the choices that the Supreme Court will face in the years ahead, except in light of still-unfolding history.

Historical Background to *Roe*

Substantive Due Process and the Fourteenth Amendment

Much of the relevant history of substantive due process and judicial enforcement of unenumerated rights has already emerged in prior chapters. As Chapters 2 and 7 briefly noted, there is a serious historical argument that the Fourteenth Amendment's framers and ratifiers understood the Privileges or Immunities Clause to protect a number of basic or fundamental liberties that the Clause does not specifically list. Prior to the Civil War, the Constitution already included a provision – the Privileges *and* Immunities Clause in Article IV – that forbade the states to discriminate against out-of-staters in regulating the exercise of those otherwise unlisted "privileges and immunities" that had long been assumed to be fundamental elements of citizenship in a free society.[6] Among these was the right to pursue a lawful trade free from unreasonable governmental regulation.

In the *Slaughter-House Cases* (1873),[7] to which Chapters 2 and 7 have referred already, a group of white butchers challenged a state scheme of slaughterhouse regulation by arguing that it violated the Privileges or Immunities Clause. According to the butchers, the right to practice a trade numbered among "the privileges or immunities of citizens of the United States." In a tortured opinion rejecting that argument, a 5–4 majority distinguished sharply between the privileges and immunities of state citizenship, on the one hand, and the privileges or immunities of national citizenship, on the other hand. As much after the ratification of the Fourteenth Amendment as before, the Court held, the most important privileges and immunities were those of state citizenship, which the states could continue to define and regulate as they chose, subject to the provision of Article IV that they must not discriminate unreasonably against out-of-staters in doing so. The Fourteenth Amendment's reference to "the privileges or immunities of citizens of the United States," the *Slaughter-House* majority insisted, encompassed only a very small set of previously recognized rights of national citizenship, most prominently including the right to travel from one state to another.

The Supreme Court's reluctance to recognize a set of privileges or immunities of citizens of the United States that included contract and other economic rights is easy to understand in the historical context of the *Slaughter-House Cases*. In the aftermath of the disastrous *Dred Scott* decision and the Civil War, the Court's majority did not wish to claim large new responsibilities likely to enmesh it in further controversy. Even so, the Court's reasoning in the *Slaughter-House Cases* is difficult to defend. With its holding, the *Slaughter-House* majority ruled that a principal provision of the Fourteenth Amendment, adopted specifically to alter the relationship between state and national governments following the Civil War, essentially changed nothing. As a dissenting opinion protested, if the majority's interpretation of the Fourteenth Amendment's Privileges or Immunities Clause were correct, its enactment would have been "a vain and idle enactment, which

---

[6] See U.S. Const. art. IV, § 2, cl. 1 ("The Citizens of each State shall be entitled to all Privileges and Immunities of Citizens in the several States.").
[7] 83 U.S. 36 (1872).

accomplished nothing, and most unnecessarily excited Congress and the people on its passage."[8] Nonetheless, the holding of the *Slaughter-House Cases* remains unaltered. Since the *Slaughter-House Cases*, the Court has treated the Privileges or Immunities Clause of the Fourteenth Amendment as a virtual constitutional nullity.[9]

Substantive Due Process in the *Lochner* Era

Ironically, within a few years of *The Slaughter-House Cases*, the Supreme Court commenced to perform under the Due Process Clause a function very similar to the one that it had refused to accept under the Privileges or Immunities Clause: The Court began to scrutinize state legislation to determine whether it unreasonably, and thus "without due process of law," interfered with substantive rights to liberty or property (rather than depriving citizens of one of "the privileges or immunities" of citizens of the United States). In the early years, moreover, the Court trained its attention principally on the reasonableness of the very kind of economic regulatory legislation that the plaintiffs in the *Slaughter-House Cases* had sought to challenge.

The era of "substantive due process" review of economic legislation under the Due Process Clause began around 1890. The assumptions that underlay the Supreme Court's decision-making are hard to recapture. The Court took for granted that the states are entitled to enact regulatory legislation to promote public health, safety, and morals. But it also assumed that regulation lacking in fundamental fairness should be deemed to deprive its targets of liberty or property "without due process of law." In the hundreds of substantive due process cases that came before the Supreme Court from the late 1800s through the 1930s, the justices asked either or both of two questions: First, does the state regulatory legislation have a valid public purpose? Second, if so, does the challenged regulation represent a fair and sensible means of pursuing that purpose?

If the notion of substantive due process makes sense at all, the Court's approach sounds reasonable. Certainly it would have sounded

---

[8] *Ibid.* at 96 (Field, J., dissenting).
[9] *Saenz v. Roe*, 526 U.S. 489 (1999) was unusual in relying on the Privileges or Immunities Clause as the constitutional home of a traditionally recognized right to travel, but the Court gave no indication that it intended any broader revitalization of the clause.

reasonable if the Court had conducted the same inquiries to determine whether challenged legislation violated the "privileges or immunities" of citizenship by unduly impairing the exercise of traditional liberties – as, but for the *Slaughter-House Cases*, it might have done. In practice, however, the Court's administration of substantive due process review reflected narrow, grudging views of what counted as valid public purposes and as reasonable means of promoting them. The Court thus became what the *Slaughter-House* majority had feared, "a perpetual censor upon all legislation of the States."

The Court began implementing substantive due process review near the dawn of the Progressive Era in American politics. During that period, legislatures recurrently enacted regulatory legislation aimed particularly at protecting miners and factory workers, including children, from brutally long hours, low wages, and oppressive conditions of employment. Often the Court found such legislative efforts invalid on the ground that they interfered unreasonably with rights to freedom of contract protected by the Due Process Clause.

Lochner v. New York (1905),[10] the decision from which this era of judicial history takes its name, exemplified the Court's approach. *Lochner* struck down a New York statute imposing a sixty-hour limit on bakery employees' work weeks. In finding the statute unconstitutional, the Court first imagined that it might have been passed for the special benefit of bakery workers, to give them an advantage in bargaining with bakery owners. But for the state simply to try to benefit one class of citizens (bakery workers) at the expense of another (their employers) was not, in the Court's view, a valid public purpose. To the Court, legislation designed to benefit only one otherwise competent group of citizens, especially by improving their situation relative to others, aimed to promote class interests, not the general public interest.

Alternatively, the *Lochner* Court imagined that the New York legislature might have enacted the statute limiting bakery workers to sixty-hour weeks for the purpose of protecting bakers' health. For the state to promote the health of its citizens was a permissible public purpose, the Court acknowledged, but it then scrutinized the state's chosen means and found them wanting. There was insufficient evidence, the Court ruled, that working more than sixty hours a week as a baker posed a significant threat to health. Absent such evidence, the state's

---

[10] 198 U.S. 45 (1905).

regulation was unreasonable and potentially tyrannical. Under the state's theory, the Court wrote, "[n]ot only the hours of employees, but the hours of employers, could be regulated, and doctors, lawyers, scientists, all professional men, as well as athletes and artisans, could be forbidden to fatigue their brains and bodies by prolonged hours of exercise."[11] Three justices dissented on this point. They believed the evidence sufficient to uphold the statute as a health measure.

Justice Oliver Wendell Holmes, later to emerge as a champion of free speech rights, dissented on more fundamental grounds. The Court, he objected, was reading the Constitution through the lens of a particular, controversial, economic philosophy that looked skeptically on all governmental regulation of economic markets. It assumed that if a factory owner and factory laborers wished to contract for seventy-hour work weeks at pennies an hour, they had a natural right to do so, and any governmental interference was a suspect deprivation of liberty. The difficulty, Holmes wrote, was that this was "an economic theory which a large part of the country does not entertain." Where the Court saw voluntary transactions among willing contractors, others perceived self-sustaining social structures conspiring to keep the poor, poor and the rich, rich. Where the Court saw natural liberty, others discerned socially constructed inequality in which some had too much bargaining power and others had too little. Given the division of views, Holmes thought that elected officials and ultimately the voters, not the justices of the Supreme Court, should chart the nation's economic and regulatory policy.

From the 1905 decision in *Lochner* through 1937, the Supreme Court conducted substantive due process review of roughly 400 economic regulatory statutes. The justices invalidated about half. The Court had difficulty distinguishing legislation promoting genuine "public" interests in protecting those not competent to protect themselves (such as children and sometimes, in the Court's view, women) from legislation that impermissibly attempted to promote some citizens' interests at the expense of others. The Court also varied in its willingness to credit evidence showing that legislation reasonably promoted worker health and safety. Nevertheless, the Court maintained its basic analytic framework in the face of unrelenting public and legislative opposition.

[11] *Ibid.* at 60.

That opposition grew angrier as time passed. Although *Lochner* was a due process case, the *Lochner*-era Supreme Court invalidated regulatory legislation under other provisions of the Constitution as well. Most notably, the Court frequently struck down federal laws regulating economic activity as lying beyond Congress's power to enact under Article I of the Constitution (the provision from which Congress derives most of its powers). From the perspective of a majority of the justices, Congress and the states had overstepped their proper roles and were trying to eliminate vital freedoms of contract that the Framers of the Constitution had regarded as God-given. From the perspective of those on the other side, the justices were unreasonably trying to impose antiquated economic notions on an unwilling nation. On this view, the justices' antiregulatory stance had become untenable in a modern industrial economy, especially when rampant unemployment made it impossible for employees – who could easily be fired and replaced – to bargain effectively with their employers for decent working conditions or a living wage.

When anger and frustration with the Court reached an apex in the mid-1930s, with President Roosevelt credibly proposing to "pack" the Supreme Court to save the New Deal, as discussed in Chapter 2, the Court abruptly altered course. With respect to substantive due process, the turning point came in *West Coast Hotel Co. v. Parrish* (1937),[12] which upheld a state law mandating a minimum wage for women. Reflecting its dramatic rejection of the *Lochner*-era assumption that an unregulated market economy provided fair opportunities for the exercise of natural liberty, the Court wrote, "The exploitation of a class of workers who are in an unequal position with respect to bargaining power and are thus relatively defenceless against the denial of a living wage is not only detrimental to their health and well being but casts a direct burden for their support upon the community."[13] In this formulation, an unregulated "free market" is neither sacrosanct nor even presumptively just. The government violates no protected liberty when it identifies economic "exploitation" and enacts regulatory legislation to correct it.

In the wake of *West Coast Hotel* and parallel decisions sustaining Congress's regulatory power under the Commerce Clause, the

---

[12] 300 U.S. 379 (1937).
[13] *Ibid.* at 399.

principal monuments of the *Lochner* era all tumbled within a few years. The Supreme Court's conservative stalwarts departed the bench, and President Roosevelt got to remake the Court with justices who shared his constitutional vision. In the jurisprudential regime that Roosevelt brought into being, it became an unquestionable premise of constitutional reasoning – shared by all or nearly all justices of the Supreme Court for a span of decades – that all economic regulatory legislation enjoys a presumption of constitutionality and should be upheld as long as it is supported by any conceivable rational basis. What is more, it became the conventional wisdom, taught to generations of law students, that *Lochner*'s underlying theory was not only erroneous but disgracefully so. Summarizing the lessons that the Court had drawn from the *Lochner* experience, Justice Hugo Black – the first man named to the Supreme Court by Franklin Roosevelt and a constitutional literalist who believed that the Due Process Clause conferred no substantive guarantees of property rights – wrote in 1963 that "[u]nder the system of government created by our Constitution, it is up to legislatures, not courts, to decide on the wisdom and utility of legislation." He continued:

> There was a time when the Due Process Clause was used by this Court to strike down laws which were thought unreasonable, that is, unwise or incompatible with some particular economic or social philosophy .... [That approach] has long since been discarded. ... It is now settled that States "have power to legislate against what are found to be injurious practices ..., so long as their laws do not run afoul of some specific federal constitutional prohibition, or of some valid federal law."[14]

Perhaps significantly, the Supreme Court has never wholly renounced the scrutiny of economic legislation under the Due Process Clause. It continues to ask whether such legislation is rationally related to a legitimate public purpose. Yet not since 1937 has the Court invalidated economic regulatory legislation on "substantive due process" grounds.[15]

---

[14] *Ferguson v. Skrupa*, 372 U.S. 726, 729–30 (1963).

[15] In *Eastern Enterprises v. Apfel*, 524 U.S. 498 (1998), however, Justice Kennedy's conclusion that an economic regulatory statute violated substantive due process was necessary to the Court's decision that the statute was unconstitutional – a conclusion that four other justices reached under the Takings Clause.

The Road to *Roe v. Wade*

Since the political and constitutional revolution that Franklin Roosevelt did more than any other single figure to shape, a broad consensus has existed that the substantive due process decisions of the *Lochner*-era Supreme Court were deeply mistaken. In the immediate aftermath of *Lochner*'s demise, the leading accounts of *Lochner*'s error focused on the concept of substantive due process and on the related view that the Constitution contemplates judicial protection of "unenumerated" constitutional rights (such as freedom of contract).

But it was not too long before thinking on these matters began to evolve, at least in some, mostly liberal, quarters. A few decisions during the *Lochner* era had upheld rights of personal liberty substantially unconnected to economic regulation. In *Pierce v. Society of Sisters* (1925),[16] the Supreme Court held that a state violated the substantive due process rights of parents to direct their children's upbringing, as well as the rights of operators of private schools, when it required children to attend public schools through the eighth grade. *Meyer v. Nebraska*[17] (1923) similarly invalidated a statute forbidding the teaching of any language other than English to students who had not completed the eighth grade. Even in the aftermath of 1937, the Supreme Court continued to cite those decisions approvingly. In addition, there was at least one *Lochner*-era case in which the Court had failed to uphold a substantive due process claim that progressives increasingly regarded as itself constituting a stain on the Court's reputation. This was *Buck v. Bell* (1927),[18] in which the Court sustained a state law providing for the compulsory sterilization of "mental defectives" in state institutions. That decision included the hauntingly callous line, "Three generations of imbeciles are enough."

Cases such as *Pierce*, *Meyer*, and *Buck* posed the question whether it was wise, humane, or even tenable to insist that the Constitution protects no rights or liberties that are not specifically listed in its text. A corollary question was whether *Lochner*'s mistake might not have lain in assuming that the Fourteenth Amendment protects some substantive liberties but in protecting the wrong unenumerated

---

[16] 269 U.S. 510 (1925).
[17] 262 U.S. 390 (1923).
[18] 274 U.S. 200 (1927), 207.

rights based on what Justice Holmes had called "an economic theory which a large part of the country does not entertain."

Although reliance on *Lochner* remained taboo, the Supreme Court began to soften its stance on the possible existence of unenumerated rights protected by the Fourteenth Amendment as early as 1942, in *Skinner v. Oklahoma*.[19] In *Skinner*, the Court held that a state statute that authorized the sterilization of people with multiple convictions for some felonies, but not for others, violated the Equal Protection Clause. Mere rational basis review was inappropriate, and "strict scrutiny" properly applied, the Court reasoned, because procreation was "a basic liberty" and "one of the basic civil rights of man." By the 1960s, as discussed in Chapter 7, the Court had also picked out a number of other rights that are nowhere specifically listed in the Constitution as being "fundamental" for purposes of equal protection analysis.

Especially in light of the creeping recognition of substantive rights protected under the Equal Protection Clause, an important test case for the Warren Court's resistance to substantive due process came in *Griswold v. Connecticut* (1965).[20] *Griswold* presented a challenge to a state statute that barred the distribution or use of "any drug ... or instrument for the purpose of [contraception]." As interpreted, the statute allowed doctors to prescribe contraceptives to protect physical and psychological health – a loophole widely exploited by physicians serving middle- and upper-class patients. But the law threatened clinics expressly offering family-planning assistance to the less affluent. By a vote of 7–2, the Court invalidated the statute, despite obvious anguish about the rationale for the result.

Writing for the majority, Justice Douglas continued to eschew reliance on the Due Process Clause. "Overtones of some arguments suggest that *Lochner* ... should be our guide ... [b]ut we decline that invitation," he wrote. In a brisk but confusing opinion, Douglas instead reasoned that several provisions of the Bill of Rights give rise to "peripheral" or "penumbral" rights that "create zones of privacy."[21] As an example, he cited the recognized First Amendment right to freedom of association, which is not expressly mentioned in the Constitution, as constituting a "penumbra where privacy is protected

---

[19] 316 U.S. 535 (1942).
[20] 381 U.S. 479 (1965).
[21] *Ibid.* at 484.

from governmental intrusion." Similar "penumbras" of privacy surround other constitutional guarantees, Douglas continued, and the relation of marital intimacy – which Connecticut sought to regulate by denying contraceptives to married couples – fell "within the zone of privacy created by" one or more of those express provisions and their penumbras, although Douglas did not say which.

Where Douglas's opinion in *Griswold* seemed to acknowledge the existence of rights that were not explicitly "enumerated," centrally including a right or rights to privacy, other justices, who wrote concurring opinions, thought it less necessary to establish that the Connecticut statute violated "some right assured by the letter or penumbra of the Bill of Rights." In the view of one concurring justice, protection for the right at issue in *Griswold* came from "the concept of ordered liberty" as guaranteed by the Due Process Clause. The Due Process Clause, Justice Harlan wrote, "protects those personal rights that are fundamental, and is not confined to the specific terms of the Bill of Rights."

Although confusing in other respects, *Griswold* clearly suggested that the most disturbing feature of the Connecticut statute was its intrusion into intimate aspects of the marital relationship, some protection for which the Constitution might reasonably be said to presuppose. But the Court abandoned that limitation on *Griswold*'s rationale in *Eisenstadt v. Baird* (1972),[22] which invoked the Equal Protection Clause to invalidate a Massachusetts law that forbade the distribution of contraceptives to single people despite their availability to married couples. "If the right of privacy means anything," the Court wrote, "it is the right of the *individual*, married or single, to be free from unwanted governmental intrusion into matters so fundamentally affecting a person as the decision whether to bear or beget a child."[23] Those portentous words may have been written with abortion as well as contraception in mind.

Roe v. Wade and Abortion Rights

Roe v. Wade, which was decided by an astonishing 7–2 majority, followed a year later. The reverberations would redirect the future of the Supreme Court and the country for decades to come.

---

[22] 405 U.S. 438 (1972).
[23] *Ibid.* at 453.

Roe and Its Immediate Aftermath

The *Roe* opinion by Justice Harry Blackmun, a former lawyer for the Mayo Clinic, was sprawling; it included a long section on the history of abortion and its legality from ancient to modern times. As even many of those who supported the result acknowledged, however, the Court's opinion was bereft of cogent legal reasoning at crucial junctures. (The literature on how the *Roe* opinion ought to have been written is vast.) Justice Blackmun's analysis can be reconstructed as unfolding in three steps.

First, the Constitution protects a right to privacy that is broad enough to encompass a woman's right to abortion. According to Justice Blackmun, the Court had no need to determine conclusively whether the privacy right was "founded in the Fourteenth Amendment's concept of personal liberty, as we feel it is, or in the Ninth Amendment." Either way, *Roe* raised questions, now associated with *Lochner*, about whether the Supreme Court had any business identifying and enforcing unenumerated rights. Precedent, including *Griswold* and *Eisenstadt*, undoubtedly offered some support for the Court's conclusion. But neither *Griswold* nor *Eisenstadt* was explicitly reasoned as a substantive due process case. In addition, abortion fit only awkwardly under the privacy rubric. The strongest constitutional objection to abortion regulation is not that it intrudes on an activity normally conducted in private but that it interferes with what might be more plausibly described as an important aspect of personal liberty and distinctively burdens women.

Second, Justice Blackmun labeled abortion as a fundamental right, any interference with which triggers strict scrutiny. In support of this characterization, Blackmun relied primarily on "[t]he detriment that the State would impose upon a pregnant woman by denying her" the choice to end an unwanted pregnancy. He did not directly address whether abortion would have been recognized as a fundamental right in 1868, when the Fourteenth Amendment was ratified. Nor did Justice Blackmun squarely face up to the challenge that opponents of the decision would press most vociferously: Unlike any previously recognized fundamental right, abortion inherently involves the destruction of a human fetus. Abortion opponents claim that there can be no right, fundamental or otherwise, to cause the loss of an innocent life.

Third, Justice Blackmun determined that the state's interest in preserving fetal life became compelling but only at the point of fetal viability. "This is so," Blackmun sought to explain, "because the fetus then presumably has the capability of meaningful life outside the mother's womb."[24] This attempted justification, as an influential critic noted with biting logic, mistakes a definition for a syllogism.[25] By definition, a viable fetus has the capacity for life outside the womb. Yet the definition supplies no answer to the question of whether the state has a compelling interest in preserving fetal life prior to the point of viability.

Justice Byron White, writing in dissent, described the Court's decision in *Roe* as "an exercise of raw judicial power" that "fashion[ed] and announc[ed] a new constitutional right ... with scarcely any reason or authority for its action." Justice William Rehnquist also dissented, maintaining that the challenged statutes easily passed the rational basis test that he thought should apply.

Viewed in retrospect, *Roe* was very much a creature of the cultural and jurisprudential era of the otherwise generally conservative Burger Court. Deciding the case amid a sexual revolution and an increasing flow of educated women into professional careers, the justices recognized the capacity of unwanted pregnancies to disrupt otherwise well-planned lives. The justices would also have been aware that *Roe*, like *Skinner* and *Griswold* before it, had an "equal rights" as well as a "fundamental rights" dimension. Beyond the obvious point that only women could become pregnant in 1973, a woman with sufficient funds and education could typically procure a lawful abortion by traveling to a state or nation where abortion was legal. By contrast, women who were poorer and less well educated often lacked access to legal abortion. Many thousands sought illegal abortions instead. According to some estimates, the mortality rate for illegal, unlicensed abortions was more than ten times higher than the mortality rate for legal abortions.[26]

Also crucial to understanding *Roe v. Wade* in its historical context is that the Burger Court included no justices who styled themselves as originalists, and even its most conservative justices were predominantly secular in orientation. From their perspective, *Roe* must have seemed a judicious compromise: It protected a woman's right to

---

[24] *Roe*, 403 U.S. at 163.
[25] John Hart Ely, "The Wages of Crying Wolf: A Comment on Roe v. Wade," 82 *Yale Law Journal* 920, 924 (1973).
[26] See, for example, Jesse H. Choper, "Consequences of Supreme Court Decisions Upholding Individual Rights," 83 *Michigan Law Review* 1, 185 (1984).

control the use of her body before the point of fetal viability, while permitting the state to protect unborn life thereafter.

As time revealed, however, the Supreme Court lacked the capacity to make the compromise stick. Abortion opponents never accepted *Roe*'s legitimacy. Within a short time after its decision, conservative presidential candidates began to promise to appoint pro-life justices. The Republican Party platform called for *Roe* to be reversed. By 1992, with the two justices who had dissented in *Roe* still remaining on the Court and the anti-*Roe* Republican Presidents Ronald Reagan and George H. W. Bush having appointed five new justices (and Democrats none), *Roe* appeared ripe for overruling.

The Supreme Court thus surprised most observers when it affirmed "*Roe*'s essential holding" in a bitter 5–4 decision in *Planned Parenthood of Southeastern Pennsylvania v. Casey* (1992).[27] Three themes dominated the *Casey* plurality opinion that was jointly authored by Justices Sandra Day O'Connor, Anthony Kennedy, and David Souter – all of whom were nominated to the Court by presidents who had pledged to seek pro-life justices. First, if *Roe* was a mistake at the time of its decision, it was not an obvious one. An unwanted pregnancy subjects women to enormous burdens. Decisions such as *Skinner*, *Griswold*, and *Eisenstadt* made it plausible to rely on precedent to hold as a matter of law that women had a fundamental right to decide whether to bear an unwanted child. Second, a generation of women had shaped their lives in partial reliance on *Roe*. They had entered relationships and built careers in the expectation that unplanned pregnancies would not force them into unwanted childbearing. Third, the plurality worried openly that the Court's "legitimacy" – by which they appeared to mean the respect that it commanded in the eyes of the public as a trustworthy interpreter of the Constitution and guarantor of the rule of law – would be compromised if it were to overrule *Roe* "under fire" and thus foster an impression that political pressure could trigger a change in constitutional law. Precisely because the authors of the *Casey* plurality opinion had been appointed to overrule *Roe*, they felt, when the occasion actually arose, that they ought not do so. *Casey* marked the first time that a Supreme Court opinion ever openly expressed such a thought – one that the six-justice majority in *Dobbs* would explicitly reject.

[27] 505 U.S. 833 (1992).

Although *Casey* preserved what it described as *Roe*'s "central holding," it granted states more flexibility than before to regulate and discourage abortion. Under *Roe*, nearly all impediments to abortion attracted strict judicial scrutiny. Under *Casey*, women retained the right to abort a fetus prior to the point of viability if they insisted on doing so, but the states could impose waiting periods and require those performing abortions to provide information on alternatives, as long as those efforts did not amount to an "undue burden" on the ultimate abortion right.

Like *Roe* before it, *Casey* represented an effort by a majority of the justices to stake out a middle ground in abortion controversies. According to polls taken at the time, moreover, the Court's decision aligned well with mainstream public opinion in allowing states to affirm their preference for childbirth over abortion but guaranteeing women the ultimate right of decision. Again as with *Roe*, however, a militant minority of pro-life abortion opponents refused to acquiesce. They continued to maintain that abortion was morally heinous and that the Constitution did not include, and could not reasonably be interpreted to include, any abortion rights whatsoever. Moreover, despite their minority status in the nation as a whole,[28] the pro-life and anti-*Roe* forces constituted strong majorities in some states and exerted a disproportionate influence in the internal politics of the Republican Party, whose campaign platforms and presidential candidates continued to call for the overruling of *Roe* and *Casey*.[29]

Dobbs

Until overruled, *Roe* and *Casey* enjoyed the formal status of binding Supreme Court precedent that all lower courts, both state and federal, were bound to follow. But conservative state legislatures enacted more and more antiabortion statutes that were patently unconstitutional under those precedents with the aim of provoking the Court to reconsider them. *Dobbs v. Jackson Women's Health Organization* arose from a Mississippi statute that barred abortion after the fifteenth

---

[28] "U.S. Public Continues to Favor Legal Abortion, Oppose Overturning Roe v. Wade," *Pew Research Center* (Aug. 29, 2019), www.pewresearch.org/politics/2019/08/29/u-s-public-continues-to-favor-legal-abortion-oppose-overturning-roe-v-wade/.

[29] Julie Johnson, "Reagan Vows to Continue Battle on Abortion," *The New York Times* (Jan. 14, 1989).

week of pregnancy or, as the Court's opinion put it, "several weeks before the point at which a fetus is now regarded as 'viable' outside the womb." In an opinion by Justice Samuel Alito that was joined by Justice Thomas and by all three of the justices whom President Donald Trump had appointed, *Dobbs* overruled *Roe* and *Casey*.

The opinion's tone was caustic. *Roe*, Justice Alito wrote, was "egregiously wrong" at the time of its decision and "deeply damaging." In support of this conclusion, Alito quoted a law professor's observation that *Roe* was "not constitutional law and g[ave] almost no sense of an obligation to try to be."[30] According to the majority, *Roe* misstated pertinent history, "was remarkably loose in its treatment of the constitutional test" that it purported to apply, and had no "sound basis in precedent." *Casey*, Alito added, failed to shore up defects in *Roe*'s reasoning. If anything, it made matters worse by characterizing the abortion right as "an integral part of a broader entrenched right" to "make 'intimate and personal choices' that are 'central to personal dignity and autonomy.'" This conceptualization was far too broad, the majority asserted. If taken seriously, it "would license fundamental rights to illicit drugs, prostitution, and the like." The majority also rejected *Casey*'s suggestion that women who had planned their personal and professional lives "in reliance on the availability of abortion in the event that contraception should fail" as having "little support in our cases." This asserted reliance interest was insufficiently concrete and depended on empirical speculations that are "hard for anyone – and in particular, for a court – to assess," Justice Alito wrote.

The majority's own constitutional analysis was complex. Justice Alito argued that in "1868, the year when the Fourteenth Amendment was ratified, three-quarters of the states, 28 out of 37, had enacted statutes making abortion a crime" and that *Roe*'s defenders were "unable to show that a constitutional right was established when the Fourteenth Amendment was adopted." Apparently on this basis, a number of commentators quickly identified *Dobbs* as an example of the conservative supermajority's originalist pretensions. But this conclusion was subtly off-base. Without seeking to supply an originalist foundation for what he took to be controlling precedent, Justice Alito recognized that the Due Process Clause "has been held to guarantee

---

[30] *Dobbs*, 597 U.S. at 228 (quoting Ely, "Wages," *supra*, at 947).

some rights that are not mentioned in the Constitution" as long as they are "'deeply rooted in this Nation's history and tradition' and 'implicit in the concept of ordered liberty.'"[31] The ultimate ground for his rejection of an abortion right lay in its failure to satisfy that traditionalist, rather than a strictly originalist, test.

Justice Alito also asserted that "[n]othing in this opinion should be understood to cast doubt on precedents that do not concern abortion" – presumably including ones upholding rights to engage in private acts of same-sex intimacy and same-sex marriage that I shall discuss later – even if they were not "rooted in our Nation's history and tradition" at the time of their decision. "As even the *Casey* plurality recognized, '[a]bortion is a unique act' because it terminates 'life or potential life,'" Justice Alito wrote. In an implicit acknowledgment that the majority opinion did not rest on originalist grounds, Justice Thomas authored a concurring opinion – which none of the other conservative justices chose to join – arguing that "we should reconsider all of this Court's substantive due process precedents."

If we ask why none of the other conservative justices adopted Justice Thomas's uncompromising position that the Due Process Clause protects no substantive rights, the reasons appear to be complex. None of the conservatives is a thoroughly consistent originalist. All of them care about precedent to at least some extent – even if not enough to save *Roe v. Wade*, which they appear to have regarded as especially morally outrageous. In addition, judicial conservatives have their own uses for substantive due process. As we saw in Chapter 6, Justice Alito has embraced substantive due process reasoning as the legal basis for the incorporation doctrine, under which the Court has held that nearly all provisions of the Bill of Rights apply against the states. Judicial conservatives have also interpreted the Due Process Clause of the Fifth Amendment as establishing a substantive prohibition against race discrimination, including affirmative action, by the federal government.[32]

The three liberal justices who participated in *Dobbs* all dissented in an opinion by Justice Stephen Breyer that could fairly be described as a paradigmatic example of living constitutionalist reasoning. Justice

---

[31] *Ibid.* at 231, 237–38.
[32] Some academic commentators now maintain that the prohibition against race discrimination by the federal government could and should be grounded in the Citizenship Clause of the Fourteenth Amendment. See, for example, Ryan Williams, "Originalism and the Other Desegregation Decision," 99 *Virginia Law Review* 493, 501 (2013).

Breyer emphasized the important role that *Roe* and *Casey* had played in protecting women's dignity and autonomy: "Respecting a woman as an autonomous being, and granting her full equality, meant giving her substantial choice over th[e] most personal and most consequential of all life decisions." The dissenters did not claim originalist support for their position, but they were unapologetic about its absence: "In 1868, there was no nationwide right to end a pregnancy, and no one thought that the Fourteenth Amendment provided one." But only men participated in the ratification, Justice Breyer wrote, "so it is perhaps not so surprising that the ratifiers were not perfectly attuned to the importance of reproductive rights for women's liberty." He continued: "[A]pplications of liberty and equality can evolve while remaining grounded in constitutional principles, constitutional history, and constitutional precedents."[33]

The full legal ramifications of the *Dobbs* decision for the availability of abortion in the United States remain to be felt. *Dobbs* made clear that states (and Congress) are now free to enact prohibitions of abortion, subject to "rational basis review" under the Due Process Clause. But imaginable forms of antiabortion legislation would pose novel and highly debatable questions, including these:

- Would a prohibition against counseling a woman to seek an out-of-state abortion by a state that criminalizes abortion violate the Free Speech Clause of the First Amendment?
- Would a prohibition against traveling out-of-state to procure an abortion, or aiding and abetting out-of-state travel for that purpose, violate a constitutionally protected right to travel?[34]
- Could an antiabortion state impose criminal penalties on an out-of-state doctor who performed an out-of-state abortion on one of its citizens on the theory that the out-of-state abortion destroyed a fetus that the regulating state had a constitutionally cognizable interest in protecting from harm?

Abortion: Concluding Observations

There can be little doubt that involvement in abortion controversies damaged the institutional reputation of the Supreme Court. The

---

[33] *Ibid.* at 376 (Breyer, J., joined by Sotomayor and Kagan, J.J., dissenting).
[34] Justice Kavanaugh suggested in *Dobbs* that it would, although he did not cite any authority in support of that conclusion.

Court's celebrators often cite the capacity for reasoned deliberation as its signal virtue. In addressing the question whether there is or should be a right to abortion, however, "reasoned deliberation" may give way too quickly to moral intuitions for judicial reasoning (on either side) to earn the respect of those who disagree with its conclusions. With abortion having been the most politically salient constitutional issue of the past fifty years, it is probably inevitable that the nominations of Supreme Court justices and ensuing confirmation debates would have become ever more politicized.

Justice Scalia used to say that the Supreme Court should keep its hands off abortion issues and leave them for resolution by democratically accountable decision-makers in Congress and the state legislatures. The majority opinion in *Dobbs* included similar intimations. But even if *Dobbs*'s holding that the Fourteenth Amendment includes no substantive guarantee of abortion rights persists indefinitely, other abortion-related questions, as we have seen, will arise under other constitutional provisions. In one form or another, the saga of abortion litigation in the Supreme Court thus seems destined to continue.

Rights of Sexual Autonomy

Griswold v. *Connecticut* recognized married couples' rights to private sexual intimacy. But there is no corresponding constitutional landmark establishing rights of unmarried heterosexual couples. Even in *Eisenstadt v. Baird*, which addressed states' power to deny access to contraceptives to single individuals, the Supreme Court stopped short of considering whether, and if so when, acts of sexual intimacy involving a man and a woman who were not married to each other might be subjected to criminal sanctions if a state wished to prohibit them.

Insofar as more clarity now exists about constitutional rights to liberty or autonomy in matters of sexual intimacy, it has come mostly from Supreme Court cases challenging state prohibitions against sodomy involving same-sex partners. Same-sex sodomy has often elicited condemnation for reasons involving religious teaching and a belief among some that "natural law" condemns acts of same-sex sexual intimacy. According to moralists within the natural law tradition, the natural and therefore exclusively proper use of male and female sex organs is for acts associated with procreation (even if procreation is not physically possible in a particular case due, for example, to the infertility of one or both of the participants).

The Supreme Court's responses to arguments for the protection of same-sex intimacy under the Due Process Clause present a case study in living constitutionalism or doctrinal evolution. As recently as 1961, every state prohibited sodomy. At that time, a Supreme Court decision invalidating antisodomy laws would have been unthinkable. Twenty-five years later, when the number of states that barred sodomy had fallen by half, a sharply divided Court upheld the enforcement of a general antisodomy law against same-sex couples in *Bowers v. Hardwick* (1986).[35] Then in 2003, when only thirteen states maintained antisodomy prohibitions, *Lawrence v. Texas*[36] overruled *Bowers* and upheld a substantive due process right to engage in private acts of sexual intimacy.

Although manifestly influenced by evolving social attitudes, the result in *Lawrence* also turned on the vote of a normally conservative Supreme Court justice, Anthony Kennedy, who repeatedly championed gay rights in both equal protection and substantive due process cases. As a measure of the significance of Kennedy's presence on the Court, it is highly doubtful whether the cohort of justices who decided *Dobbs* in 2022 would have ruled the same way that the Court in *Lawrence*, with Kennedy writing the majority opinion, did. (The moderate conservative Justice O'Connor also concurred in the judgment, but on narrower equal protection grounds.) We thus may have reason to question whether the story of rights to engage in same-sex intimacy under the Due Process Clause has reached a stable equilibrium as the Court has cycled from *Bowers* to *Lawrence* to *Dobbs*.

Bowers involved a challenge to a Georgia statute that forbade heterosexual as well as same-sex sodomy. In practice, however, prosecutions for consensual heterosexual sodomy never occurred. Criminal prosecutions for same-sex sodomy were also rare, but unusual circumstances resulted in the filing of charges against Michael Hardwick: When police arrived at his home to question him about another matter, a roommate led them directly to Hardwick's bedroom, where they observed him engaged in an act of same-sex sexual intimacy. Although the state ultimately dropped the prosecution, Hardwick decided to

---

[35] 478 U.S. 186 (1986).
[36] 539 U.S. 558 (2003).

press the issue. He sought a judicial ruling that the antisodomy statute deprived him of a constitutionally protected fundamental right to sexual autonomy in the privacy of his bedroom.

The Supreme Court rejected Hardwick's claim. Several threads ran through the Court's opinion and the concurring opinions of the justices in the 5–4 majority. The first involved anxiety about the judicial role in recognizing fundamental rights under the Due Process Clause amid the ongoing fallout from *Roe v. Wade*. Writing for the Court, Justice Byron White, one of the two dissenters in *Roe*, observed that "[t]he Court is most vulnerable and comes nearest to illegitimacy when it deals with judge-made constitutional law having little or no cognizable roots in the language or design of the Constitution."[37] He further maintained that the Court could properly treat as "fundamental" only those rights that are either "implicit in the concept of ordered liberty" or "deeply rooted in this Nation's history and tradition." This formulation seemed intentionally ambiguous about – if not flatly inconsistent with – *Roe*, even though two members of the *Bowers* majority had also joined the majority opinion in *Roe*.

The second, sometimes latent, theme in the Court's opinion was contempt for homosexual conduct. The Court refused to consider whether the Constitution would permit application of the Georgia statute to heterosexual sodomy. Citing historical prohibitions against sodomy, the majority opinion caustically concluded that "to claim that a right to engage in [same-sex sodomy] is 'deeply rooted in this Nation's history and tradition' or 'implicit in the concept of ordered liberty' is, at best, facetious."[38]

A third strand in the Court's opinion involved an unwillingness to recognize a fundamental privacy or autonomy right embracing all forms of private, voluntary sexual conduct. The Court said that "it would be difficult, except by fiat, to limit the claimed right to homosexual conduct while leaving exposed to prosecution adultery, incest, and other sexual crimes even though they are committed in the home."

Justice Harry Blackmun wrote a powerful dissenting opinion. In it, he derided the majority's preoccupation with the anatomical details of private, consensual acts of sexual intimacy. At stake, he wrote, was not an isolated right to engage in same-sex sodomy but

---

[37] *Bowers*, 478 U.S. at 194.
[38] *Ibid.* at 194.

"the fundamental interest all individuals have in controlling the nature of their intimate associations with others." In Justice Blackmun's view, longstanding moral judgments about the propriety of homosexual conduct did not alone permit Georgia to prosecute citizens for making choices about the most intimate aspects of their lives. The Constitution presupposed a right of all persons to engage in voluntary conduct in the privacy of their homes that posed no palpable threats to themselves or others, he maintained. He thought it cruel and bigoted to deny members of the LGBTQ community the lawful opportunity for sexual intimacy that others take for granted.

Seventeen years later, the Court largely adopted Blackmun's position when it squarely overruled *Bowers* in *Lawrence v. Texas*. Because the Texas statute involved in the case prohibited only same-sex and not heterosexual sodomy, the Court might have held that even if all sodomy could be prohibited, the distinction between same-sex and heterosexual sodomy was simply irrational and therefore unconstitutional under the rational basis test. (Justice O'Connor took this position in a concurring opinion.) But Justice Kennedy, who wrote the majority opinion joined by four other justices, insisted on going further to make clear that a state could not prohibit same-sex sodomy even if it also barred heterosexual sodomy.

Bowers's mistake, Kennedy insisted, was to frame the claim of right before the Court as one "to engage in certain sexual conduct." At issue, according to the *Lawrence* majority, was a right that heterosexual and especially married couples have long taken for granted – a right to engage in intimate private conduct, including sexual relations, potentially as an aspect of or a gateway to an enduring relationship. Justice Kennedy also made clear the majority justices' central concern with the dignity of those members of the LGBTQ community who faced a realistic threat of prosecution or harassment for engaging in private sexual intimacies: "When homosexual conduct is made criminal by the law of the State, that declaration in and of itself is an invitation to subject homosexual persons to discrimination both in the public and in the private spheres .... [*Bowers*'s] continuance as precedent demeans the lives of homosexual persons."[39]

The three justices generally viewed as the Court's most conservative members – Chief Justice William Rehnquist and Justices

---

[39] Lawrence, 539 U.S. at 575.

Antonin Scalia and Clarence Thomas – filed a strident dissent. Written by Justice Scalia, it argued that the Court had abused its authority by taking a partisan position in a "culture war" between liberals and social and religious conservatives and by "largely sign[ing] on to the so-called homosexual agenda ... [of] eliminating the moral opprobrium that has traditionally attached to homosexual conduct."[40]

Will *Lawrence* survive *Dobbs*? On the one hand, as I have said, it seems unlikely that the Supreme Court's current conservative supermajority would find the right upheld in *Lawrence* to be "deeply rooted in [our] history and tradition" if the question were one of first impression. Justice Kennedy labored in *Lawrence* to describe the right as one to engage in intimate private conduct – a formulation that could plausibly pass muster under the applicable "history and tradition" test. But Justice Alito's *Dobbs* opinion faulted the Court's opinion in *Planned Parenthood v. Casey*, which *Dobbs* overruled, for relying on a similarly broad formulation of the right that it purported to enforce. At the same time, *Dobbs* supplies supporters of *Lawrence* with a specific, textual, basis for hope. The Court said specifically in *Dobbs* that "[n]othing in this opinion should be understood to cast doubt on precedents that do not concern abortion." Given that assertion, *Lawrence* remains binding on the lower courts unless and until the Supreme Court reverses it. And the justices may have enough commitment to stare decisis to prefer to leave *Lawrence* undisturbed, at least for the intermediate term. As noted earlier, the number of antisodomy laws on the books had dwindled even before *Lawrence*, and actual prosecutions for violating the few that remained on the books were vanishingly scarce. Today, following Justice Kennedy's departure from the Court, the enduring character of the change in constitutional law that *Lawrence* wrought – if it does indeed endure – may be attributable to a background shift in public attitudes toward private acts of sexual intimacy between unmarried couples, including same-sex partners.

Marriage

A number of Supreme Court cases have characterized the opportunity to marry as a "fundamental" right protected by the Due Process Clause, the Equal Protection Clause, or both. *Skinner*

---

[40] *Ibid.* at 602 (Scalia, J., joined by Rehnquist, C.J., and Thomas, J., dissenting).

v. Oklahoma, which described procreation as "one of the basic civil rights of man," also linked marriage with procreation in being "fundamental to the very existence and survival of the race." In *Loving v. Virginia* (1967),[41] the Court held that a statute barring marriage between people of different races not only violated equal protection but also infringed a fundamental liberty right protected by the Due Process Clause. "The freedom to marry has long been recognized as one of the vital personal rights essential to the orderly pursuit of happiness by free men," Chief Justice Warren wrote.[42]

Roughly fifty years later, the Supreme Court, by a vote of 5–4 in an opinion by Justice Kennedy, built on *Loving* to uphold a fundamental due process right to same-sex marriage in *Obergefell v. Hodges* (2015).[43] Like *Lawrence v. Texas*, in which Justice Kennedy also wrote the majority opinion, *Obergefell* marked a dramatic advance in the recognition of constitutional rights for gays and lesbians. Again like *Lawrence*, it also highlighted a deep and recurring methodological issue in the definition of constitutionally protected fundamental rights under the Due Process and Equal Protection Clauses that also figured prominently in *Dobbs* and will undoubtedly continue to challenge the justices.

The divisive methodological issue involves how to define the scope of rights that are, according to a formulation that a Court has frequently employed, "deeply rooted in [our] history and tradition" and "implicit in the concept of ordered liberty."[44] At first blush, marriage appears to satisfy that formula almost uniquely well. But does the historically recognized right to marry encompass "same-sex marriage," as in *Obergefell*, or "interracial marriage," as in *Loving*? As we saw in Chapter 6, lawyers and judges often describe questions such as these as raising issues about the "level of generality" at which rights, or the tradition in which rights are grounded, should be described. This was the central methodological issue in *Obergefell*, as it had been in *Bowers* and *Lawrence*.

In the often-cited case of *Washington v. Glucksberg* (1997),[45] which rejected a claimed fundamental right not to be denied the assistance of a willing physician in ending one's life, the Supreme Court

---

[41] 388 U.S. 1 (1967).
[42] *Ibid.* at 12.
[43] 576 U.S. 644 (2015).
[44] For example, *Dobbs*, 597 U.S. 231; *Washington v. Glucksberg*, 521 U.S. 702, 721 (1997).
[45] 521 U.S. 702, 721 (1997).

insisted that "we have required in substantive-due-process cases a 'careful description' of the asserted fundamental liberty interest" as defined and limited by specific historical practices. That asserted methodological limitation on substantive due process adjudication probably cannot be squared with the results in *Roe* and *Casey,* as Justice Alito emphasized in overruling those decisions in *Dobbs.* As is more important for present purposes, it might appear hard to reconcile with Court's rulings in *Lawrence, Obergefell,* and possibly *Loving* as well.

But Justice Kennedy, who had joined the Court's opinion in *Glucksberg,* concluded that the *Glucksberg* formula did not control in *Obergefell* because the Court's precedents called for a different approach in cases involving "marriage and intimacy." "If rights were defined by who exercised them in the past, then received practices could serve as their own continued justification and new groups could not invoke rights once denied," he reasoned. And that conclusion would be incompatible with the Court's interpretations of the Equal Protection Clause, to which, Justice Kennedy found, the Due Process Clause is "connected in a profound way." Under the Equal Protection Clause, Kennedy asserted, "the Court has recognized that new insights and social understandings can reveal unjustified inequality within our most fundamental institutions that once passed unnoticed and unchallenged."[46] On that "living constitutionalist" basis, Justice Kennedy and the *Obergefell* majority upheld the challengers' claim of a fundamental right to same-sex marriage. Effective exclusion of gays and lesbians from the institution of marriage, the Court found, deprived them of the social and familial stability, respect, and self-respect that marriage has traditionally afforded.

Chief Justice Roberts and Justices Scalia, Thomas, and Alito all wrote impassioned dissents in *Obergefell.* "The fundamental right to marry does not include a right to make a State change its definition of marriage," the chief justice maintained. In his view, "the majority's approach has no basis in principle or tradition, except for the unprincipled tradition of judicial policymaking that characterized discredited decisions such as *Lochner.*" The chief justice also argued that "[t]he marriage laws at issue here do not violate the Equal Protection Clause, because distinguishing between opposite-sex and same-sex couples is rationally related to the States' 'legitimate state interest' in

[46] *Obergefell,* 576 U.S. at 673.

'preserving the traditional institution of marriage.'" In a separate, even more plaintive dissent, Justice Alito protested that "[i]t is far beyond the outer reaches of this Court's authority to say that a State may not adhere to" the traditional understanding of marriage as involving one man and one woman. He warned that the *Obergefell* decision would "be used to vilify" as "bigots" those "who are unwilling to assent to the new orthodoxy."[47]

When the dissenting opinions in *Obergefell* are viewed in conjunction with the more recent decision in *Dobbs*, they leave little doubt that if *Obergefell* came before the Supreme Court for the first time today, the current conservative supermajority would reach a different result. But it does not follow that *Obergefell* is ripe for overruling. Lower courts and other public officials remain bound by it. And the argument that *Obergefell* should not be overruled seems strong under traditional understandings of stare decisis. A significant factor in determining whether a prior decision should be overruled is whether it has generated significant reliance interests. Today, there are nearly 750,000 married same-sex couples in the United States, many if not all of whom have organized their lives in reliance on the promise that their marriages will carry the same privileges and entitlements as anyone else's.[48] Still, one cannot be sure. In the domain of substantive due process adjudication, the Court looks very different following the retirement of Justice Anthony Kennedy than it did before.

Conclusion

From *Dred Scott* and *Lochner* through *Roe*, *Lawrence*, *Obergefell*, and *Dobbs*, substantive due process adjudication by the Supreme Court has always provoked controversy. No one would defend all of the Court's substantive due process decisions. There may be no other area of constitutional law in which the Court's interpretations of formally unamended constitutional language have exhibited more reversals of course. Nonetheless, some have always believed that substantive due process, coupled with the related premise that the

---

[47] *Ibid.* at 741 (Alito, J., joined by Scalia and Thomas, J.J., dissenting).
[48] Zachary Scherer, "Key Demographic and Economic Characteristics of Same-Sex and Opposite-Sex Couples Differed," *United States Census Bureau* (Nov. 22, 2022), www.census.gov/library/stories/2022/11/same-sex-couple-households-exceeded-one-million.html.

Constitution presupposes the existence of unenumerated but judicially enforceable rights, represents a crucial check against the tyranny of the majority within the American scheme of government.[49]

In an era of frequent paeans to originalism and textualism, the Supreme Court's enthusiasm for substantive due process adjudication has undoubtedly waned, as exhibited by *Dobbs*. Strikingly, however, the Court has never renounced the proposition that the Due Process Clause protects some otherwise unenumerated substantive rights. Nor do a majority of the justices seem likely to do so in the near future. Although heated debates persist about whether particular claimed rights exist and about how, methodologically, protected rights should be identified, there is thus more agreement than is often recognized about a possibly surprising fundamental premise: Most conservative as well as liberal justices embrace the premise that the Constitution implies or presupposes the existence of more judicially enforceable rights than its language creates explicitly.

---

[49] See, for example, James Fleming, *Constructing Basic Liberties: A Defense of Substantive Due Process* (Chicago, IL: University of Chicago Press, 2022).

9 THE SHRINKING YET STILL FORMIDABLE POWERS OF CONGRESS

The Supreme Court's most momentous ruling of 2012 came in *National Federation of Independent Business (NFIB) v. Sebelius*.[1] The case posed the most testing questions about the scope of Congress's power that the Court had confronted since 1937, when, in an about-face recounted in Chapter 2, the Court had upheld Congress's power to enact central elements of the New Deal. At stake in *NFIB* was the constitutionality of the Affordable Care Act (ACA) or, as some called it, Obamacare. The ACA, which aimed to guarantee health care to virtually all Americans, was the proudest achievement of the Obama administration, enacted in 2010. On the night when the bill passed the House, by a vote of 219–212, the president had delivered a short, triumphant speech celebrating the accomplishment. Banner headlines appeared in newspapers the following day. Two years later, the nation braced for another cliffhanger vote on the ACA, this time by the Supreme Court.

NFIB presented multiple questions, most of which would probably have struck nonlawyers as abstruse. Perhaps the most basic was whether Congress could force Americans to purchase health insurance. In public debates, those challenging the constitutionality of the ACA had sought to analogize that question to whether Congress could compel people to buy broccoli. Although that question seems

---

[1] 567 U.S. 519 (2012).

readily comprehensible, to understand the significance of *NFIB* to the development of constitutional law, it is necessary to bear in mind two points that many may find counterintuitive. First, no provision of the Bill of Rights gives Americans an individual "right" not to be forced to buy health insurance (or broccoli). A few years earlier, when Massachusetts had enacted a statute effectively compelling some of its residents to purchase health insurance, the rights-conferring provisions of the Constitution posed no obstacle. Second, it did not follow from the fact that Massachusetts could require residents to procure health insurance that Congress could impose a similar mandate. Unlike some state governments, the government of the United States has long been understood to be one of limited or "enumerated" powers. In order for laws enacted by Congress to be valid, Congress must be able to point to a specific constitutional provision authorizing it to enact them. Most of the authorizations come in Article I, but there are a few in other Articles of the original Constitution as well. In addition, the Thirteenth, Fourteenth, and Fifteenth Amendments all conclude with authorizations of Congress to enforce their guarantees "by appropriate legislation."

To justify Congress's mandate that some Americans had to purchase health insurance, defenders of the ACA placed principal reliance on Article I, Section 8, Clause 3, which authorizes Congress "[t]o regulate Commerce with foreign Nations, and among the several States." To anyone not versed in constitutional law, the Commerce Clause might seem a poor candidate to support a congressional dictate to buy health insurance. But since the New Deal, and indeed before, the Commerce Clause had emerged as the go-to provision for justifying federal laws that regulate the national economy or any activities with a "substantial effect" on the quantity of goods and services that are ultimately shipped in "Commerce ... among the several States." The purchase and sale of insurance are economic activities. And the market for health care, which insurance helps to finance, is hugely economically consequential. Examples of kinds of legislation that Congress has enacted under the Commerce Clause, based on the rationale that they regulate economic activities with a "substantial effect" on interstate commerce, include minimum wage and antidiscrimination laws, environmental regulations, prohibitions against the possession and sale of obscenity and narcotic drugs, and workplace safety requirements. Given these precedents, lawyers involved in drafting the ACA had confidently expected that the statute's "individual mandate" would easily pass constitutional muster under the Commerce Clause. If Congress can require businesses to sell goods and services to people with whom they would rather not do business – as it does, for example, when it enacts antidiscrimination laws – why couldn't Congress insist that people purchase health insurance that they would rather not buy?

In 2012, the Supreme Court, by nearly all counts, included four liberal and five conservative justices. The four liberals all agreed that under the Court's precedents, the individual mandate survived scrutiny under the Commerce Clause as a regulation of the interstate insurance and health care markets. But the Court's five conservative members ruled that it did not. In their view, past cases had pushed the interpretation of Congress's power "[t]o regulate Commerce ... among the several States" to, and possibly beyond, any reasonable limit as defined by original historical understandings. And whatever paring back the conservatives might or might not want to consider in future cases, they agreed strongly that they should tolerate no further expansions. The individual mandate was different from any provision that the Court had upheld before, they reasoned, because it required people who were not already engaged in insurance or health care markets to become commercial actors. Congress could regulate those who had voluntarily entered interstate markets or who otherwise engaged in economic activity that substantially affected commerce, but the Commerce Clause, the conservative justices agreed, granted Congress no authority to require people to participate in economic markets or activities that they wished to eschew.

Chief Justice John Roberts announced the decision in the ACA case and, as per custom, explained the majority's rationale for its holdings. As he completed his explanation that Congress had no authority to enact the individual mandate under the Commerce Clause, most observers in the courtroom assumed – and at least one television network breathlessly reported – that the mandate was therefore invalid. But Roberts had not finished. Having held that Congress could not enact the individual mandate under the Commerce Clause, he turned next to an argument on which the government, in defending the ACA, had placed little reliance: What the statute termed a "penalty" for failing to buy health insurance could instead be characterized as a "tax" on those who did not purchase coverage.

Now joined by the four liberal justices and over the dissents of the other conservatives, Roberts announced that a tax on the failure to buy health insurance lay within Congress's power to impose under the Constitution's Taxing and Spending Clause.[2] Although Congress did not call the ACA's penalty a tax, Roberts reasoned, it was collected by the Internal Revenue Service and had many of the hallmarks of a tax. And in the case of reasonable doubt about whether Congress had the power to enact legislation, he wrote, it was the job of the Supreme Court to get out of the way and let the politically accountable institutions of government – Congress and the president – decide. The four other conservative justices objected angrily, but to no avail, that the individual mandate, which Congress had chosen not to label as a tax, could not be upheld based on bait-and-switch techniques.

From the perspective of those who favor expansive interpretation of Congress's Article I powers, the Supreme Court's reliance on Congress's power to tax to sustain the ACA's individual mandate was a short-term victory that exacted a longer-term cost. In upholding what Congress had labeled a "penalty" as a "tax," Chief Justice Roberts found it necessary to draw a distinction between taxes, which Congress can enact under Article I, Section 8, Clause 1, and "penalties" that have a regulatory rather than a revenue-raising purpose. Because the tax for failure to purchase health insurance was less than the cost of some available policies, Roberts determined that it was not coercive. Indeed, it might raise some revenue from people who preferred to pay the tax as an alternative to the higher insurance premiums. But that reasoning committed the Court to drawing a distinction between permissible taxes and impermissible penalties, only the former of which could be justified under the Taxing and Spending Clause, that the Court had not previously attempted to enforce since prior to 1937. As a result, the effect of the Court's decision to uphold the individual mandate under the Taxing and Spending Clause, but not the Commerce Clause, was to leave Congress with less regulatory power under Article I than many constitutional lawyers had thought it possessed when Congress initially enacted the ACA.

I have begun this chapter on congressional power with this partial, abbreviated discussion of *NFIB v. Sebelius* because it is the Supreme Court's most recent major pronouncement on the scope of

---

[2] U.S. Const. art. I, § 8, cl. 1.

Congress's powers under Article I. As I shall make clear going forward, I believe *NFIB* reveals a lot, not only about what the current law is but also about the concerns that have preoccupied and are likely to continue to preoccupy the conservative justices. That said, *NFIB* certainly does not tell us everything we might want to know. In 2012, at the time of the *NFIB* decision, John Roberts was the Court's "swing" justice on issues of congressional power. According to press reports, Roberts's decision-making in the ACA case was swayed by his dislike for the optics of a Supreme Court majority consisting of five conservative justices, all appointees of Republican presidents, invalidating the signature achievement of the Democratic Obama administration over the votes of four justices appointed by Democratic presidents. With the Court now having a six-justice conservative supermajority, Roberts's capacity to be the difference-maker has waned. If the question whether the ACA's individual mandate could be upheld under the taxing power were to come to the Court for the first time today, there is no assurance that the conservative supermajority would decide the same way that the Court did in 2012. It is also possible that the conservative supermajority, in the years ahead, may consider not only refusing to extend Congress's recognized powers under Article I but also overturning precedents stretching back to 1937 that have construed Congress's powers very liberally. In order to gauge that possibility, the remainder of this chapter first looks backward to relevant history and then traces the arc and processes of constitutional change in the interpretation of the powers of Congress as they have unfolded up to the present day.

Historical Background to Modern Issues

Proximate Origins of *NFIB*

The precedents that form the background to the Supreme Court's decision in *NFIB v. Sebelius*, and that frame a number of the choices that the Court will face going forward, mostly begin with the 1937 "switch in time." As Chapter 2 explained, prior to the fateful spring of that year, the justices had invalidated important New Deal legislation by distinguishing between interstate commerce, which Congress can regulate, and manufacturing and agriculture, which the Court insisted lay beyond Congress's Commerce Clause authority. Even when Congress sought to regulate the interstate shipment of goods, the

Court had sometimes struck down federal laws that it viewed as having the purpose or intent of controlling what happened in manufacturing facilities and on farms that were located in a single state. In *Hammer v. Dagenhart* (1918),[3] for example, the Court had ruled that Congress overstepped its Commerce Clause authority by barring interstate transportation of goods produced through the use of child labor. The obvious purpose of the law, a majority of the justices held, was to achieve effective regulation over processes of manufacturing.

The Court began its climbdown from decisions that narrowly construed Congress's commerce power with its decision in *NLRB v. Jones & Laughlin Steel Corp.* (1937).[4] That case upheld the application of the National Labor Relations Act, which protected union organizing, to a large steel manufacturer that sold most of its products in interstate commerce. Although "manufacturing itself is not commerce," the Court reasoned in a 5–4 decision, manufacturing practices, such as discharging employees for unionizing activities, become subject to federal regulation "if they have such a close and substantial relation to interstate commerce that their control is essential or appropriate to protect that commerce from burdens and obstructions" such as "industrial strife" and work stoppages.

The decisiveness of the turnaround exhibited in *Jones & Laughlin Steel* became clear in two cases decided in 1941 and 1942 that remain leading precedents today. *United States v. Darby*[5] (1941) upheld Congress's Commerce Clause authority to regulate wages, hours, and working conditions in manufacturing facilities on either of two alternative bases. First, Congress can forbid the shipment of goods in interstate commerce if the conditions of their manufacture – including employees' wages and hours – fail to satisfy federal standards. Second, Congress can regulate "activities intrastate," such as manufacturing, if they have a "substantial effect" on commerce. *Wickard v. Filburn*[6] (1942) underlined the breadth of that second ground. *Wickard* upheld the imposition of a penalty on a farmer who had grown 239 more bushels of wheat than his marketing allotment under the federal Agricultural Adjustment Act, even though the excess went entirely to home consumption. That home consumption might have only a "trivial" effect on the interstate

[3] 247 U.S. 251 (1918).
[4] 301 U.S. 1 (1937).
[5] 312 U.S. 100 (1941).
[6] 317 U.S. 111 (1942).

wheat market if viewed in isolation. But when farmer Filburn's actions were "taken together with [those] of many others similarly situated," their cumulative effect on prices for and interstate sales of wheat would be sufficiently "substantial" to justify federal regulation under the Commerce Clause, the Court held. When Justice Robert Jackson showed a draft of his majority opinion in *Wickard* to his law clerk, the clerk remarked that if the Court issued the opinion as written, it would never again be able to hold that a congressional regulation of intrastate economic activity exceeded Congress's commerce power. Jackson replied that he did not disagree.[7]

During the same period that the Supreme Court abandoned its *Lochner*-era construction of the Commerce Clause, it offered comparably broad interpretations of Congress's power to impose taxes and make expenditures to promote the general welfare under Article I, Section 8, Clause 3. It was up to Congress, not the courts, to determine which expenditures would effectively promote the general welfare, as distinguished from that of particular groups or individuals, the Court ruled in a 1937 decision sustaining the Social Security Act's federally funded pension scheme.[8]

When *Darby* and *Wickard* are viewed in conjunction with parallel decisions upholding Congress's power to tax and spend to promote the general welfare in enacting statutes such as the Social Security Act, they mark a wholesale transformation in prevailing understandings of Congress's powers under Article I. That recasting was enabled, and indeed propelled, by what was in effect a peaceful political revolution. As president, Franklin Roosevelt advanced, and persuaded a large majority of the American people to adopt, a vision of national government in the United States that took responsibility for taming the business cycle, ensuring safe conditions and living wages for workers, and establishing a social safety net for the involuntarily unemployed, the disabled, and the aged. From 1933, when Roosevelt took office, to 1969, when Lyndon Johnson departed, Democratic presidents occupied the White House for twenty-eight of thirty-six years, interrupted only by the moderate Republican Dwight Eisenhower. In addition, Democrats continued to dominate congressional elections for more

---

[7] See Barry Friedman, *The Will of the People: How Public Opinion Has Influenced the Supreme Court and the Meaning of the Constitution* (New York, NY: Farrar, Straus and Giroux, 2009), 235.
[8] *Helvering v. Davis*, 301 U.S. 619 (1937).

than a decade thereafter. Throughout this period, Congress enacted progressively more legislation implementing and sometimes expanding the big-government agenda of Roosevelt's New Deal. Signal additions included the 1964 Civil Rights Act, which banned race and sex discrimination in much of the economy, and landmark environmental and workplace safety legislation.

The politics and the constitutional law of this era were, unsurprisingly, closely interconnected. Roosevelt's extraordinary success in winning elections allowed him to reshape the Supreme Court. By 1941, he had appointed seven of the nine justices who decided *Darby* and *Wickard* by unanimous votes. In constitutional law as in politics, moreover, even most conservatives and Republicans in the decades immediately following the 1937 turnaround acquiesced in the assumption that the Constitution made nearly pervasive national regulation – much if not most of it adopted under the Commerce Clause – a permissible political choice for Congress, subject only to the constraints imposed by the Constitution's expressly rights-creating provisions such as the First Amendment. The culminating ratification of these assumptions came in 1964, when the Supreme Court affirmed Congress's power under the Commerce Clause to bar race discrimination by a relatively small restaurant, Ollie's Barbecue, that catered exclusively to a local clientele. By unanimous vote, the Court, in *Katzenbach v. McClung* (1964),[9] largely echoed the reasoning of *Wickard v. Filburn*. It was plausible to think that the cumulative effects of discrimination by small restaurants throughout the country might discourage travel by racial minorities and reduce the quantities of food sold in interstate commerce, the Court explained. As late as 1981, the Court upheld environmental legislation by observing even more casually that "we cannot say that Congress did not have a rational basis for concluding that surface coal mining has substantial effects on interstate commerce."[10]

Critical Perspectives

The question whether the post–New Deal developments in Commerce Clause doctrine comported with the Constitution's original meaning has been, and continues to be, much debated. The Founding

---

[9] 379 U.S. 294 (1964).
[10] *Hodel v. Virginia Surface Mining & Reclamation Ass'n*, 452 U.S. 264 (1981).

generation never imagined a national government that would perform all of the functions that the national government discharges today. But what the Framers imagined or anticipated does not necessarily define the meaning of Article I's grants of congressional power. To take a plain example, the Framers could not foresee air travel, but no one doubts that Congress can regulate interstate commerce that occurs via air, not ground transportation, or that the Article I authorizations "to raise and support Armies" and to "provide and maintain a Navy" adequately empower the creation of an Air Force and more recently a Space Force.

With respect to Congress's power to regulate "commerce" among the several states, Samuel Johnson's famous eighteenth-century *Dictionary of the English Language* defined "[c]ommerce" as "[i]ntercourse: ... interchange of any thing; trade; traffick."[11] This entry is consistent with the frequent observation that the Founders differentiated between manufacture, on the one hand, and commerce, on the other. But insofar as Congress prohibits trade in an item, such as any commodity produced by workers paid less than a minimum wage, is it not regulating commerce? According to Johnson's dictionary, "regulate" meant "[t]o adjust by rule or method" or "direct," as in "[r]egulate [a patient] in his manner of living."[12] Similarly, the Founding generation would have found the Social Security system, funded by employment taxes, to be unimaginable, but it is a different question whether the system fits within the language of Article I empowering Congress to "lay and collect Taxes ... to ... provide for the ... general Welfare of the United States."

It would, of course, be far too simplistic to seek to identify original constitutional meanings by examining dictionary entries alone. Constitutional provisions need to be understood in a broader context of widely shared assumptions and purposes. But the historical purposes of the Commerce Clause are hard to reconstruct in a neutral way because the Framers and ratifiers inhabited a political, economic, and intellectual world so different from ours. On the one hand, the Framers clearly anticipated that the states, not Congress, would be the principal lawmakers. They also appeared to contemplate that the states would

---

[11] Samuel Johnson, "Commerce," *A Dictionary of the English Language*, 4th ed. (1773; reprinted 1978).
[12] *Ibid*, "Regulate."

retain what they called the "police power" – probably to the exclusion of Congress – to enact legislation to protect the public health, safety, and morals. On the other hand, the Framers apparently viewed the Constitution as empowering Congress to deal with all matters of genuinely national dimension.[13]

An additional element of the Framers' worldview further complicates the picture. The Founders regarded each of the states as a "sovereign" that retained its sovereignty even after the ratification of the Constitution. To the eighteenth-century mind, "sovereignty" implied supremacy. Reconciliation of state sovereignty with national sovereignty thus would appear to have required that there be no overlap of state and national powers: If the federal government could regulate the same conduct as a state, and thereby displace state legislation, this would have implied that the state was not really sovereign or supreme. Operating with this categorical scheme, many members of the Founding generation appear to have assumed – as we have seen – that there was a distinction between the manufacture of products, which should be subject only to state and not to congressional regulation, and the shipment and sale of goods in interstate commerce, which would come within Congress's commerce power. But suppose that a manufacturing plant spews pollution into the atmosphere, that the pollution flows across state lines, and that it damages agriculture, health, and thus economic productivity in other states. Should Congress today be deemed powerless to enact regulatory legislation because of an anachronistic eighteenth-century understanding that the regulation of manufacturing is a power reserved to the states? Is pollution not a genuinely national problem today, with profound effects on interstate commerce, even if it was not in 1787?

Questions about the original meaning of the Commerce Clause and Congress's other Article I powers are further complicated by different possible answers' ideological stakes, as the debate about the ACA's individual mandate brought out. On the whole, political liberals tend

---

[13] See Jack N. Rakove, *Original Meanings: Politics and Ideas in the Making of the Constitution* (New York, NY: Knopf, 1996), 177–80 (describing the Constitutional Convention's efforts to give determinate meaning to a proposal to confer national legislative power "in all cases to which the separate States are incompetent, or in which the harmony of the United States may be interrupted by the exercise of individual Legislation," *ibid.* at 177 [quoting James Madison, *Notes on the Constitutional Convention* (May 29, 1787), in 1 *The Records of the Federal Convention of 1787*, at 17, 21 (Max Farrand ed., rev. ed. 1937)]).

to favor a broad interpretation of Congress's commerce power as necessary to permit the enactment of economic, environmental, and workplace safety legislation. To be effective, such regulation often must occur at the national level. For example, as congressional majorities believed when enacting the ACA, it may be difficult if not impossible for one state to make health insurance available to all its residents by requiring that insurance companies offer policies at affordable rates even to those who are already sick. Any state that tried to do so would become a magnet for sick people and bad insurance risks who could no longer afford market-rate policies in the states where they had resided previously. If insurance companies responded by refusing to do business in the state on foreseeably money-losing terms, the state program would collapse. Similarly, it might be impossible for a single state to protect its environment effectively if unregulated air or water pollution from other states would continue to sweep across its borders.

But where liberals tend to favor broad congressional power, conservatives characteristically exhibit skepticism – and not simply because they have different views about the nature or significance of the Constitution's original meaning. Part of their opposition reflects resistance to one-size-fits-all national regulation. In at least some cases, state and local governments may enjoy advantages in tailoring legislation to local problems and values. Many conservatives also adhere to the libertarian view that "that government is best which governs least." Recognition of sweeping federal regulatory power increases the likelihood that regulation will be enacted at some level of government. According to conservatives, regulation should be hard to impose. It directly and obviously diminishes individual liberty, and it also threatens to hamper economic efficiency.[14]

As in other areas of constitutional law, one might argue that these liberal and conservative views should be irrelevant to matters of interpretation: The justices' job is to ascertain what the Constitution means, not to make policy judgments. But for judges and justices forced to decide which strand of "original understanding" to emphasize and how to construe relatively vague constitutional language, considerations of which interpretation would lead to the "best" results

---

[14] For a reading of the Commerce Clause in light of views such as these, see Richard A. Epstein, "The Proper Scope of the Commerce Power," 73 *Virginia Law Review* 1387 (1987).

almost inevitably exert a potent influence. The division between conservative and liberal justices in *NFIB v. Sebelius* illustrates this general proposition.

Political and Constitutional Realignment

In his first inaugural address in 1981, President Ronald Reagan pronounced that "government is not the solution to our problem; government is the problem."[15] Although that sentiment was by no means unanimous, it concisely expressed an important thread of emerging public opinion. By 1981, commitments to the political and constitutional visions of governmental power that had characterized what some political scientists described as "the New Deal settlement" were coming unsettled. By then, the country had entered into a new political cycle in which Republican presidents would occupy the White House in twenty-eight of the forty years from 1969 to 2009. In addition, Ronald Reagan, like Franklin Roosevelt, had a constitutional vision to match his policy agenda. During the Reagan administration, the Federalist Society was founded, and Attorney General Edwin Meese helped to sponsor the originalist movement in constitutional interpretation. Believing that constitutional liberals had hijacked the Constitution beginning in 1937 and then under the Warren Court, one of Reagan's appointees to one of the lower federal courts coined the phrase "the Constitution-in-exile."[16] With it, he captured the belief of growing numbers of conservatives that prevailing constitutional doctrine – including those aspects involving the powers of Congress – had drifted far out of line with the Framers' design. Again adapting the strategies of Franklin Roosevelt for conservative purposes, Reagan sought to use nominations of Supreme Court justices to reshape constitutional law. By 1991, Republican presidents had appointed seven of the nine justices of the Supreme Court. At no time since then has there ever been a majority of justices nominated by Democratic presidents.

Since the Reagan years, the Court has embarked on a course correction in cases testing the limits of congressional power, but one that, so far, has been relatively mild. Unlike presidents, justices of the

---

[15] Ronald Reagan, "Inaugural Address," *Ronald Reagan Presidential Library* (Jan. 20, 1981), www.reaganlibrary.gov/archives/speech/inaugural-address-1981.
[16] See Douglas H. Ginsburg, "Delegation Running Riot," *Regulation* (Winter 1995), 83, 83–84 (book review).

Supreme Court do not have a veto pen. They cannot simply invalidate legislation that they dislike. They need to offer explanations for their decisions that they are prepared to live with when lower courts apply them in the future. In light of the public's settled expectations and reliance interests, the justices must also decide which precedents they are prepared to, or feel that they must, grudgingly accept. To offer one anchoring example, we can expect even the most conservative justices to think hard, and then to think some more, before adopting a rationale for decision in a Commerce Clause case that would raise serious questions about the soundness of the decisions that upheld the 1964 Civil Rights Act. In many eyes, including those of some conservatives, a ruling invalidating the central federal statutory prohibition against race discrimination would invite shocked and resentful comparisons with now-vilified cases from prior eras that condoned race discrimination, including *Korematsu v. United States* (1944).[17] The justices would likely find it at least as hard, and possibly harder, to decide at this late date that the Social Security Act – on which more than fifty million Americans depend for retirement income – exceeds the scope of congressional power under the Taxing and Spending Clause.

Congress's Regulatory Power under the Commerce Clause Today

The Supreme Court began its exercise in limiting congressional power under the Commerce Clause in *United States v. Lopez* (1995).[18] *Lopez* held by 5–4 that Congress lacked Commerce Clause authority to enact a statute that criminalized possession of a gun within a school zone. At the time of its decision, *Lopez* delivered a shock. It marked the first time since before 1937 that the Court had found that a statute regulating activities by private parties lay beyond the reach of Congress's commerce power. Even so, the *Lopez* opinion took a cautious approach. Chief Justice William Rehnquist began by charting the scope of Congress's authority as defined by prior cases. Congress, he acknowledged, could regulate the use of the channels of interstate commerce, could protect instrumentalities of commerce and interstate travelers, and could regulate intrastate activities with substantial effects

[17] 323 U.S. 214 (1944).
[18] 514 U.S. 549 (1995).

on interstate commerce. Having recognized these seemingly capacious powers, Rehnquist sought to establish that the Gun-Free School Zones Act attempted to stretch the limits of congressional authority further than any prior case. In particular, the Court emphasized that the chain of reasoning linking guns in school zones to school violence and school violence to "substantial effect[s]" on interstate commerce was too attenuated. Any argument predicated on a regulated activity's substantial effects on interstate commerce must mark or at least contemplate a meaningful limit to federal power, the majority insisted.

A few years later, the Court again found that Congress had overstepped the bounds of its commerce power in *United States v. Morrison* (2000),[19] which invalidated the federal Violence Against Women Act (VAWA). The VAWA authorized victims of "gender-motivated violence" to bring suits for civil damages against their abusers. Once again, the Court's majority took the tack of arguing that the statute before it was unlike any law that the Court had previously upheld under the Commerce Clause. In distinguishing prior cases, the majority maintained that the gender-motivated violence that the VAWA forbade was not a principally "economic activity." Congress, the Court allowed, could regulate economic activities (such as manufacture and sales of goods), even if they occurred wholly within a single state, but not noneconomic intrastate activities (such as violence against women), on the basis of their substantial cumulative effects on the flow of goods in interstate commerce. As in *Lopez*, the Court overruled no prior decisions. Because the VAWA was an important statute, *Morrison*'s invalidation of it was an important ruling. Nevertheless, *Morrison*, like *Lopez*, had little effect in threatening the continued validity of most of the statutes that Congress enacted under the Commerce Clause in the era of the New Deal settlement. Minimum wage laws, antidiscrimination laws, most antipollution laws, and prohibitions against the transportation of marketable commodities, including drugs and obscenity, all regulate economic activities that, in the aggregate, substantially affect interstate commerce.

Perhaps partly because *Morrison* left the previously recognized scope of Congress's authority unscathed, Justice Clarence Thomas, who joined the majority opinion, also concurred separately to say he thought the Court should overrule cases permitting Congress to regulate

---

[19] 529 U.S. 598 (2000).

intrastate activities based solely on their "substantial effects" on interstate commerce. But no other justice joined him. Although none of the other conservative justices explained why, one possible implication of Thomas's proposal would be to raise questions about the continuing validity of *Katzenbach v. McClung*, which had sustained the application of the antidiscrimination provisions of the 1964 Civil Rights Act to a restaurant with an almost exclusively intrastate clientele.

NFIB v. Sebelius, the case that introduced this chapter, imposed a further limitation on Congress's commerce power, but, again, one that did not represent an acknowledged cutback. The ACA was a complex statute that included provisions enacted under the Taxing and Spending Clause, to which I have referred already and about which I shall say more shortly. Congress relied on the Commerce Clause principally to defend the constitutionality of two mandates. First, the ACA required insurance companies to sell health insurance policies to would-be purchasers with preexisting conditions. Second, to provide those companies with a compensatory revenue stream for being required to insure customers on whom they were virtually certain to lose money, Congress enacted the individual mandate, requiring a number of healthy people to buy insurance that they did not want to pay for.

As discussed earlier, the *NFIB* majority denied that the Commerce Clause authorized Congress to enact the individual mandate by relying on the no-extension-beyond-settled-precedents rationale of *Lopez* and *Morrison*. As Justice Ginsburg's dissenting opinion argued, however, that rationale did not clearly and unquestionably apply. According to the majority, prior cases under the Commerce Clause had authorized the regulation of voluntary economic activity, not compulsions of relevantly inactive individuals to purchase an unwanted product. But virtually everyone will participate in the market for health care at some point, and requiring the procurement of insurance as a payment mechanism can plausibly be viewed as a way of regularizing inevitable future economic transactions in an interstate market. Insofar as people are market participants, it is well settled that Congress possesses commerce power to compel them to do business on terms that they dislike (e.g., by requiring the payment of minimum wages) or with people with whom they would prefer not to deal at all (e.g., by enacting antidiscrimination laws). Still, the line that the Court laid down is an intelligible one, even if it may be hard to draw in some cases. After *NFIB*, the Commerce Clause permits the regulation of economic activity, not the compulsion of those who would prefer to be inert to engage in unwanted transactions.

Outside the context of the ACA, the significance of *NFIB*'s ruling that the Commerce Clause does not permit Congress to regulate economic inactivity remains to be seen. It is hard to imagine realistic scenarios under which Congress would wish to require individuals to purchase unwanted products other than health insurance. (The hypothetical mandate that people buy broccoli would be a clear political nonstarter.) Moreover, and perhaps more significantly, none of the parties to *NFIB v. Sebelius* doubted that Congress could require insurance companies, as participants in an interstate economic market, to sell insurance to parties to whom they would have preferred not to sell it at rates that they thought unreasonably low.

If we ask why the Court's conservative justices so strongly resist what they take to be extensions of Congress's previously recognized Commerce Clause power, some of the explanation likely lies in what Randy Barnett calls "the gravitational force of originalism":[20] They believe that the Court's precedents have been out of alignment with the Constitution's original meaning at least since 1937, and they do not wish to exacerbate that situation. So far, however, the doctrine of stare decisis and the settled expectations and reliance interests of much of the American public appear to have dissuaded the conservative justices from rolling back central aspects of the Commerce Clause power as it has existed since the New Deal. It is not impossible, but neither does it seem assured, that a conservative Court may wish to go further. What would be truly astonishing is any extension of Congress's commerce power to encompass any novel form of regulation.

The Necessary and Proper Clause

At the end of a list of enumerated congressional powers, Article I, Section 8, Clause 18 of the Constitution includes an additional grant of congressional authority "to make all Laws which shall be necessary and proper for carrying into Execution the foregoing Powers." *McCulloch v. Maryland* (1819),[21] which was discussed in Chapter 2,

---

[20] See Randy E. Barnett, "The Gravitational Force of Originalism," 82 *Fordham Law Review* 411, 420 (2013).
[21] 17 U.S. 316 (1819).

is still the most important case interpreting that provision. Besides upholding Congress's power to create a Bank of the United States despite the absence of any specific authorization, *McCulloch* established two important points about the Necessary and Proper Clause. First, that provision is an affirmative grant of congressional authority, not a limiting stipulation that Congress may not legislate under other provisions conferring legislative power except insofar as doing so is "necessary and proper." Second, even when Congress relies on the Necessary and Proper Clause as a source of ancillary authority, Chief Justice John Marshall held that the word "necessary" need not mean "absolutely necessary." It suffices if a law is "convenient" or "useful" for achieving a valid federal purpose, Marshall wrote.

Through the years of the New Deal settlement, the Supreme Court interpreted the Commerce Clause so expansively that it seldom had occasion to depend on the Necessary and Proper Clause as a further source of congressional authority. Interestingly, however, the conservative Justice Antonin Scalia relied on it in an opinion concurring in the judgment in *Gonzales v. Raich* (2005),[22] which upheld the application of a federal antidrug law to homegrown medical marijuana that would never cross state lines. Even in the absence of a substantial effect on interstate commerce, regulation of intrastate noneconomic activity may be necessary and proper as "part of a larger regulation of economic activity," such as a prohibition against the production and sale of marijuana in interstate markets, "in which the regulatory scheme could be undercut unless the intrastate activity were regulated,"[23] Scalia concluded. That rationale could plausibly help to explain a number of long-accepted forms of federal regulation more commonly grounded directly in the Commerce Clause, such as prohibitions against possession of narcotics or materials that had previously traveled in interstate commerce.

Any reason to believe that the modern conservative justices might begin to construe the Necessary and Proper Clause as a significant grant of supplemental congressional authority proved short-lived, however. Seven years later, in *NFIB v. Sebelius,* five conservative justices rejected an argument that the individual mandate to purchase health insurance could be sustained as "necessary and proper" to the

---

[22] 545 U.S. 1 (2005).
[23] *Ibid.* at 36 (Scalia, J., concurring in the judgment) (quoting *Lopez,* 514 U.S. at 561).

attainment of permissible ends of the ACA. The conservatives cited two closely related grounds for their conclusion. First, Chief Justice Roberts advanced an anti-bootstrapping rationale. In his view, the power that Congress claimed to require individuals to purchase health insurance was "vast" and "novel," not incidental to any previously recognized authority. Congress could not leverage a lesser power to regulate insurance markets to justify exercise of a larger, unenumerated power to compel people to participate in markets that they wished not to enter. Second, Roberts determined that "[e]ven if the individual mandate [was] 'necessary' to the Act's insurance reforms, such an expansion of federal power [was] not a 'proper' means for making those reforms effective."[24] By making assessments of whether challenged legislation is "proper" independent of whether it is "necessary," this analysis introduced a potentially independent obstacle to reliance on the Necessary and Proper Clause as a source of congressional regulatory authority. Although the conservative justices did not seek to spell out the full implications of their holding, the majority opinion plainly exhibited wariness about reliance on the Necessary and Proper Clause to support new, expansive claims of federal regulatory power.

The Taxing and Spending Power

Historical Evolution

As the Commerce Clause stands to modern congressional power to regulate the national economy, so stands Congress's power to "lay and collect Taxes" and to spend money to "provide for the common Defence and general Welfare" to many modern programs of benefits distribution, including Social Security and Medicare. As with the Commerce Clause, the original understanding of this provision is uncertain. James Madison, who played one of the lead roles in drafting the Constitution, maintained that Congress was empowered to tax and spend only to fund the exercise of other powers that the Constitution specifically confers on it (such as raising armies and maintaining post offices). By contrast, Alexander Hamilton, another prominent participant in the Constitutional Convention and, like Madison, a coauthor of *The Federalist Papers*, contended that the taxing and spending power

[24] *NFIB*, 567 U.S. at 560.

was an independent one, permitting Congress to expend funds in any way that it thought appropriate to promote the general welfare.[25] Since the New Deal era, the Court has adhered to the latter, broader, view. In upholding the Social Security Act's provision of age-based pensions, Justice Benjamin Cardozo wrote that Congress has broad discretion to identify what the general welfare requires. He added: "Nor is the concept of the general welfare static. Needs that were narrow or parochial a century ago may be interwoven in our day with the well-being of the nation."[26] Today, as I have suggested previously, Social Security and other federal spending programs funded out of tax revenues seem too deeply rooted to be vulnerable to constitutional attack.

Nevertheless, there are limits on Congress's power to tax. As discussed in the introductory section of this chapter, Chief Justice Roberts was joined by the four liberal justices in *NFIB v. Sebelius* in voting to sustain the ACA's individual mandate either to buy insurance or pay a penalty as imposing a permissible "tax." In doing so, however, he emphasized that the power to tax is not, and may not be wielded as, a power to coercively compel: Taxes must not be "punitive" and must have the purpose or effect of raising revenue. These conditions would stop a Congress whose Commerce Clause powers had been trimmed from simply recasting what once were regulations of commerce as prohibitively high taxes on activities that Congress would actually prefer to forbid.[27]

The Spending Power as a Lever to Influence or Compel Behavior

Constitutional questions about the limits of Congress's power under Article I, Section 8, Clause 3 have also arisen when Congress has sought to influence or effectively compel behavior through the exercise of its spending power. Prior to 1937, the Supreme Court had

---

[25] See *United States v. Butler*, 297 U.S. 1, 65–66 (1936) (describing Madison and Hamilton's views).
[26] *Helvering v. Davis*, 301 U.S. 619, 641 (1937).
[27] The validity of the "mandate" was challenged in the Supreme Court once again after Congress, in 2017, lowered the tax on noncompliance to $0. Challengers argued that in the absence of any liability for failure to procure insurance, the mandate, which remained a part of the US code, could no longer be justified as an exercise of Congress's power to tax to promote the general welfare. In *California v. Texas*, 593 U.S. 659 (2021), the justices dismissed the suit by 7–2 on the ground that the plaintiffs lacked standing since they were not adversely affected by the effectively unenforceable mandate.

held in *United States v. Butler*[28] (1936) that Congress could not wield its power of the purse to entice behavior that lay within "a subject reserved to" regulation by the states. After 1937, that restriction withered as expansive interpretations of the Commerce Clause undercut the assumption that there are subjects, including manufacturing and agriculture, that are necessarily and exclusively reserved to state regulation, regardless of their effects on interstate commerce.

Even after 1937, the Court continued to insist that valid exercises of the spending power must not be "coercive," but for decades it administered that stipulation with a light touch. Taking advantage of the broad leeway afforded to it, Congress has frequently attempted to influence conduct by both private individuals and the states by attaching conditions to proffered grants of funding. When Congress provides federal support for activities and programs subject to requirements that recipients spend the money to advance Congress's goals, there is typically no ground for complaint. For example, few would object when the federal government insists that states spend federal grants to improve highways on roads, not education, or Medicaid funding on providing aid to the poor, not subsidizing the arts. Nevertheless, when states grow overwhelmingly dependent on federal grant money, champions of federalism understandably worry that Congress may employ its power of the purse to undermine the constitutional stature and independence of the states.

South Dakota v. Dole (1987)[29] – which for thirty-five years was the Supreme Court's leading case on the subject – epitomizes the potential problem. In 1984, Congress wanted a uniform national drinking age of twenty-one. But the Twenty-First Amendment, which arguably makes the regulation of alcohol distinctively subject to state regulation,[30] rendered it doubtful that Congress could have mandated a minimum drinking age under the Commerce Clause, and the Supreme Court assumed (without holding) that it could not have done so. Instead, Congress sought to achieve the effect that it wanted by providing that any state with a drinking age of less than twenty-one would forfeit 5 percent of the federal highway funds that it otherwise

---

[28] 297 U.S. 1 (1936).
[29] 483 U.S. 203 (1987).
[30] See U.S. Const. amend. XXI, § 2 ("The transportation or importation into any State, Territory, or possession of the United States for delivery or use therein of intoxicating liquors, in violation of the laws thereof, is hereby prohibited.").

would have received. South Dakota complained that Congress's threat to withhold highway funds offended principles of constitutional federalism by diminishing its quasi-sovereign autonomy to determine a legal drinking age within its borders, but the Supreme Court disagreed.

In an opinion by Chief Justice Rehnquist, the Court said that conditions on federal funds were permissible as long as they required otherwise lawful behavior, were clearly stated in advance, and were germane to the purposes for which Congress had provided grants to the states in the first place. The statute in *South Dakota v. Dole* satisfied the last condition, the Court reasoned, because a twenty-one-year-old drinking age would help to promote enhanced highway safety by making it less likely that young drivers would imbibe alcohol before getting behind the wheel. The Court then added a final qualification: "[T]he financial inducement offered by Congress [must not] be so coercive as to pass the point at which pressure turns into compulsion."[31] On the facts of *South Dakota v. Dole*, the Court found this condition to be satisfied as well, since only a small percentage of federal highway funding was at stake. From 1987 until 2012, the Court never found a statute conditioning a state's receipt of federal money on its compliance with a federal requirement to be impermissibly coercive.

The Court therefore broke new ground in 2012 when it held in *NFIB v. Sebelius*, by a vote of 7–2 on this point, that a provision of the ACA that required the states to expand their Medicaid programs (to provide health care to more low-income people) or forfeit *all* federal Medicaid funds was unduly coercive and therefore violated principles of constitutional federalism. According to Chief Justice Roberts, Congress could have refused to give "new funds to States that will not accept the new conditions" of federally mandated Medicaid eligibility, but it could not "threaten[] to withhold ... existing Medicaid funds" without crossing the line into forbidden coercion. Taken in isolation, the Court's holding makes sense. (The ruling on this point did not affect the validity of the rest of the ACA, including the individual mandate.) Federal Medicaid funds make up as much as 10 percent of some states' total budgets. As Roberts wrote, a threat to withdraw all of that money "is a gun to the head."[32] Even two of the Court's liberal justices

---

[31] *Dole*, 483 U.S. at 211.
[32] *NFIB*, 567 U.S. at 581.

in *NFIB* concurred in that assessment, as a majority of the current justices undoubtedly would as well.

But how will the Court draw the line between conditions on funding that are coercive and those that are not? As Justice Ruth Ginsburg noted in an opinion dissenting on the Medicaid funding issue in *NFIB*, the conditions that Congress imposed on states' receipt of Medicaid funds would surely have been permissible if Congress were establishing the Medicaid program for the first time. The Court said that the threatened withdrawal of funding was coercive, but the chief justice offered no clear guidance concerning the criteria that lower courts should use to differentiate coercive from noncoercive conditions on the acceptance of federal funds in future cases. Sometimes the modern Court insists that if no clear line can be drawn, it should or must defer to decisions by the political branches. But other times, as in *NFIB*, a majority of the justices are satisfied if they think it clear that the challenged action in a particular case goes "too far." For now, it seems a reasonable guess that the Court is likely to hold conditions attached to federal spending programs to be impermissibly coercive only when large amounts of money are at stake and Congress abruptly alters "the terms of participation in entrenched [state-federal] cooperative programs."[33]

Congressional Power to Enforce the Civil War Amendments

The Thirteenth Amendment, which abolishes slavery, the Fourteenth Amendment, which includes the Due Process and Equal Protection Clauses, and the Fifteenth Amendment, which bars race discrimination in state and national elections, all include clauses that authorize Congress to "enforce" their substantive provisions "by appropriate legislation." The modern Supreme Court has interpreted these provisions increasingly restrictively. Indeed, with surprising frequency, the Court has shown greater reluctance to uphold congressional assertions of power to enforce the Reconstruction Amendments than enactments under the Commerce and Spending Clauses of Article I.

The Court's most recent important decision came in *Shelby County v. Holder* (2013).[34] In *Shelby County*, the Court, by 5–4, invalidated a provision of the Voting Rights Act (VRA) of 1965, enacted to

---

[33] Samuel Bagenstos, "The Anti-leveraging Principle and the Spending Clause after NFIB," 101 *Georgetown Law Journal* 861, 864 (2013).
[34] 570 U.S. 529 (2013).

enforce the Fifteenth Amendment, that required states with histories of restricting voting rights as of the 1964 elections to secure approval from the Justice Department before changing their election procedures. Since 1965, Congress had reauthorized the VRA on multiple occasions but without altering the "coverage formula" that used the 1964 elections as a reference point. In support of its ruling, the Court cited a lack of adequate, modern evidence that jurisdictions that once had infringed voting rights continued to do so. "The [Fifteenth] Amendment [wa]s not designed to punish for the past; its purpose is to ensure a better future," Chief Justice Roberts wrote. He continued: "To serve that purpose, Congress – if it is to divide the States [by imposing restrictions on some that it does not impose on others] – must identify those jurisdictions to be singled out on a basis that makes sense in light of current conditions."[35] In support of its conclusion, the Court relied on what it described as an "equal sovereignty" principle, which it viewed as implicit in the Constitution's structure and found reflected in the Court's case law, that precluded Congress from subjecting some states to restrictions that it did not impose on others.

In an impassioned dissent, Justice Ginsburg objected that between 1982 and 2006, when Congress had most recently reenacted the VRA, the Department of Justice had blocked over 700 changes in voting schemes by covered jurisdictions based on determinations that they were discriminatory. She also protested the application of the equal sovereignty principle – which had previously been applied to hold that new states entered the union on an equal footing with their predecessors – to the domain of voting rights that Congress had sought to secure under the Fifteenth Amendment. Justice Ginsburg also noted that when enacting regulatory and spending legislation under Article I, Congress has frequently differentiated among states. Echoing this point, Leah Litman has interpreted *Shelby County* as holding that structural constitutional principles more stringently limit Congress's power to provide safeguards against constitutional violations under the Reconstruction Amendments than to enact other types of legislation under Article I.[36]

The Roberts Court's decision in *Shelby County* marked the culmination, to date, of an evolutionary change in constitutional doctrine

---

[35] Ibid. at 553.
[36] Leah M. Litman, "Inventing Equal Sovereignty," 114 *Michigan Law Review* 1207, 1215 (2016).

that has unfolded since the heyday of the Warren Court. The Warren Court generally welcomed congressional efforts to expand civil rights and voting rights, including under the enforcement provisions of the Civil War Amendments. *Katzenbach v. Morgan*[37] (1966) was that era's leading decision. At issue was a provision of the VRA, enacted to enforce the Equal Protection Clause, that prescribed that no one who had completed the sixth grade in a non-English-speaking school in Puerto Rico could be denied the right to vote due to lack of English literacy. An earlier case, *Lassiter v. Northampton County Board of Elections* (1959),[38] had upheld an English-literacy requirement against an equal protection challenge. In light of *Lassiter*, New York election officials argued that legislation barring New York from insisting on English literacy as a voting requirement could not qualify as appropriate legislation to "enforce" the Fourteenth Amendment. Rather than "enforc[ing]" the Equal Protection Clause, they maintained, Congress had attempted to go further than the Fourteenth Amendment required in restricting states' capacity to establish voter qualifications.

The Supreme Court disagreed. Justice William Brennan's majority opinion offered three theories on which, despite *Lassiter*, Congress's limited prohibition against literacy tests might count as "appropriate legislation" to "enforce" the Fourteenth Amendment. All three relied on the premise that the Court owes broad deference to Congress in assessing the validity of legislation to enforce Amendments enacted in the wake of the Civil War, manifesting a distrust of the states to define and enforce the rights of racial minorities, and further evidencing a reliance on Congress to ensure racial justice.

The first theory was remedial and preventative. According to Brennan, Congress could rationally have concluded that unconstitutional discrimination against Puerto Ricans occurred in a variety of settings, not limited to voting but also including public schools, welfare administration, and law enforcement. Brennan suggested that Section 5 of the Fourteenth Amendment authorized Congress to provide a remedy for those violations, and a safeguard against their recurrence, by vesting Puerto Ricans with an expanded right to vote. The right to vote, he quoted from precedent, was "preservative of all rights."[39]

---

[37] 384 U.S. 641 (1966).
[38] 360 U.S. 45 (1959).
[39] *Katzenbach*, 384 U.S. at 652 (quoting *Yick Wo v. Hopkins*, 118 U.S. 356, 370 [1886]).

Brennan's second theory postulated that Congress could justify the enactment of legislation to "enforce" the Fourteenth Amendment by invoking its "specially informed" fact-finding abilities. In upholding the particular literacy test that was challenged in *Lassiter*, the Supreme Court had not held that all literacy tests were constitutionally valid; they would be invalid if enacted for the discriminatory purpose of excluding as many racial minorities as possible from being able to vote. Based on its own knowledge and the facts presented by the parties in *Lassiter*, the Court was unwilling to presume that most literacy tests were enacted for discriminatory purposes or that they were not a "necessary or appropriate means" of furthering legitimate state ends.[40] But Congress, Brennan suggested, might know better. If Congress concluded that many or most literacy tests were adopted for the discriminatory purpose of disqualifying minority voters or were otherwise unnecessary to further legitimate state interests, the Court should defer to these largely factual judgments and should uphold the challenged prohibition against literacy tests as "appropriate" to "enforce" the Fourteenth Amendment.

Finally, and most controversially, Justice Brennan hinted that when legislating under Section 5 to enforce constitutional rights, Congress could permissibly define those underlying rights at least slightly more broadly than the Supreme Court would otherwise define them. Under this theory, which commentators dubbed the "ratchet theory,"[41] Brennan maintained that Congress had "no power to restrict, abrogate, or dilute [constitutional] guarantees," but he suggested that Congress might indeed have power to ratchet up the level of constitutional protection beyond that afforded by the Court.

If accepted, *Katzenbach v. Morgan*'s ratchet theory would have dramatically expanded the scope of congressional authority and correspondingly diminished the centrality of the judicial role. In effect, it would have called for the Supreme Court to share its power to interpret the Constitution. Under the ratchet theory, the Court's rulings would establish the minimum content of constitutional guarantees but not necessarily the maximum. Perhaps troubled by this implication, the Court pointedly failed to embrace the ratchet theory

---

[40] Ibid. at 654.
[41] See, for example, Douglas Laycock, "RFRA, Congress, and the Ratchet," 56 *Montana Law Review* 145, 155 (1995).

in a couple of subsequent cases, but without expressly renouncing it either.⁴²

Equivocation ended in *City of Boerne v. Flores* (1997),⁴³ decided over thirty years after *Katzenbach v. Morgan* by the more conservative Rehnquist Court, which was less disposed than the Warren Court to embrace Congress as a partner in expansively defining and enforcing Fourteenth Amendment rights. *City of Boerne* disavowed the ratchet theory and, more generally, sharply limited Congress's enforcement powers under the Thirteenth, Fourteenth, and Fifteenth Amendments. Specifically at issue in *Boerne* was the constitutionality of the Religious Freedom Restoration Act (RFRA). Congress had enacted the RFRA in response to the Supreme Court's decision in *Employment Division v. Smith* (1990),⁴⁴ discussed in Chapter 4, which narrowed the protections that the Court had previously afforded under the Free Exercise Clause. As originally interpreted, *Smith* almost never required the government to grant exemptions to parties whose free exercise of religion was impaired by generally applicable laws. Invoking its power under Section 5 of the Fourteenth Amendment, Congress passed the RFRA with the aim of restoring the pre-*Smith* regime under which the government must justify the denial of religious exceptions as necessary to a compelling governmental interest.

With no justice dissenting on this point, *City of Boerne* held that Congress has no power "to enact legislation that expands the rights contained in [Section] 1 of the Fourteenth Amendment" (including those, such as free exercise rights, that the Fourteenth Amendment "incorporates" under the incorporation doctrine discussed in Chapter 2). Congress's power is to enforce constitutional rights as defined by the Court, not to define constitutional rights for itself, the justices ruled. Having dismissed the ratchet theory, the Court acknowledged that Congress could provide remedies for constitutional rights violations

---

⁴² On the surface, the ratchet theory might appear inconsistent with *Marbury v. Madison*, 5 U.S. 137 (1803), and especially with its celebrated assertion that "[i]t is emphatically the province and duty of the judicial branch to say what the law is." Ibid. at 177. But *Marbury* need not be read to hold more than that courts must determine whether legislative enactments comport with the Constitution. If Section 5 of the Fourteenth Amendment gives Congress a limited power to interpret constitutional guarantees, *Marbury* could be construed to require only that the Court assess whether legislation enacted under Section 5 comes within the Section 5 grant of congressional power.

⁴³ 521 U.S. 507 (1997).

⁴⁴ 494 U.S. 872 (1990).

and, under some circumstances, could legislate to prevent them – provided that what counted as a constitutional rights violation was defined by the courts, not Congress. But the Court insisted that in order to be permissible, preventive and remedial legislation must exhibit "congruence and proportionality" to an underlying pattern of identified constitutional violations. The Court suggested that the legislation involved in *Katzenbach v. Morgan* met this test: "The provisions restricting and banning literacy tests ... attacked a particular type of voting qualification ... with a long history as a 'notorious means to deny and abridge voting rights on racial grounds.'" Even if not every literacy test had this invidious purpose, many of them did, and the statutory prohibition was thus congruent and proportional to the problem that it addressed. By contrast, the Court said, the RFRA was wholly "out of proportion to a supposed remedial or preventive object"[45]: Congress was trying to redefine the rights guaranteed by the Free Exercise Clause, not to remedy or prevent violations of the narrow right that the Court had identified in *Employment Division v. Smith*.

In applying *Boerne*'s demand that remedial legislation under Section 5 of the Fourteenth Amendment must be congruent with and proportional to an identified pattern of judicially cognizable constitutional violations, the Supreme Court has invalidated parts of a number of other important federal statutes. In *United States v. Morrison*, which held that Congress lacked power to enact the VAWA under the Commerce Clause, the government also maintained that congressional authority existed under Section 5. State officials far too frequently failed to prosecute perpetrators of domestic violence, the government argued, and Congress had sought to provide victims with a private right to sue partly to remedy the states' failure to afford them the equal protection of the laws. But the Court found no adequate demonstration of congruence and proportionality between the asserted constitutional wrongs and the attempted statutory remedy of authorizing women alleging domestic violence to bring suits for money damages in federal court. The Court applied a similar logic in *Shelby County*: Even if the coverage formula of the 1965 Voting Rights Act was congruent and proportional to an identified pattern of constitutional violations at the time of its initial enactment, it had ceased to satisfy that stricture by 2013.

---

[45] *Boerne*, 521 U.S. at 532.

Although neither *City of Boerne* nor *Shelby County* was decided by today's Supreme Court, both decisions almost certainly reflect the prevailing attitudes of a majority of the current justices in at least three relevant respects. First, the Court continues to be very jealous of its distinctive authority to interpret the Constitution and, indeed, the law more generally. The justices are therefore acutely wary of legislation manifesting a congressional judgment different from the Court's own about the substantive content of constitutional rights.

Second, the conservative justices of the current era are concerned about protecting constitutional federalism. Because the Constitution generally creates rights only against the government and its officials, legislation to enforce the Reconstruction Amendments often applies only to state and local governments and their employees and limits their authority. By invalidating legislation that Congress has enacted to enforce the Thirteenth, Fourteenth, and Fifteenth Amendments, the Court views itself as upholding the states' sovereign prerogatives.

Third, it is also revealing that neither in *City of Boerne* nor in *Shelby County* did the prevailing Supreme Court majority engage deeply with evidence of the Constitution's originally understood or intended meaning. Many commentators believe that the Reconstruction Congress that drafted the Fourteenth Amendment understood it as endowing Congress with an interpretive authority to enforce the Amendment's substantive guarantees to their reasonable outer limits.[46] Without carefully considering historical arguments to this effect, *Shelby County*, in particular, relied heavily on what it took to be a general structural principle – which it did not attempt to support with either close textual or original historical analysis – establishing the states' equal sovereignty. In doing so, the Court offered no sustained response to the obvious criticism that the Civil War Amendments reflected a rejection of understandings of state sovereignty that had prevailed previously. To repeat a phrase that I used earlier, a majority of the current justices are at least as conservative as they are originalist.

---

[46] See, for example, Jack M. Balkin, "The Reconstruction Power," 85 *NYU Law Review* 1801, 1805 (2010) (arguing that Reconstruction Congresses included the enforcement clauses in the Civil War Amendments because they did not trust the courts to enforce civil rights); Michael W. McConnell, "The Supreme Court, 1996 Term – Comment: Institutions and Interpretation: A Critique of Boerne v. Flores," 111 *Harvard Law Review* 153, 183 (1997) (maintaining that *Boerne*'s "conclusion that judicial interpretations of the provisions of the Amendment are the exclusive touchstone for congressional enforcement power finds no support in the history of the Fourteenth Amendment").

Concluding Observations

All in all, Congress's Article I powers under the Commerce, Necessary and Proper, and Taxing and Spending Clauses remain vast. An increasingly conservative Supreme Court would manifestly like to restrict those powers, which swelled to their current expanse beginning in 1937 and through the ensuing decades of the New Deal settlement. But a constitutional counterrevolution in the field of congressional power has proved hard for the justices to bring off due partly to reliance interests (e.g., in Social Security) and partly to widespread public understandings of some potentially vulnerable statutes as historic national achievements (for instance, the 1964 Civil Rights Act). Short of full constitutional counterrevolution, the supermajority of conservative justices seems set against further expansion of big federal government. They may be looking for further acceptable limitations, such as the one adopted in *NFIB*, when the Court insisted that although Congress can regulate economic activity, it cannot mandate action, such as the purchase of health insurance, by people not already engaged in market-related behavior. So far, however, Justice Clarence Thomas has stood alone in calling for a comprehensive realignment of judicial doctrine to reflect what he takes to be the original understanding of Congress's Article I powers.

In construing Congress's power to "enforce" the Civil War Amendments, the Supreme Court has taken a somewhat more aggressive stance by maintaining that the power to "interpret" the Constitution is its alone. Under this interpretation, enforcement legislation must demonstrate "congruence and proportionality" to a documented pattern of judicially cognizable constitutional violations. Equally controversially, the Court has maintained that enforcement legislation must not disparage the states' "equal sovereignty," even under Amendments crafted to define and enforce minorities' civil rights against the states.

In developments reminiscent of the run-up to the 1937 "switch in time that saved nine," the Supreme Court's modern commitment to rein in the regulatory powers of Congress has provoked political progressives increasingly to view the Court as an obstacle to the achievement of social justice. Otherwise, however, the current climate exhibits few obvious similarities to the era of the Roosevelt Revolution in American politics and constitutional law.

10 THE POWERS OF THE PRESIDENT AND THE EXECUTIVE BRANCH IN A PERIOD OF FERMENT

Some of the Roberts Court's most far-reaching revisions of constitutional law have involved the powers, prerogatives, and immunities of the president and the executive branch. The leading decisions form a quasi-paradoxical pattern. On the one hand, the Roberts Court has expanded the personal powers and prerogatives of the president. On the other hand, the Court has taken aggressive steps to diminish the power of federal regulatory agencies, such as the Environmental Protection Agency (EPA) and the Consumer Financial Protection Bureau, which are a part of the executive branch that the president heads. Both strands of the Court's decisions reflect positions that today are associated with political conservatism, though what has counted as a conservative position regarding executive power has varied over time. Some of the modern Court's rulings purport to reflect original constitutional meanings and to disdain decision-making based on pragmatic or functional considerations, but others put pragmatic concerns at the forefront of their analysis. Whatever the formal basis for the Court's decisions, there can be no doubt that the conservative justices are keenly aware of their rulings' likely implications. As noted in Chapter 3, all of the conservative justices except for Justice Barrett served in the executive branch before being named to the Court, and she was a scholar of the judicial role in constitutional and statutory interpretation during her academic career.

No decision better illustrates the conservative supermajority's commitment to protecting the personal prerogatives of the president than *Trump v. United States* (2024).[1] The case originated as a federal prosecution of then former President Donald Trump for alleged crimes committed while in office. The indictment claimed that Trump illegally conspired to overturn the results of the 2016 presidential election by asserting knowingly false claims of election fraud, seeking to obstruct the counting of ballots in contested jurisdictions, and plotting to block the certification of vote counts and slates of electors eligible to vote in the electoral college.

When Trump's lawyers initially asserted that he enjoyed "immunity" from prosecution for crimes allegedly committed in his capacity as president, most legal experts scoffed. The clause of the Constitution that provides for presidential impeachment seems to contemplate that a former president would be subject to prosecution for crimes committed while in office. It says, "Judgment in Cases of Impeachment shall not extend further than to removal from Office, and disqualification to hold and enjoy any Office of honor, Trust or Profit under the United States: *but the Party convicted shall nevertheless be liable and subject to Indictment, Trial, Judgment and Punishment, according to Law.*"[2] In 1974, after Richard Nixon had resigned the presidency amid the Watergate scandal, President Gerald Ford pardoned him, and Nixon accepted the pardon. Both assumed, as nearly everyone else did at the time, that without it, Nixon would have faced prosecution.

In *Trump v. United States*, however, the Supreme Court's conservative majority, by a vote of 6–3, confounded once-widespread expectations by holding that presidents enjoy broad immunity from criminal prosecution for abuses of their official authority. The decision, which Chief Justice Roberts wrote, was not originalist. It adduced no substantial evidence that the Framers or Founding generation understood the Constitution as endowing past presidents with immunity from prosecution for crimes committed while in office. In lieu of historical evidence, the chief justice relied principally on "[t]he Framers' design of the Presidency" and on the Court's precedents addressing other issues involving presidential prerogatives. He placed particular weight on *Nixon v. Fitzgerald* (1982),[3] which held that the president

---

[1] 603 U.S. 593 (2024).
[2] U.S. Const. art. I, § 3, cl. 7 (emphasis added).
[3] 457 U.S. 731 (1982).

enjoyed absolute immunity from private suits for civil damages arising from the president's official acts.

Viewed from the perspective of the present, *Fitzgerald* had two notable features. First, like many other decisions of the Burger Court, Justice Powell's majority opinion made no pretense of being either originalist or textualist. Its reasoning emphasized practical concerns, maintaining that, in the absence of absolute immunity, presidents would be easy targets for suits for damages by disgruntled citizens. If presidents were not immune from suit, the Court reasoned, fear of civil liability might sometimes deter them from unflinching action in the public interest. The Roberts Court frequently disparages precedents from the Burger Court as meriting little respect because of what current justices regard as their predecessors' undisciplined reliance on policy-based reasoning. Second, the Burger Court precedents on which Chief Justice Roberts predicated the Court's ruling in *Trump* would have been easy to distinguish. *Nixon v. Fitzgerald* had differentiated private suits for damages, from which it found the president to be immune, from prosecutions for violating the criminal law. There was a greater public interest in enforcing the criminal law than in allowing private citizens to recover civil damages from presidents and former presidents, *Fitzgerald* suggested. But no matter. "If a former President's official acts are routinely subjected to scrutiny in criminal prosecutions, 'the independence of the Executive Branch' may be significantly undermined" in contravention of the constitutional design, the majority reasoned in *Trump*.[4]

The *Trump* opinion divided claims of presidential immunity from criminal prosecution into three categories. First, the Court accepted the parties' stipulation that "a former President can be subject to criminal prosecution for *unofficial* acts committed while in office." Second, it posited that the president is entitled to "absolute immunity" from prosecution for actions taken in the "exercise of his core constitutional powers." Third, it ruled that the president is further entitled to some form of immunity from prosecution for all other official acts, though it declined to decide pending further development of the case whether that immunity would also "be absolute, or instead whether a presumptive immunity" would suffice. A presumptive immunity would shield a former president from criminal liability, the majority implied,

---

[4] 603 U.S. at 613–14.

"unless the Government can show that applying a criminal prohibition to [a particular] act would pose no 'dangers of intrusion on the authority and functions of the Executive Branch.'" Although this formulation leaves many questions unsettled, proving the utter absence of "dangers of intrusion" on presidential functions would appear to be a stringent standard for prosecutors to meet.

Within the categorical scheme that *Trump* creates, perhaps the most crucial issue involves how to differentiate between a president's official and unofficial acts. Although the majority did not lay down clear lines, it pointedly declined to locate any of former President Trump's allegedly illegal actions in the case before it as definitively falling within the "unofficial" category. To begin its analysis, the Court affirmed that a president's motives were irrelevant to whether an action should be classified as official or unofficial. It then ticked through various allegations in the indictment. First, the Court determined that alleged directives to officials in the Justice Department to press state officials to replace legitimate slates of electors with fraudulent substitutes fell squarely within the core presidential responsibility to manage the executive branch.

Second, the Court ruled that Trump had at least presumptive immunity from counts averring that he had pressured the vice president to refuse to certify validly chosen electors from states in which Trump maintained that the vote counts were fraudulent. "[O]ur constitutional system anticipates that the President and Vice President will remain in close contact regarding their official duties," the chief justice posited.[5]

Third, the Court found that determining whether Trump's alleged interactions with state officials and private parties aimed at altering vote tallies and organizing sham slates of electors involved official or unofficial acts would require fact-specific analysis best conducted by the lower court. But the majority emphasized the president's broad mandate to discuss matters of public interest with state officials and "to encourage them to act in a manner that promotes the President's view of the public good." Turning finally to allegations of criminal wrongdoing based on Trump's tweets and public statements prior to the assault on the Capitol that occurred on January 6, 2021, the Court recognized the president's broad authority to utilize "the

---

[5] *Ibid.* at 621–22.

office's 'bully pulpit.'" It thus concluded that "most of a President's public communications are likely to fall comfortably within the outer perimeter of his official responsibilities" before acknowledging that a president might occasionally "speak[] in an unofficial capacity – perhaps as a candidate for office or party leader."[6] Accordingly, the Court once again called for the lower court to conduct a fact-specific analysis of the president's claims to immunity. In doing so, however, it ruled that actions taken by a president in an official capacity could not be introduced into evidence to help prove a charge based on unofficial conduct. Justice Barrett, who joined the remainder of the Court's opinion, dissented from this aspect of its decision.

The Court's three liberal justices filed an impassioned dissenting opinion, written by Justice Sotomayor. "Today's decision to grant former Presidents criminal immunity reshapes the institution of the Presidency" by permitting the president to evade basic obligations to obey the criminal law, Justice Sotomayor wrote. Under the logic of the majority opinion, she continued: "When [the President] uses his official powers in any way, ... he will now be insulated from criminal prosecution. Orders the Navy's Seal Team 6 to assassinate a political rival? Immune. Organizes a military coup to hold onto power? Immune. Takes a bribe in exchange for a pardon? Immune." "In every use of official power," Justice Sotomayor added, "the President is now a king above the law."[7]

With the Court's ruling having at best uncertain foundations in the Constitution's text and history, one can fairly ask why the majority was moved to rule as it did. Some critics have charged a conservative Court with displaying undue sympathy to the claims of a former Republican president who had appointed three of its members. But the majority opinion, unsurprisingly, avowed another motivating concern involving the prospect of tit-for-tat criminal prosecutions of former presidents by partisan Justice Departments in successive administrations. In response to the dissenting opinion's "extreme hypotheticals about a future where the President 'feels empowered to violate federal criminal law,'" Chief Justice Roberts countered with what he termed "the more likely prospect of an Executive Branch that cannibalizes itself, with each successive President free to prosecute his predecessors,

---

[6] *Ibid.* at 598.
[7] *Ibid.* at 685 (Sotomayor, J., joined by Kagan and Jackson, J.J., dissenting).

yet unable to boldly and fearlessly carry out his duties for fear that he may be next."[8] The chief justice continued:

> Virtually every President is criticized for insufficiently enforcing some aspect of federal law (such as drug, gun, immigration, or environmental laws). An enterprising prosecutor in a new administration may assert that a previous President violated ... [a] broadly worded criminal statute that can cover "'any conspiracy for the purpose of impairing, obstructing or defeating the lawful function of any department of Government.'" Without immunity, such types of prosecutions of ex-Presidents could quickly become routine. The enfeebling of the Presidency and our Government that would result from such a cycle of factional strife is exactly what the Framers intended to avoid.

Whether the majority or the dissenting opinion better appraised the practical stakes of the *Trump* ruling is a question that appears to have divided legal commentators along roughly the same ideological lines as it split the Justices.

The Roberts Court's other most dramatic decision concerning the powers of the president and the executive branch, *Loper Bright Enterprises v. Raimondo* (2024),[9] substantially diminished the power of federal administrative agencies. The case is difficult to explain, as are many aspects of the functions of federal regulatory agencies and what is often referred to as the administrative state. To a first approximation, administrative agencies are governmental bodies, located within the executive branch, that possess powers assigned by Congress to implement federal statutes. Some agencies have existed nearly since the beginning of US history with responsibility for such matters as distributing public lands, issuing patents and copyrights, and calculating and collecting customs duties. Many view the Interstate Commerce Commission, with was established in 1887 with various responsibilities for regulating interstate commerce, including the power to prescribe interstate railroad rates, as the first modern administrative agency. Many other agencies have been created since, especially through bursts of lawmaking during the New Deal and in the 1960s and 1970s, as Congress enacted increasingly ambitious and complex regulatory legislation.

---

[8] *Ibid.* at 640.
[9] 144 S. Ct. 2244 (2024).

Because agencies' functions involve the administration of statutes, the scope of agencies' practical authority depends partly on their capacity, if any, to interpret those statutes authoritatively. In crafting legislation to deal with complicated problems, Congress cannot reasonably be expected to speak directly to every issue that might arise in applying statutory policies to complex and sometimes unforeseeable facts. In the environmental area, for example, Congress can decide that factories may not emit dangerous quantities of toxic waste into the air or water, but it may lack the resources to determine exactly which wastes should be deemed toxic at exactly which concentrations. To bridge the gap between general policies and the details of their application, Congress has often vested agencies with the authority to write rules or regulations with the force of law, giving concrete content to vague or ambiguous statutory language. Under other statutes addressing other regulatory challenges, Congress has sometimes charged agencies with adjudicating in the first instance whether a vaguely worded statute applies to particular cases, typically with an opportunity for the losing party to appeal an agency's quasi-judicial decision to an Article III court. Some administrative agencies possess both rulemaking and adjudicative powers.

In the iconic case of *Chevron U.S.A., Inc. v. National Resources Defense Council, Inc.* (1984),[10] the Supreme Court held that when a statute is vague or ambiguous, courts should defer to any reasonable agency interpretation, even if the court might otherwise have interpreted the statute differently. If a statute spoke clearly and unequivocally to a disputed matter, Congress's directive would control. But if not, the Court pronounced, a court should accede to the judgment of the administering agency. The Supreme Court issued its ruling in *Chevron* by a unanimous vote in an opinion written by Justice John Paul Stevens and joined by both the Supreme Court's most conservative and its most liberal members.

In the ensuing years, "the *Chevron* doctrine" did not initially divide judicial liberals from conservatives. Agencies, the justices agreed, possess relevant expertise concerning technical issues. In addition, judicial deference to agencies promotes political accountability – ultimately by the president – for controversial decisions. Justice Antonin Scalia, who was a conservative champion, also believed that *Chevron* helped

[10] 467 U.S. 837 (1984).

cabin what otherwise would be a troublingly broad scope of judicial discretion in interpreting vague statutes. Over time, however, sentiment grew on the political right that *Chevron* ceded too much power to bureaucrats to make important decisions, including ones hobbling economic development and tyrannizing ordinary Americans. Those sentiments drove the decision in *Loper Bright*, which overturned *Chevron* by a vote of 6–3. Courts, not agencies, must determine authoritatively what statutes mean and, in doing so, should exercise independent judgment, the Court ruled.

All of the current Court's conservative justices concurred in the *Loper Bright* result. Chief Justice Roberts authored the decision. His opinion did not rest directly on the Constitution but, instead, concluded that *Chevron* had misinterpreted a federal statute called the Administrative Procedure Act (APA). The APA, the chief justice held, required courts, in reviewing agencies' actions, to render independent determinations on all questions of law. But the majority also hinted, without holding explicitly, that *Chevron* might have violated the constitutional separation of powers, under which, the Court had said in the seminal case of *Marbury v. Madison* (1803),[11] "[i]t is emphatically the province and duty of the Judicial Department to say what the law is." The majority opinion in *Loper Bright* pointedly quoted that language.[12]

The practical effect of *Loper Bright* is to render the rules issued by agencies to implement their authorizing statutes substantially more vulnerable to challenges, including by members of regulated industries, than they were before. In more symbolic terms, it also reflects an agenda of the current Supreme Court, which does not appear yet to be complete, of diminishing the powers and limiting the independence of federal regulatory agencies.

The remainder of this chapter offers a necessarily partial overview of the development of presidential and executive branch powers over US history with a heavy emphasis on recent developments. I assume throughout that by grasping how we got to where we are, we can gain insights into likely future developments.

---

[11] 5 U.S. (1 Cranch) 137, 163 (1803).
[12] When the Supreme Court decided *Chevron* in 1984, it had not thought it was undermining *Marbury*. In its view, the Court discharged its constitutional and statutory obligations when it determined that a vague statute was reasonably susceptible to multiple interpretations and that courts should understand Congress as having delegated authority to resolve indeterminacies to administrative agencies, not courts.

The President and Executive Power in Historical Perspective

Today we refer to the presidency as the most powerful office in the free world. It was not always thus. The United States did not initially occupy a prominent space on the world stage. Furthermore, the nature and size of the federal government, and of the president's position within it, have evolved starkly over time. In 1789, fewer than 1,000 people worked for the federal government.[13] The State Department had only nine employees;[14] the War Department began with just two.[15] The government's primary day-to-day concerns were collecting taxes and delivering the mail. Without a proper staff, the first president, George Washington, relied on just four men to advise him: the members of his cabinet.[16]

Even in the absence of a well-staffed executive branch, Congress from early on began delegating expansive powers to the president. For example, the first Congress passed lump-sum appropriations and, within broad limits, left it to the president to determine how the money should be spent.[17] Congress also granted President Washington enormous discretion in foreign affairs. An early statute "authorized" the president "to permit the exportation of arms, cannon and military stores, the law prohibiting the exportation of the same to the contrary notwithstanding," as long as he acted in "cases connected with the security of the commercial interest of the United States, and for public purposes only."[18] During a period of tensions with France, Congress imposed an embargo on French trade but specified that if

---

[13] Formal statistics on total federal employment before 1816 are not available. See Bureau of the Census, *Historical Statistics of the United States: Colonial Times to 1970* (Washington, DC: US Department of Commerce, 1975), 2:1103. One detailed review of available records puts the number of federal employees at 780 in 1792, not including deputy postmasters, who likely numbered several hundred. See Leonard D. White, *The Federalists: A Study in Administrative History* (New York, NY: Macmillan, 1948), 255.

[14] James Q. Wilson et al., *American Government* (Boston, MA: Wadsworth & Cengage Learning, 2011), 403–04.

[15] White, *Federalists, supra* note 8, at 146.

[16] Thomas Engeman and Raymond Tatalovich, "George Washington: The First Modern President? A Reply to Nichols," in *George Washington and the Origins of the American Presidency*, ed. Mark J. Rozell et al. (New York, NY: Greenwood Press, 2000), 37, 61.

[17] Early Act of September 29, 1789, ch. 23, 1 Stat. 95; see also Act of March 26, 1790, ch. 4, § 1, 1 Stat. 104; Act of February 11, 1791, ch. 6, 1 Stat. 190 (conferring similar discretion).

[18] Act of March 3, 1795, ch. 53, 1 Stat. 444, 444.

France "disavow[ed]" and "refrain[ed]" from various aggressive acts, "it shall be lawful for the President of the United States, being well ascertained of the premises, to remit and discontinue the prohibitions and restraints hereby enacted and declared."[19]

Multiple reasons underlay delegations such as these. Congress cannot always foresee the specific problems that will arise in the future. And when problems develop, it can be difficult for Congress to respond expeditiously. Congress is a large, often fractious institution. All members have constituencies to which and for which they attempt to speak. When one party controls the House while the other has a majority in the Senate, coordination can be difficult to achieve. By contrast, the executive branch is headed by the single president of the United States, who is much more capable of decisive and accountable leadership.

Given Congress's relevant incapacities, even presidents who came into office as ideological skeptics of broad executive powers have sometimes seized them even in the absence of congressional delegations. Thomas Jefferson sent marines to fight the Barbary pirates who preyed on merchant ships off the coast of Africa. He also negotiated the Louisiana Purchase, which he presented to Congress as a fait accompli, even though he felt qualms about his constitutional authority to do so. Subsequent presidents have continued the pattern. After the southern states announced their secession in 1861, Abraham Lincoln began raising armies and imposed a blockade of southern ports without waiting for Congress to come back into session. Later during the Civil War, Lincoln unilaterally issued the Emancipation Proclamation, which declared the abolition of slavery in the states that had left the Union, as a war measure.

Presidential responses to warlike acts against the United States and its citizens may pose special issues, and the Civil War, in which the most fundamental presuppositions of the constitutional order were contested on battlefields, was undoubtedly unique. Nevertheless, military threats, some existential in character, illustrate the historically continuing challenge of maintaining adherence to constitutional norms well-suited to ordinary times in exigent circumstances of various kinds. Although the range of issues and decisions involving the scope of executive power to address perceived emergencies is sprawling, constitutional lawyers typically regard *Youngstown Sheet & Tube Co. v.*

---

[19] Act of June 13, 1798, ch. 53, §5, 1 Stat. 565, 566.

Sawyer[20] (1952) as the leading Supreme Court decision involving presidential authority. Curiously, however, majorities of the justices have often treated a concurring opinion by Justice Robert Jackson as more authoritative than the majority opinion.

Youngstown arose when, with the nation at war in Korea, President Harry Truman ordered federal officials to seize and operate the nation's steel mills to avert a planned strike. Truman maintained that an interruption in steel production would threaten the war effort and the safety of troops in the field. Had he wished to do so, Truman could have invoked a federal statute, the Taft–Hartley Act, and obtained a judicial order forbidding a strike for eighty days, during which time he could have sought emergency legislation from Congress. But Truman was a Democratic president with an important union constituency. The Taft–Hartley Act, which the unions despised, had been passed over his veto. Spurning the course available under the Taft–Hartley Act, Truman asserted power directly under the Constitution to seize the steel mills and to run them, presumably on terms acceptable to the Steelworkers Union, until the dispute was settled. As authority for his action, Truman cited his constitutional power as "Commander in Chief"[21] of the US Armed Forces and provisions of Article II empowering the president to "take Care that the Laws be faithfully executed"[22] and vesting him with "[t]he executive Power."[23]

By a vote of 6–3, the Supreme Court held that none of these provisions empowered the president to take over the steel mills. Justice Hugo Black – a proto-originalist and textualist who claimed to read the Constitution literally – wrote the majority opinion. According to Black, the steel mills were too remote from any battlefield for the president's commander-in-chief power to be relevant. Black further maintained that both the "take Care" power and the grant of executive power limited the president to executing laws that Congress had enacted. As read by Black, the Constitution carefully and specifically assigned lawmaking power to Congress and restricted the president to executing congressionally enacted laws. For the president to order seizure of the steel mills in the absence of authorizing legislation was too much like lawmaking, Black thought, possibly because it interfered with the

---

[20] 343 U.S. 579 (1952).
[21] U.S. Const. art. II, §2, cl. 1.
[22] Art. II, §3.
[23] Art. II, §1, cl. 1.

private property rights of the mills' owners. Although Congress could adjust or limit property rights, or even authorize the taking of private property for "public use" (subject to the payment of "just compensation" under the Takings Clause of the Fifth Amendment),[24] the president could not.

Justice Black's analysis reflects what scholars have subsequently termed a "formalist" approach to separation-of-powers issues. He assumed that a categorical divide exists between the lawmaking powers given to Congress and the law-executing powers given to the executive, with the content of both categories fixed by the Constitution's plain language and original historical understandings. In this way of thinking about separation-of-powers issues, crises and changing needs play no central role. If this approach were pressed to its logical extreme, it would probably yield the conclusion (as pointed out by the dissenting opinion) that President Lincoln acted unconstitutionally when he issued the Emancipation Proclamation, which asserted a presidential power to alter property rights previously recognized by law, not merely to carry out statutes passed by Congress.

Sharply contrasting with Justice Black's opinion was that of Justice Jackson, a former attorney general under Franklin Roosevelt and a special prosecutor at the Nuremberg trials of Nazi war criminals. More pragmatic than doctrinaire, Jackson was also one of the best writers ever to serve on the Supreme Court, a gifted stylist who never finished law school but who drew heavily on Shakespeare and the Bible. He was the author of many much-quoted epigrams, including an observation that the Constitution is not "a suicide pact" and that judicial interpretation should not turn it into one. Although Jackson agreed with Black about how the *Youngstown* case should come out, his opinion argued that the president's powers are not rigidly fixed under the Constitution, as Black maintained, but at least partly adjustable.[25] Within Jackson's framework, one crucial variable involves the stance taken by Congress. When Congress authorizes the president to act, the politically accountable branches of the national government accord in their judgment about the practical necessity or desirability of executive authority, and courts should give strong deference to their

---

[24] U.S. Const. amend. V ("[N]or shall private property be taken for public use, without just compensation.").
[25] See *Youngstown*, 343 U.S. at 635–38 (Jackson, J., concurring).

determination. In contrast with cases in which Congress has authorized presidential action, Jackson identified instances in which Congress has acted to curb presidential authority. In such cases, Jackson thought that presidential power sank to its "lowest ebb." Between the poles of congressionally authorized and congressionally forbidden assertions of executive authority, Jackson identified a third category that he dubbed a "zone of twilight." Within this category, he suggested, presidential power might depend on practical considerations, including the gravity of the problem that the president confronted.

Commentators have described Justice Jackson's opinion as epitomizing a "functionalist" approach to separation-of-powers issues (in contrast with Black's "formalism"). As the term is usually used, "functionalism" recognizes that the lines separating executive from legislative from judicial power are often blurry and variable; that ebbs and flows of power are permissible as long as each branch retains its core functions and a capacity to check and balance power grabs by other branches; and that practical considerations matter in determining what the Constitution requires and permits, at least in otherwise doubtful cases.

Under Justice Jackson's framework, a presidential seizure of the steel mills might have appeared defensible in a true national emergency, if no practical alternative existed. (Indeed, in the months immediately preceding the United States's entry into World War II, President Roosevelt had averted a crippling strike by seizing a California plant that produced one-fifth of the nation's airplanes, and he had done so with the approval of his attorney general, who was none other than Robert Jackson!). In *Youngstown*, however, the president had another, statutorily authorized, means to protect the national interest: He could have obtained an injunction barring a strike for eighty days under the Taft–Hartley Act and, if the union still threatened to walk out at the end of that period, could have sought congressional authorization for a seizure. What is more, by enacting the Taft–Hartley Act, Congress had at least implicitly signaled its intent to deny the president the broader, more drastic power simply to order federal takeovers of important industries.

Given that Justice Black's formalism and Justice Jackson's functionalism both pointed to the same result, the *Youngstown* Court almost surely reached the right decision. But which of these two formidable justices had the better of the argument remains a debatable question on which reasonable minds can differ. As we will see, there can be no question that Justice Jackson's framework better explains the overall pattern of the Supreme Court's decisions, both before and after *Youngstown*, especially during the era of the New Deal settlement. But there also can be no doubt that the current Supreme Court's frequent reliance on textualist and originalist methodologies to resolve constitutional cases replicates assumptions that underpinned Justice Black's majority opinion in *Youngstown* – even though a competition between formalist and functionalist approaches to constitutional interpretation remains live. As illustrated by the Court's nonoriginalist, substantially functionalist opinion in *Trump v. United States* – which rests heavily on (contestable) practical judgments about recurring needs for bold and unhesitating presidential action – the balance of influence may be shifting, but no rout has yet occurred.

Delegated Powers: Vague Agency Mandates and the Nondelegation Doctrine

When Justice Jackson wrote in *Youngstown* about presidential power, he expressed openness to, not a skepticism of, congressional delegations to the executive branch. At the end of the *Lochner* era, and just before the "switch in time that saved nine," the Supreme Court struck down two pieces of New Deal legislation on the ground that they impermissibly attempted to delegate Congress's lawmaking powers to the executive by authorizing agency officials to promulgate rules with the force of law.[26] The Constitution, the Court reasoned, assigned the legislative power exclusively to Congress. In the years since, the Court has never formally abandoned the "nondelegation doctrine," but neither has it ever found that an explicit grant of rulemaking authority to the president or an administrative agency went further than the Constitution will allow.

At the time of *Youngstown* and for decades thereafter, the leading case upholding rulemaking by executive agencies to implement vague congressional mandates was the World War II decision in *Yakus v. United States* (1944).[27] To combat wartime inflation,

---

[26] See *Panama Refining Co. v. Ryan*, 293 U.S. 388 (1935); *A. L. A. Schechter Poultry Corp. v. United States*, 295 U.S. 495 (1935).
[27] 321 U.S. 414 (1944).

Congress established a federal agency charged with limiting wage and price increases to those that would be "fair and equitable." The authorizing statute, the Emergency Price Control Act, obviously left enormous discretion to the agency, which needed to develop detailed codes specifying permissible and impermissible price increases for diverse commodities throughout the country. Nonetheless, the Supreme Court upheld the delegation.

Its reasoning had two elements. First, the Court suggested that Congress had already done all the required lawmaking in the constitutional sense because it had established a legislative policy – that only fair and equitable price increases should be permitted – and left the agency with the job of implementing the law, not making it. Although the Court thus purported to honor the nondelegation doctrine, it tolerated a delegation of enormous scope, as the second strand of the Court's reasoning acknowledged. That second strand was avowedly pragmatic or functionalist: "The Constitution as a continuously operative charter of government does not demand the impossible or the impracticable."[28] Congress and the president had reasonably concluded that the stresses of wartime required anti-inflation rules. Yet to develop such rules in their necessary details – determining, for example, how much could be charged for a used car or a loaf of bread – lay beyond Congress's practical competence.

Yakus set a precedent much exploited by subsequent Congresses and extending well beyond wartime demands. Within a few decades, a host of agencies possessed the power to issue legally binding regulations involving such matters as entitlements to federal benefits, workplace safety, environmental quality, and forbidden employment practices. Congress did all that the Constitution required of it, the Supreme Court held, if it supplied "an intelligible principle" for agencies to follow in implementing vague mandates with detailed codes of rules.[29] As we have seen, moreover, in the years of the New Deal settlement, the Court complemented its broad tolerance of delegated executive power with the *Chevron* doctrine, described in the introduction to this chapter, under which courts deferred to agency interpretations of the statutes that Congress had charged them with implementing.

---

[28] Ibid. at 424.
[29] See *Whitman v. American Trucking Assn's, Inc.*, 531 U.S. 457, 472 (2001) (citing *J. W. Hampton, Jr., & Co. v. United States*, 276 U.S. 394, 409 [1928]).

More recently, the winds of change have quartered. The prevailing trends are now conservative, formalist, and skeptical of agency power to regulate citizens' traditional liberties. The *Loper Bright* decision, which overruled *Chevron* and its regime of deference to agencies' statutory interpretations, offers one clear example. Another comes from a case decided in 2019 in which three conservative justices, writing in dissent, voted to invalidate a federal statute on nondelegation grounds and another said that he, too, would "support" efforts to "reconsider" whether the doctrine should be revitalized if a majority of his colleagues were willing to do so.[30]

Even absent a formally reinvigorated nondelegation doctrine, the modern Supreme Court has developed a partial surrogate in what it has dubbed "the major questions doctrine." The major questions doctrine is a Court-formulated rule of statutory interpretation. Under it, courts interpreting statutes that otherwise delegate power to administrative agencies will presume that Congress – at least in the absence of very specific language – would not have intended to authorize the agencies to adopt regulations of especially large "economic and political significance."[31] A central and controversial decision in the doctrine's development was *West Virginia v. EPA* (2022),[32] which concluded that Congress had not sufficiently clearly authorized the EPA to enact a regulation limiting carbon emissions by existing power plants. The Court's opinion justified the major questions doctrine on two related grounds. First, the majority maintained that the doctrine implements constitutional "separation of powers" principles by insisting that Congress take clear responsibility for enacting or authorizing important regulations. Justice Gorsuch amplified this rationale in a concurring opinion that Justice Alito joined. "The framers believed that the power to make new laws regulating private conduct was a grave one that could, if not properly checked, pose a serious threat to individual liberty," he wrote. Second, the Court posited that the major questions doctrine reflects independently well-founded assumptions about Congress's likely intent: If Congress has not said so explicitly, it is unlikely to want to give agencies free rein to enact rules of great economic and political consequence.

---

[30] See *Gundy v. United States*, 139 S. Ct. 2116, 2131 (2019) (Gorsuch, J., joined by Roberts, CJ., and Thomas, J., dissenting); *id*. at 2131 (Alito, J., concurring in the judgment).
[31] See *West Virginia v. EPA*, 597 U.S. 697, 721 (2022) (quoting *FDA v. Brown & Williamson Tobacco Corp.*, 529 U.S. 120, 159–60 [2000]).
[32] 597 U.S. 697 (2022).

Justice Kagan filed a vehement dissent, protesting that the regulation that the majority invalidated in *West Virginia v. EPA* came squarely within the language of a statutory provision authorizing the EPA to select the "best system of emission reduction" for power plants emitting greenhouse gases. Noting that the justices in the majority often claim to be "textualists" who interpret legislation according to its plain or ordinary meaning, she retorted that "[t]he current Court is textualist only when being so suits it." She continued:

> When that method would frustrate broader goals, special [interpretive] canons like the "major questions doctrine" magically appear as get-out-of-text-free cards. Today, one of those broader goals makes itself clear: Prevent agencies from doing important work, even though that is what Congress directed.[33]

The majority parried that claim by arguing that textualist premises call for reading statutes "in context" and that the relevant context supported its conclusion that the EPA lacked authority to issue the challenged regulation. However one judges that argument, the major questions doctrine significantly limits the regulatory powers of administrative agencies under a number of important statutes.[34]

Appointment and Removal Powers

The Constitution provides for a federal government consisting of legislative, executive, and judicial branches. Many of the agencies that have traditionally administered federal regulatory and benefits-dispensing statutes have long been housed in Cabinet departments, subject to presidential oversight that is typically enforced through the president's power to appoint – and, as we shall see, to remove – their heads. Such agencies are generally referred to as "executive agencies." During the twentieth century, however, the idea gained currency that some functions of modern government made it necessary, desirable, or appropriate for some agencies to be independent of direct

---

[33] *Ibid.* at 779–80 (Kagan, J., joined by Breyer and Sotomayor, J.J., dissenting).
[34] See also 600 U.S. 477 (2023) (applying the major questions doctrine to hold that the Secretary of Education did not possess delegated authority to forgive a designated category of student loans); *National Federation of Independent Business v. OSHA*, 595 U.S. 109 (2022) (per curiam) (applying the major questions doctrine to stay the Department of Labor's vaccine mandate during the COVID-19 pandemic).

political control by the president. For example, when the Federal Trade Commission (FTC) determines whether the specific trade practices of specific companies violate the law – subject to further review in a court – it seems plausible to think that its decisions should not be influenced by political pressure to reward the president's allies or to punish the president's political opponents. With that thought in mind, Congress has sometimes created what are commonly referred to as "independent agencies." Although even independent agencies are almost always located within the executive branch, the statutes that establish them often seek to safeguard their partial independence by protecting their heads from removal by the president except for specified causes.

Although loosely "functionalist" reasoning led to the broad acceptance of statutes designed to protect some agencies' independence from direct presidential control through most of the twentieth century, since the Reagan administration, proponents of presidential power have mounted a forceful attack, grounded on what they take to be the clear language of Article II of the Constitution. Article II begins with the proclamation that "[t]he executive Power shall be vested in a President of the United States of America." Building on that and other language in Article II, critics of the concept of agency independence have developed a formalist theory notable for its elegant simplicity. The "unitary executive theory" holds that the Constitution establishes one president, vested with the entire "executive power" of the United States, and that the president must therefore be able to supervise and control all officials who work in the executive branch. According to the unitary executive theory, presidential control requires that the president must possess exclusive power not only to appoint high federal officials but also to dismiss them. Proponents claim that this theory promises to deliver coherent, politically accountable presidential administration.

Since the 1970s, the Supreme Court has agreed that the president must have the power to appoint all high federal officials charged with executing the law.[35] In doing so, the Court has relied on the language of Article II, Section 2, Clause 2, which directs that the president "shall nominate, and by and with the Advice and Consent of the Senate, shall appoint" certain named officials and "all other Officers of the United States, whose Appointments are not herein otherwise provided for."

---

[35] The leading modern case is *Buckley v. Valeo*, 424 U.S. 1 (1976).

A complication arises from a clause that follows almost immediately: "[B]ut the Congress may by Law vest the Appointment of such inferior Officers, as they think proper, in the President alone, in the Courts of Law, or in the Heads of Departments." Given this stipulation, the Supreme Court has struggled to draw the line between "principal" officers, whom the president must appoint, and "inferior" officers, whose appointments can be assigned to "heads of Departments" or courts of law. Recent cases appear to have established a relatively bright-line test: An official is an "inferior" officer if there is some higher-up official who can countermand his or her decisions.[36] By contrast, an official whose decisions are not subject to someone else's direct countermand is a principal officer. (Virtually all agree that lower-level employees of the government – indeed, nearly all those beneath the top echelon of management – are not "Officers" in the constitutional sense and that other provisions for their appointment are therefore permissible. For example, no one thinks that clerks and janitors require presidential or cabinet-level appointments or confirmation by the Senate.)

Partly because Article II does not speak explicitly about whether the president possesses inherent constitutional authority to fire executive officials, the scope of the president's removal powers has engendered recurring debate. *Myers v. United States*[37] (1926) grew from the president's insistence on removing a postmaster despite a federal statute protecting postmasters from dismissal except for good cause. In an opinion by Chief Justice William Howard Taft, himself a former president, the Court invalidated the statutory limitation on the president's authority. The president was responsible for the administration of the entire executive branch, Taft reasoned, and he must therefore be able to dismiss any subordinate who did not enjoy his full confidence.

A few years later, however, the Court considerably complicated its analysis of the president's removal powers. In *Humphrey's Executor v. United States* (1935),[38] involving a statute that limited the president's power to remove commissioners of the FTC, the Court adopted a "functionalist" approach aiming to take account of what it viewed as considerations of good government. *Humphrey's Executor* distinguished *Myers* based on the duties performed by federal trade

---

[36] See *Edmond v. United States*, 520 U.S. 651 (1997).
[37] *Myers v. United States*, 272 U.S. 52 (1926).
[38] 295 U.S. 602 (1935).

commissioners. Whereas Myers performed traditional executive functions, Congress had empowered the FTC to adjudicate in the first instance, subject to judicial review, whether violations of federal law had occurred. According to the Court, when Congress creates "quasi-legislative or quasi-judicial agencies," it can limit the president's removal powers in order to protect the independence of those performing legislative and especially judicial functions.

The highwater mark for functionalist analysis of presidential removal powers may have come in *Morrison v. Olson* (1988),[39] which upheld a statute protecting an "independent counsel" investigating crimes at the upper echelons of the executive branch from removal by the attorney general (presumably acting at the behest of the president) except for "good cause." The Court was nearly unanimous, with the conservative Chief Justice William Rehnquist writing for an 8–1 majority. Although the majority found the independent counsel's functions to be executive in nature, it could "not see how the President's need to control" the counsel's decisions was "so central to the functioning of the Executive Branch as to require as a matter of constitutional law that the counsel [must] be terminable at will by the President." The sole dissenting vote came from Justice Scalia, who insisted that the president must be able to exercise "supervision and control" over all officers of the United States performing purely executive functions.[40] Scalia also objected to the Court's framework for analysis, which he took to be so ad hoc in its assessment of permissible and impermissible intrusions on the president's authority as to be effectively ungoverned by law.

In the years since *Morrison v. Olson*, the modern Supreme Court has almost wholly embraced Justice Scalia's position. In *Seila Law LLC v. Consumer Financial Protection Bureau* (2020),[41] the Court, in an opinion by Chief Justice Roberts, explained that its "precedents have recognized only two exceptions to the President's removal power." One came in *Humphrey's Executor*, which "held that Congress could create expert agencies led by a *group* of principal officers [such

---

[39] 487 U.S. 654 (1988).
[40] The majority, he wrote, "fails to explain why it is not true that – as the text of the Constitution seems to require, as the Founders seemed to expect, and as our past cases have uniformly assumed – all purely executive power must be under the control of the President." *Ibid.* at 734–35 (Scalia, J., dissenting).
[41] 591 U.S. 197 (2020), 204.

as the commissioners of the FTC] removable by the President only for good cause." The other exception involved cases such as *Morrison*, which the chief justice described as holding that "Congress could provide tenure protections to certain *inferior* officers with narrowly defined duties." Taking the constitutional norm to be that the president's power to remove executive officials must be unrestricted, the Court invalidated a statutory provision permitting dismissal of the sole director of the Consumer Financial Protection Bureau only for inefficiency, neglect, or malfeasance. Over the objection of four dissenters, the Court rejected any role for functionalist considerations in the constitutional analysis.

Recent historical work has cast significant doubt on claims that "the unitary executive theory," which seems to drive the Supreme Court's recent decisions concerning the president's removal powers, accurately reflects the original understanding for Article II.[42] Nonetheless, a majority of the current justices appear committed to it in cases involving the appointment and the dismissal of "officers" of the executive branch. Although *Seila Law* purported to distinguish *Humphrey's Executor*, the functionalist rationale of the latter has now been almost thoroughly undercut in modern cases governing the president's removal authority.

Unilateral Claims of Executive Power

Although the removal cases are controversial, it has always been recognized that the Constitution endows the president with some independent powers not dependent on congressional delegation. The Constitution grants some such powers explicitly. These include the power to issue pardons and, as we have seen, to nominate judges, justices, and "principal" officers in the executive branch. But many other unilateral presidential powers are implicit.

The most debated of the president's unilateral powers relate to waging war. As noted earlier, throughout American history, presidents have claimed authority to send troops into battle without awaiting a congressional declaration of war. By one count, "[f]rom 1798 to

---

[42] See generally Cass R. Sunstein and Adrian Vermeule, "The Unitary Executive: Past, Present, Future," 2020 *Supreme Court Review* 83; Julian D. Mortenson, "Article II Vests the Executive Power, Not the Royal Prerogative," 119 *Columbia Law Review* 1169 (2019).

2000, there were over 200 cases where the President transferred arms or other war material abroad or actually sent troops [into hostile environments], all without Congressional involvement."[43]

Some of the arguments supporting presidential war powers are pragmatic or functionalist: American lives and interests would be compromised if the president could not respond swiftly to foreign threats or attacks. Other arguments appeal to historical practice. Still others claim that those who wrote and ratified the Constitution intended to permit the president to initiate war-making. Although scholars are divided, some maintain that Congress's power to declare war is a narrow one, which merely triggers the international laws of war,[44] and need not be exercised in order to authorize military action by the United States. On this view, the president can launch military operations unilaterally, subject only to constraints arising from Congress's power to deny funding. The contrary view is that although the president has inherent constitutional authority to repel sudden attacks and to protect lives imminently at risk, Congress possesses exclusive power to commit the country to a sustained war, whether declared or undeclared.[45]

Congress reviewed the pattern of executive war-making during the early 1970s, when a Democratic Congress sought to impose modest strictures on the president, then a Republican, by enacting the War Powers Resolution (WPR). The WPR provides that whenever presidents initiate or respond to military hostilities, they should notify House and Senate leaders within forty-eight hours and that presidentially directed military actions should cease after not more than sixty days (with a provision for extension to ninety days in cases of "unavoidable military necessity") unless authorized by Congress. By nearly everyone's account, the WPR has proved a failure. Presidents have occasionally ignored or defied it. Some have argued insistently that the WPR is unconstitutional.

Although debates about the president's unilateral war-making powers have occurred frequently in political fora and scholarly

---

[43] John E. Nowak and Ronald D. Rotunda, *Constitutional Law* (St. Paul, MN: West Group, 2000), 255.

[44] See, for example, John C. Yoo, "The Continuation of Politics by Other Means: The Original Understanding of War Powers," 84 *California Law Review* 167, 242 (1996).

[45] See, for example, John Hart Ely, *War and Responsibility: Constitutional Lessons of Vietnam and Its Aftermath* (Princeton, NJ: Princeton University Press, 1993), 3; Harold Hongju Koh, *The National Security Constitution: Sharing Power after the Iran-Contra Affair* (New Haven, CT: Yale University Press, 1990), 74–77.

journals, courts have seldom weighed in. A number of lower courts refused to rule on the constitutionality of American involvement in the Vietnam War on the ground that the challengers presented "political questions" that lay beyond the constitutional and practical competence of courts to adjudicate. Decades after Vietnam, the United States Court of Appeals for the District of Columbia Circuit dismissed a suit contending that President Bill Clinton's commitment of troops to the then ongoing war in Yugoslavia violated the WPR based on a determination that the plaintiffs lacked "standing" to sue.[46]

Despite the traditional reluctance of judges and justices to define the president's inherent authority to commit troops to hostilities, it should not be assumed that the Constitution and arguments about its proper interpretation have no practical influence. Verdicts in "the court of public opinion" matter – and the American public has generally appeared to accept that the Constitution requires congressional authorization for large-scale and drawn-out military operations, even if not for smaller fights of shorter duration. Events surrounding the 1991 Persian Gulf War and the 2003 invasion of Iraq illustrate how the division of war powers between Congress and the president has tended to work. In both instances, the president's representatives initially maintained that he could conduct large-scale military operations without congressional approval. Again in both cases, however, the president ultimately found it politically untenable to commit large forces to battle until after seeking and obtaining congressional authorization.

Recent years have presented few cases testing the response of the current Supreme Court to claims of unilateral presidential power not involving the appointment and removal of high federal officials. But the sitting justices' support for a broad removal power, based on a theory of the unitary executive branch, would not necessarily imply endorsement of other claims of inherent presidential authority. In *Medellín v. Texas* (2008),[47] all of the conservative justices then serving on the Court agreed that the president could not compel Texas courts to reopen their consideration of a criminal case involving a Mexican citizen as the defendant. President George W. Bush had directed the Texas courts to take that action in order to bring the United States into

---

[46] See *Campbell v. Clinton*, 203 F. 3d 19 (DC Cir. 2000).
[47] 552 U.S. 491 (2008).

conformity with a ruling by the International Court of Justice (ICJ), which held that Texas officials had breached US obligations under an international treaty when they failed to inform Medellín of his right to have the Mexican consulate notified of his arrest and detention. In rejecting the president's claim of authority to dictate action to the Texas courts by a vote of 6–3, the Court emphasized that the Senate, in ratifying the treaty under which Medellín claimed his rights, had not agreed to make decisions of the ICJ directly binding on the United States or its officials. The Court also rejected an argument that the president's action lay within an inherent presidential authority to resolve disputes with foreign nations.

By contrast, in *Zivotofsky v. Kerry* (2015),[48] the Supreme Court held that the president possessed a unilateral power to grant formal recognition to foreign nations. In light of that presidential authority, the Court ruled that Congress overstepped constitutional bounds when it sought to compel the State Department to issue passports listing Israel as the birthplace of US citizens who were born in Jerusalem.

Executive Privilege and Immunity

Issues involving claims of presidential immunity and executive privilege are closely related but easily confused. As I shall use the terms, presidential *immunity* signifies a constitutional protection of the president against liability to criminal prosecution or suits for civil damages. By contrast, *executive privilege* functions as a shield sometimes entitling the president, and others who work for or advise the president, to resist demands to provide testimony or other evidence in connection with judicial trials or congressional investigations.

With respect to both presidential immunity and executive privilege, the leading cases have emerged from the presidencies of Richard Nixon and Donald Trump. As discussed earlier, *Nixon v. Fitzgerald* held the president absolutely immune from suits for civil damages arising from even illegal and unconstitutional actions within the "outer perimeter" of the president's official duties. The Supreme Court that decided *Fitzgerald* divided 5–4, with most of the Court's conservative justices joining the majority and most of the liberals in dissent. There was a similar conservative versus liberal division in *Trump v. United*

[48] 576 U.S. 1 (2015).

States. In both cases, the dissenting opinions claimed that the conferral of absolute presidential immunity effectively placed the president above the law. (In a partially analogous context, judges, including Supreme Court justices, also enjoy absolute immunity from suits for damages based on actions taken in a judicial capacity.)

The central cases defining the scope of executive privilege have yielded complex outcomes and, notably, have not exhibited such sharp divisions among the justices as the presidential immunity decisions. The issue of executive privilege first came before a federal court in *United States v. Burr* (1807),[49] a criminal prosecution of a former vice president on charges of treason. When Burr's lawyers moved for a subpoena compelling the production of documentary evidence by President Thomas Jefferson, Jefferson asserted a constitutional prerogative to resist the demand. Chief Justice John Marshall, who was effectively acting as a lower court judge "riding circuit," rejected Jefferson's claim to an absolute executive privilege. Nevertheless, he allowed that the president might be entitled to refuse to make some disclosures on narrower grounds, such as the existence of "state reasons" why some documents "cannot be introduced." Since *Burr*, courts have recognized a privilege not only of the president but also of other high executive officials to withhold information the disclosure of which would threaten national security. Marshall's opinion in *Burr* also recognized that courts should refuse to enforce "vexatious and unnecessary subpoenas" against the president.

In the leading modern case on executive privilege, *United States v. Nixon* (1974),[50] the Supreme Court held unanimously that the need for confidentiality in communications between presidents and their advisors justifies "a presumptive privilege for Presidential communications." The Court reasoned that "[c]ertain powers and privileges flow from the nature of [the president's] enumerated powers," even though none explicitly creates a power to resist demands for evidence material to judicial processes. But the Court then held that the president's presumptive privilege needed to be balanced against, and was outweighed by, "the demonstrated, specific need for evidence in a pending criminal trial."[51]

---

[49] 25 F. Cas. 30 (CCD Va. 1807) (No. 14,692d).
[50] 418 U.S. 683 (1974).
[51] *Ibid*. at 713.

The Supreme Court applied a similar balancing approach in two more recent cases involving President Trump. In *Trump v. Vance* (2020),[52] the Court held by 7–2 that the president had no absolute executive privilege to resist subpoenas for financial records issued in connection with a state criminal inquiry into "business transactions" by him and his affiliated businesses. Having done so, the Court remanded the case to the lower courts to determine whether Trump's constitutionally grounded challenges to specific subpoenas might succeed. *Trump v. Mazars USA, LLP*[53] (2020) similarly concerned subpoenas seeking information about Trump's finances, but this time the parties demanding disclosure were three committees of the House of Representatives. In an opinion by Chief Justice Roberts, the Court ruled that the lower court should assess both Congress's need for information and the extent of burdens on the president in determining whether particular demands for information could be enforced. The decision appears to strengthen the president's hand in negotiations with Congress about whether, when, and how to respond to congressional demands for information. It does so by establishing time-consuming litigation as a plausible option for the president if Congress refuses to be satisfied by the president's voluntary disclosures.

Conclusion

Overall, the modern Supreme Court's cases involving the powers and privileges of the president and the executive branch do not align neatly with one another. For the most part, the Court is wary of, and has taken significant steps to curb, the regulatory authority of federal agencies administering congressionally enacted statutes. A majority of the justices plainly believe that agency rulemaking and adjudication of citizens' rights pose significant threats to individual liberty and are in tension, if not incompatible, with the Framers' constitutional design. In overruling or limiting precedents that helped to establish and sustain schemes of economic and environmental regulation that had grown familiar since the New Deal, the Court often relies on "formalist" reasoning and derides appeals to considerations of policy and expediency as constitutionally irrelevant. By contrast, in cases involving disputes

---

[52] 591 U.S. 786 (2020).
[53] 591 U.S. 848 (2020).

about the powers and prerogatives of the president – insofar as they can be distinguished from those of the executive branch that the president heads – the Court sometimes engages in more nearly "functionalist" reasoning in which concerns about the practical consequences of its rulings loom large. For example, originalism and textualism play little role in the Court's decisions concerning presidential immunity and executive privilege. Nearly without exception, the trend lines of the Court's rulings register as "conservative" in one or another sense of that protean term. But the conservatism is sometimes more substantive than methodological – and it is definitely not the brand of conservatism that resists judicially driven change.

11 LAW AND CHANGE IN THE SUPREME COURT

This book has presented two overlapping narratives of constitutional law and constitutional change. One is a long-term story, involving shifting interpretations of the Constitution throughout its history. The other is a presentist portrait, focused on the current Supreme Court, which is dominated by a 6–3 majority of conservative justices.

The long-term narrative has portrayed the Court's practice in adopting evolving interpretations of a little-changed written Constitution as perennial. Multiple factors have contributed to the churn. Much of the Constitution is written in vague language, which renders it amenable to diverse understandings. Also, the Constitution is exceptionally hard to amend formally. The difficulty of amendment creates incentives not only to advance interpretations that serve specific policy goals at particular times but also to adopt styles of constitutional exegesis that facilitate ongoing adaptation.

Frequently, of course, leading actors in political and constitutional dramas have disagreed with each other, and sometimes with the Supreme Court, about what would constitute wise or even tenable interpretive conclusions. This pattern developed early in constitutional history. In 1798, Federalists and their Jeffersonian opponents differed vehemently about whether the Sedition Act, which made it a crime to criticize the president, violated the Free Speech Clause of the First Amendment. A similar division emerged about whether a statute by which the Jeffersonians abolished the offices of thirteen "Midnight Judges" who had been installed by the lame-duck Adams administration contravened Article III, which protects federal judges from removal during "good behavior." On both sides of these controversies, as with many that have unfolded subsequently, contending constitutional interpretations largely reflected the political interests and affiliations of their proponents. Similarly, ideological divisions are, and long have been, common among the justices of the Supreme Court. Under these circumstances, changes in the Court's membership – sometimes even of a single justice – can produce, and often have produced, rapid revisions of prevailing constitutional doctrines.

Another prominent feature of the story of long-term constitutional change is that the Supreme Court operates within what political scientists have characterized as politically constructed boundaries. This thesis, which prior chapters have invoked repeatedly, has both a harder and a softer aspect. On the hard side, there are some conceivable judicial decisions that dominant political actors would either refuse to obey or take efficacious measures to reverse with the public standing behind them. For example, in an infamous episode during World War II, President Franklin Roosevelt credibly threatened to defy the Court if it did not permit the trial of would-be Nazi saboteurs apprehended in the United States, one of whom happened to be a US citizen, in a military tribunal without a civilian jury.[1] In the perilous context of wartime, the justices felt compelled to accede to the president. Almost immediately after hearing arguments in the case, the Court summarily rejected the defendants' constitutional objections to their mode of trial and, in a departure from usual protocol, announced that an opinion explaining its reasoning would follow at a later date. By the time the Court's opinion issued, the military trial had been completed and the US citizen who was a defendant in the case had already been executed. Short of actual or threatened defiance of judicial rulings, a softer version of the politically constructed bounds of judicial power comes into play when Supreme Court decisions incite a backlash at the

---

[1] The resulting doctrinal change had reverberations in a later generation in helping to justify the use of military commissions, not Article III courts, to authorize detentions of suspected enemy combatants in the War on Terror. For discussion of the relevant decisions, including the circumstances surrounding the World War II case *Ex parte Quirin*, 317 U.S. 1 (1942), see Richard H. Fallon Jr. and Daniel J. Meltzer, "Habeas Corpus Jurisdiction, Substantive Rights, and the War on Terror," 120 *Harvard Law Review* 2029, 2072–80 (2007).

ballot box and the election of a president who has pledged to appoint justices who will overturn unpopular rulings. In the 1968 election, as Chapter 2 recounted, Richard Nixon achieved success partly by making the Warren Court's criminal procedure decisions a campaign issue. His judicial appointments transformed the Court and launched a process of conservative doctrinal revisionism that began tentatively but has accelerated over time.

One further aspect of the long-term story of constitutional change via Supreme Court decision-making deserves emphasis: It has long been accepted within our constitutional order that prior Court decisions provide legally permissible reasons for rulings in subsequent cases, sometimes without regard to whether the precedents may have deviated from the Constitution's originally understood meaning. To reframe the point in more practical terms, the justices can claim a lawful entitlement, or sometimes even an obligation, to base their current and future decisions on past rulings that they might have regarded as unsupportable on first principles. Some cite the doctrine of substantive due process, including the interpretation of the Due Process Clause of the Fifth Amendment to bar race discrimination by the federal government, as illustrative of this phenomenon. In the critics' view, substantive due process is a judicial invention of which the Supreme Court has made, and under the doctrine of stare decisis can continue to make, recurring, sometimes innovative, use. But the doctrine of stare decisis, it has long been recognized, is not an absolute command. If the justices so choose, they can reconsider past decisions and, within politically constructed bounds, can embark on new paths of constitutional development that they think are more consonant with original constitutional meanings. By one tally, as of 2024, the Supreme Court had overruled one of its prior decisions on more than 200 occasions.[2]

The presentist story of constitutional change that I have told in this book is, of course, continuous with the long-term account, but there are important elements of contrast, too. In maintaining that we have entered a distinctive era of Supreme Court history, prior chapters have emphasized four themes. First, the current coterie of justices is more attentive to issues of constitutional interpretive methodology

---

[2] See "Table of Supreme Court Decisions Overruled by Subsequent Decisions," *The Library of Congress* (2024), https://constitution.congress.gov/resources/decisions-overruled/ (recording 236 decisions overruled between 1798 and 2024).

than their predecessors in any prior period. Originalism and textualism have achieved unparalleled prominence. The Court frequently cites original constitutional understandings and the analytical deficiencies of predecessor Courts in ignoring or misrepresenting original meanings as bases for reversals of course. Decisions under the Establishment Clause and the Second Amendment furnish examples. A sense among the conservative supermajority that the law has drifted objectionably far from the original constitutional design also helps to explain a number of the Court's recent rulings limiting congressional power under Article I and curbing the authority of federal regulatory agencies.

Second, however, the Supreme Court of the present era is not consistently originalist. Doctrinal enclaves remain in which references to original constitutional meanings play little role. Examples include the Free Speech Clause of the First Amendment and the Equal Protection Clause of the Fourteenth Amendment. The conservative justices have also declined to reject the concept of "substantive due process," though they have sought to limit it to cases involving rights grounded by history and tradition. Given the Court's apparent inconsistency, critics often charge the ostensibly originalist justices with hypocrisy. The Court's defenders reply that nearly all versions of originalism acknowledge a role for stare decisis in constitutional adjudication.[3] With the dispute thus framed, it is characteristic of the modern age that the justices argue frequently and sometimes impassionedly about whether the vague and flexible principle of constitutional stare decisis applies to particular cases. When they do so, they often divide along ideological lines.

Third, the current Supreme Court is very conservative as defined by nearly any substantive measure. In particular, the members of the conservative block control the outcome in a high proportion of publicly salient cases. The conservative justices tend to be cohesive partly because of the careful vetting that preceded their nominations and confirmations. But it also matters crucially that the current conservative majority is a 6–3 supermajority. Parties contending for conservative results can afford to lose one otherwise conservative justice and still prevail.

---

[3] See, for example, Amy Coney Barrett, "Originalism and Stare Decisis," 92 *Notre Dame Law Review* 1921, 1921–22 (2017).

Fourth, the current conservative Court may be less constrained by politically constructed limits on judicial power than the members of conservative majorities in other recent times. A number of the current Court's most headline-grabbing decisions have proved unpopular. The decision overruling *Roe v. Wade*[4] (1973) is a notable example. In addition, the Court's approval ratings in public opinion surveys have plummeted in recent years. But our closely divided politics, in conjunction with Senate filibuster rules, make any effective political retaliation against the Court by Congress, such as Court-packing, highly unlikely.

Law and Politics in the Supreme Court

This book's account of the Supreme Court's role in recurrently changing the content of constitutional doctrine under a mostly unamended written Constitution raises questions about whether the Constitution meaningfully binds the Court and whether the justices behave lawfully or legitimately when they selectively choose either originalist or nonoriginalist premises to justify revisions of constitutional doctrine. The answer to both of these questions is yes, I believe, but only if we adopt a flexible understanding of what it means for the Court to be bound or constrained by the Constitution and a capacious view of the Court's lawful authority.

In thinking about whether the Constitution meaningfully constrains the Supreme Court, analysis should begin with the premise – which almost no one would deny when not worrying about the Supreme Court – that the Constitution is law in, and indeed the "supreme Law" of,[5] the United States. In support of that premise, we should note that the Constitution has many clear provisions, such as those stipulating that the president serves for a term of four years and that each state has two senators. Rarely does anyone suggest that provisions such as these have no binding force, even in the Supreme Court. It is the Constitution, after all, that structures the government of the United States and gives the Court its authority. The Court cannot both depend on the Constitution as the foundation for its powers and function free of constitutional limitations. The same constitutional norms that empower the Court work in conjunction with provisions

---

[4] See 410 U.S. 113 (1973), overruled by *Dobbs v. Jackson Women's Health Organization*, 597 U.S. 215 (2022).
[5] U.S. Const., art. VI.

establishing other institutions of government and conferring individual rights to limit what the Court can lawfully do. To take an extreme example, if the Court, by a vote of 6–3, were spontaneously to decree that the presidential term of office shall henceforth be three or five years rather than four, the response of other officials and the general public, I am quite confident, would be that the Court's order was utterly lawless and should not be accepted.

I cite the likely response by political officials and the American people to a transparently unlawful or legally illegitimate assertion of Supreme Court authority to make an important point about the most fundamental constitutional constraints that apply to the Court. Although the justices are subject to the criminal law, many possible abuses or attempted abuses of their offices would not be crimes. An imagined ruling by the justices that the president's term is either more or less than four years furnishes an example. Nevertheless, even though the justices could not be punished criminally for such a ruling, neither should they, or we, anticipate that so lawless a decision would command obedience and that the Court, after issuing it, could continue to function as before. If other officials and the public viewed a Supreme Court holding as utterly beyond the pale of properly judicial power under the Constitution, the justices would predictably encounter resistance in some form. Possibilities include defiance, impeachment, and Court-packing.

Recognizing the significance of what others would regard as constitutionally unauthorized judicial decisions that would warrant some form of resistance by the political branches is, I believe, crucial to understanding how the Constitution simultaneously empowers and constrains the Supreme Court. To see why requires a brief consideration of the foundations of constitutional law and, indeed, of all legal authority. If we ask why the Constitution is legally binding in the United States, the short answer – which many people find counterintuitive and some regard as terrifying – is that the Constitution is legally binding only because it is accepted as legally binding by a sufficient number of relevant people. The dictates of the British Parliament once were law in the thirteen colonies that initially became the United States. But British law ceased to be law in the United States when enough people stopped accepting it as such. The Articles of Confederation then enjoyed the status of law for a time, but they in turn lost that status when enough people accepted the Constitution as binding in the Articles' stead.

Specifying whose acceptance is necessary for the existence of law, and in particular to establish the written Constitution as the fundamental law of the United States, requires introduction of a further complication and partial qualification of the premise that the foundations of law lie in acceptance. H. L. A. Hart, who was the most influential philosopher of law in the twentieth century, posited that judges and justices form the core constituency whose acceptance of fundamental norms lies at the foundations of a legal system.[6] To denominate the ultimate criterion, rooted in acceptance, by which judges and other officials differentiate law from nonlaw, Hart coined the term "the rule of recognition."[7] According to Hart, the content of the rule of recognition is a matter of empirical fact that is not itself subject to legal validation: "[T]he rule of recognition ... is in effect a form of judicial customary rule existing only if it is accepted and practised in the law-identifying and law-applying operations of the courts."[8] But while Hart emphasized the role of judges and courts in accepting and enforcing ultimate norms of legal validity, he also suggested that many others must be prepared to acquiesce in judges' practices in identifying and applying the law. If we distinguish acceptance from acquiescence, some groups' acquiescence to judges' and justices' practices may be as necessary to the maintenance of a legal order as the justices' acceptance of ultimate criteria of legal validity.

At some point along a spectrum, the general question of whether the Constitution meaningfully constrains the Supreme Court blends with the question of whether and, if so when, its assertions of constitutional authority to revise constitutional doctrine will be sufficiently broadly accepted or acquiesced in by other officials and the public. As I have emphasized throughout this book, the Constitution needs to be interpreted. And in considering whether the Court acts within the bounds of its constitutionally legitimate authority in interpreting the Constitution to resolve a particular contested question one way or the other, we should recognize that there can be an important difference between the Court's making a legally legitimate decision and the Court's deciding a disputable question correctly. Precisely because constitutional questions are often reasonably debatable, we need an

---

[6] See H. L. A. Hart, *The Concept of Law*, 3rd ed. (Oxford, UK: Oxford University Press, 2012).
[7] See *ibid.* at 94–95, 100–10.
[8] *Ibid.* at 256.

ultimate arbiter such as the Court to rule authoritatively in particular cases. For the Supreme Court to be able to play that role, moreover, we must recognize that the justices can, and typically do, behave legally legitimately even when they reach decisions that many, if not most, citizens, judges, and other officials view as mistaken. To err is human. So recognizing, we must accept that not every error by the Supreme Court is an illegitimate one that lacks constitutional entitlement to be obeyed by lower court judges and other conscientious officials. It is only when the Court engages in a clear overreach or errs unusually egregiously that it can be said to have acted beyond the scope of its lawful authority or behaved legally illegitimately.

With this complex jurisprudential and conceptual background in place, we are at last ready to consider whether the Supreme Court behaves lawfully or legally legitimately when it revises what once had appeared to be settled constitutional doctrine. Given the distinction between deciding a constitutional issue legitimately and deciding it correctly, we should begin with the presumption that the Court's decisions are legitimate or within the scope of its constitutional mandate to resolve disputable questions authoritatively even when we think the Court decided incorrectly. To be clear, I do not mean to suggest that the set of constitutionally unauthorized or legally illegitimate decisions by the Supreme Court is an empty one. To take just one example, I would side with the many who have assigned *Dred Scott v. Sandford*[9] (1857) to that category.

Although I could not reasonably attempt to parse every case in which critics have accused the Supreme Court of rendering legally illegitimate decisions, it may be useful for me to say a few words about two grounds on which some have lodged allegations of lawless behavior against the justices. A few originalists have argued that because the Constitution is, as the Supremacy Clause contained in Article VI says, "the supreme Law of the Land," the justices can have no lawful authority to decide cases on the basis of precedents that deviate from the Constitution's "real," which some take to be its original, meaning. On the other side, when angered by Supreme Court decisions overturning precedents that they support, such as *Roe v. Wade*, liberal "living constitutionalists" have sometimes maintained that decisions overruling iconic cases are inherently lawless or illegitimate.

[9] 60 U.S. 393 (1857).

Neither of these positions is sustainable. Just as the Constitution's legal validity depends on and reflects its acceptance, the same is true of norms of constitutional adjudication that make prior Supreme Court rulings permissible bases for future decisions by the Court even if they deviate from the Constitution's original meaning. So far as I am aware, all justices of the Supreme Court, including those currently sitting, have accepted one or another formulation of the principle of stare decisis that permits even originally erroneous constitutional rulings to control the outcomes of subsequent cases. Moreover, it should be equally clear that the long-accepted principle of stare decisis has never been understood by the justices to be categorically binding on them in constitutional cases and that some of the Court's decisions overruling past iconic interpretations are now celebrated. Virtually no one would argue today that the Court behaved illegitimately in overruling *Lochner v. New York*[10] (1905) or in abandoning the interpretation of the Fourteenth Amendment adopted in *Plessy v. Ferguson* (1896).[11] Judges and other officials have accepted the legal legitimacy of these and other decisions overruling once iconic constitutional precedents, and the public has broadly acquiesced.

In sum, the standards that fix the bounds of legally permissible constitutional interpretation by the Supreme Court – some of which may be directly traceable to the Constitution but others of which are grounded in judicial and official acceptance and public acquiescence – accord the Court extraordinary flexibility or opportunity for the exercise of practical, sometimes moral, judgment. It would even be accurate to say that the legal norms governing constitutional interpretation by the Supreme Court are functionally indistinguishable in some instances from rules authorizing constitutional change. Still, there are limits on the Court's powers, enforced in part by the willingness of other officials and ultimately the American public either to accept or to acquiesce in the Court's claims of interpretive authority.

I said earlier that some find the thought that the foundations of constitutional law lie in patterns of "acceptance," and not in any timeless guarantee, to be a frightening one. Today I would describe it as a settled rule of constitutional law, grounded in acceptance, that reasonable Supreme Court decisions of disputable constitutional questions

---

[10] 198 U.S. 45 (1905).
[11] 163 U.S. 537 (1896).

bind the parties before the Court. But imagine that a future president defied a Court decision that the president maintained was mistaken. During the Watergate era, President Richard Nixon intimated that he might refuse to obey a Supreme Court ruling that he must surrender recordings of selected White House conversations for possible use as evidence in a criminal trial. In the context of the time, it became evident that defiance of the Court's decision in *Nixon v. United States*[12] (1974) would lead to the president's impeachment and removal from office. In the face of that reality, Nixon surrendered the tapes. But with the *Nixon* case we can contrast Thomas Jefferson's implied threat of disobedience if the Supreme Court had ruled against his administration in *Marbury v. Madison*[13] (1803) and Franklin Roosevelt's warning that he would ignore a decision requiring trial by jury for German saboteurs apprehended in the United States. If one asks "What would happen if a future president defied a Supreme Court ruling?" an honest answer would need to include a recognition that "it depends." There are many potential variables reflecting the unsettling truth that the foundations of law, and perhaps especially constitutional law and judicial power, lie in the potentially shifting sands of official acceptance and public acquiescence.

Appraising Constitutional Law and Constitutional Change

The long-term and presentist depictions of constitutional law and constitutional change that I have offered in this book both invite normative assessment. But in presenting my own appraisal, I do not expect all others to agree with me. Readers should feel competent at this point to judge for themselves.

In assessing a practice of constitutional adjudication in the Supreme Court that, from the beginning, has included shifting interpretations of a substantially unchanged text, I think it vital to start with an evaluation of the written Constitution. Although many Americans hold the Constitution in worshipful regard, in my view, it is far from ideal. It was mostly written in the eighteenth century by men who could not have anticipated many future developments and twenty-first-century problems. The nation would have a better basis for going forward if we

[12] 418 U.S. 683 (1974).
[13] 5 U.S. (1 Cranch) 137 (1803).

had a well-designed modern constitution that responded more directly to the needs, expectations, and prevailing values of the people of the United States of the twenty-first century. But a well-designed twenty-first-century constitution is not on the table as a viable alternative to our actual Constitution. Moreover, even if one or more clear options existed, what would impress some as ideal would hold no allure for, and might even repel, others. Under these circumstances, appraisal of our practice of constitutional adjudication by the Supreme Court as an ongoing process of interpretive change requires assessing how well the Court and the nation have done with what they have had to work with.

Although our current Constitution is far from perfect, one of its signal virtues – viewed in relation to our legal culture and political order – has lain in its adaptability. As prior chapters illustrate, the Supreme Court, with the acceptance and acquiescence of relevant constituencies, has developed interpretive methods that permit, even if they do not require, transformations of prevailing doctrines to accommodate evolving needs and values. Originalists sometimes deride Court-driven change that contravenes their view of original constitutional meanings as exhibiting a democratic deficit. According to some of them, the Constitution was ratified by democratic supermajorities, and democratically legitimate constitutional change can occur only through constitutionally specified supermajoritarian processes. In my opinion, our eighteenth-century Constitution, which was drafted exclusively by white males and ratified by processes from which all women and nearly all people of color were excluded, has suffered democratic shortfalls since its inception. That Constitution also makes formal amendment far too hard for it to furnish a sufficient corrective. Viewed against this background, evolutionary reshaping of constitutional law through judicial interpretation has provided at least some opportunity for historically evolving public values to exert influence. Although the political processes by which presidents nominate and the Senate confirms justices were never perfect substitutes for formal constitutional revision by an engaged public, over the course of history I believe that they have helped to produce a more workable and just constitutional order than we would have had otherwise. There have been bleak periods, to be sure. Nevertheless, in my judgment, our constitutional history is a happier one than it likely would have been if prevailing interpretations had been fixed early on and had remained static thereafter.

My appraisal of the present period in Supreme Court history is more troubled. Among other differences, peculiar recent circumstances have enabled one political party, which has not at any relevant point enjoyed a broad and deep national mandate, to install a supermajority of justices with an aggressive agenda of change. My assessment would undoubtedly be more cheerful if the current Court's conservative values aligned more closely with my own. But they do not. Compounding my sense of disaffection, the political processes of presidential nomination and Senate confirmation of justices seem unlikely to offer the same opportunities as they have in the past for political rebalancing of the Court through what once would have counted as the normal operation of the political system. The "hardball" tactics that resulted in the Senate's refusal to consider President Obama's nominee to succeed Justice Scalia and the rushed confirmation of Justice Barrett to replace Justice Ginsburg only weeks before a presidential election appear to have shattered traditional norms of political fair play. In addition, there is good reason to anticipate that the current conservative justices will hold their seats for far longer than the historic average of their predecessors and will time their resignations to permit Republican presidents to name their replacements unless Democrats enjoy an unprecedented skein of success in presidential elections. Overall, I fear that the unhealthy state of our contemporary politics and culture – which are marked by uncivil discourse, reckless partisanship, and tribal instincts – has given us a Supreme Court whose decisions and divisions too often reflect, rather than ameliorate, the pathologies that surround it.

Despite the difficulties of the current situation, I do not assume that our constitutional order is doomed to irreversible decline and an ultimate fall. Nor have I abandoned long-term hopes for the Supreme Court as an institution. Just as the country has come successfully through troubled times before, so has the Court, and both may do so again. I hope for the best. But if history teaches anything, it is that there are no assurances that the future will be like the past. In constitutional law as in much else, the advent of change – whether for worse or for better – may be the only certainty.

INDEX

303 Creative LLC v. Elenis, 13n19, 126

Abington School District v. Schempp (1963), 89n22
abortion, 3, 5, 54, 57, 61, 67, 69, 75, 95, 137, 195, 210, 222–30. *See also specific decisions*
Abrams v. United States (1919), 108
academic freedom, 162
Adams, John, 19, 29
Administrative Procedure Act, 275
affirmative action, 2–3, 5–6, 8, 54–55, 61, 75, 161–63, 169, 174, 176–80, 185, 194, 208, 228
Affordable Care Act. *See* Patient Protection and Affordable Care Act
Affordable Care Act case. *See National Federation of Independent Business v. Sebelius* (2012)
agency fees by nonunion employees, 125
A.L.A. Schechter Poultry Corp. v. United States (1935), 36n3, 281n26
Alexander v. South Carolina State Conference of the NAACP (2024), 200n85
Alito, Samuel, 57, 61, 69–71, 97, 122, 127, 149, 227, 236, 283

Allegheny, County of v. ACLU (1989), 86n13, 86n14, 86n15, 88
American Legion v. American Humanist Association (2019), 88
American Supreme Court, The (McCloskey), 41n18
anticanon, 170
Articles of Confederation, 22, 24, 300
association, freedom of, 104, 131–33, 221

Baker v. Carr (1962), 199n83
balancing test, 112, 130, 135, 154, 293
Bank of the United States, 39, 255
Barnett, Randy, 254
Barrett, Amy Coney, 4, 72–73, 76, 153, 158, 306
Betts v. Brady (1942), 52n36
Biden, Joseph, 72, 75
Bill of Rights, 20–21, 51–52, 106, 149, 221–22, 228, 240. *See also specific amendments*
Bipartisan Campaign Reform Act, 122
Black, Charles, 42, 168
Black, Hugo, 104, 170, 219, 278
Blackmun, Harry, 54, 223, 232
Boerne, City of v. Flores (1997), 264, 266
Bolling v. Sharpe (1954), 172

308 / Index

Bostock v. Clayton County (2020), 71n26, 193
Bowen v. Roy (1986), 93n34
Bowers v. Hardwick (1986), 231–33
Boy Scouts of America v. Dale (2000), 133
Bradwell v. Illinois (1872), 185n53
Brandeis, Louis, 108, 109, 110–11
Brandenburg v. Ohio (1969), 109–11, 116
Braunfeld v. Braun (1961), 92n30
Breedlove v. Suttles (1937), 198n80
Brennan, William, 92, 262–63
Breyer, Stephen, 75, 98, 119, 142, 147, 150, 154, 208, 228
broadcast media, 138–39
Brown v. Board of Education (1954), 14, 51, 53, 64, 162, 171–72, 174, 176, 200
Brown v. Board of Education (II) (1955), 172n27
Brown v. Entertainment Merchants Association (2011), 130
Brown v. Socialist Workers '74 Campaign Committee (1982), 132
Buck v. Bell (1927), 220
Buckley v. Valeo (1976), 121, 285n35
Burford, Anne Gorsuch, 70
Burger, Warren, 12, 53, 55, 142, 175
Burwell v. Hobby Lobby Stores, Inc. (2014), 95n44
Bush, George H. W., 55, 59, 68, 74, 83, 225
Bush, George W., 60, 66, 69, 71, 207, 290
Bush v. Gore (2000), 207–8, 306
busing, 53, 175

cable television, 139
California v. Texas (2021), 257n27
Cardozo, Benjamin, 257
Carson v. Makin (2022), 78–80, 84, 90
Carter v. Carter Coal Company (1936), 36n4

categorical rules, 98, 112, 126, 165, 248, 271, 279
Catholics, 82–83
censorship, 104
Central Hudson Gas & Electric Corp. v. Public Service Commission (1981), 118
Chaplinsky v. New Hampshire (1942), 117n34, 127–28
Chase, Samuel, 38
Chevron U.S.A., Inc. v. National Resources Defense Council, Inc. (1984), 274
child pornography, 129
Church of the Lukumi Babalu Aye, Inc. v. City of Hialeah (1993), 90
churches. *See* religion
Citizens United v. Federal Election Commission (2010), 3, 122–24
citizenship, 46–47, 150, 165, 196, 214, 216
civil rights, 15, 50, 109, 132, 165, 169–70, 172, 176, 235, 262, 267
Civil Rights Act of 1964, 71, 172, 193, 246, 251, 253, 267
Civil War, 24, 38, 39, 42, 45–46, 163, 164n5, 213–14, 260, 262, 266, 266n46, 267, 277
Clark v. Community for Creative Nonviolence (1984), 114n29
clear and present danger, 107–10
Clinton, Bill, 71, 74, 188, 190, 290
Coase, Ronald, 118
Cohen v. California (1971), 115–16, 128
Colegrove v. Green (1946), 199n82
Collin v. Smith (1978), 116n33
Collins, Susan, 72
Commerce Clause, 36, 218, 240–55, 258, 265
commercial speech, 117
Congress, U.S.
    Article I and, 15, 25, 36, 40, 48, 218, 240, 242–43, 245, 247, 267
    commerce power. *See* Commerce Clause

enforcement power, 262, 264, 267
House of Representatives, 23, 25, 38, 42, 293
powers of, 15, 239–67
Senate, 3–4, 23, 25, 30, 37–38, 59, 174, 199, 277, 286, 291, 299, 306
spending power. *See* Taxing and Spending Clause
state governments and, 258–60
war powers, 289–90
Connick v. Myers (1983), 135
conservatism, 62, 103, 139, 179, 268, 294
Constitution, U.S.
amendments to, 5, 295
Article I, 15, 25, 240, 242–43, 245, 247–48, 254, 257
Article II, 16, 25, 278, 285–86, 288
Article III, 29–30, 65, 203, 274, 296n1
Article IV, 44, 213, 214
Article VI, 302
Articles of Confederation and, 300
Bill of Rights. *See* Bill of Rights
Constitutional Convention, 22, 25, 27
due process. *See* due process
equal protection. *See* equal protection
interpretation of, 6, 16, 20, 22, 25, 32–33, 55, 61, 86, 158, 179, 250, 281, 296, 303
judicial review. *See* judicial review
race and. *See* race
ratification of, 18, 20
reach of, 21
slavery and. *See* slavery
Supreme Court and. *See* Supreme Court
women and. *See* women
content-based regulation, 13, 103–15, 125, 130
corporate expenditures, 13
COVID-19, pandemic, 73, 284n34
Craig v. Boren (1976), 186
Crawford v. Marion County Election Board (2008), 206

criminal procedure, 53, 297
Cutter v. Wilkinson (2005), 99n55

Danforth, John, 68
Debs v. United States (1919), 107, 109–10
Debs, Eugene, 107–8
Declaration of Independence, 163
Democratic-Republican Party, 23, 30–31, 105
Democrats, 56, 199, 203–6, 225, 245, 306
Dennis v. United States (1951), 109
Department of Agriculture v. Moreno (1973), 182–83
discrimination, 14, 46, 51, 54, 71, 79–80, 91, 96, 98, 101, 126, 132, 162, 164, 166–67, 169, 172, 175–76, 182–83, 185, 187, 189–90, 193
discriminatory purpose, 183–84, 263
District of Columbia v. Heller (2008), 142, 145–49
Dobbs v. Jackson Women's Health Organization (2022), 6, 15, 57, 195, 226–29
Douglas, William O., 111, 196, 221
draft cards, 113. *See also United States v. O'Brien*
Dred Scott v. Sandford (1857), 43–45, 170, 211, 213, 302
due process, 14–15, 20, 37, 44, 48, 52, 54, 58, 149–50, 164, 169, 172, 180, 191–92, 195, 211, 213, 215, 218, 220–21, 223, 228, 234, 237, 297
economic legislation, 215–19
equal protection and, 195–96
fundamental rights and, 195, 212, 232, 235
incorporation doctrine. *See* Fourteenth Amendment
substantive due process, 48, 210–38
Duncan v. Louisiana (1968), 52n36
Dworkin, Ronald, 166n9

Eastern Enterprises v. Apfel (1998), 219n15
Edmond v. United States (1997), 286n36
education, 55, 78–80, 82, 84, 101, 104, 161–62, 170, 181, 188, 195
  discrimination and, 170–72
Eisenstadt v. Baird (1972), 222, 225, 230
elections
  campaign contributions, 3, 121, 132
  campaign expenditures, 122, 132
  districting, 198–99, 201–6
  voting and, 166, 195, 198, 206–7
Ely, John Hart, 54, 194
Emancipation Proclamation, 277, 279
Emergency Price Control Act, 282
Employment Division v. Smith (1990), 12, 94, 97, 101, 264–65
Engel v. Vitale (1962), 89n22
Epperson v. Arkansas (1968), 89–90
equal protection, 8, 21, 47, 51, 161–209
  affirmative action. *See* affirmative action
  classifications and, 166, 173, 175, 180, 182–83, 188–89, 194
  disparate impact, 183–85
  districting and, 198, 201
  due process and, 195
  fundamental rights and, 194–96
  integration, 175–76
  race. *See* race
  sex discrimination, 182, 185–90
  sexual orientation, 190–93
  voting and, 196–200
Espinoza v. Montana Department of Revenue (2020), 85n12
Espionage Act, 13, 106
Establishment Clause, 77–78, 80–85
  ceremonial deism, 85
  Free Exercise Clause and, 80, 99
  Lemon test, 83–84, 86, 89
  neutrality rationale, 85
  original understanding, 81
  public schools and, 88–90
  strict separationism, 78–79, 83, 86

Everson v. Board of Education (1947), 81
Ex parte Merryman (1861), 45n24
Ex parte Quirin (1942), 296n1
executive branch, 28, 31, 268, 271–72, 275, 281, 285–86, 288, 290, 293. *See also* President
  Chevron doctrine, 274, 282
  unitary executive theory, 285, 288
executive immunity, 269–71
executive privilege, 291–93
expressive organizations, 132–33

fairness doctrine, 138
FCC v. Beach Communications, Inc. (1993), 180n44
FCC v. Pacifica Foundation (1978), 138–39
Federal Communications Commission, 138
Federal Reserve Board, 7
Federal Trade Commission, 285–86, 288
federalism, 55, 258–59, 266
Federalist Papers, 18, 24n6, 28n15, 29n17, 256
Federalist Party, 29, 37
Federalist Society, 60–61, 250
Feingold, Russell, 122
Ferguson v. Skrupa (1963), 219n14
Fifteenth Amendment, 21, 46–47, 164–65, 197, 260–61, 266
Fifth Amendment, 44, 169, 172, 228, 279, 297
  Due Process Clause. *See* due process
First Amendment, 2, 12, 21, 51, 147, 154, 221, 246, 295
  Establishment Clause. *See* Establishment Clause
  Free Exercise Clause. *See* Free Exercise Clause
  freedom of association. *See* association, freedom of
  freedom of speech. *See* Free Speech Clause
  original understanding, 81, 105, 123

Fisher v. University of Texas (2016), 178n40
Fitzgerald v. Racing Ass'n of Central Iowa (1999), 181n46
flag burning, 114
formalism, 280
Fourteenth Amendment, 8, 21–22, 46, 50, 52, 64, 149, 155, 298, 303
   Due Process Clause. *See* due process
   equal protection. *See* equal protection
   incorporation doctrine, 52, 228, 264
   original understanding, 46, 51, 150, 164–66, 213
   ratification of, 22
   section 5 of, 262–67
Frankfurter, Felix, 112, 171–72, 199
Free Exercise Clause, 12, 77–80, 90–98
   Establishment Clause and, 79–80, 99
   exemptions and, 91–98
   ministerial exception, 96
   most favored nation approach, 97
   original understanding, 94
   Smith and, 94–95
   strong free exercise interpretation, 79
   wall of separation, 12, 82, 84
Free Speech Clause
   Black and, 104
   Brandeis and, 108
   broadcast media. *See* commercial speech
   child pornography, 129
   content discrimination, 104–15
   corporate speech, 123
   expressive conduct, 113–15, 126
   fighting words, 9, 103, 116
   forum doctrine, 136–38
   government speech, 134–35
   hate speech, 13, 116–17
   Holmes and, 106–9, 111, 120, 128, 217
   incidental restrictions on, 113
   libel. *See* libel
   managerial domains, 133, 138
   marketplace of ideas, 108, 120, 123, 128
   obscenity, 9, 13, 103, 118, 128–29, 240, 252
   persuasion principle, 9, 13, 103, 114, 119–21, 124, 131
   public forum, 136–37
   public school students' speech rights, 136
   unprotected categories, 127–31
Frontiero v. Richardson (1973), 186, 188
Fulton v. City of Philadelphia (2021), 95n45, 96
functionalism, 280
fundamental rights, 47, 197–98
   equal protection and, 194–96
   substantive due process and, 210–38
   unenumerated rights, 213, 221, 223

Garcetti v. Ceballos (2006), 135n68
gay rights, 4, 56, 61, 75, 182, 190–91, 231
   don't ask, don't tell, 190
   gay marriage, 70, 72, 190, 192, 228, 235–36
gender issues, 53, 187–89. *See also* equal protection, sex discrimination
gerrymandering, 202–6, 306
Gienapp, Jonathan, 26n10
Ginsburg, Ruth Bader, 4, 68, 72, 76, 185–86, 188, 208, 253, 260–61, 306
Gonzales v. Raich (2004), 255
Gore, Al, 207
Gorsuch, Neil, 4, 70–71, 84, 89, 98, 193, 283
government speech, 134–35
Great Depression, 15, 35, 48
Greece v. Galloway (2014), 87–89
Griffin v. Illinois (1956), 195n71
Grutter v. Bollinger (2003), 177–78
Gundy v. United States (2019), 283n30
guns, 2, 141–42, 144–46, 149–50, 153, 156, 160, 252. *See also* Second Amendment

Hague v. Committee for Industrial Organization (1939), 137n76
Hamilton, Alexander, 18, 28, 256
Hammer v. Dagenhart (1918), 48n29, 244
Harlan, John Marshall, 169
Harlan, John Marshall, II, 222
Harper v. Virginia Board of Elections (1966), 196, 206
Hart, H. L. A., 301
hate speech, 13, 116–17
Hazelwood School District v. Kuhlmeier (1988), 136n73
Heller, Dick, 141, 145
Hodel v. Virginia Surface Mining & Reclamation Ass'n (1981), 246n10
Holder v. Humanitarian Law Project (2010), 125
Holmes, Oliver Wendell, 106–9, 111
  Lochner and, 217
  marketplace of ideas and, 108, 120
homosexuality, 190. *See also* equal protection; gay rights
Hosanna-Tabor Evangelical Lutheran Church and School v. Equal Employment Opportunity Commission (2012), 96
Hughes, Charles Evans, 35
Humphrey's Executor v. United States (1935), 286, 288

immunity
  absolute, 270, 291
  presidential, 269–73, 291
impeachment, 33, 38, 269, 300, 304
incorporation doctrine. *See* Fourteenth Amendment
independent agencies, 72, 285
intermediate scrutiny, 147, 151, 187, 189
International Court of Justice, 291
International Covenant on Civil and Political Rights, 102
internet, 22
interracial marriage, 164, 172–73, 235
Iraq War, 290

Jackson, Ketanji Brown, 2, 75
Jackson, Robert, 124, 245, 278–79, 280–81
Jacobellis v. Ohio (1964), 129n56
Janus v. American Federation of State, County, & Municipal Employees, Council 31 (2018), 125, 134
Japanese internment. *See Korematsu v. United States*
Jay, John, 18–19, 28–29
Jefferson, Thomas, 23, 37, 81–82, 105, 277, 292, 304
Johanns v. Livestock Marketing Association (2005), 134
Johnson, Andrew, 45
Johnson, Lyndon, 245
Johnson, Samuel, 247
judicial review, 24, 287
  Article III and, 27
  foundations of, 32
  history of, 19, 27
  judicial restraint, 50, 180
  Marbury and, 28, 31, 34
  Marshall and, 31
  politics and, 31–33
judicial supremacy, 11, 28, 32–33

Kagan, Elena, 2, 63, 74, 88, 125, 127, 204, 284
Katzenbach v. McClung (1964), 246, 253
Katzenbach v. Morgan (1966), 262–65
Kavanaugh, Brett, 4, 71–72, 153, 159
Kennedy, Anthony, 4, 55, 67, 70–71, 75, 87, 89, 119, 148, 178, 192, 225, 231, 233–37
Kennedy v. Bremerton School District (2022), 84, 87, 89–90, 135
Klarman, Michael, 23, 171n23
Korean War, 278
Korematsu v. United States (1944), 169–70, 172, 251
Kramer v. Union Free School District (1969), 196
Ku Klux Klan, 110, 116

Lassiter v. Northampton County Board of Elections (1959), 262
Lawrence v. Texas (2003), 192, 231, 233, 235
Lee v. Weisman (1992), 89
Lemon v. Kurtzman (1971), 82
Levi, Edward, 59
libel, 128
liberalism, 3, 8, 12–13, 50, 58, 63, 66, 95, 98, 118, 126, 128, 144, 211, 248
liberty interests, 236
Lincoln, Abraham, 45, 86, 277, 279
Litman, Leah, 261
living constitutionalism, 212, 228, 231, 236, 302
Lochner v. New York (1905), 15, 170, 211, 213
   aftermath of, 15, 221
   Holmes and. *See* Holmes, Oliver Wendell
   Lochner era, 48–51, 58, 119, 125, 151, 180, 211, 215–18, 220, 281
   repudiation of, 218, 220
   Warren Court and, 221
Locke v. Davey (2004), 79, 91
Loper Bright Enterprises v. Raimondo (2024), 273–75, 283
Lorillard Tobacco Co. v. Reilly (2001), 119
Loving v. Virginia (1967), 173, 195n70, 235
Lynch v. Donnelly (1984), 86
Lyng v. Northwest Indian Cemetery Protective Association (1988), 93n35

Madison, James, 18, 24, 26, 30, 81, 256
Mahanoy Area School District v. BL (2021), 136
major questions doctrine, 283–84
majority-minority districts, 200–1, 204
Marbury, William, 30–31, 34

Marbury v. Madison (1803), 19, 26–32, 37, 42, 45, 49, 275, 304
marriage, 70, 164, 172, 190–91, 234–37
Marshall, John, 28–29, 31–32, 34, 37–38, 40–41, 44, 255, 292
   state laws and, 38
Marshall, Thurgood, 68, 74, 162
Martin v. Hunter's Lessee (1816), 39, 42
Masterpiece Cakeshop v. Colorado Civil Rights Commission (2018), 95n46
McCain, John, 122
McCarthy, Joseph, 109
McCloskey, Robert, 41
McConnell, Mitch, 3–4
McConnell v. Federal Election Commission (2003), 122, 125
McCreary County v. ACLU (2005), 86n13, 87n16
McCulloch v. Maryland (1819), 39–41, 66, 254
McDonald v. City of Chicago (2010), 149–51
Medellín v. Texas (2008), 290
Medicaid, 259–60
Medicare, 256
Meese, Edwin, 55, 250
Meyer v. Nebraska (1923), 220
Miami Herald Publishing Co. v. Tornillo (1974), 124, 126
Miers, Harriet, 60, 69
Mikhail, John, 26n9
militias, 142–44, 146, 148
Miller v. California (1973), 129, 138
minorities, 47, 50–51, 92, 111, 175, 193, 199, 246, 262, 267. *See also* equal protection
Miranda v. Arizona (1966), 3, 51
Mobile v. Bolden (1980), 200
Moody v. NetChoice, LLC (2024), 126–27
Mormon Church, 91
Morrison v. Olson (1988), 287

most favored nation approach. *See* Free Exercise Clause
Myers v. United States (1926), 286

NAACP v. Alabama (1958), 131
Naim v. Naim (1955), 172
National Association for the Advancement of Colored People, 131, 170
National Federation of Independent Business v. OSHA (2022), 284n34
National Federation of Independent Business v. Sebelius (2012), 239–42, 253, 255, 259
National Rifle Association, 144
Native American Church, 94
natural rights, 105n5
Necessary and Proper Clause, 254–56
New Deal, 15, 35, 37, 46, 49, 55, 58, 118, 181, 218, 239, 243, 254, 257, 273, 281, 293
    New Deal settlement, 50, 125, 250, 252, 267, 281
New York Rifle & Pistol Association v. Bruen (2022), 63n12, 151–55, 160
New York Times Co. v. Sullivan (1964), 106n6, 128
Nineteenth Amendment, 197
Ninth Amendment, 212, 223
Nixon tapes case. *See United States v. Nixon*
Nixon v. Fitzgerald (1982), 269–70, 291
Nixon, Richard, 53, 56, 269, 291, 297, 304
NLRB v. Jones & Laughlin Steel Corp. (1937), 244
nondelegation doctrine, 281–83

Obama, Barack, 3, 56, 73–74, 239, 243, 306
Obergefell v. Hodges (2015), 70, 190, 192, 235–37
O'Connor, Sandra Day, 55, 75, 87, 95, 122, 177, 225, 231, 233
originalism, 1, 8, 10, 20, 55, 61–66, 85, 101, 142, 179, 205, 238, 294, 298

original intent, 55, 75
original public meaning, 55, 61, 75
original understanding, 13, 174, 197, 249, 256, 267, 288

Palko v. Connecticut (1937), 52n36
Palmore v. Sidoti (1984), 173
Panama Refining Co. v. Ryan (1935), 281n26
Parents Involved in Community Schools v. Seattle School District No. 1 (2007), 176, 185
parochial schools, 78, 82–83, 101
party presentation principle, 63–64
Patient Protection and Affordable Care Act, 67, 75, 239, 248, 256, 259
Payne v. Tennessee (1991), 65n16
Persian Gulf War, 290
Pickering v. Board of Education (1968), 135
Pierce v. Society of Sisters (1925), 220
Planned Parenthood of Southeastern Pennsylvania v. Casey (1992), 3, 57, 225–28, 234
Plessy v. Ferguson (1896), 47, 167–71, 303
political parties, 23, 33, 204, 306
political question doctrine, 199, 203, 290
polygamy, 91
Post, Robert, 134
Powell, Lewis, 55, 161–63, 177, 270
precedent, 6, 8, 14, 28, 32, 52, 57, 64–65, 72, 90, 123, 148, 150, 179, 198, 223, 226, 228, 240, 244
predominant factor test, 201
President, 9, 16, 23–25, 28, 32, 268–94. *See also specific presidents*
    agencies and, 284–88
    appointment power, 285
    Article II and, 25, 278
    delegated powers, 282
    executive privilege, 291–93
    immunity, 269–73
    impeachment and, 269, 304
    removals and, 286–88

unitary executive theory, 285
veto power, 24
war powers, 289. *See also* war powers
prior restraint, 105, 107
privacy, 222–23, 232
Privileges and/or Immunities Clause, 46–47, 51, 150, 164–65, 197, 212–14
Progressive Era, 216
prohibition, 92
Protestants, 83, 89
public forum doctrine, 137
public schools. *See* education

race, 14, 132, 161–64, 167–79, 183, 185–86, 191, 194, 201–2, 246, 260
  affirmative action. *See* affirmative action
  discrimination and. *See* discrimination
  equal protection and. *See* equal protection
  minority groups, 177, 184, 194
  voting and, 201
racially disparate impact, 183–85
racism, 116, 132
ratchet theory, 263. *See also* *Katzenbach v. Morgan*
rational basis test, 180–83, 192, 196, 221, 224, 229, 246
  heightened rationality review, 192
Reagan, Ronald, 55, 69, 83, 225, 250
Reconstruction period, 20, 45–46, 172, 179, 266
Red Lion Broadcasting Co. v. FCC (1969), 138
Reed v. Reed (1971), 185n55
Regents of the University of California v. Bakke (1978), 161–63, 177
Rehnquist, William, 3, 53, 55, 67, 79, 84, 117, 133, 224, 233, 251, 259, 287
religion, 12, 20, 48, 52, 77–101, 135, 167, 180, 194, 264

Amish groups, 93
conservative coalition, 95
Establishment Clause. *See* Establishment Clause
exemptions and, 92–98
Free Exercise Clause. *See* Free Exercise Clause
governmental aid to, 82
public schools and, 88–90
symbolic support of, 78, 87
Religious Freedom Restoration Act, 264
Reno v. American Civil Liberties Union (1997), 139
Republicans, 3, 11, 45–46, 53, 55, 60, 67, 199, 202, 205–6, 225–26, 246, 272, 306
Reynolds v. Sims (1964), 196–200
Reynolds v. United States (1878), 91
Roberts, John, 3, 7, 53, 55, 66, 67n18, 70, 76, 130, 176, 203, 241, 243
Roberts, Owen, 37
Roberts v. U.S. Jaycees (1984), 132–33
Roe v. Wade (1973), 2, 4, 6, 15, 54–55, 57, 67, 72, 195, 210, 222–25, 299
Rogers v. Lodge (1982), 200
Romer v. Evans (1996), 191–92
Roosevelt, Franklin, 35–37, 48–49, 173, 218–20, 245, 250, 279–80, 296, 304
  court-packing, 36–37, 49, 218
Rucho v. Common Cause (2019), 202–6
Rudman, Warren, 59
Rust v. Sullivan (1991), 137n75

Saenz v. Roe (1999), 215n9
San Antonio Independent School District v. Rodriguez (1973), 195n72
Scalia, Antonin, 1, 3–4, 7, 12, 55, 64, 69–70, 73, 94, 97, 123, 130–31, 142, 145–48, 230, 234, 236, 255, 274, 287, 306
Schenck v. United States (1919), 106–8, 128
schools. *See* education
Second Amendment, 2, 141–60, 298
  original understanding, 145–46

seditious libel, 105
Seila Law LLC v. Consumer Financial
    Protection Bureau (2020), 287
separate but equal. See Plessy v. Ferguson
separation of powers, 275, 283
Seventh Amendment, 149
sex discrimination. See equal protection,
    sex discrimination
sexual autonomy rights
    married couples, 222
    same-sex couples, 231–34
sexual revolution, 224
Shapiro v. Thompson (1969), 195n68
Shaw v. Reno (1993), 201
Shelby County v. Holder (2013), 260–61
Sherbert v. Verner (1963), 92, 97
Skinner v. Oklahoma (1942), 195n69,
    221, 235
Slaughter-House Cases (1873), 46, 166,
    180, 214–15
slavery, 20, 24, 42–43, 45–46, 163,
    166, 172, 211, 260, 277
Smith, Jack, 111
Smith, William French, 67
Snyder v. Phelps (2011), 115
social rights, 168
Social Security, 23, 35, 37, 39, 49, 93,
    245, 247, 251, 256, 267
Sorrell v. IMS Health, Inc. (2011), 119
Sotomayor, Sonia, 73–74, 159, 179, 272
Souter, David, 55, 59, 208, 225
South Dakota v. Dole (1987), 258–59
speech, freedom of. See Free Speech
    Clause
stare decisis, 17, 57, 64–65, 70, 90,
    146, 234, 237, 254, 297–98, 303
Starr, Kenneth, 71
state action doctrine, 21
states
    appeals from, 39, 42
    citizenship and, 214
    constitutions of, 196
    sovereignty of, 261, 266
    subsidies and, 78, 83
Steel Seizure case. See Youngstown
    Sheet & Tube Co. v. Sawyer

Stevens, John Paul, 56, 59, 74, 94, 123,
    142, 146, 150, 176, 201, 206,
    208, 274
Steward Machine Co. v. Davis (1937),
    37n7
Stewart, Potter, 92, 129
Stone v. Graham (1980), 90
Strauder v. West Virginia (1880), 167
Strauss, David, 9, 103
strict scrutiny, 93, 96–97, 112,
    147, 174, 178, 180, 186, 195,
    221, 223
Stuart v. Laird (1803), 30n19, 37n11
Students for Fair Admissions
    (SFFA) v. President and Fellows
    of Harvard College (2023),
    161, 163, 174, 178–80,
    184, 194
Supremacy Clause, 302
Supreme Court
    appointments to, 4, 18, 58, 76.
        See also specific Justices
    conservatism. See conservatism
    constraints on, 300–2
    judicial review. See judicial review
    jurisdiction of, 31, 39
Swann v. Charlotte-Mecklenburg Board
    of Education (1971), 175

Taft, William Howard, 286
Taft–Hartley Act, 278, 280
Takings Clause, 279
Tandon v. Newsom (2021), 96
Taney, Roger, 42, 44–45, 211
taxation, 40
Taxing and Spending Clause, 15, 36,
    242, 253, 256–60
    original understanding, 256
television, 139
Tenth Amendment, 41
Texas Monthly, Inc. v. Bullock (1989),
    99n53
Texas v. Johnson (1989), 114
textualism, 1, 8, 10, 71, 142, 194, 238,
    270, 294, 298
thanksgiving, 81, 86

Thirteenth Amendment, 20–21, 24, 163, 260
Thomas, Clarence, 55, 59, 68, 151, 178, 200, 207, 234, 252, 267
Tinker v. Des Moines Independent Community School District (1969), 104n3, 136
Trinity Lutheran Church v. Comer (2017), 85n12
Truman, Harry, 170, 278
Trump, Donald, 4, 66, 70, 72, 110, 227, 269, 291
Trump v. Hawaii (2018), 170n20
Trump v. Mazars USA, LLP (2020), 293
Trump v. United States (2024), 268–73, 281, 292
Trump v. Vance (2020), 293

unenumerated rights, 213, 221, 223
United States v. Burr (1807), 292
United States v. Butler (1936), 258
United States v. Carolene Products Co. (1938), 50, 177n37
  footnote four, 50, 52, 194
United States v. Darby (1941), 244
United States v. Eichman (1990), 114
United States v. Lee (1982), 93n33
United States v. Lopez (1995), 251–52
United States v. Miller (1939), 144, 146
United States v. Morrison (2000), 252–53, 265
United States v. Nixon (1974), 292
United States v. O'Brien (1968), 113–14, 155
United States v. Playboy Entertainment Group (2000), 139n79
United States v. Rahimi (2024), 155–59
United States v. Schwimmer (1929), 111n21
United States v. Seeger (1965), 100n56
United States v. Stevens (2010), 129–30
United States v. Virginia (1996), 188–89

Valentine v. Chrestensen (1942), 117n35
Van Orden v. Perry (2005), 86n13

Vermeule, Adrian, 12n17, 49n31, 288n42
Vidal v. Elster (2024), 158n15
Vietnam War, 113, 115, 290
Vinson, Fred M., 171
Violence Against Women Act, 252
Virginia Military Institute, 188
Virginia State Board of Pharmacy v. Virginia Citizens Consumer Council (1976), 117
voter ID laws, 206–7
voting rights, 14, 47, 164, 196–209, 261–62, 265
Voting Rights Act, 200, 260, 265
voucher program, 78–79, 84

Walz v. Tax Commission (1970), 83
war powers, 289
War Powers Resolution, 289
Warren, Earl, 12, 50–53, 171, 197
Washington v. Davis (1976), 183–84
Washington v. Glucksberg (1997), 235
Washington, George, 30, 37, 81, 276
Welsh v. United States (1970), 100n57
West Coast Hotel Co. v. Parrish (1937), 218
West Virginia State Board of Education v. Barnette (1943), 124
West Virginia v. EPA (2022), 283–84
White, Byron, 70, 224, 232
Whitman v. American Trucking Assn's, Inc. (2001), 282n29
Whitney v. California (1927), 108, 111
Wickard v. Filburn (1942), 244, 246
Wills, Garry, 143
women, 21, 23, 53, 57, 98, 133, 163, 182, 185–89, 194, 210, 218, 224, 226, 252, 305
World War I, 13, 88, 106, 109
World War II, 170, 280–81, 296

Yakus v. United States (1944), 281
Youngstown Sheet & Tube Co. v. Sawyer (1952), 277–81

Zelman v. Simmons-Harris (2002), 84
Zivotofsky v. Kerry (2015), 291

Printed by Integrated Books International,
United States of America